PRODUCTION STUDIES, THE SEQUEL!

Production Studies, The Sequel! is an exciting exploration of the experiences of media workers in local, global, and digital communities—from prop masters in Germany, Chinese film auteurs, producers of children's television in Qatar, Italian radio broadcasters, filmmakers in Ethiopia and Nigeria, to seemingly autonomous Twitterbots. Case studies examine international production cultures across five continents and incorporate a range of media, including film, television, music, social media, promotional media, video games, publishing, and public broadcasting.

Using the lens of cultural studies to examine media production, *Production Studies, The Sequel!* takes into account transnational production flows and places production studies in conversation with other major areas of media scholarship including audience studies, media industries, and media history. A follow-up to the successful *Production Studies*, this collection highlights new and important research in the field, and promises to generate continued discussion about the past, present, and future of production studies.

Miranda Banks is Associate Professor of Visual and Media Arts at Emerson College and a research fellow in the Emerson Engagement Lab. She is the author of *The Writers: A History of American Screenwriters and Their Guild* and co-editor of *Production Studies: Cultural Studies of Media Industries.*

Bridget Conor is Lecturer in the Centre for Culture, Media and Creative Industries at King's College London. She is the author of *Screenwriting: Creative Labour and Professional Practice* and the co-editor, with Rosalind Gill and Stephanie Taylor, of *Gender and Creative Labour.*

Vicki Mayer is Professor of Communication at Tulane University. She has published widely on media production and producers, and is the author of *Below the Line: Producers and Production Studies in the New Television Economy* and *Producing Dreams, Consuming Youth: Mexican Americans and Mass Media.*

PRODUCTION STUDIES, THE SEQUEL!

Cultural Studies of Global Media Industries

*Edited by
Miranda Banks,
Bridget Conor,
and Vicki Mayer*

Routledge
Taylor & Francis Group

NEW YORK AND LONDON

First published 2016
by Routledge
711 Third Avenue, New York, NY 10017

and by Routledge
2 Park Square, Milton Park, Abingdon, Oxon OX14 4RN

Routledge is an imprint of the Taylor & Francis Group, an informa business.

Library of Congress Cataloging-in-Publication Data
Production studies
   Production studies, the sequel! : cultural studies of global media industries /
edited by Miranda Banks, Bridget Conor, and Vicki Mayer.
      pages cm
   Includes bibliographical references and index.
   1. Television—Production and direction.   2. Motion pictures—Production
and direction.   3. Mass media and culture.   I. Banks, Miranda J., 1972–
editor.   II. Conor, Bridget, 1980– editor.   III. Mayer, Vicki, 1971– editor.
   PN1992.75.P78 2015
   302.23—dc23
   2015003243

ISBN: 978-1-138-83168-1 (hbk)
ISBN: 978-1-138-83169-8 (pbk)
ISBN: 978-1-315-73647-1 (ebk)

Typeset in Bembo
by Apex CoVantage, LLC

CONTENTS

V. Transnational Circuits   173

VI. Redefining the Industry   211

PREFACE

"The worst thing the French ever gave us is the auteur theory," [Vince Gilligan, creator of *Breaking Bad*,] said flatly. "It's a load of horseshit. You don't make a movie by yourself, you certainly don't make a TV show by yourself. You invest people in their work. You make people feel comfortable in their jobs; you keep people talking."[1]

"The productive forces are the result of man's practical energy, but that energy is in turn circumscribed by the conditions in which man is placed by the productive forces already acquired, by the form of society which exists before him, which he does not create, which is the product of the preceding generation."[2]

In newspapers and magazines, at awards ceremonies, and in social media we often see the profiles of individual media makers who through a combination of grand vision, great charisma, divine inspiration, and decisive action create something beloved to audiences, viewers, or listeners. While significantly more researched and nuanced in their evaluations, many media studies texts, as well, focus on the single-handed efforts of one great man—less so on those of one great woman—within a production process. In this book, we complicate personal stories by locating them within larger cultural studies of discrete production communities, their material cultures, and their historical contexts.

Media production is an imbricated and prolonged process, one that can simultaneously be highly individualized and fully collaborative. Even labor that practitioners conduct while working alone is not produced in a vacuum: directors have producers, artists have grants from foundations or organizations, and journalists have a community of sources—who now also tweet their own news-bytes. Through an even wider lens, their physical organization and its infrastructure rely on a host of invisible others: from the East Congolese tin miner to the London film school professor. Without collapsing the distinctions between these various networks and their attendant political economies, it bears emphasis that the status of the media producer depends on unequal forces of production. As television showrunner Vince Gilligan said in an interview, auteurism is often the fantasy of a viewer watching a film rather than the reality of the production process. Yet Gilligan is among the few people on the crew whom journalists want to interview, and thus among the fewer whom audiences might remember.

The phrase 'production culture' in this volume signals this tension between individuals' agency and the social conditions within which agency is embedded. Rather than reify the binary of singular creativity against structural constraints, the idea of production cultures allows for a more coherent examination of producers as they work, live, and organize together. The (ironically) social construction of producers as singular is reflected in media contents. Even when media makers clearly state that they work with a team, the process of celebrating the individual regularly masks production labor as well as the exercise of asymmetric forms of power and control.[3] As Bev Skeggs and Helen Wood point out, television now appears to be offering numerous "lessons in individualization" both on-screen and off-, offering "incitements for 'ordinary' people to perform their own self-awareness, self-work and ultimately, self-transformation."[4] Skeggs's earlier work illustrated that this 'self' is a bourgeois political project, one in which middle-class interests are consolidated while working-class values are constructed as the 'constitutive limit' of those interests.[5] Thus, for Skeggs and Wood, who focus on reality television and its audiences, their concern is about how "relations of personhood are relayed and circulated" through the specific fabric(s) of this textual form.[6] In the following chapters, our contributors reinforce the importance of studying these processes of circulation within film, publishing, the games industry, radio, and the Internet.

As a scholarly approach, production studies examines specific sites and fabrics of media production as distinct interpretative communities, each with its own organizational structures, professional practices, and power dynamics. Like cultural studies and media studies scholarship, our research exists in a nexus between disciplines and fields. Production studies provides grounded analyses of media makers' experiences, observations, conversations, and interactions, and in the process, investigates what Skeggs and Wood call these distinct 'relations of personhood.' This observational, on-the-ground research allows scholars better access to determining the nuances of language, behavior, ritual, and subjectivities. Grounded data throws into perspective our scholarly understandings of production communities in light of shifts in policy, economic imperatives, industrial organizations, national politics, globalization, and local or regional dynamics.

We are less interested in the strategies of media industries or corporations or governments or their various institutions (although these goals are often constitutively important), but in the goals of producers, in their own words. Without sliding into a naïve empiricism, the voices of multiple people involved in media production give new insights into otherwise opaque industrial processes. They frequently sit alongside, and often in juxtaposition to voices found in trade literatures, popular press, and other readily available archives. While savvy and self-reflective, the foregrounding of producers as human subjects also illuminates their similarities, their diversity, and their own internal contradictions. Production studies hence fills the gaps found in other kinds of media production research, albeit in partial and incremental ways. Production studies cannot claim to understand all variations of media producers and modes of production, or even approach the validity of a statistical sample of all writers, or even all 'American writers,' 'British copy editors' (etc.).

The hallmark of a successful production study for us is marked more by depth than by breadth. Our situated sources of producers' knowledge reflect their everyday experiences in the office, the home, or other work worlds. The collection and analysis of cultural texts, from stray posts on the Internet to formal interview responses, and from ethnographic field notes to other lay forms of narration, should paint a picture of a production culture: its common languages, practices, and frameworks for understanding. Drawing on the insights contributed by American-inflected cultural studies and continental social theory, production studies points to these cultures as sites of simultaneous privilege and struggle, whether by class, race, and/or gender. In this, the sociological concepts of counter-knowledges, hidden transcripts, and tactics of the weak become relative within multiple contexts, from that of a single organization to those of competing media industries, production regions, and global geographies. By stretching the micro politics of production across various scales and scenarios, production studies understands producers as interpretative communities within media industries that wield considerable power, but do not distribute that power to all producers equally.

The original volume, *Production Studies*, was born out of a need for greater connection between scholars who studied media production in this particular way, but who worked across different departments and divergent scholarly traditions. 'Production studies' was not coined to infer a new methodology or field of inquiry—nor did we intend to position our book as a declaration of a new beginning. Rather, the original contributors grappled with the work of many scholars who had already contributed significant work on the micro politics of media production cultures, among them Leo Rosten, Hortense Powdermaker, and Todd Gitlin, not to mention John Caldwell, Laura Grindstaff, Serra Tinic, Vicki Mayer, and Elana Levine. At the time, in the early 2000s, ethnographically inspired studies of production did not fit comfortably within the academy. In the humanities, the research pendulum had swung to understanding audience cultures over those of producers.[7] In the social sciences, the discussions of media industries at the time rarely included their organizational cultures or the voices of workers in them, although there were some noteworthy exceptions.[8] Given the lack of a common disciplinary home or academic community, as well as the editors' own locations, the first anthology highlighted past and present scholarship, but it also focused on film, television, and some digital media industries in the English-dominant world. In doing so, the chapters in the collection homed in on the formation of producers' subjectivities within professional, creative, economic, or cultural contexts, as well as the geographic dimensions of production identities, networks, and rituals. This was the starting point for making production studies visible, and continues to be a central feature of its definition.

Five years later, studies of workplace cultures, invisible and precarious labor practices, and trade mythologies, as well as social relationships and power dynamics, are now regular elements of a well-rounded industrial critique of the media. The varied work of production studies researchers continues to provide a range of self-reflexive, interdisciplinary approaches to examining the roles of cultural producers and lay theories of their practices. Since the publication of *Production Studies*, many excellent single-authored books and edited volumes have interrogated cultures of production and economies of media labor.[9] An increased number of university film and media studies programs push the idea of integrating production and theory. Meanwhile, the economic and symbolic power of global media industries has continued unabated, fueled by the digital convergence strategies of media industries and the deregulation of public service and trade provisions that permit their expansion. We felt that the time was ripe to once again assess where cultural studies of media production are going, and where they may take us next.

Production Studies, The Sequel! pushes the original agenda of *Production Studies* further, examining local, regional, and national cultures of global media production through the perspectives of a diversity of media makers. Together, the chapters cover more industries with an eye toward the new centers and sites for global media production, as well as the transformation of traditional media industries and conventional production practices. This second volume challenges what can sometimes be read as a myopic view of what media production is and where it happens. It includes studies of social media, music, video games, publishing, promotional media, and radio, as well as those forms known as film and television. Crucially, we devote a section of this volume to public service production cultures that have long been dominant (in the United Kingdom and Western Europe, for example), as well as multiple chapters that emphasize the blurred lines that separate media producers, audiences, and other workers in deregulating and decentralizing media industries. In other words, we are more attendant to the ways people live with the consequences of transforming political economies and regulatory regimes. Chapters in this volume showcase archival research and historical analysis, political economy, actor-network theory, ethnographies, oral histories, interviews, participant observations, and artist- and practitioner-led research. We are also delighted to highlight new research from international scholars who have conducted local and regional studies that examine production in more than thirteen countries. All of these authors have worked to chart the theoretical and methodological trends toward production studies in their respective fields, while adding their own unique approaches and insights gained from their most recent research.

It should also be noted that a second volume does not presume to have resolved some of the fundamental challenges that arise from grounded research. Production studies needs to further challenge the wide-eyed ethnographer's assumption that the text from an interview is more insightful or authentic than other sorts of textual readings, from trade texts to social media posts to the textual elements they actually produce. Our concern, of course, is part of an older debate, for which we hearken back only to the 1990s.[10] Like production studies today, reception studies advocated a detour from the psychoanalytic and content-centric readings of films. In a well-cited critique, Jane Feuer writes that the empirical audience researcher ultimately reads the audience as a text "without the benefit of the therapeutic situation . . . in which case there is the tendency to privilege the conscious or easily articulated response."[11] This cautioning is relevant to the study of producers who both author and are inscribed in a variety of textual communities.

What we hope remains salient in doing production studies, then, is the research setting, the position of the researcher in relation to the field and its subjects. This was the thrust of Jackie Stacey's response to Feuer and was demonstrated powerfully in her examination of interviews with British women about postwar film stars. She theorized that each one of her interactions involved a "trialogic circuit": from the expectations of the interviewees, to their image of themselves in the past, to the imagined community of their peers in the present.[12] While the questions of projections may play out differently in the contexts in which researchers study 'up' or even 'sideways' across lines of class privilege and social hierarchies, the lessons for production studies are clear. Any production study must circle back ultimately to the reasons why any field site is necessarily constrained and in any case necessarily limited, not simply by a lack of access or more subjects, but by the conditions through which we understand 'producers.'

We hope that the various cases and positions within this book enable this kind of self-reflection, not to hinder but to further its explanatory uses. To say production studies focuses on small case studies that do not claim to be universal does not mean the cases should not be useful toward the formation of social theory. The connections between structure and agency continue to be a theoretical project that carries over from audience studies into production studies.[13] The attraction of Pierre Bourdieu, Bruno Latour, and Tiziana Terranova in studies of media—as a field, as actors, and as labor, respectively—is precisely the ability to work from the empirical toward broader understandings of media production in society. These are not easy leaps. For example, as Nick Couldry's critique of Bourdieu's field theory makes clear, it is necessary to go beyond middle-range theory in showing how the concrete exchanges of symbolic capital within specific fields contribute to the pervasive exercise of media power in society at large.[14] Otherwise we end up either not seeing the forest for the trees, or, worse, creating forests from a few of our arboreal samples.

All of this is to say that production studies methods should be guided and made transparent within the politics of the research. This breeds a healthy skepticism toward abstract generalities, avoiding a false dichotomy between the "bad text" and the "good producer."[15] It also frees us to see the linkages across industries, professions, and workers not otherwise put into comparison. It should inspire a cultural studies of social praxis, which, in the terms Stuart Hall set out, offers a challenge to the prevailing common sense.[16] This is important to, first, challenge the "overdetermined cultural mystique" that assigns media industries such author-ity over their own processes, but also, second, to build bridges with other workers, whether deemed 'creative' or not, 'artistic' or not, 'professional' or not.[17]

Structure of this Volume

The first volume pointed to intersections between the contributors' disciplinary fields through four parts: (1) histories of media production studies; (2) producers: selves and others; (3) production spaces: centers and peripheries; and (4) produc-tion as lived experience. While traces of these themes are present throughout many of the chapters in this second volume, we were inspired by the contribu-tors' scholarship to highlight other critical issues and motifs. *Production Studies, The Sequel!* is organized into six areas of interdisciplinary, intellectual inquiry into media production and culture.

Part I, Tools of the Trade, offers three different chapters that explore how manual and digital instruments used in media making not only transform the final product, but also the processes of media production and the identities of media producers. Those products range from bots, to props, to synthespians. Jobs are redefined, positions are added or dropped, and the hierarchies of power within production communities are often shaken, reassembled, or reimagined. These chapters examine technologies, materialities, and production practices, analyzing moments of change as well as the implications of these shifts on per-formances, spaces, and production communities. Part II, Being the Brand, high-lights analyses of commercial and promotional production and labor. These three chapters illuminate both individuals and organizations—'booth babes,' pop stars, and 'on-brand' television makers—and the affective and performative labor rela-tions that typify these kinds of promotional production. The chapters in Part III, Production Pedagogies, all examine distinct types of teaching and learning that happen among institutions, media makers, aspirants, and audiences. Contribu-tors examine screenwriting education in Denmark, the pedagogies and ethics of 'poverty porn' production in the Philippines, and 'group writing' in the Czech Republic. Part IV, Putting the Public Back in Public Service, explores four unique communities that incorporate analyses of public service media production, as well as independent, private, and commercial forms of production. Contributors here explore questions around regulation, policy, and institutional power, and Part IV includes studies of public service television in the United Kingdom and Germany, artist-produced television in Canada, and radio production in Italy. Part V, Transnational Circuits, highlights four distinctly local studies that are simultaneously transnational in scope and reach. Their subjects range from location filmmaking in China and Taiwan to video film production in Nigeria and Ethiopia to game production work linking 'dominant' and 'emerging' production locations from San Francisco to Warsaw. Part VI, Redefining the Industry, presents four chapters concerned with processes of establishing and maintaining industrial boundaries, particularly in contexts of technological and transnational change. These chapters focus on pan-Arab children's television production, digital magazine production, the comics industry, and North American television regulation. In a fitting final section to this second volume, our chapter authors investigate the ways industries define and redefine their modes of production, distribution, and regulation.

As editors, our collaboration with each other on this project as well as with our contributors and Routledge Press has been engaging, illuminating, and deeply enjoyable. As we worked on this book as well as our own individual projects, we were regularly reminded how our scholarship stands on the shoulders of those who laid the groundwork for production studies as we understand it today. There are three people in particular whose pioneering work, whose creative ideas, and whose careful guidance permeate this collection. We consider this sequel part of a continuing conversation with them. Thus, we dedicate this book to our mentors, John T. Caldwell, Rosalind Gill, and Ellen Seiter, with gratitude for their works and for their enduring influence on us all.

NOTE FROM THE COVER ARTIST: "CHANGING THE GUARD: FROM 'SEMPER FI PANAVISION' TO 'INSURGENT CROWD-SOURCING'"

What gives with the self-conscious war footing that fuels many forms of film and television production? From the start, outsider film 'artists' posed as mass culture's agitating vanguard; basically embracing a Napoleon-era conceit for twentieth-century entertainment aesthetics. But this avant-garde was largely illusory and merely the tip of a much bigger and unexceptional sort of production culture posturing informed by militarism. Even the legions of workers making films and series for Hollywood and mainstream TV corporations regularly rationalized their activities by invoking paradigms of violent contestation. Even if Hollywood's genre visions may have been uninspired (and their screen content unremarkable), committed gaffers, grips, and ACs regularly described their creative work, qualitatively, in masculinist, military terms. If avant-garde elites tilted at mass-culture windmills, then more anonymous below-the-line craft workers and their department heads rationalized that their many shooting locations were indeed beachheads to be conquered—irrespective of whatever capitalist fantasies their producer overlords may have had in mind.

The image I painted for the first edition of *Production Studies* (2009)— *Semper Fi Panavision*—reflected this rationalization of war footing among mainstream, below-the-line craft workers. Their daily challenge was to survive unrealistic producer demands, through collective teamwork, in a heavy industry defined by militaristic, top-down, command-and-control management. The flag-waving Iwo Jima Marine Corps monument I riffed on had circulated in the background as a trade icon for struggling camera operators in the United States. Yet the icon also resonated, I discovered, with crew-speak in the Anglophone countries (Canada, Great Britain, Australia) featured in that edition of our book. Yet Panavision soon declared bankruptcy, and quickly vanished as a big-gear battle-tattoo separating the men from the boys soon after our book appeared. During my Hollywood fieldwork from 1995 to 2008 I had the nagging sense that I was documenting something not unlike the decline and fall of the Roman Empire. Used equipment and rental houses bulged at the seams with unused, dust-covered, and increasingly obsolete equipment. Digital technologists sold producers on sky-is-falling futurism, while the crafts unions simply dug in more deeply into once-trusty cultural bunkers now abandoned in the face of runaway production and endless outsourcing. A century of leaden inertia, and cults of professionalism, had kept the heavy mode of production in place as a marker of exceptionalism. At the same time production's symbolic war footing faded as an effective salve against labor's ever greater underemployment.

The second volume of *Production Studies* extends well beyond the Anglophone countries and tangles globally with slippery, shifting, and unruly modes of production. Traditional forms of media war footing no longer resonate in the same way in a world of crowd-sourcing, YouTube celebrity branding, riot porn, Pentagon Twitter spins, hacked Pentagon Facebook pages, on-screen ISIS beheadings, and—well— 'real war' (in the Middle East, Africa, Ferguson, Missouri, and elsewhere). Yet contestation in public spaces, by media makers armed with cameras and recorders, is very much alive. The online space is full of activist media makers and corporate liars marching to the drumbeat of production culture's war footing. The cover painting for the second volume—titled *Insurgent Crowd-Sourcing*—is my attempt to reflect on the notion of a changing of the guard: that the cultural ground under our feet is giving way; that the old iconic fantasies of masculinist Hollywood stand tattered on crumbling walls while a new generation of media makers turns to face the onslaught. As I have argued elsewhere, production cultural expressions increase in quantity and intensity during times of struggle and instability. The fact that making a living wage in professional production work is now largely a thing of the past for most media workers worldwide may be the very reason that media makers must now showcase and accelerate their discourses of war footing as compensation. That is, war talk may serve as a form of symbolic deprivation pay that media insurgents deploy to be seen in a cluttered global media market.

During the eighteen years that I both taught production at the university level and hosted guest lectures from media professionals, I was always amazed at how quickly talk in the classroom or lab turned from the craft or technical task at hand to anecdotes, trade narratives, and, yes, war stories. At first, I guessed that these expressions must form a shared 'cultural skin' around technical tasks, which in turn served to animate and give students an odd (but clearly practical) sort of solidarity and collective mission. Eventually I began to see that film and media production practices cannot be easily separated from either the communities who manage them; or from the production cultures that constantly sanction and legitimize them. That new iterations and icons of militarism and war footing still fuel production's sanctioning and legitimation is no small matter in my mind. I hope the cover image for this new volume serves readers as a useful portal to the innovative essays and key case studies that follow.

—John T. Caldwell, UCLA
January 25, 2015

Notes

1 Brett Martin, "Inside the Breaking Bad Writers' Room: How Vince Gilligan Runs the Show," *The Guardian*, September 20, 2013. www.theguardian.com/tv-and-radio/2013/sep/20/breaking-bad-writers-room-vince-gilligan.

2 Karl Marx, "Letter to Annenkov" (1846) in *Marx Engels Collected Works*, translated by Peter and Betty Ross, v. 38 (International Publishers, 1975), 95.

3 One often wants to attribute greatness to the individual—and Vince Gilligan deservedly received a fair share of such praise during the five years his series *Breaking Bad* aired on Anglophone television. But even the article that cites Gilligan saying how the work is collaborative fails to present the work as such. In this newspaper profile, the author documents how Gilligan throws out ideas and staff writers are there as his sounding board. When these other writers speak, it is not as individuals with their own backgrounds but as "one of the writers."

4 Bev Skeggs and Helen Wood, *Reacting to Reality Television: Performance, Audience and Value* (Abingdon: Routledge, 2012), 4.

5 Bev Skeggs, *Class, Self, Culture* (London: Routledge, 2004).

6 Skeggs and Wood, *Reacting to Reality Television*, 4.

7 At the time of preparing and 'producing' *Production Studies*, there were a few books just out that were already noted as a turn toward the study of producers including, among others, Michael Curtin, *Playing to the World's Biggest Audience: The Globalization of Chinese Film and TV* (Berkeley: University of California Press, 2007) and Timothy Havens, *Global Television Marketplace* (London: British Film Institute, 2008).

8 Here we are thinking of Georgina Born, *Uncertain Vision: Birt, Dyke and the Reinvention of the BBC* (London: Vintage, 2005); Arlene Davila, *Latinos Inc.: Marketing and the Making of a People* (Berkeley: University of California Press, 2001); and the contributors to the groundbreaking volume *Media Worlds: Anthropology on New Terrain*, edited by Faye Ginsburg, Lila Abu Lughod, and Brian Larkin (Berkeley: University of California Press, 2002).

9 For example: Tom O'Regan, Ben Goldsmith, and Susan Ward, *Local Hollywood: Global Film Production and the Gold Coast* (St. Lucia: University of Queensland Press, 2011); David Hesmondhalgh and Sarah Baker, *Creative Labour: Media Work in Three Cultural Industries* (Abingdon, Oxon: Routledge, 2011); Vicki Mayer, *Below the Line: Producers and Production Studies in the New Television Economy* (Durham, NC and London: Duke University Press, 2011); Tejaswini Ganti, *Producing Bollywood: Inside the Contemporary Hindi Film Industry* (Durham, NC: Duke University Press, 2012); Mark Banks, Rosalind Gill, and Stephanie Taylor, eds., *Theorizing Cultural Work: Labour, Continuity and Change in the Cultural and Creative Industries* (Abingdon: Routledge, 2013); Aswin Punathambekar, *From Bombay to Bollywood: The Making of a Global Media Industry* (New York: New York University Press, 2013); Petr Szczepanik and Patrick Vonderau, eds., *Behind the Screen: Inside European Production Cultures* (New York: Palgrave MacMillan, 2013); Bridget Conor, *Screenwriting: Creative Labour and Professional Practice* (Abingdon: Routledge, 2014); Michael Curtin, Jennifer Holt, and Kevin Sanson, *Distribution Revolution: Conversations about the Digital Future of Film and Television* (Berkeley: University of California Press, 2014); Miranda J. Banks, *The Writers: A History of American Screenwriters and Their Guild* (New Brunswick, NJ: Rutgers University Press, 2015). Journal articles abound but unfortunately, because of space restrictions, it would be prohibitive to include them here.

10 It would be foolish here to try to trace out the centuries-long debates over naïve empiricism that continue to occupy critical studies today.

11 Feuer is drawn from a conference paper first cited in David Morley, "Changing Paradigms in Audience Studies," in *Remote Control: Television, Audiences and Cultural Power*, edited by Ellen Seiter, Hans Borchers, Gabriele Kreutzner, and Eva-Maria Warth (New York: Routledge, 1989), 24.

12 Jackie Stacey, "Hollywood Memories." *Screen* 35, no. 4 (1994): 326.

13 See, for example, an overview of this project in Ellen Seiter, *Television and New Media Audiences* (Oxford: Oxford University Press, 1999).

14 Nick Couldry (2003), "Media, Symbolic Power and the Limits of Bourdieu's Field Theory," Media@LSE Electronic Working Papers, No. 2, edited by Rosalind Gill et al., London: Media@LSE. www.lse.ac.uk/media@lse/research/mediaworkingpapers/pdf/ewp02.pdf.

15 This phrasing is actually borrowed from a phrase Charlotte Brunsdon used in critiquing any formalization of a reception studies agenda because it would result in the bifurcation of the "bad text" and the "good audience."

16 This summary statement is expanded on eloquently in Helen Davis, *Understanding Stuart Hall* (London: Sage, 2004).

17 John Caldwell makes this first point in "Cultural Studies of Media Production: Critical Industrial Practices," in *Questions of Method in Cultural Studies*, edited by Mimi White and James Schwoch (London: Blackwell, 2004), 109. The second point is argued in more depth in Vicki Mayer (2011) *Below the Line*.

I

TOOLS OF THE TRADE

1

I LIKE MY BOTS LIKE I LIKE MY PEOPLE: WEIRD, MIXED, ALWAYS ACTING

Chris Peterson

"I like my husbands like I like my orthodoxy: prevailing, communist, always correct."
—@ilikelikeilike[1]

@ilikelikeilike tells jokes on Twitter. This is not unusual: many of Twitter's several hundred million accounts tell jokes. Unlike most of them, however, @ilikelikeilike tells *only* jokes; stranger still, it tells versions of *only one* joke, over and over again, as it has every three hours since June 2013. @ilikelikeilike can perform this comic feat, which would seem to require inhuman stamina and ingenuity, because @ilikelikeilike is not a human: it is a bot.

Twitter bots programmatically generate and post tweets. The proximate programmer of @ilikelikeilike is Joel McCoy, a software developer from Somerville, Massachusetts, who designed the bot to automatically generate variations of a formulaic joke by pseudo randomly selecting nouns and verbs from an online dictionary. Being random, the jokes are funny only accidentally, but this, according to McCoy, is precisely the point. "[I am] making bots for all the bad and lazy jokes people make so that no one has to spend time on them," he told *WIRED*. "It's the automated labor theory of humor: let machines do the work so people have the time to think."[2]

Bots have always been about labor. The word 'bots' began as a simple contraction of its parent, 'robot,' the etymology of which the *Oxford English Dictionary* traces to an eponymous "central European system of serfdom, by which a tenant's rent was paid in forced labour or service."[3] In 1922, during the Lochner era of laissez-faire capitalism, the *New York Times* noted approvingly that "Robots were by all means better for use in factories and in armies, making cheap labor material, and not causing any troubles as strikers."[4] By 1990, 'bots' had diverged sufficiently to warrant their own definition as "automated program[s] on a network (esp. the Internet), often having features that mimic human reasoning and decision-making."[5] Stuart Geiger, in his study of the bots that help bring order to Wikipedia, describes them as "articulations of delegation" that work to "simultaneously produce and rely upon a particular vision of how the world is and ought to be."[6]

@ilikelikeilike

```
I like my <%= person %> like I like my <%= object %>:
<%= desc0 %>, <%= desc1 %>, <%= junc %> <%= desc2 %>
```

I have reproduced here the formula at the heart of @ilikelikeilike. Each time it runs, the bolded variables (my emphasis) are populated with a noun, adjective, or conjunction drawn from a word list either written by McCoy or provided by the online dictionary Wordnik.

Word lists may seem banal, but they are not neutral. Lists enable what Ian Bogost calls "ontographical cataloguing": the process of registering the things understood to exist. McCoy's person *list, for example, contemplates and constructs a cast of characters who might properly be the subject of a sexually freighted joke:*

```
["men", "women", "ladies", "fellahs", "partners",
"hook-ups",  "pairings",  "lovers",  "husbands",
"wives", "spouses", "senpai"]
```

This list reflects and reproduces McCoy's values—to an extent. "I mixed male-gendered, female-gendered, and gender-neutral terms there, consciously," McCoy told me. "[But as] to what the robot might say about any or all of those groups, I don't exercise any prior restraint or even guidance."

Instead, what @ilikelikeilike says about those characters is determined on the fly as they collide with objects pulled randomly from Wordnik. Cofounded by a lexicographer and an engineer, Wordnik has developed its own canon, assembled its own corpora, authored its own lists. All these undoubtedly reflect cultural codes as well, but they are blackboxed to @ilikelikeilike, which simply requests a random noun, as well as three adjectives associated with that noun, and blindly inserts them into the joke ("I like my women like I like my upheaval: political, violent, and not domestic").

Wordnik presently allows programs to query its database up to 15,000 times per hour at no charge. @ilikelikeilike can freely exploit all the work done upstream by dictionary editors, marketing associates, and relational databases. If, however, Wordnik 'goes on strike,' and stops providing words for any reason (because its employees demand more money, because its servers demand more power, and so on), then @ilikelikeilike will be forced to shut down.

Bots, like all computer programs, are thus designed to do what their designers want them to do. The semiotics of labor discipline are deeply embedded in the culture of computation, and have been ever since the word 'computer' meant not a machine made of metal, but rather a human *hired* to perform complex calculations.[7] Eric Grimson, an influential computer scientist and an architect of the undergraduate computer science curriculum at MIT, introduces students to computational thinking through the paradigm of "imperative programming," which he defines as "methods of ordering a computer to do something."[8] Cormen and his colleagues, in their foundational textbook *Introduction to Algorithms*, describe algorithms as a "well-defined computational procedure that takes some value, or set of values, as *input* and produces some value, or set of values, as *output*."[9] As Nick Seaver argues, the 'values' that algorithms define and (re)produce should be understood and examined sociopolitically as much as arithmetically.[10]

In this context it is tempting to read Twitter bots as the vanguard of a media production dystopia: as inexpensive, inexhaustible creative delegates of the technicians who build them. And, as other authors argue in this volume, there really *is* a shift toward computationally assisted forms of media production and an accompanying redistribution of the work available to (and shaped by) human labor. Adding ontological insult to economic injury, McCoy's automated theory of humor would seem to endanger even *comedy*, that last bastion of uniquely human creativity. These bots aren't only taking our jobs, they're telling our jokes!

@metaphorminute

In spring 2012 Darius Kazemi, another prolific botmaker based in Somerville, created @metaphorminute, which generates absurd, evocative metaphors by populating a template with words randomly selected from Wordnik ("a celery is a philosopher: inquiring and panic-stricken").

A few days into its young life, however, @metaphorminute tweeted "a faggot is a gadfly: case, but not heterosexual." Kazemi was horrified by the metaphor his bot had made. It was "as though my bot gained sentience but turned out to be a

> homophobic asshole," he wrote on his blog. "I'd been jokingly referring to the bot as 'my child' but now it had reached an age where it was mouthing off using words it didn't fully understand, and I had to really think about where to draw the line."
>
> While searching the Web, Kazemi found a blacklist of 458 'bad words' that had been compiled as a resource for developers. However, he felt the list, which contained words like 'hacker' and 'dominatrix,' was overbroad. "After discussing it with my spouse," he wrote, "I determined that what I really cared about were 'oppressive' words of various stripes—terminology used to denigrate specific groups of people." So he rewrote it to include ~forty-five words he believed @metaphorminute should not be allowed to say, washing his child-bot's mouth with programmatic soap.
>
> By doing so, Kazemi—and his wife—labored to inscribe their politics in @metaphorminute. But who labored to teach Kazemi and his wife to consider the oppressiveness of words, and what resources helped them decide which words are sufficiently oppressive to blacklist? Who taught Wordnik that it was acceptable to include these words, and who decided to add them to the legacy print dictionaries that Wordnik originally imported? In order to account for all the politics and labor in the bot, we must consider what Bruno Latour calls pre-inscription: "all the work that has to be done upstream of the scene and all the things assimilated by an actor . . . before coming to the scene as a user or as an author."
>
> Distance creates uncertainty for the proximate programmer. "Merely writing the code for a piece of software does not make me some sort of god who has fully exhausted everything about that software," Kazemi concluded. He's right, but not right enough, for even gods can be surprised by their creations. As sins go, @metaphorminute's was old, even original. A bot is a human: disobedient and fallen.

But although it may seem straightforward to conclude that these Twitter bots replace human labor, that is, that of the human wits who may otherwise have tweeted, or from whose own tweets these bots steal scarce attention, the truth is more complex. It turns out to be unexpectedly tricky to evaluate and ascribe authorship of the creative labor that goes into any given tweet by any bot. Who can be seen to stand behind a Twitter bot—who has worked so that it works—depends on where and how you look.

Upon first glance @ilikelikeilike may seem like a trivial technical toy. Yet, upon further inspection, this apparently simple bot can be seen to require a surprising amount of labor before it can execute even the most insignificant, unfunny joke. McCoy must maintain his server and pay for its power, which itself flows through an immense public/private electrical grid. The Wordnik application programming interface (API) must make available to @ilikelikeilike words from a corpus its developers labored to construct, a corpus that itself relies on legacy print

dictionaries its editors labored to create and classify. A litany of as yet unenumer-
ated actors (the node.js development team, the free or fair trade coffee that fuels
late night programming sessions, the multinational corporate entity of Twitter
itself, and countless others excluded for want of word count) bravely buttresses
the entire enterprise, which would quickly collapse without such actors' hidden
support.

Even keeping time—the most apparently simple, taken-for-granted computational task—requires staggering amounts of work. A computer's system time is
commonly kept by counting the number of ticks that have occurred since the
beginning of an arbitrary epoch, such as the conventional Unix Epoch that began
at 00:00:00 GMT 1 January 1970. This counting has been historically done by
physical chips, called Real Time Clocks (RTCs), that periodically pulse and inter-
rupt the central processing unit, rudely reminding it to permanently increment
the count of ticks that have transpired since the dawn of system time. These chips
are inanimate but not insensate: quartz RTCs often used in computers typically
speed or slow their rate of oscillation by one microsecond per degree Celsius
change in temperature, and even oven-controlled quartz clocks may unpredict-
ably wander several seconds over the course of a year.

Because the complexity of contemporary capitalism requires coordinated
timekeeping, the Internet Engineering Task Force (IETF), an ad hoc coalition
of network engineers, developed the Network Time Protocol, which facilitates
the regular recalibration of local system time against an international standard.
Thus system time is not truly kept, but *negotiated*. The stable-seeming clock in the
corner of your computer screen in fact represents a temporary resolution in an
ongoing argument between the demands of late capitalism and a quivering quartz
crystal.

From one perspective, @ilikelikeilike requires barely any human labor to tell a
joke; from another, it requires a massive network of engineers and standards and
chips just to tell when it is *time* to tell a joke, and when it speaks, it is in a chorus
of these many distributed actors. If any of these human and nonhuman actors stop
working, at any time, so too will @ilikelikeilike, which suddenly seems less like a
bot (that performs labor) than a factory (that aggregates it).[11] Rather than *replace*,
then, these bots should be understood to *displace* labor, like a boat displaces water,
moving it out of position but never eliminating that upon which it floats. Indeed,
sociologist Bruno Latour defines work as displacement: the translation, delegation,
shifting-out performed by one actor to support another.[12] The labor never disap-
pears; it simply moves further upstream, obscured by a fog shrouding the lands just
beyond proximate cause.

With bots, there may be proximate programmers, but there are not clear
authors, just more or less legible author functions.[13] Thus, while bots are artifacts that both prescribe and perform a politics, the precise politics in a bot is as
indeterminate as the labor in a bot, and for the same reasons.[14] Nobody knows

this better than the programmers themselves, who are as frequently surprised as anyone else by what their bots say. So while it is tempting for nontechnical critics to see bots as a kind of political prosthesis for the technicians inside them, the infinite regress of actors contained in each bot means that, as Seaver has argued, there isn't actually anyone inside or outside algorithms.[15] Depending on the shape of the network, some of us may be closer, and some further away, but in the end, we are simultaneously internal *and* external; entangled and eutectic.

@LatourLiturgies

In late 2013 I tweeted "Idea: Latour Liturgies." The pun was intended to play simultaneously on Ian Bogost's lists of "Latour Litanies"; the worshipful deference with which Latour is sometimes treated by his academic acolytes; the oracular tone of Latour's many aphorisms; and Latour's personal Catholicism. Shortly thereafter, I decided to make my idea into a bot.

Like the other bots I've described, @LatourLiturgies is randomly generated, only more so. Instead of populating random words into a fixed template, @LatourLiturgies downloads hundreds of tweets from @LatourBot (a bot that tweets quotes from Latour's writings) and @SpeakOLord (which tweets verses from a Catholic Bible) into a file. The bot then operates a Markov process over the combined corpus to probabilistically generate sentences inflected by both voices but decidedly distinct from either ("The LORD is a stronghold for the sociologists and sociologists learn from the lack of a thing!").

Unlike Kazemi and McCoy, I didn't write most of the code that animates my bot. Instead, I edited code posted freely by Jacob Harris, a developer at the Times, and modified by Nate Matias, a classmate at MIT. I've hosted other bots on my own servers, but this code uses iron.io, a service that allows (limited) free use of its computational resources for running bots and scripts. I didn't even make the avatar myself: I just downloaded a famous portrait of Latour smiling enigmatically, downloaded a cartoon halo and angel wings, and used Photoshop to superimpose the latter on the former.

As I write this @LatourLiturgies has issued more than 1,000 tweets. But who has authored them? Surely not Latour, and surely not the Bible; surely not the administrators of either of the bots I use as sources; surely not Harris or Matias, or iron.io. I connected the plumbing that made @LatourLiturgies possible, but I'm as surprised as anyone else when I read what it says because what I intend it to do is to say something I, by definition, don't intend it to say! @LatourLiturgies voices recombinant riddles: the wisdom of bots talking past each other, mixed up by math, and served pseudo randomly to readers, as far removed from a single human author as a bologna is from a boar.

Nor is this blended character unique to the bot form. As Oli Mould showed in an earlier volume of this series, both media productions and media producers are always temporary, contingent, mixed. Actors and actresses depend on writers and stages and smoothies and each other. Cameras depend on lights and videographers and electricity and emulsions. Jokester bots and standup comedians alike can either be blackboxed as stable objects or exploded open into their constitutive networks, depending on how you look at them. With apologies to Raymond Williams: there are in fact no people, only ways of seeing networks as people. Ontologically speaking, we're all already hybrids.

The a priori indeterminacy of objects is both a bug and a feature of actor-network theory (ANT) as an approach for studying production culture. The point of ANT is to follow the actors and describe what one sees, tracing the associations that tie the object of study together rather than taking the object as a given to be situated in a larger structure. As Latour, a godfather of ANT, writes: "I can now state the aim of this sociology of associations more precisely: there is no society, no social realm, and no social ties, but there exist translations between mediators that may generate traceable associations."[16] Because ANT places no limits in advance on the researcher's range as she travels down, up, and across the regress, it is up to her to trace or erase the linkages that allow the account to hang together. The production culture does not preexist her study of it; it is what she establishes in order to study it.

This methodological freedom places a heavy rhetorical burden on the researcher, but it also makes ANT an exceptionally sharp and flexible approach for studying media production. A skilled practitioner of ANT knows which connections to bring to the fore and which to allow to sink out of sight, and tests her skill by writing descriptions that are more or less convincing depending on the connections she chooses to trace between the actors themselves. Fundamentally, to do ANT is to allow actors to grant their own agency, tell their own story: "to describe, to be attentive to the concrete state of affairs, to find the uniquely adequate account of a given situation."[17] If she does her job well, and stays true to their trail, then an ANT approach can help her realize the truly transformative and underappreciated work done by spouses and servers, Catholics and quartz.

Notes

1 @ilikelikeilike Tweet, February 16, 2014. https://twitter.com/ilikelikeilike/status/434981168304635904.

2 Klint Finley, "Twitter 'Joke Bots' Shame Human Sense of Humor," *Wired.com*, August 22, 2013. www.wired.com/wiredenterprise/2013/08/humor-bots/.

3 "robot, n.1". OED Online, Oxford University Press. www.oed.com/view/Entry/275486?rskey=SeiRe7&result=1&isAdvanced. e.g.: "The Robot had been limited in 1800 by the Ragusa government to ninety days a year, and minimum standards had been set for the keeping of the peasant during this period."

4 "robot, n.2". OED Online, Oxford University Press. www.oed.com/view/Entry/1666
41?rskey=r6o0U9&result=2&isAdvanced=false.

5 "bot, n.3". OED Online, Oxford University Press. www.oed.com/view/Entry/25128
0?rskey=xzvc0Q&result=3&isAdvanced=false.

6 Stuart Geiger, "The Lives of Bots," in *Critical Point of View: A Wikipedia Reader*, edited by
Geert Lovink and Nathaniel Tkacz (Amsterdam: Institute of Network Cultures, 2011).
www.networkcultures.org/_uploads/%237reader_Wikipedia.pdf, 78.

7 "computer, n.". OED Online, Oxford University Press. www.oed.com/view/Entry/37
975?redirectedFrom=computer.

8 See, e.g., the lectures of 6.001.x, available on edX.org.

9 Thomas H. Cormen et al., *Introduction to Algorithm, Second Edition* (Cambridge: MIT
Press, 2001).

10 Nick Seaver, "Knowing Algorithms," *Media in Transition 8*, Cambridge, MA (2013).
http://nickseaver.net/papers/seaverMiT8.pdf.

11 Stuart Geiger, "Bots, Bespoke, Code and the Materiality of Software Platforms." *Information, Communication & Society* 17, no. 3 (2014): 342–56.

12 Jim Johnson, "Mixing Humans and Nonhumans Together: The Sociology of a
Door-Closer." *Social Problems* (1988): 298–310.

13 Michel Foucault, "What Is an Author?" in *The Foucault Reader*, edited by Paul Rabinow
(New York: Pantheon, 1984), 101.

14 Bryan Pfaffenberger, "Technological Dramas." *Science, Technology & Human Values* 17,
no. 3 (1992): 282–312.

15 Seaver, "Knowing Algorithms."

16 Bruno Latour, *Reassembling the Social: An Introduction to Actor-Network-Theory* (Oxford:
Oxford University Press, 2005), 108.

17 Latour, *Reassembling the Social*, 144.

2

PERFORMANCE, LABOR, AND STARDOM IN THE ERA OF THE SYNTHESPIAN

Mary Desjardins

In 2008, John Caldwell argued that systematic struggles over control determine contemporary media authorship, as they did in the studio era of film production. However, the increased competition and the blurring of labor categories in both production and postproduction "triggers pressure to symbolically value craft distinctions and innovation in public ways."[1] This chapter is an exploration of how contemporary media authorship has been expressed and contested in public ways through press and industry discourses that account for the emergence of the part human, part computer-generated 'synthespian.' Specifically, I examine these discourses' assumptions about labor and its relation to the commodity image (e.g., the star) in the contemporary film industry between the late 1990s, when the term first came into wide use in the trade and popular press, and 2003, when discussion turned toward speculation that motion-capture performer and voice artist Andy Serkis would receive an Oscar nomination for his contribution to Gollum, the digitally created character in *The Lord of the Rings: The Two Towers* (2002). The issues that crystalized around the serious industrial and critical attention given to Andy Serkis's digitally enabled performance were not new, but they seemed to indicate a turning point in public discussions about the status of acting in contemporary Hollywood films, especially action-oriented blockbusters. For example, in response to speculations around Serkis's chances for an Oscar nod, Jim Morris, who was at the time president of Lucas Digital, told *Daily Variety*, "It's a given that major movies don't get made now without digital characters." In the same article, Tim Sarnoff, president of Sony Pictures Imageworks, asserted, "Nobody looks at shot count any more as the single criteria as for what makes a great f/x movie. . . . They now look at *performance*."[2]

While the claims of these industry executives might be representative of the hyperbole that is part of the corporate toolbox for public self-scrutiny, film scholar Pamela Robertson Wojcik reassesses the concept of acting in light of the Serkis example. She suggests the actor's snubbing by the Academy was not due just to his collaborative performance with new technologies, but also to the fact that his vocal performance was interpreted as "unfastened from the body." She argues that the issue raised by Serkis's contribution to *The Two Towers* and the increasing reliance on digitally enabled performances in Hollywood films "points to a crisis in the conception of acting ... [i.e.,] the issue of acting in the digital age."[3]

So what is a synthespian, and how does it differ from characters and actors typical of previous eras of film production? A synthespian is a specific kind of 'virtual actor,' a photo-realistic, computer-generated film character created from the combination of several discrete computer processes including, most significantly, motion capture of a carbon-based actor. Media scholars Mark Wolfe, Tom Gunning, and Stephen Prince have emphasized the continuity between the virtual actor in recent digitized cinematic contexts and actors in the history of the analog-based cinema. For instance, they relate chronophotography and rotoscoping, previous analog-era processes of 'capturing' the motion of acting bodies for animated or special effects shots, to the capacity of contemporary digital processes to use actors for raw data rather than holistic performances. Gunning suggests the shared investment in synthespians by contemporary film creators and audiences exemplifies a continued fascination with cinema's capacity to show the human body in motion, a fascination that goes back to the very first films, including animated films.[4]

Whether or not this fascination with synthespians is actually a continuance of earlier audience responses to 'bodies in motion,' journalists and industry workers have not typically referred to traditional animated film characters as synthetic thespians, synthespians, virtual actors, or vactors, even though they share fundamental features with contemporary virtual actors—for example, like synthespians, traditional animated characters don't exist as discrete, material beings in pro-filmic reality; they may, too, have the source of their motion from the traced movements of a carbon-based performer (e.g., rotoscoping); and their voices or sounds are usually produced by actors, even famous stars, of film and other media.[5] Despite these similarities, there is a discursive divide between the ways industry and press discuss synthespians and the traditional animated characters who appeared in what was once understood by the category 'animated films.'

Synthespians, created from the use of human motion as raw data for digital transformation, are now identified by terms suggesting that these entities are not merely animated characters functioning within filmic narrative and spectacle, but are, themselves, authors—or, at least authoring agents of a particular sort. The term 'synthespian' (portmanteau word for 'synthetic thespian') does not connote a singular agent or consciousness authoring a performance, or the bodily presence we typically think is fundamental to transforming an actor's choices into action. Synthespians would seem to act without consciousness or presence. Despite any unease that might emerge from terms like these that co-join the inanimate with the animate—that suggest authored performance whose author is not singular, 'natural,' or perhaps even locatable—company executives and representatives of various Hollywood industry crafts, as well as the press that regularly quotes them, use these terms in negotiating the status of authorship in an industry increasingly reliant on the production of special effects-driven films.

The term 'synthespian' was coined and trademarked by digital artists Jeff Kleiser and Diana Walczak in 1989. For the next decade, the term was used within the special interest groups researching and employing soft- and hardware tools to create 'synthetic' computer-human performance capabilities.[6] 'Synthespian' took off as a popular term in the late 1990s, after William Gibson used it in his novel *Idoru* (about a synthetic Japanese pop star), after Virtual Celebrities Productions was formed to buy the digital rights to dead film stars, such as Humphrey Bogart and Marlene Dietrich, and after blockbuster films started to rely on photorealistic computer-generated characters (often creatures), which may or may not have employed (the still primitive) motion capture of carbon-based actors.[7] At this time, discussions of the virtual actor, now more and more synonymous with the term 'synthespian,' appeared in hundreds of articles in the trade press, fan publications, and entertainment sections of newspapers and magazines. Writers for the trade press, in their first mentions of synthespians, were concerned about the phenomena of computer-generated characters and virtual actors in terms of industry economies, labor, and technological developments. In the popular press, however, discourses about synthespians tended to proliferate when writers and journalists emphasized these figures not only in those aforementioned terms, but also as possible new media stars.[8]

Stars are unique in media labor categories in that they are both labor and commodity. The star performer labors to create the star image through acting, transforming the body (e.g., working out), posing for photos, giving interviews about craft and/or private life, and so forth, but this star performer also materially *embodies* the commodity, even if his or her physical presence is not necessary for the commodity's circulation. Synthespians, as digitally created figures, have no indexical relation to a real, carbon-based body, although Gunning argues that the use of motion capture could be said to "reference" a real body.[9] And, of course, synthespians cannot labor on behalf of their own creation as stars—performers enacting motions for capture on computer, computer artists who paint the features of the synthespian or match scanned images onto the motion capture, and performers who provide voices are the laborers who construct the synthespian. Although real, flesh-and-blood stars are also created out of the labor of others, a point to which I will return shortly, these striking dissimilarities between stars and synthespians suggest that what the press and increasingly the industry mean by 'synthespian as star' must derive from other commonalities between 'real' stars and 'synthespian' stars.

In distinguishing the difference between actor and star, Barry King argues that a film actor subsumes the self—"a personal identity, operative behind all roles and settings—into a character in a limited social setting."[10] Stars may act; however, they don't surrender their public personalities to the demands of characterization, instead "remain[ing] the same in a variety of contexts, locations, and environments," a status that makes stars "transfilmic entities."[11] The emergence of companies such as Virtual Celebrities Productions to create and market computer-generated reanimations of dead stars testifies to the way media industries and family estates continue to extract value from the fetishized star commodity and prove that the star is transfilmic—that is, the star image embodied by a carbon-based actor maintains a sameness in a variety of contexts, locations, and environments even after death.

The rationale guiding Virtual Celebrities Productions suggests that traces of actor labor can continue in their commodity form as long as some legal entity labors and barters on their behalf. However, the typical synthespian is not reanimated from a dead star. Like a carbon-based actor, it is subordinated to character in a specific narrative, plot, and visual spectacle. Yet film and computer effects companies, in collusion with the popular press, try to construct these kinds of virtual actors as 'transfilmic entities.' For example, Dr. Aki Ross, the lead synthespian character in *Final Fantasy: The Spirits Within* (2001), a film populated entirely by synthespians and the first motion picture produced by a computer game company, has become, like many flesh-and-blood stars, a magazine cover girl. The same computer artists who created her look as a brilliant scientist in the film stripped her down to a skimpy, string bikini for the cover of *Maxim* magazine's "Hot 100 babes" supplement a couple of months before the film's release.[12] All this suggests that stars and synthespians are alike, or can be alike, in the way they are promoted as transfilmic commodity fetishes, rather than (primarily) as laborers.[13]

Stars and synthespians are also alike in that their construction and circulation are the result of collaborative labor that is structured, and often obscured, by the industry's management of labor and the promotion of stars or synthespians as commodity fetishes. During the studio era of filmmaking, specific management strategies were geared toward a hierarchization and division of labor practices, which subordinated studio contract and casual employees to studio management.[14] Make-up and hair styling artists, wardrobe designers, dance, voice, and elocution teachers, stand-ins, stunt doubles, and even some writers, directors, and cinematographers, were directed by producers to help construct, enhance, and maintain the star images of specific acting laborers, who were contractually held to perform in certain films, pose for photos, give press interviews, and so forth.

Even in the post-studio era of filmmaking (roughly since the 1960s), in which stars and other production employees are usually independent agents, actor-laborers work in collaboration with other laborers to construct a unique star persona. The current inflation of star salaries not only attests to their continuing value to producers in guaranteeing a film's box office success, but also recognizes the need for stars to hire personal trainers, assistants, dieticians, hair and make-up stylists, and so forth to help construct, enhance, and maintain their image. These needs are in addition to the needs fulfilled by below-the-line laborers paid for by the production company to work for and with the star during the production and then the postproduction marketing phases of a specific film. Although dystopic discourses about the star image construction and exploitation have been produced since the silent era of filmmaking, much of the contemporary popular press discourse about stars glosses over the degree to which stars not only work for their image, but work with others to produce and promote it. In other words, this particular discourse deflects attention away from stars' position as laborers among other laborers, to promote them as sites of audience identification and desire.

It is the star's possession of a marketable, transfilmic identity that gives him or her leverage in making deals with studios or production companies concerning how that labor is to be expended, used, and compensated. Synthespians have no indexical relation to their creators and are not living beings with the agency to enact or withhold their labor. However, because labor creates synthespians, issues about working conditions and compensation are still relevant to their status in the industry. The collusion between industry and press enabling the marketability of the synthespian as a transfilmic entity obscures aspects of the collaborative labor in creating the synthespian, and also contributes to the relatively powerless position of computer technicians and artists and motion-capture performers in the film industry.

Arguably, these production groups have, to date, contributed the most to the creation of the synthespians, but like animation artists and models who collaborated in the creation of characters in earlier forms of animation during the studio era, they have little leveraging power with production companies. Furthermore, since 1997, which is the year the term 'synthespian' starts appearing in the press with any regularity, trade papers like *Variety* and *Hollywood Reporter* have documented both the periodic lay-offs of computer technicians at large FX companies and the inability for them to be represented by existing industry-related unions.[15] By the early 2000s, when FX companies had more work than they could handle, these nonunionized, lower-level, below-the-line workers were expected to work in exploitative conditions.[16]

Although the trade and popular press accounts of the creation of synthespians often mention or even focus with concern on the possibilities that standard talent labor categories—stuntmen, extras, cinematographers—might be or have been diminished, and appear obsessed with tracing the technical processes and artistic choices that result in the synthespian, their discourses are often compatible with the industry's need to keep such below-the-line digital effects workers a casual labor force.

The Screen Actors Guild seems to have picked up on this trend and, in response, has expended some effort in changing the discourse about motion capture. The Guild, which not only represents most motion picture and television actors, but took over the representation of extras in the mid-1990s, formed a committee in 1998 to study the interactive relation among actors, computers, and computer technicians in the process of motion capture, which is necessary for the realistic animation of the synthespian. In early 1999, the committee reported to members in an article in the Guild's *Screen Actor* magazine.[17] The article assures its readers that digital actors are rarely used *instead* of actors, but in *addition* to actors. This reassurance, however, is somewhat curious given that the Guild encompasses stunt doubles and extras, as well as actors with speaking parts. Even if an argument can be made that digital actors will not significantly replace most flesh-and-blood actors cast in speaking parts in a film, some of the first press discussions of synthespians were in the context of their replacement of extras for background (in *Titanic*); many of the articles about job re-skilling or declining work opportunities for performers since the emergence of digital actors concern stunt performers or stunt doubles. While the predominance of so many effects-driven action films has increased the *amount of work* for registered SAG stunt performers, the actual number of laborers the in this category registered with the Guild has dropped by almost 50 percent between 1997 and 2003, the same period in which the synthespian emerged as a significant, new performing category.[18]

The *Screen Actor* article is significant in its emphasis on the authorial status of the actor's contribution to computer-generated characters. It begins with a reminder that the 1998 negotiations between the union, the Alliance of Motion Picture and Television Producers (AMPTP), and television networks revealed that production management did not consider motion capture an area of contract coverage. The special committee's findings, as revealed in this article, provide a platform for SAG to assert that actors involved in the motion-capture process author their moves, and that henceforth, whenever motion capture involves actors it should be referred to as 'performance capture.' The way this new term gives actors leverage in negotiating contracts with computer FX and film companies is still unclear; however, to a large extent, SAG has succeeded in changing the discursive terms of this technological process. Almost all the computer artists, producers, and so forth interviewed in the trade press and the popular FX fan magazines since the publication of the SAG report in 1999 have begun referring to the process as 'performance capture,' and give at least lip-service praise to the contribution of actors in the creation of the synthespian.

Evidence from a few of the FX fan magazines suggests that the magazines and the production talent interviewed therein seem quite invested in the SAG perspective that actors author their moves in performance capture. For example, in

Cinefantastique, one of the oldest and best-selling magazines read by fans devoted to special effects films, the motion capture line producer for *Final Fantasy* praises the 'artistry' of actors he worked with for the necessary motion capture to create the synthespians that populate this film:

> We cast actors based on their performances. We're looking for the most talented people to work with. . . . It's not about having someone here with mime skills, it's about having someone who's a very good actor. You'll see that with the motion capture performance capability, every nuance and subtlety of the performance is captured. If somebody overacts, you see it, it stands out. We're trying to get the subtleties of human movement into the computer. That's the key of what we're doing here.[19]

This same producer makes similar claims about the film in an article in *Empire*, a British film fan magazine. Colin Kennedy, the article's author, asserts that "the performances are so accurate that the mother of one of the stuntmen recognized her son's gait from a set of moving dots."[20]

Of course not all laborers involved in creating synthespians share the belief that performance-capture actors are significant or functional authors. *Final Fantasy's* animation supervisor, Andy Jones, explains in *Cinefex* how animators hand-animated or 'keyed' most of the psychological movements for the characters played by the synthespians. He claims that because the motion capture stage was so big, most of the actors overplayed their parts—and consequently, performance capture was only used for broad movements; "we found that it was just easier to keyframe those subtle things."[21]

Jones's remarks suggest that performance capture actors are replaceable, not only by other similarly sized but anonymous actors for broad movements, but also by the animators themselves, who often use a mirror to look at the expressions on their own faces to key in subtle movements that will allow the synthespian to project psychological depth. Computer animators using their own expressions as models for facial movement to render virtual actors is mentioned in most articles about films populated by virtual actors. This animator practice of self-representation in creating characters goes back to earlier animation practices. For example, famous Disney animators Frank Thomas and Ollie Johnston argued that both actors and animators use gestures and expressions in their work of creating characters, but while "the actor can rely on his inner feelings to build his portrayal, the animator must be objectively analytical."[22] It is worth noting here that Thomas and Johnston give authorial credit to actors through their reliance on or cultivation of inner feelings, but they also imply gestures and expressions "naturally emerge" from the actors' feelings—that is, actors perform a character from inside out. Animators, by contrast, are authors because they "analytically" figure out how to communicate the feelings of a character from the outside by trying on different physical expressions and gestures using their own bodies.

In the terms I have been developing here, the ubiquity of this 'animator as author' discourse, at least until the early 2000s, suggests that both animators and actors providing performance capture for films were not typically considered as 'transfilmic entities,' but as conforming to an actorly role generalizable to their craft—the mother's recognition of the gait of her stuntman son in the synthetic film character notwithstanding. During the studio era, talent generalizable to their craft was always likely to be most of the casual workforce, and this seems to be proven true as well in the new media economy that is committed to making special-effects, action-oriented films that rely as much or more on craft as they do on star names to capture a world market. What is somewhat ironic about animation director Jones's attitude toward actors' lack of functional authorship in *Final Fantasy* is that the media industry also views computer technicians or artist-animators as generalizable to craft, and hence the relatively low starting range for these jobs (about $30,000 a year in the early 2000s), and the periodic, but predictable, announcements of their lay-offs after films are produced or go over budget.

Journalists writing in-depth articles about *Final Fantasy* and other FX films using synthespians for fan-oriented magazines tend to employ discursive practices that reiterate these logics of industry and effects workers at the high end of the labor hierarchy by placing emphasis in their essays on the 'artistic' choices made in creating the synthespian, rather than on the management practices that divide and hierarchize the labor practices in an FX house. This fetishizes the production process, but does not necessarily position typical FX laborers in places of control. It is not uncommon for articles to describe the routinized aspects of the synthespian animation process in passive, actually subjectless grammatical constructions. For example, the following description of creating synthespians for *Final Fantasy* appeared in *Cinefantastique*: "Sequences involving the phantom-like alien creatures, flying vehicles and other props, and even certain actions of the 'synthespians' were created using traditional, time-consuming, key-frame computer animation. Shots went through the various stages of production—lighting, visual effects (smoke, explosions, dust, etc.)."[23] One can read this passage and conclude that the entire film was automated without human labor. In the case of *Final Fantasy*, magazines typically mention and discuss the role of Hironobu Sagakuchi, the creator of the original series of computer games, producer Chris Lee, performance capture line producer Remington Scott, and animation supervisor Andy Jones, both quoted earlier in this chapter, and a few other positions relatively high on the labor hierarchy of the production. The hundreds of computer animators and other staffers are of course never mentioned by name, and are rarely mentioned in terms that suggest an accurate number count.

Statements by key personnel of *Final Fantasy* reveal how they foreground their control over the transfilmic possibilities versus the actorly function of the synthespian. For instance, several of the magazines quote producers Chris Lee and Jun Aida as claiming that many of the features of the lead synthespians of the film were constructed to connote a generalized notion of how a star is supposed to appear physically—the perfect skin, chiseled jaw, and so forth. Yet they also claim the greatest skill was expended on Dr. Sid, the synthespian with wrinkles and age spots, that is, with details that might be read as contributing to a more realistic, complex texture, and that requires more subtle artistry on the part of the animator. Lee and Aida claim that if the company had software improvements earlier or enough capital to lengthen production time, their teams could have expended the skill and artistry to make all the characters have more individualized textures.

This brings us back to Serkis, the actor providing the voice and body movements for Gollum. The 2002–3 marketing discourse for *The Lord of the Rings: The Twin Towers* and the press reporting the film's use of synthespians position him as a contender for a best supporting actor Oscar. While these discourses are concerned with production processes, animation supervisors, and the film's director, Peter Jackson, they also shift more to a focus on the actor who provides the raw data through performance capture and voice recording. Jackson and the film's visual effects producer, Dean Wright, claim that Serkis's work represents unprecedented contribution of an actor to the creation of a synthespian. Press articles never fail to mention that he worked longer on the film than any other of the film's actors, including those who perform in all three parts of the trilogy—acting his part twice in real time with the other actors, once in a motion capture suit, then performing on a stage for computer artists, and finally contributing postproduction voice dubbing. Although Serkis's contributions are to some extent generalizable to the craft of character acting, the extent to which he went beyond the usual demands of not only acting with performers during principal photography, but also in performance capture usually done only in postproduction, is used by press reporters and film crew alike to fetishize him as a transfilmic entity—one deserving of mention of having a 'private' persona, performance authorship, and an Oscar-worthy talent.[24] This campaign also elevates Jackson as a visionary director who recognized that a believable computer-generated character might only be possible with the contribution of an actor authoring a coherent, emotion-based performance and of an FX team that can create a fantastic bodily form to accompany that performance. One New Line executive claims that "Peter would talk to the animators as though he were talking to an actor,"[25] while Serkis was quoted in the trade press as saying, "Peter wanted all the emotion and physicality to come from a single performance."[26]

Press accounts about *The Two Towers* and its successful Gollum synthespian present the collaboration between Andy Serkis and FX animators as unprecedented and Jackson's authorial decisions as innovative. In doing so, they make implicit claims that these individuals' labors represent discrete authorial contributions. However, this chapter argues that these claims are driven by what is actually the erosion of discrete labor categories in the contemporary film industry. While Serkis failed to receive an Oscar nomination, the marketing and press discourses about *The Two Towers* exemplify how the synthespian functioned in the early years of its existence as a mediating figure and discursive term for both industry workers and the press in negotiating how to make sense of a new media environment, especially around issues of authorship and labor.

Notes

1 John T. Caldwell, *Production Culture: Industrial Reflexivity and Critical Practice in Film and Television* (Durham, NC: Duke University Press, 2008), 324.

2 Marc Graser, "The Clone Wars," *Daily Variety*, January 21, 2003, A1. Emphasis mine.

3 Pamela Robertson Wojcik, "The Sound of Film Acting." *Journal of Film and Video* (Spring 2006), reprinted in Heather Addison and Charles Berg, eds., *Annual Editions* (Dubuque, IA: McGraw Hill Contemporary Learning Series, 2007–8), 31.

4 Stephen Prince, *Digital Visual Effects in Cinema: The Seduction of Reality* (New Brunswick, NJ: Rutgers University Press, 2012); Thomas Gunning, "Gollum and Golem: Special Effects and the Technology of Artificial Bodies," in *From Hobbits to Hollywood: Essays on Peter Jackson's Lord of the Rings*, edited by Ernest Mathijs and Murray Pomerance (Amsterdam: Rodopi, 2006), 319–49; Mark J. P. Wolf, "The Technological Construction of Performance." *Convergence* 9, no. 4 (2003): 48–59.

5 By traditional animated films, I mean analog, stop-motion animated films that characterized most animation (whether cellular animation or Claymation, etc.) before the 1990s.

6 Jeff Kleiser, "Synthespianism and Anthropomorphization of Computer Graphics," gives the history of how the first synthespians were conceptualized, named, and technologically developed. www.kurzweilai.net/synthespianism-anthropomorphization-of-computer-grapics.

7 For representative discourses on enterprises reanimating dead stars, see Bruce Weber, "High-Tech Casting: Death Is No Drawback," *The New York Times*, March 11, 1994, B1, B16; Marla Matzer, "L.A. Firm Gives Digital Life to Stars of Yesteryear," *Los Angeles Times*, June 10, 1998, D1, D5; Bruce Haring, "Digitally Created Actors: Death Becomes Them," *USA Today*, June 24, 1998; Karen Kaplan, "Old Actors Never Die; They Just Get Digitized," *Los Angeles Times*, August 9, 1999; Megan Turner, "Back from the Dead: It's a Digital Disgrace—Hollywood Legends Recast with Modern Actors," *New York Post*, August 17, 1999; Austin Bunn, "Tech 2010: #26 Heaven Sent, The Dead Celebrity Who Comes Back to Life," *The New York Times*, June 11, 2000. See Lisa Bode, "No Longer Themselves? Framing Digitally Enabled Posthumous 'Performance.'" *Cinema Journal* 49, no. 4 (Summer 2010): 46–70, for a scholarly take on digitally enabled performances for stars/actors who died before shooting was finished on a production.

8 Some of the first articles in the trade and popular press that report and reflect on the advances from computer-generated characters to actual synthespians include: Ellen Wolff, "3-D, Digitally Speaking," *Daily Variety*, March 23, 1995; Katharine Stalter, "Synthespians Target H'w'd," *Daily Variety*, January 16, 1997; "Mirage Making Magic," *Weekly Variety*, January 26, 1997; Rex Weiner, "Exec Sees No Windfall on 'Titanic,'" *Daily Variety*, May 23, 1997; Carl DiOrio, "ILM [Industrial Light and Magic] in Labor

on Virtual Humans," *Hollywood Reporter,* June 18, 1997; John Voland, "'Titanic' F/X Spawn: New Digital Doman Offshoot Station X Bows," *Daily Variety,* January 22, 1998; Max Glaskin, "Virtual Actors Do Stunts at the Double," *The Sunday Times,* June 7, 1998; Guy Walters, "Coming Soon to a Cinema Near You: Animation Man," *The Times,* October 14, 1998; Patti Hartigan, "Digital Actors: Computers Make It a Virtual Certainty," *Chicago Sun-Times,* June 20, 1998; Ron Magid, "Digital Actors: This Year's Model," *Hollywood Reporter,* March 2, 2000, S6–9; Ruth La Ferla, "Perfect Model: Gorgeous, No Complaints, Made of Pixels," *The New York Times,* May 6, 2001, Arts and Leisure section 1, 8.

9 Motion capture (aka 'mo-cap') involves attaching light sensors or reflectors onto the actor's body, which, when filmed and scanned, provide computer data of the body and/ or face in motion for further manipulation. Computer animators can construct new and/or fantastical bodies and faces out of the data provided by the actor's mo-cap to create a synthetic character—a synthespian.

10 Barry King, "Stardom as an Occupation," in *The Hollywood Film Industry,* edited by Paul Kerr (London: Routledge & Kegan Paul, 1986), 158.

11 King, "Stardom as an Occupation," 169.

12 See La Ferla, "Perfect Model."

13 Others have argued this point from different perspectives, including Mary Flanagan, Kimberly Speight, Adam Faier, and Anna Notaro.

14 By "studio era," I mean the period of vertically integrated studios, roughly from the mid-1920s to about 1960, after which long-term contracts for stars were mostly over, and court-mandated divestment of exhibition sites and absorption by conglomerates put an end to large-scale, mass production of films by stand-alone companies.

15 See "IATSE Pacts to Represent Digital Domain Crew," *Weekly Variety,* January 6, 1997; Denise Hamilton, "Defense Vets Morph into New Jobs," *Los Angeles Times,* January 13, 1997; Stalter, "Synthespians Target H'w'd"; Katharine Stalter, "Digital Domain Axes Staffers," *Daily Variety,* March 7, 1997; Stephen McGinty, "Computers Kill off Cinema's Death-Defying Stuntmen," *The Sunday Times,* May 18, 1997; Paul Karon, "Domain Shrinking: F/X Houses Make 54 Staffers Disappear," *Daily Variety,* October 9, 1997; Anthony Breznican, "Pixels Replace Stunt Performers," *Austin Chronicle,* October 24, 1999; Sheigh Crabtree, "Digital Domain Lays off 17," *Hollywood Reporter,* April 3, 2001; Marc Graser, "F/X Houses Spring Back to Life," *Weekly Variety,* January 14, 2002; Marc Graser, "Tech Wizards Eye New Directions," *Daily Variety,* January 14, 2002; Rob Driscoll, "Hollywood Asks Who Needs Actors?" *Financial Times,* October 25, 2002; P. J. Huffstutter, "In With a Big Bang, Out With a Whimper," *Los Angeles Times,* April 20, 2003; Marc Graser, "F/X Gridlock Seizes Studios," *Daily Variety,* June 30, 2003; Ellen Wolff, "Prod'n Pace Hobbled by Ambitious F/X," *Daily Variety,* July 28, 2003. Many of the 1997 articles revolve around issues of FX labor at Digital Domain, which produced the synthespian extras and other FX for *Titanic* (1997).

16 See Huffstutter, "In With a Big Bang"; Graser, "F/X Gridlock," for documentation of work conditions for ordinary digital effects workers. Graser, in another article, "Tech Wizards," focuses on higher up in the effects hierarchy, specifically F/X supervisors, noting that there are differences in how they are treated by the studios and at facilities such as ILM, Sony Pictures Imageworks, and Digital Domain, where they can be treated like superstars. See also Matt Stahl, "Privilege and Distinction in Production Worlds: Copyright, Collective Bargaining, and Working Conditions in Media Making,"

in *Production Studies: Cultural Studies of Media Industries*, edited by Vicki Mayer, Miranda J. Banks, and John T. Caldwell (New York: Routledge, 2009), 54–67.

17 "New Technologies Committee Working Hard on 'Performance Cap.'" *Screen Actor* 40, no. 4 (March 1999).

18 Weiner, "Exec Sees No Windfall," and Walters, "Coming Soon to a Cinema Near You" for early discussions of computer-generated figures and/or synthespians replacing extras. For reports about effects of synthespians and computer-generated figures on stunt performers, see Breznican, "Pixels Replace"; Michael Mallory, "New Moves They Must Learn," *Los Angeles Times*, September 10, 2000; "Thomas Jane Training with SEALS for Punisher Movie," *USA Today*, June 13, 2003. www.earthsmightiest.com/movies_tv/news/?a=277; Richard Verrier and P. J. Huffstutter, "A New Risk in the World of Film Stunts," *Los Angeles Times*, September 2, 2003.

19 Bill L. Peterson, "Once upon a Time in the Future . . . *Final Fantasy*: Will CG Adventure Find an Audience Beyond Seasoned Game Players?" *Cinefantastique* 33, no. 4 (August 2001): 9.

20 Colin Kennedy, "Electric Dreams." *Empire* 147 (September 2001): 89.

21 Jody Duncan, "Flesh for Fantasy." *Cinefex* 86 (July 2001): 42.

22 Quoted in Prince, *Digital Visual Effects*, 104, from their 1981 book, *The Illusion of Life: Disney Animation* (New York: Disney Editions).

23 Peterson, "Once upon a Time," 11.

24 Michael Fleming, "Oscar Hopeful Serkis 'Towers' Over CGI Brethren," *Daily Variety*, November 21, 2002; Susan Wloszczyna, "Actor Gives Voice—and Body—to Vile Gollum," *USA Today*, December 17, 2002; Gregory M. Lamb, "The Rise of 'Synthespians,'" *The Christian Science Monitor*, December 18, 2002; Matt Hurwitz, "Gollum's Flying Serkis," *Daily Variety*, January 21, 2003; Ben Berkowitz (Reuters), "The Man Behind the Gollum Is a Shakespearean Actor," *Yahoo! News*, January 31, 2003; Ivan Askwith, "Gollum: Dissed by the Oscars?" *Salon.com*, February 18, 2003; Susan Wloszcyna, "Gollum Longs to Follow You Around," *USA Today*, February 31, 2003, identifies one of the transfilmic properties of the synthespian Gollum, which seems to distinguish him (and Serkis) from the mere actor John C. Reilly, who was up for an Oscar for best supporting actor (for *Chicago*) the year Serkis was denied a nomination: the Gollum has a "deluxe 11-inch talking doll built in his image."

25 Hurwitz, "Gollum's Flying Serkis."

26 Fleming, "Oscar Hopeful."

3

HOW GLOBAL IS HOLLYWOOD?

Division of Labor from a Prop-Making Perspective[1]

Patrick Vonderau

In July 2011, international media widely reported that film director George Lucas had lost a *Star Wars* copyright case in the UK Supreme Court. Lucasfilm, a company committed to aggressively protecting its intellectual property rights relating to the *Star Wars* franchise, had sued a hitherto unknown British prop designer named Andrew Ainsworth over replica storm trooper outfits. Ainsworth, who built the original storm trooper helmets while working out of his small design studio in Twickenham, South London on 1977's *Star Wars*, had been selling the costumes based on his original molds online for years. Lucas had repeatedly claimed the designer was breaching his copyright and in 2006, he won a $20 million judgment in the United States, resulting in a ruling from the U.S. District Court for the Central District of California that barred Ainsworth from importing his *Star Wars* products. In 2008, Lucasfilm took the case to Britain's High Court and in 2009 to the Court of Appeal, before finally bringing it to the Supreme Court in 2011. Meanwhile, Ainsworth continued selling small batches of storm trooper helmets, armor, and replicas of weapons, the Dark Lord costume, or the original R2D2 droid (complete with lights and wheels) for prices ranging between 300 and 2,500 British pounds per item. The courts unanimously concluded that props such as the storm trooper helmets were not art and thus not subject to British copyright laws, rejecting Lucasfilm's claim to enforce the earlier U.S. copyright judgment in the United Kingdom.[2]

In many ways, the Ainsworth-Lucas dispute seems to expose and challenge a division of labor ingrained in today's globalized media production systems. Since Adam Smith and the beginnings of classical political economy, the sphere of production has been viewed as an arena of continual subdivision between tasks and workers that leads to both increased productivity and human costs. For Marxists, division of labor means a mechanism for linking productivity, exploitation, and social control—a way of governing production processes that builds on the fragmentation of work, alienation, deskilling, and low labor.[3] This division may even take on a geographical dimension when the technical division of labor within a given organization disintegrates into a social division of labor between organizations in different countries.[4] A rich body of media industries scholarship has pointed to the effects a "new international division of labor" may have had on media workers' rights and identities, collaborative processes, local labor markets, or capital flows since the 1970s.[5] Long before *Star Wars*, U.S. copyright policies separated, or indeed created authors and non-authors, conferring proprietary rights on creative talent, and denying such rights to crafts workers.[6] And long before the Ainsworth-Lucas case, U.S. runaway productions had been at the center of disputes over the unequal conditions of work that may separate local, contracted 'below-the-line' wage workers such as prop makers or costume designers from incoming, contracted U.S. 'above-the-line' talent such as directors, art directors, or actors.[7]

The legal dispute between Ainsworth and Lucas both exposes and challenges this view on division of labor in the media industries. In their court reporting, British media described "Ainsworth, 62" as a "father-of-two" who had struggled to pay his children's school fees before discovering the props' value when selling two dusty storm trooper helmets at an auction back in 2004.[8] Ainsworth, who had worked as a prop designer for other U.S. productions shot at Shepperton Studios in the 1970s, such as *Superman* (1978, Richard Donner) and *Alien* (1979, Ridley Scott), thus fits into the picture of David battling Goliath[9] over the exploitation of value derived from runaway production labor. Even the courts came to agree that Lucasfilm's $20 million compensation claims were overblown, given that Ainsworth had sold his items to the value of "not more than $30,000 in the United States,"[10] and irrespective of the fact that props manufactured for European productions are regularly commodified and sold online there. Think, for instance, of prop-heavy British-German-French coproduction *The Three Musketeers* (Paul W. S. Anderson, 2011) whose props and costumes were still on sale at Hollywood retailer premiereprops.com as of September 2014; or think of director Quentin Tarantino, who was rumored to have sold props from *Inglorious Basterds* (2009), also shot on stage at Studio Babelsberg (Germany), via eBay for extra income. In this context, Ainsworth appeared to turn capitalism against itself, testifying to the possibility of worker resistance and of regaining authority over the conditions and possibilities of production labor. As he stated in an interview with the BBC, "this is a massive victory, a total victory . . . If there is a force, then it has been with me these past five years."[11]

This chapter suggests a different perspective on the division of labor in the media industries. It does so by following the cracks that also appear in this picture—the inconsistencies, contradictions, and paradoxes that permeate stories of unjust media work such as the above, on all levels, be they individual, organizational, legal, or even philosophical. For one, Ainsworth's media appearance as an anonymous loner defeating 'the industry' defied his actual career trajectory as an industry designer and entrepreneur, during which he had owned factories to produce and globally distribute kayaks, sportswear, and patented sport games before 'revisiting' his prop-making facility, Shepperton Design Studios, in 2004.[12] Ainsworth was hardly less skillful than Lucas in playing the press; while both claimed victory after the UK court ruling, both had in fact partly lost their cases. The court decided not to enforce U.S. copyright, nor did it grant Ainsworth the ownership over the copyright to the helmets as he in turn had requested.[13]

Ainsworth's as well as Lucas's entrepreneurial strategies were also both clearly situated within the same changing geography of globalization. Underlying their respective earnings from *Star Wars* was a model of economic development that appears as rather different from the 'new international division of labor' that had informed production when the original 1977 film was made. Today's post-Fordist media industry system dissolves traditional notions of 'core' versus 'periphery' as it sees low-wage, low-skill sweatshop factories emerge in former core regions (such as Southern California), and high-skill, industrial agglomerations proliferate in former production peripheries (such as the United Kingdom, Germany, or the Czech Republic).[14] It is a system marked by disintegrated industrial networks in which a large number of diversified firms interrelate.[15] In this contemporary environment, where creative output is often managed through the office of the production designer, cinema may be said to have turned into a "networked design practice," and Hollywood into a "digitally networked neighbourhood."[16] Consequently, studios aim at keeping control over this new mode of production that primarily appears as a constant reproduction—as a "production of continuous working copy as extendable Intellectual Property (IP)."[17] Their way of doing so is to construct closed spheres of innovation that limit the commercial use of their content in the networked environment.[18] Designer Ainsworth interfered in the order of this new economy, while being himself part of it.

The most surprising paradox, however, is that both Ainsworth and Lucas insisted on the storm trooper helmets being art because their opposing claims of copyright ownership would require such a definition. Thus, while Lucasfilm's attorneys suggested that the props were art in order to prevent any future commercial use of their content, Ainsworth's attorneys proposed that his work was art in order to underline his future artistic rights. This led three British courts into perennial, complex debates that became deeply entangled in theoretical and philosophical issues, such as the difference between art and non-art, for instance, or the specific difference between real helmets used for war and those used only in fictitious combatting on screen—both debates that go beyond the purview of copyright legislation and so far have hardly been an issue for political economy. My main point in this chapter is that they should. For how are we to answer questions about ownership, division of labor, or exploitation in contemporary media production processes without taking into account the various individual, organizational, legal, or philosophical layers of these processes?

Studies of production and the media industries ought to acknowledge the meaning of the objects produced (such as props), the ways production knowledge and agency are distributed between workers and their tools (such as prop molds), and the aesthetics of a production itself (such as prop making). Acknowledging industrial workers as producers means to move below the surface of macro-geographical issues or media institutions.[19] This certainly is not to say that a political economy confined to studying such institutions would be 'simplistic,'[20] or that media work wouldn't be precarious—in this latter respect, media resemble other industries. But it means to say that a political economy studying design processes in today's postindustrial, digitally networked production environments needs more refined analytical instruments in order to account for what makes media production conceptually or historically *specific*, as compared to other industry practices. While it is hardly new to point out the need for such refined and integrative approaches,[21] the following argument differs in *how* these layers are analytically integrated. Taking its cue from Alfred Gell's anthropology of art, and based on ethnographic fieldwork that investigated prop making in the context of U.S. runaway productions at Studio Babelsberg, Germany between 2010 and 2012, the remaining part of this chapter suggests a methodological triangulation that combines the *semiotics of objects*, the *knowledge of technologies*, and the *aesthetics of practices* in its study of production. As any production ethnographer would acknowledge, such an approach also necessitates thinking through these layers while doing the analysis itself.[22] And here we are, already in the midst of the field.[23]

At the Gates of the Studio: Notes from the Field Diary

October 13, 2010. I am to meet Ben Palmer, a British prop maker and animatronix engineer now living in Berlin, in front of the prop workshop at Studio Babelsberg.[24] It's a rainy afternoon in October. *The Three Musketeers*, Constantin Film's international coproduction starring Orlando Bloom, Milla Jovovich, and Logan Lerman, is shooting for the second day on a stage. Ben arrives and informs me that a large part of the work has already been accomplished elsewhere, on location in Bavaria. I find myself in the middle of the shoot, in the middle of the day, entering an ongoing process at a point where everyone's willingness to share insights is limited by missed deadlines, overdrawn budgets, and increasing 'IP' anxiety. Ben is patient and accommodating, however, and he walks me through the workshop. I see workbenches, tools, a few coworkers, weapons made from rubber, molds that are "cost-saving measures," as he briefly explains. Everyone is silently tinkering with something. A few drawings are lying around, but the project doesn't come alive as a whole. The fragmentation of work necessarily appears first to the beholder; the process is divided up in ways that deny access to the field. Ben seems to deliberately ignore the whole of the film, the larger organization in which his workshop forms part, but not because he would be alienated from his work, rather to the contrary—in order to get the work done. It's like Hennion wrote of the production of pop music: the doors of the studio have to be closed, the industry has to be forgotten, the outer world.[25] The workshop is small, unheated, provisional—Ben tells me it is cleared out after each project, only to then be set up anew. For Ben, this new film is just another project, hard to delineate against other projects he is simultaneously working on; the projects blend into each other in terms of repeated collaborations (relations between workers), uses of workspace, artifacts produced. . . .

We are walking outside, it has stopped raining, looks dreary, we are in the muddy periphery of the studio lot. Ben walks me over to a shipping container he rents—it is where he keeps his tools when a project ends. The workshop is remote from where the shooting takes place. There is an implied topography of the studio that has nothing to do with the real estate property we are standing on or with 'Studio Babelsberg' as a branded historical site. Babelsberg appears as a *bricolage*, ad hoc and fractured, a shape-shifting ensemble of companies, financing plans, and contracts worked out elsewhere. All these metaphors of production—'workshop,' 'factory,' 'network,' and 'culture'—imply a sense of place, a spatial order. They invoke traditional crafts and art systems, Taylorist models of divisions of labor, projectification or spaces of flow, and historically grown infrastructures on which networks of production can thrive. Yet in order to get into the field, I have to build on a more deterritorialized notion of culture, and a more process-oriented notion of place. What about the *temporal* dimension of production? What is Babelsberg if not a "practiced place?"[26]

While we are slowly walking over to the main part of the lot, I start to realize that this production space is organized in circles, each circle having its own temporality. What follows the silent tinkering in the prop workshop is the collaborative fever of the art department with its models, designs, and artists, and then we are moving on stage, where I am to marvel at the grand complexity of set construction. Leading from one place to another is a network of communication channels, a division of inputs, processing, storage, and usage established in answer to the questions: What will be required, when, and why? The closer you get to the shooting, the less autonomous you are, more and more technology comes in, the 'smell of creation.' The final stage is the shooting stage, upgraded technologies and screens everywhere, man-machines walk around, whispering to each other. Functionally divided units of workers—the producers, directors, the sound department—camp in tents around the star, while the star himself remains invisible, literally screened off. Zero access, tension is in the air, the time of the star is in dire need of protection. Ben and I get a glimpse of Bloom and Jovovich performing alone in front of a green screen, in what is to become the most boring moment of my entire visit. Why am I here where time comes at the highest expense? The periphery as preferred site for mapping the social topographies of production.

Inside Prop World: Dividing Labor and Production Control

Prop making is a craft labor profession in feature film and television production and notably different from what prop masters or production designers do.[27] While getting instructions, designs, or ideas from these groups prior to and during the shoot, prop makers independently budget, plan, and create props in autonomously organized workshops. Using a limited variety of materials, techniques, and tools, they manufacture any props that cannot be bought or rented, and they modify existing props according to production needs. In today's post-studio, project-based era, U.S. runaway productions coming to Germany usually employ freelance prop makers who organize in semi-permanent work groups, that is, in specialized project teams moving from project to project.[28] In the 2006–14 period, such groups of prop makers were constituted and stabilized through a system of accounting, deal-making, and contracting practices that centered around Studio Babelsberg as one key site in Germany giving foreign investors access to coproduction partnerships, and to federal and regional film subsidies. A roster of design-intensive action films including *Mission Impossible III* (2006, J. J. Abrams), *Speed Racer* (2008, The Wachowski Brothers), *Ninja Assassin* (2009, James McTeigue), *Unknown Identity* (2011, Jaume Collet-Serra), and *Witch Hunters* (2013, Tommy Wirkola) came to foster the growth of a local network of about thirty prop builders and model makers who would work repeatedly in different constellations together. The "design interest"[29] inherent in this particular genre of high-budgeted U.S. action entertainment thus created particular employment conditions for prop makers. Trade union Ver.di described these conditions as above the average of regular German film production in terms of hourly wages, reputation building, and the length of project employment that could well exceed six months of continuous prop work.[30] Compared to Pinewood (UK) or Barrandov (Czech Republic), however, Studio Babelsberg and the Berlin-Brandenburg region have not yet developed the same depth of infrastructure that would secure equally large numbers of international projects in the future, with local attempts to develop such an infrastructure remaining largely contingent on the existence of the German Film Fund established in 2007.

As one of just a handful of senior prop makers, Benjamin Palmer regularly took turns in supervising the Babelsberg workshop, a task that includes budget calculation and sourcing work for the group. Prop makers are conventionally part of the art department and subordinated to either a prop master or a set decorator, who in turn reports to the production designer and assistant director. Yet such conventional hierarchies are not determining working conditions given the relative autonomy of the prop workshop. Rather, the central locus of control within this working environment—in the sense of both a managerial division of labor and of self-governance—is time. As Palmer put it:

> Prop making follows pretty much the same principle for every film. There are of course different needs for what has to be fabricated. But if you have done it a while, you have done it before. All I have to do is juggle the time. Time is the hard one; it's not juggling how to make them [i.e., the props, P.V.], it's *just* the time. Deadlines are always close, and they always change.... At the end of the day, material isn't that expensive; it's the labor cost that is expensive, so we are pushed all the time, "cheaper cheaper faster faster" [*laughs*]; it's all about speed and effectiveness.... You always try to keep it to the best, but sometimes they move the schedule, other things come in, so you have to have something on that day.[31]

As in other fields of film and television production, management only sets the general pacing and timing of work.[32] At the beginning of each project, a basic shooting schedule based on a breakdown of the script becomes—together with designs (drawings) circulating in the art department, and the daily call sheet later in the process—the key informational input on which the organizing of work in the workshop is based. The script itself is less significant, as it "does not necessarily tell you anything about the props."[33] Based on the shooting schedule, the supervising prop maker works out a budget, allocating costs to labor hours and materials for each of the objects to be produced. Throughout all the different projects a prop maker may work on, he or she may use the same few materials—silicon, glues, polyurethane casting resin such as Fast Cast, or chemiwood (a block of chemical wood), to name a few. What specifies the division of labor in a given prop-making process are not just these material inputs, the schedule, or overall conditions of work: it is also the props themselves, the tools required to work with them, and the aesthetic engagements of the prop-making craft.

The Career of a Prop

Simply put, a prop is an item handled or used by an actor during the filming of a show. This may include objects such as bottles or newspapers, but also guns, grenades or knives, fake food, and personal props such as rings and eyeglasses. Ultimately, a prop is defined by "whose responsibility, whose budget it comes from," making the question a "political" one.[34] Objects may circulate between prop masters, set dressers, stunt coordinators, special effects, or costumes, engaging their various departments in negotiations of look, functionality, and responsibility. For *The Three Musketeers*, for instance, a flamethrower was built by the special effects department, then 'dressed' by the prop-making team, shot on stage, and finally enhanced by VFX in postproduction. Such division of labor is obviously also mediated by the artifact itself. How prop work collaboration develops, and how tightly diversified and deeply connected workers within a given project's group are, depends on the character of the produced object in the first place. The specially designed and time-consumingly built life-sized cars for *Speed Racer* embody different attachments between the prop makers and their tools, and between the departments involved, than the large batches of identical historical weapons made for *Inglorious Basterds*. Thus, instead of explaining prop work as being determined by an abstract, uniform 'context' of production, props can be seen as variably co-organizing prop work, mediating the relations between the participants in the process.[35] Props, in other words, have some agency, a 'biography' or 'career' that extends beyond the actual shoot. Once a prop is finished, it moves into the storage (or prop store), where it "waits until it needs to go on set, and when they are finished with it, it will go back."[36] A prop then continues its career in a complex reuse economy. This may include prop masters buying props from production in order to rent them out to another film, production companies auctioning off props via Christie's and other memorabilia traders, and even directors or actors keeping or selling items they worked with during filming. Props thus move smoothly in and out of the film and the studio, crossing different layers of reality associated with cinematic fiction—the reality of the work whose relations they mediate, the pro-filmic reality in front of the camera, the diegetic universe of Jedi knights or Musketeers fighting evil, and the afilmic worlds of those renting, selling, or owning them.[37]

Managing Work through the "Toby Mold"

Props play a part in the organizing of the labor process; they have 'meaning' that reflects their circulation both inside and outside the studio and even on the ways the labor market for prop makers is structured, given that some types of stories generate more work than others. Yet props are certainly not the only actors that are relevant for understanding how conventional principles of division of labor are situated and localized within this specific topography of production. Equally instructive is to study the relation between prop makers and their tools. Such tools, especially the 'big machinery' a freelancing senior prop maker may bring into production as part of his services, such as table saws, grinding machines, turning lathes, or air compressors, are a way to ensure getting onto a new project, and to set one's services off against those of competitors.[38] The right tools assist in managing the inner hierarchy of group collaboration in this field, and they are of course also essential for coping with the time and cost management pressure exerted by production. Of particular importance in this contexts are molds. This is because prop making is primarily a reproductive activity:

I copy [*laughs*]. At the end of the day, we copy articles, we reproduce pieces or design pieces. For example, if there is a bottle, and they can find one but can't buy another twenty to match it, we need to reproduce it twenty times. We take a mold for the original, we reproduce it and ... for example, we do it in breakaway effects or something. Sometimes it can be just me, one person. In Babelsberg, we had a lot of shoot 'em up films where we made replica guns. When it's more fancy, a sci-fi or period piece ... it's getting more interesting, and it also starts getting more people.[39]

Molds for casting copies of artifacts using silicon or rubber are traditionally made from plaster or fiberglass, yet Palmer's group adopted another technology that was introduced by a visiting supervising British prop maker, Toby Shears, during production of *In 80 Days Around the World* (2004, Frank Coraci). The 'Toby Mold,' as they refer to it, is made of medium-density fiberboards (MDF) and delivers a more precise cast. It also speeds up the casting process, allowing a focus on the work with prototypes, that is, with the creation of new objects for subsequent reproduction, a task that accompanies the more routine aspects of prop work. Finally, the mold is reusable. While production owns the look of a film, and a prop master often takes the props, it is the senior prop maker who owns his tools and masters the molds.

The Aesthetics of Making Rubber Guns

With the question of ownership, the argument leads back to where this chapter began. A prop maker does not own a mold, so what about his or her owner-ship in the creation of a film, as debated in the Ainsworth-Lucas case? There is, of course, an odd anachronism in relating a traditional understanding of artistic production in the sense of *creatio ex nihilo*, of solitary origination, to the reproduc-tivity of prop making, and to today's networked production systems at large. At the same time, acknowledging the reproductive character of prop work does not preclude the possibility of aesthetic significance in the objects, processes, and per-sonal judgments involved. Prop makers regularly translate and interpret designs. For instance, making a specific prop such as Athos's (Matthew McFayden) fantasy umbrella harpoon gun, an item whose design became essential for the experience conveyed in the opening of *The Three Musketeers*,[40] necessitated working from a drawing that provided only a general idea of the design, without any technical specifications given. The idea of the prop as accessible through the drawing had to be translated into a first material artifact, or prototype. A first studio representa-tion of such a fictitious artifact may consist of a photocopy glued on cardboard; it may be cast in silicon or carved from chemical wood in order to negotiate the scale and weight of the future prop, and to understand how it will align with an actress's or actor's bodily performance. Subsequent transformations of this first mock-up into a functional prototype of the prop may take weeks and even involve elements disassembled from real-world artifacts, such as gun triggers. Throughout the process, translations and interpretations are unavoidable because a drawing is "two-dimensional, and when you start producing three-dimensional, then it doesn't quite work as they had the vision; it's too small perhaps, or it doesn't quite work."[41] In other words, prop making continuously requires an engagement that is nothing but aesthetic in character, prompted by constant "clashes with the material world"[42] on one hand, and conflicts with those in charge of having the 'vision' and signing off on the props on the other. Prop making then, is, in a Kantian sense, all about aesthetic subjectivity that feels itself via judgments of taste occasioned by objects. But is it also about art?

Conclusion

Revisiting the Ainsworth-Lucas case, I contend that a tension between an original and a reproduction, as well as one between the 'upper view' and those executing the view, is endemic to the division of labor in prop making for feature film production. And yet it would be utterly misleading to identify this tension with the questions brought up during the Lucasfilm dispute; that is, the question of ownership over props, the nature of props as art, and of an industry seemingly allowing for creative authorship only along an above/below-the-line demarcation. There is, as I would like to conclude, a conceptual gap that keeps political economy (and even lawyers, as it seems) from identifying what makes this form of production specific. It is an unnoticed conceptual gap that persists between art and aesthetics, law and ethics, the social and the cultural. In assuming these concepts could be flatly equated, political economists tend to collapse worker subjectivity, authorship, and ownership into each other. These observations show that prop making is part of a production culture that is temporal rather than spatial, with processes, tools, languages, communities of practices, and managerial forms of control predicated on time. Production's social topography, in turn, appears as marked by differences that are not simply fixed oppositions as the above/below-the-line scheme suggests, but rather circular, following from the phasing of inputs on the way to the shoot. As Benjamin Palmer aptly observes in the industrial context of networked design practices:

> We are the middle men, only the prop makers, but at the end of the day, isn't everybody a middle man? Even producers have bosses, and in the making of a movie, on the ground everybody will have somebody above them.[43]

Given the closed sphere of innovation that enables the production of working copy as extendable IP, it remains an uncontested truth among prop makers that they do not hold ownership in the designs they are working with. In this sense,

Hollywood indeed has become a globally networked neighborhood. This legal truth, however, is not to be conflated with the ethical attitude a prop maker may show toward his personal involvement in a given production. "You might feel you own the look, but nothing is yours," as Palmer asserts. "If it looks good on the screen, you feel, 'that's mine,' but if it looks bad?" implying that, sometimes, not to have owned or authored a design can become the advantage of a middle man who rejects that design on aesthetic grounds. Paradoxically, some of the prop makers within the Babelsberg group expressed an ethical distance from the look and storylines of those 'shoot 'em up films' whose 'lower' genres had allowed the establishment of the group in the first place.

This leads finally back to the ultimate philosophical question: Are props art? As I suggested earlier, a prop's career entails a journey leading through different realities associated with cinematic fiction, and answering the question about a prop's status as art thus ultimately requires an acknowledgment of the changing status of the object at hand. While a storm trooper helmet would not be considered art in its capacity to co-organize the division of labor that went into its making (or as a helmet used by storm troopers in the fictional world of the story), it well may become art in the outer, afilmic world of those selling or owning it. Such a processual concept of props as art runs counter to the substantial definition brought up in the Lucasfilm case, when the helmets were compared to sculptures and real-world artifacts (helmets used in the Second World War) by means of some 'function' understood as intrinsic to them. Whatever truth there is in the legal philosophy of this argument, it is a fact that Ainsworth's storm trooper helmets became an instance of post-conceptional art that both evokes and transcends the historical ontology of the artwork when, in October 2013, Damien Hirst and other British artists transformed the helmets into objects to be displayed at the Saatchi Gallery.[44] As if having waited for this final step in the career of the prop, British property law was changed in 2014 in the United Kingdom's Intellectual Property Act to include a new criminal offense for the copying of registered designs—just in time to accommodate Lucasfilm's shooting of *Star Wars Episode VII* in the country.[45]

Notes

1 With special thanks to Ben Palmer for generously discussing his work with me. I would also like to acknowledge the contribution made by John T. Caldwell, Petr Szczepanik, Eva Redvall, and Dorota Ostrowska in discussing earlier versions of this research with me.

2 For the press coverage of this ruling and the debates that preceded it, see, for instance, "Lucasfilm Wins Legal Battle," *Variety*, October 11, 2006; Sarah Knapton, "Court to Rule in Star Wars Costume Battle," *The Guardian*, April 7, 2008; Ben Child, "George Lucas Defeated over Star Wars Stormtrooper Replicas," *The Guardian*, July 27, 2011; Diana Lodderhose, "Lucasfilm Loses U.K. Court Battle," *Variety*, July 27, 2011; "Lucas Loses Star Wars Copyright Case at Supreme Court," *BBC News*, July 27, 2011.

3 Toby Miller, "The New International Division of Cultural Labor," in *Managing Media Work*, edited by Mark Deuze (Thousand Oaks, CA and London: Sage, 2011), 87–100.

4 Allen J. Scott, *Geography and Economy: Three Lectures* (Oxford: Clarendon Press, 2006), 38–9.

5 See, among others, James F. Tracy, "Whistle While You Work: The Disney Company and the Global Division of Labor." *Journal of Communication Inquiry* 23, no. 4 (1999): 374–89; Serra Tinic, *On Location: Canada's Television Industry in a Global Market* (Toronto: Toronto University Press, 2005); Ben Goldsmith and Tom O'Regan, *The Film Studio: Film Production in the Global Economy* (Lanham, MD: Rowman & Littlefield, 2005); Greg Elmer and Mike Gasher, eds., *Contracting Out Hollywood: Runaway Productions and Foreign Location Shooting* (Lanham, MD: Rowman & Littlefield, 2005); Toby Miller, Nitin Govil, John McMurria, Richard Maxwell, and Ting Wang, *Global Hollywood 2* (London: British Film Institute, 2005), 111–72; Vicki Mayer, *Below the Line: Producers and Production Studies in the New Television Economy* (Durham, NC and London: Duke University Press, 2011); John T. Caldwell, "Stress Aesthetics and Deprivation Payroll Systems," in *Behind the Screen: Inside European Production Cultures*, edited by Petr Szczepanik and Patrick Vonderau (New York: Palgrave Macmillan, 2013), 91–112; Michael Curtin and John Vanderhoef, "A Vanishing Piece of the Pi: The Globalization of Visual Effects Labor," in *Television & New Media* 16(2), 2015.

6 Matt Stahl, "Privilege and Distinction in Production Worlds: Copyright, Collective Bargaining, and Working Conditions in Media Making," in *Production Studies: Cultural Studies of Media Industries*, edited by Vicki Mayer, Miranda J. Banks, and John T. Caldwell (New York and London: Routledge, 2009), 54–68.

7 'Above' and 'below the line' refer to a convention in U.S. film production budgeting, where creative work is accounted for above the line and craft and technical expenses are accounted for below the line in a given project budget. For a study on U.S. runaways in Europe in the 1950s and 1960s, see Daniel Steinhart, "A Flexible Mode of Production: Internationalizing Hollywood Filmmaking in Postwar Europe," in *Behind the Screen: Inside European Production Cultures*, edited by Petr Szczepanik and Patrick Vonderau (New York: Palgrave Macmillan, 2013), 135–52.

8 "Lucas Loses Star Wars Copyright Case at Supreme Court," *BBC News* (UK edition), July 27, 2011. www.bbc.co.uk/news/uk-12910683.

9 "Lucas Loses Star Wars Copyright Case at Supreme Court."

10 *Judgment: Lucasfilm Limited and others (Appellants) v Ainsworth and another (Respondents), given on July 27, 2011*. supremecourt.uk.

11 "Lucas Loses Star Wars Copyright Case at Supreme Court."

12 Andrew Ainsworth, *CV 1965–2007* (two parts), to be downloaded from his storm trooper retail Web site, originalstormtrooper.com.

13 Royal Court of Justice, Court of Appeal, *Judgment before Lord Justice Rix, Lord Justice Jacob and Lord Justice Patten, given on 16th of December 2009 (EWCA Civ 1328)*. www.bailii.org/ew/cases/EWCA/Civ/2009/1328.html. See also Jill Lawless, "Battle over 'Star Wars' Outfit Settled (Sort of)," *Los Angeles Times*, August 1, 2008; "Split Decision in 'Star Wars' Case," *Variety*, August 3, 2008.

14 John T. Caldwell, *Production Culture: Industrial Reflexivity and Critical Practice in Film and Television* (Durham, NC: Duke University Press, 2008).

15 Allen J. Scott, *On Hollywood: The Place, the Industry* (Princeton, NJ: Princeton University Press, 2005).

16 Damian Sutton, "Cinema by Design: Hollywood as a Network Neighbourhood," in *Design and Creativity: Policy, Management and Practice*, edited by Guy Julier and Liz Moor (Oxford and New York: Berg, 2009), 174–90.

17 Sutton, "Cinema by Design," 175.

18 Andrew Currah, "Hollywood, the Internet and the World: A Geography of Disruptive Innovation." *Industry and Innovation* 14, no. 4 (2007): 359–84.

19 Vicki Mayer, "Where Production Takes Place." *The Velvet Light Trap* 62 (2008): 71–3; Timothy Havens, Amanda D. Lotz, and Serra Tinic, "Critical Media Industry Studies: A Research Approach." *Communication, Culture & Critique* 2 (2009): 234–53.

20 For what appears as a misrepresentation of newer production studies' approaches, see Janet Wasko and Eileen R. Meehan, "Critical Crossroads or Parallel Routes: Political Economy and New Approaches to Studying Media Industries and Cultural Products." *Cinema Journal* 52, no. 3 (Spring 2013): 150–7.

21 Apart from many of the publications mentioned elsewhere in this chapter, see, for instance, Elana Levine, "Toward a Paradigm for Media Production Research: Behind the Scenes at *General Hospital*." *Critical Studies in Media Communication* 18, no. 1 (2001): 66–82; or, most recently, Derek Johnson, Derek Kompare, and Avi Santo, eds., *Making Media Work: Cultures of Management in the Entertainment Industries* (New York and London: New York University Press, 2014), 1–24.

22 See Sherry Ortner, "Access: Reflections on Studying Up in Hollywood." *Ethnography* 11, no. 2 (2010): 211–33; Nathaniel Kohn, *Pursuing Hollywood: Seduction, Obsession, Dread* (Lanham, MD and New York: Rowman & Littlefield, 2006); and the work of Georgina Born, especially *Uncertain Vision: Birt, Dyke and the Reinvention of the BBC* (London: Vintage, 2005).

23 The following production ethnography is based on three main sources: a field diary kept in both written and audio-recorded form; extensive background interviews; and repeated observations on site.

24 What follows is a long excerpt from my field diary (originally kept in German) that has been translated and edited for use in this chapter.

25 Antoine Hennion, "An Intermediary between Production and Consumption: The Producer of Popular Music." *Science, Technology & Human Values* 14, no. 4 (Autumn 1989): 400–24.

26 Michel de Certeau, *The Practice of Everyday Life* (Berkeley: University of California Press, 1984).

27 See Stephen M. Levine, *Hollywood from Below the Line: A Prop Master's Perspective* (Bandeon, OR: Robert D. Reed Publishers, 2014), especially 1–5.

28 See Helen Blair, "Winning and Losing in Flexible Labour Markets: The Formation and Operation of Networks of Interdependence in the U.K. Film Industry." *Sociology* 37, no. 4: 677–94.

29 Goldsmith and O'Regan, *The Film Studio*, 2–3.

30 Kathlen Eggerling, Ver.di/Connexx, interview with the author, Berlin, March 31, 2011.

31 Benjamin Palmer, interview with the author, Berlin, December 1, 2010.

32 See Helen Blair, "'You're Only as Good as Your Last Job': The Labour Process and Labour Market in the British Film Industry." *Work, Employment & Society* 15, no. 1 (2001): 162.

33 Palmer, interview.

34 Palmer, interview; see also Levine, *Hollywood from Below the Line*, passim.

35 My argument here elaborates on a new strand within the sociology of art first proposed in Hennion, "An Intermediary between Production and Consumption," and by anthropologist Alfred Gell in *Art and Agency* (Oxford: Oxford University Press, 1998), later taken up by Sara Malou Strandvad in her PhD thesis, "Inspiration for a New Sociology of Art: A Socio-Material Study of Development Processes in the Danish Film Industry" (Copenhagen: CBS, 2009) and by Georgina Born, "The Social and the Aesthetic: For a Post-Bourdieuian Theory of Cultural Production." *Cultural Sociology* 4, no. 2 (2010): 171–208. See also the contributions in Petr Szczepanik and Patrick Vonderau, eds., *Behind the Screen: Inside European Production Cultures* (New York: Palgrave MacMillan, 2013).

36 Palmer, interview.

37 I am relating to the analytic terminology introduced by philosopher Étienne Souriau, "La structure de l'universe filmique et le vocabulaire de la filmologie." *Revue internationale de Filmologie 2* (7–8) (1951): 231–40 and to Gell, *Art and Agency*. Souriau has not been translated into English yet.

38 Benjamin Palmer, interview with the author, Berlin, October 13, 2010.

39 Palmer, interview, October 13, 2010.

40 In *The Three Musketeers'* opening sequence, it is the appearance and unconcealed spectacle of the props, the technical functionality of the weapons and gadgets put on display, that firmly places this period picture within the canon of the contemporary action movie, and that also endows its fantastic storyline with a sense of haptical or material reality.

41 Palmer, interview, October 13, 2010.

42 Anonymous source, interview with the author, Potsdam-Babelsberg, February 26, 2011.

43 Palmer, interview, October 13, 2010.

44 For the exhibition, see "Art Wars." http://artwars.net. For a discussion of conceptual and post-conceptual art, see Peter Osborne, *Anywhere or Not at All: Philosophy of Contemporary Art* (London and New York: Verso, 2013).

45 "Changes to Design and Patent Law," press release. www.gov.uk. Several media outlets attributed this change to the Ainsworth case.

II
BEING THE BRAND

4

WORKING THE BOOTH

Promotional Models and the Value of Affective Labor

Nina B. Huntemann

In recent years, key sites of my research in games studies have included live events, namely industry trade shows and game conventions. My attention was drawn to the trade show as a site for studying production cultures in games because the trade show plays an important role in defining industry trends, debuting new technology, and promoting video games and game culture to global consumers. Despite significant demographic shifts in both the consumers and producers of its products, long-held assumptions about how women use technology for work and play, and the persistent use of women's bodies in service of work and play structure the gender divisions that persist in the games industry. Trade shows are part of the insider world of technology development and diffusion, and as such offer a behind-the-scenes look at the industrial logics and promotional practices that perpetuate those gender divisions.

Trade shows, also known as trade fairs, trade exhibitions, or expos, are often a key component of a company's marketing communication strategy. Trade show events occur across a diversity of industrial sectors, from agriculture, fashion, and construction to health care, tourism, and firearms. According to the Global Association of the Exhibition Industry, approximately 31,000 trade shows are held annually worldwide, exhibiting the products and services of more than 4 million companies, and hosting 260 million visitors.[1] At these multiday events, companies reveal new products, attendees can see and try out products firsthand, and exhibitors meet with journalists and industry representatives. In line with the business-to-business focus, most trade shows are closed to the public. Important trade shows in the games industry include the Electronic Entertainment Expo (Los Angeles), the Consumer Electronics Show (Las Vegas), the China Digital Entertainment Expo and Conference (Shanghai), the Tokyo Game Show, and G-Star (Korea).

While conducting fieldwork about women game developers at the 2009 Electronic Entertainment Expo (E3), I met Jessica,[2] who was working as a promotional model, colloquially called a 'booth babe.' I witnessed a group of male expo attendees approach her for a photo, each one taking a turn putting his arm around her for the shot. Jessica was not a celebrity, and the hundreds of people who took photos with her that day rarely asked for her name. And yet, in the days after the convention, she appeared anonymously in dozens of popular online photo galleries devoted to games and gaming culture. While a full-time student at a local college and working part-time at a coffee shop, she picked up four days of employment through an event staffing and modeling agency. For $25 an hour, she was paid to stand for ten hours at a product booth, greet the mostly male convention attendees, and keep them engaged until company representatives who were busy with other visitors could speak with them about their products.

I interviewed her about her work at E3. What struck me about her comments and, eventually, what led me to further investigate promotional modeling in games and technology, was her matter-of-factness about the encounter with the men. For her, it was quite common and just "part of the job." She also indicated that the expo-goers I had witnessed were nice and polite, even if a bit awkward. She told me stories of rude, belligerent, "overly touchy" attendees whose hands lingered too long and wandered too far. While some of the other women she knew working at E3 were at booths with men who were essentially hired bouncers, she had none and had to manage the hands-y attendees for herself. The terms 'strip' or 'dance' club were common descriptions expressed to me by other women and men when I asked them about the presence of promotional models at E3.

Universally, the trade show attendees and booth staff I have interviewed since meeting Jessica in 2009 characterize the use of promotional models as consistent with the dominant culture of games, which, despite increasing numbers of women and girls playing games, continues to assume a heterosexual male consumer. Correspondingly, the use of promotional models is frequently described as a regular part of the history of not only selling technology and games, but also the business of making technology and games. The female trade show models and event staff I have spoken with often explain that promotional models came with the 'boys' club' attitude carried over from the Consumer Electronics Show in the years before the games industry split to form E3 in 1995.

Despite her perennial presence at exclusive industry events, the promotional model is characterized as existing outside the industry, a temporary interloper. Her existence is regularly presented as evidence of the continued 'gender problem' in games and technology, an unwelcome remnant of a bygone era. The 'booth babe' is often caricatured by the media, critics, industry spokespeople, and trade show attendees as a Barbie doll with little to no knowledge of the industry, employed to bring sex appeal to unsexy products (e.g., external hard drives and console cooling systems) and who, despite her flirtatious demeanor, has no 'real' interest in the trade show attendees with whom she is paid to engage. She is marginalized by the industry she represents and, therefore, her contribution to the production of economic and cultural value that is central to media and technology industries is often ignored. At a time when women are increasingly the producers and consumers of the technologies on display, promotional models are among both the most visible and the least valued women working in the games industry. This chapter offers a more complex understanding of what promotional models do, and what their continued presence at trade shows reveals about the gendered promotional practices of media and technology companies.

Promotional Models at the Trade Show

Promotional models are common at expositions for construction tools, audio equipment, guns, cycling gear, cell phones, cameras, computers, and many other consumer electronics, as well as enterprise-level products like solar energy installations and data security systems. The use of promotional models in the United States dates back at least to the mid-twentieth-century automobile show, and is an international phenomenon repeated at trade shows around the world. The role has evolved from simple product adornment—lying naked on a car—to product evangelist. Models are often expected to speak knowledgably about the gadget they are hocking while engaging in coquettish conversation with attendees.

Employment for a promotional model is generally booked through a modeling and events staffing agency and is temporary, lasting the duration of the trade show, plus a few days of product education and costume or uniform fitting prior to the event. She may be familiar with the product and have worked for the company previously, or have no previous experience as a promotional model. Her attire can vary greatly: tight t-shirts and shorts, business casual, workout gear, ball gowns, cocktail dresses, and specially made costumes that represent company mascots or comic book, movie, or video game characters.

Promotional models rarely work booths alone. They are, in many ways, hostesses to attendees and companions to exhibitors, working in concert with the story of the brand, the character of the industry, and the spectacle of the trade show. Most promotional models are hired locally in part to save on staff travel expenses, but more important, cities like Los Angeles, Las Vegas, and Tokyo host dozens of trade shows a year and thus have a robust local market for experienced trade show talent.

In their best-selling 1999 book *The Experience Economy*, business consultants Joseph Pine and James Gilmore wrote that trade shows and other business-to-business events are like theater, with actors, audiences, props, scripts, and stages.[3] When Steve Jobs delivered product announcements at Mac World, Apple evoked classical platform theater where actors perform on a raised stage above the audience. At a trade show, this type of promotion is billed as the main event and journalists, industry analysts, and buyers flock to be the first to hear and see the technology on display. Pine and Gilmore also identify a second type of theater happening at the trade show that is not on an elevated platform, but down on the floor. Company booths and the people who work them are like street theater, they write. Akin to "jugglers, magicians, storytellers, puppeteers, acrobats, clowns and mimes," their job is to draw people in, captivate this found audience, and make the sell. Their performances are as planned and rehearsed as the platform stage product announcements, but are customized for each audience member who passes by.[4]

The promotional model—also referred to as a spokesmodel, brand ambassador, brand representative, convention model, trade show model, and booth babe—is an important actor on this street stage, performing her role of luring, entertaining, and selling. She is encouraged to interact with trade show attendees by chatting up passersby, handing out flyers and other promotional items, posing for photos, and giving personal demonstrations of the booth products. Booths are often purposefully understaffed with corporate representatives in order to cultivate a feeling of exclusivity and limited access. Models are expected to keep visitors entertained while representatives attend to other customers. This is accomplished by engaging in what one young woman I interviewed called "bar talk," a flirtatious banter that resembles a pickup conversation. The goal of this talk, she said, is to keep people at the booth and cultivate a "good feeling" about the company. Rory, a more experienced model who had represented her employer at previous trade shows, described booth talk as gatekeeping in that she used the conversation to identify "serious people" and "real media, not just bloggers" who should be guided toward company representatives. Through her talk, she protected the value of the time that company representatives spent engaging with attendees, maintaining an environment of exclusive access.

Working the Booth at E3

The Electronics Entertainment Expo (E3) is an annual exhibition event held in Los Angeles and devoted exclusively to video and computer games and game-related hardware. It is the primary industry venue in the United States for announcements and first looks at upcoming hardware and software products. E3 is not open to the public, but the amount of company-driven publicity and media coverage provides plenty of opportunities for the general public to see and get excited for the latest gadgets on display. In fact, the business-to-business meetings occurring at E3 are, literally, behind closed doors. The series of the events on the trade show floor are orchestrated to encourage industry and mainstream press coverage, and the booths are purposefully constructed as aural and visual spectacles to attract the camera's attention.[5] The aesthetic appeal of staff is part of the booth visuals.

The Nintendo floor space at E3 2014 is among the largest at the expo. Like rival console manufacturers Sony and Microsoft, Nintendo has multiple products on the market: a console (Wii U), a portable device (3DS), several controllers (Wii U GamePad, Nunchuck, and Balance Board), as well as a dozen new game titles. All of these products are housed in the Nintendo area, which is illuminated by shifting blue, green, and purple lights. Two-story-tall display cubes featuring Nintendo's famous game characters and franchises—Mario, Link, Metroid, and various Pokémon creatures—loom over the space, and loud booms from multiple games compete for aural attention.

As I walk by attendees standing in line at banks of monitors to play the latest Wii U games, a Nintendo representative approaches me. She is wearing the E3 Nintendo 'uniform': a grey, cotton t-shirt atop black bottoms and black shoes, which in her case is a mini-skirt and knee-high, high-heeled boots. "Do you want to try *Harvest Moon*?" she asks, offering me a Nintendo 3DS handheld console. As I take the device from her open hand, my eyes follow a cable from the 3DS to a box attached to a belt that is cinched around her hips. A second cable snakes out from the box on her hip to another 3DS, which is in the hands of a fellow E3 attendee engrossed in the console screen. The three of us stand in a three-foot triangle, as two of us push buttons and play our way through *Harvest Moon: The Lost Valley*. I am acutely aware of the space between the Nintendo representative and me; my attention is divided between playing the game and maintaining slack on the cable for fear of pulling on her like she is on a leash. After a few minutes I get stuck in the game, which the representative notices immediately. She instructs me on how to move forward, kindly adding that she "had that happen" her first time playing as well. This shared experience is momentarily comforting, and relieves my embarrassment at not finding my own way. But I soon hand the controller back, relieved to be free of the sense of control I had over her body through the tethered console.

At E3 in 2010, Nintendo unveiled its latest handheld game console, the 3DS. For the first time at that convention, attendees could put their hands on the device and test drive its games. To enable product demonstration, Nintendo hired female promotional models to walk around the expo floor with the 3DS tethered hip belt. This unique product demonstration proved a success and the company has used it since. The method secures the device, eliminates the need to dedicate fixed floor space to the hardware, and takes advantage of attendees wandering around the booths or waiting in line to try other Nintendo products. The use of promotional models in this way is, perhaps, the most observable example at E3 of using a woman's body as a tool. Her body replaces security cords and a kiosk, while adding mobility to the product demonstration. She facilitates a greater number of interactions between the technology and users by embodying the portability of the handheld device and, in doing so, transcending the physical limitations of the trade show floor.

As I pass between the West and South Halls of the LA Convention Center, I spot three tall women whose attire and demeanor stand out from the khaki pants or blue jeans and loose-fitting t-shirt common among E3 attendees. They are each wearing a cropped denim jacket over a black, form-fitting t-shirt with the title of a game across their bosom, and black, high-cut shorts and black, high-heeled boots. Their long hair falls below their shoulders and their faces are made up with thick mascara on false eyelashes, deep blush, and dark lipstick. They stand together handing out cardstock flyers and repeating to attendees rushing by, "Visit us in the South Hall!" I take a flyer and make my way to their booth.

A New York public relations and marketing firm hired the twentysomething Los Angeles women to represent a Korean game development team. The Korean developers, who hired the PR firm, are at E3 for the first time. The female PR representative, Cindy, revealed how new entrants to the industry learn about and perpetuate the practice of using promotional models: "I worked in the music industry for more than two decades before I started [a technology-focused marketing] company. I didn't know about the [promotional] models, but I looked around the tech shows. They're everywhere." She concluded that it was a common part of the technology trade show culture, and began regularly hiring promotional models for her clients. When asked about the effectiveness of the models for her clients' goals, she admitted, "These girls are eye candy," but added that "a good model brings people to the booth, makes them curious, doesn't put off or intimidate. Like anyone you pay, if she's good at her job, she's good for your company." This description of an effective promotional model as one who is attractive and personable was common among the staffing and marketing agency executives I interviewed.

During the interview process, agencies look for models who can hold a conversation, appear "lively," and "make you want to talk to them." In order to identify models who are likely to attract attendees and not intimidate them, job calls use words such as "must be outgoing, friendly, a people person." Several models I spoke with are keenly aware of these expectations and play up their interest in the job. One woman told me she lied during an interview about playing video games: "I don't really, but it doesn't matter. I just wanted to make a good impression."

The physical demands of the work—standing for long periods of time—is frequently stated in job calls for promotional models, but the social requirements are not stated as explicitly. Good banter requires skill, endurance, and emotional containment in order to maintain the positive and outgoing persona expected. Models describe these conversations with attendees as "exhausting" and "repetitive." E3 veteran model Ashley stated, "They [the trade show attendees] often think they are being cute. I've heard the same line forty times before my first break." While attendees may experience these exchanges as fleeting moments of flirtation, for the model these social interactions are her work.

Exploiting a promotional model's affective skills has obvious benefits for the exhibitor. However, the affective skills and product knowledge required of promotional models has not brought greater respect for women performing these roles. Instead, in an industry that historically employs more women in promotional roles than design, development, or executive positions,[6] the 'booth babe' is discounted at best, ridiculed at worst. The marginalization of the promotional model is, in part, a result of the casualization of labor in the twenty-first century generally and the precarity of media work specifically. Managing risk in a global economy and adapting to swift changes in technology has led media companies to increasingly rely on a flexible labor force that can swell as needed and be reduced and relocated quickly. However, the longevity of the promotional model throughout significant industry and market changes highlights the endurance of an industrial logic that continues to frame women as escorts to the technologies of contemporary work and leisure.

Notes

1   The Global Association of the Exhibition Industry (March 2014), *Global Exhibition Industry Statistics* (Levallois-Perret, France: Author, 2014). www.ufi.org/Medias/pdf/thetradefairsector/surveys/2014_exhibiton_industry_statistics.pdf.
2   All informants' names have been changed to maintain anonymity, per request of interviewees.
3   B. Joseph Pine II and James H. Gilmore, *The Experience Economy, Updated Edition* (Cambridge, MA: Harvard Business Review Press, 2011).
4   Pine and Gilmore, *The Experience Economy*, 201.
5   Michael Andreae, Jinn-yuh Hsu, and Glen Norcliffe, "Performing the Trade Show: The Case of the Taipei International Cycle Show." *Geoforum* 49 (2013): 193–201.
6   "The 12th Annual GD Magazine Salary Survey," *Game Developer Magazine*, April 2013. http://twvideo01.ubm-us.net/o1/vault/GD_Mag_Archives/GDM_April_2013.pdf.

5

FROM BROADCAST DESIGN TO 'ON-BRAND TV'

Repositioning Expertise in the Promotional Screen Industries[1]

Catherine Johnson and Paul Grainge

In April 2012 at the London headquarters of communications agency Red Bee Media we brainstormed creative storytelling ideas as part of a workshop to develop an online content strategy for a hair-care brand owned by a multinational consumer goods company. In the room were representatives from a number of companies responsible for the brand's promotional strategy. The head of Mobile and a range of account planners from advertising agency JWT sat alongside the global planning team from media agency Mindshare. Meanwhile, social media experts from social agency Endelman Digital shared ideas with the brand directors for the hair-care range. Steering the day's activities were creatives, strategic planners, account managers, and business directors from Red Bee's creative division. Badged 'On-Brand TV,' the workshop was used by Red Bee to sell eight lessons from television broadcasting that could enrich the brand's use of online video to engage consumers.

As brands seek new ways of reaching and engaging increasingly fragmented audiences, promotional communication emerges as a fundamental component of the work of contemporary organizations.[2] This is accompanied by the growth of a burgeoning sector around audiovisual brand communication, promotion, and design that we term the 'promotional screen industries.' This chapter uses the example of Red Bee Media to interrogate the role the promotional screen industries play in the production of audiovisual content for media and non-media brands. As we argue elsewhere, the promotional screen industries cannot be understood as a clearly defined sector, but rather exist as a fast-moving and nebulous field of media production made up of an array of companies and occupations that function within and between three main areas: advertising, film and television, and digital media design.[3] Writing of the screen industries, John Caldwell suggests that the "dense interaction of film, television and marketing today makes the aggregate industry 'a mess' for scholars to research."[4] This "mess" applies to the promotional screen industries as well. This sector involves complex networks and interactions between a range of players, from advertising and media agencies, to broadcasters, studios, and digital design and communications specialists. It was precisely these constituents who gathered for Red Bee's On-Brand TV workshop.

Red Bee Media is a world-leading broadcast and digital communications company. Blending technology and creative expertise, the company specializes in linear television playout services, the digital delivery of media content (including storage, access, navigation, search metadata, and interface design), and the creative promotion of programs and channel brands. This chapter focuses on the creative division within Red Bee that is responsible for producing trailers, idents, and multiplatform promotions. Despite working largely in broadcast promotion, Red Bee's creative division also sells its expertise to non-media brands that are attempting to develop online audiovisual content strategies. In this chapter we use an analysis of the development of Red Bee's creative division from 2000 to 2015 as a case example to address the ways the skills of broadcast marketing and design have been repositioned in the production and distribution of new forms of promotional-storytelling hybrids for both broadcast and nonbroadcast clients. Specifically, we argue that Red Bee Media is indicative of a broader industrial blurring between advertising, broadcasting, and digital design where the production of 'content' and 'promotion' is increasingly porous.

Between January 2012 and April 2013 we undertook fieldwork and more than thirty interviews with personnel within the creative division of Red Bee, including strategic planners, account directors, creatives, and those involved in the production of promotional and multiplatform content (from high-end trailers to idents and apps). We followed a number of projects from client brief to realization, some of which form the basis of the case studies within this chapter. At the same time we undertook interviews with staff at advertising and media agencies and in-house television marketing departments in the United Kingdom. By situating the analysis of Red Bee within this larger context, this chapter paints a broader picture of the transactional markets that are emerging around the skills of broadcast promotion and design in the first decades of the twenty-first century. A case study of Red Bee, a UK company that operates globally (with regional offices in France, Spain, Germany, and Australia and clients from Europe, America, the Middle East, and East Asia), also contributes to the body of work in screen studies that expands the analysis of production cultures beyond the United States.[5]

From Broadcast Design to Advertising: The Prehistory of Red Bee Media

Over the 1990s the BBC instituted extensive organizational change in which external and internal competition was encouraged.[6] When the BBC's charter renewal in 1996 endorsed the provision of commercially funded services, the corporation announced the development of a number of wholly owned commercial subsidiaries that sold expertise developed in house to external clients for the first time. This included, in December 2000, the development of BBC MediaArc, formed of the corporation's design units in London, Bristol, Birmingham, and Belfast. In a move that recognized a potential market for the corporation's internal skills in broadcast design, BBC MediaArc sold expertise in graphic design, animation, and branding to commercial broadcasting clients, such as digital broadcaster OnDigital. However, it also created advertising content for non-media clients, such as HSBC, Royal Britannia, and Wessex Water.[7] The corporation attempted to strengthen its commercial offer in these areas in 2002 by incorporating BBC MediaArc into a new commercial subsidiary named BBC Broadcast Ltd that included the BBC's 'creative services' division (responsible for trailers, promotional campaigns, and idents for the corporation) and the corporation's broadcast services of playout and subtitling.[8] As Luke Satchell commented of the impending deal in trade magazine *Broadcast*,

> It would clear the way for the corporation to raise revenues by developing promotional campaigns for third-parties as well as selling its expertise in the running, transmission and presentation of channels to advertisers and other commercial operators.[9]

BBC Broadcast continued to work for both broadcast and nonbroadcast clients and hired an experienced advertising executive, Andy Bryant, to head up its creative division and "lead it towards a commercial future."[10] Bryant introduced the ad agency discipline of strategic planning into BBC Broadcast's operations and structured the creative division around the typical ad industry roles of account managers, strategic planners, and creatives. This differentiated BBC Broadcast from the in-house marketing departments of television broadcasters that are typically organized around marketing and creative directors.[11] If BBC Broadcast adopted the disciplines and structures of advertising, however, these were combined with an in-house production department and staff with backgrounds in program production, editing, animation, graphics, and new media design. In effect, BBC Broadcast's creative division structured itself as a creative agency that combined the specialisms of television, design, and advertising.[12]

In June 2005, BBC Broadcast was sold for £166 million to Australian investment fund bank Macquarie Capital Alliance Group (MCAG) and was renamed Red Bee Media three months later.[13] Beyond political debates about the marketization of public services, the prehistory of Red Bee is a suggestive site where the boundary between advertising (produced by ad agencies) and television marketing (produced by in-house broadcast promotion specialists) comes under pressure. On one hand, Red Bee (as with BBC Broadcast and BBC MediaArc before it) sought to compete with ad agencies in the production of advertising for nonbroadcast clients. On the other hand, in selling its in-house broadcast promotion and design division the BBC opened up its creative promotional work—contracted until 2015 to Red Bee and two advertising agencies, Karmarama and RKCR/Y&R—to nonbroadcast specialists.

If Red Bee reveals an industrial blurring between the worlds of advertising and television marketing, this is not without its challenges. When BBC Broadcast was sold to MCAG, 91 percent of its turnover came from BBC-driven business, a percentage that MCAG aimed to reduce.[14] Despite this, in 2012 the majority of Red Bee's creative work still came from its contract with the BBC and was in the area of broadcast promotion. Given that most UK broadcasters produce their promotional content in-house, there is a limited domestic market for the expertise in broadcast promotion that is the mainstay of the commercial offer of Red Bee's creative division and Red Bee is particularly vulnerable to the fortunes of its key broadcast clients in this area, the BBC and UKTV.[15] When we began our fieldwork with Red Bee in 2012 the company was facing the dual challenges of broadcasters looking to reduce their marketing spending in the face of the global recession and the threat of the loss of the BBC contract for creative services, which was up for renewal in 2015. This placed pressure on the need to extend its client base, which has only intensified since the announcement in July 2014 that the BBC would not be renewing its contract with Red Bee and would be taking the majority of its promotional work back in house.[16]

Yet at the same time, there have been a number of changes to the media landscape since Red Bee was formed in 2005. In particular the rise of online video and the uptake of technologies that offer new ways of engaging with television present challenges for both broadcasters and advertisers.[17] Red Bee's response to these changes was to identify the provision of transmedia promotion for broadcasters and content strategies for nonbroadcast clients as specific areas of potential growth. This coalesced around two strategic priorities for the company in 2012: social television and On-Brand TV. 'Social television' refers to the production of content, such as apps, that facilitates social interaction around television viewing through mobile platforms. 'On-Brand TV' is a term Red Bee coined that refers to the production and scheduling of online video content for non-media brands. These are areas of wider significance across the promotional screen industries and Red Bee is not alone in attempting to move into these markets. Indeed, if Red Bee's historical origins reveal a site in which the boundary between advertising and television marketing came under pressure, the cases of social television and On-Brand TV are particularly 'messy' sites in which, as we shall see, a range of players are attempting to stake territory.

Social Television

'Social television,' a term that Gerard Goggin claims was coined in 2007, was nominated as the most important emerging technological trend by *MIT Technology Review* in 2010.[18] While 'social television' can refer to audience interaction beyond the specific moment of viewing, industry research reveals that a significant proportion of audiences uses other media devices while watching television, what is referred to as 'second screening.'[19] During the 2013 Wimbledon men's tennis final, for example, 1.1 million people worldwide tweeted 2.6 million times using hashtags associated with the broadcasting of the match.[20] Hye Jin Lee and Mark Andrejevic argue that "*second screen* is a credible candidate for 2012 buzzword of the year in the television industry."[21] However, debates about how to capitalize on social television and second screening not only took place within the walls of television broadcasters. Technology developers, content owners, platform owners, television marketers, and advertisers all jostled to take advantage of the potential opportunities of these socio-technological developments.[22]

Amid industry uncertainty about how best to make use of social television Red Bee Media promoted itself as a navigator able to guide its clients "through the maze of new market opportunities" presented by changes in media consumption.[23] This was perhaps most clearly articulated through 'Tomorrow Calling,' a year-long program of research, think tanks, white papers, and industry events undertaken by Red Bee in 2011–12. 'Tomorrow Calling' was an instance of industrial self-theorizing[24] in which Red Bee aimed to establish its 'thought leadership' in predicting and preparing clients for an uncertain future. As part of 'Tomorrow Calling,' Red Bee produced (in conjunction with digital media consultancy Decipher) three white papers on 'dual screening,' defined as "the concurrent use of devices while watching TV."[25] While offering a generalized discussion of the second screen landscape, these white papers enabled Red Bee to make a case for the kinds of content that it had the skills and expertise to produce. Specifically, Red Bee argued that broadcasters should focus on the potential that second screening offered in relation to 'companion experiences,' the production of apps, games, and Web sites designed to accompany and enhance the experience of watching television.

In fact, the insights from 'Tomorrow Calling' formed the basis of a presentation that Red Bee took directly to potential clients (broadcasters, content owners, and producers) in order to pitch for work in producing companion apps. It was through one such presentation that FX approached Red Bee to create a second screen experience around its highest rated show, *The Walking Dead* (2010–).[26] This zombie series is an AMC production distributed internationally by Fox International Channels, based on a long-running comic series of the same name. The Walkers' Kill Count app created by Red Bee for FX allowed viewers to predict the number of zombie kills before each episode, including which weapon would be used and which character would be responsible. Using innovative audio-synching technology that linked the app to the broadcast, the app counted the kills as they happened, measured against the viewers' predictions and augmented by a 'thrill meter' and heartbeat sound synched to the zombie attacks in each episode. The app integrated with Twitter and Facebook so that viewers could play along with friends and comment through the app while watching the episode. In addition, the app included trailers for forthcoming episodes, push notifications that alerted viewers to the broadcast of the next episode, and a range of stats and video clips that fans could engage with after the broadcast.

For FX, the creation of a second screen app was a marketing endeavor, a way of promoting the series to heavy Internet users who avoid traditional advertising. In its execution the app clearly had a promotional intention, aiming to encourage live viewing of the program as well as providing a site through which trailers and other promotional materials could be delivered directly to viewers. However, it also blurred the boundaries between marketing and programming, functioning as a piece of transmedia content in a number of ways. The thrill meter and heartbeat added an additional sensory layer (both haptic and aural) to each episode. The ability to predict and compete with other online viewers turned the experience of watching the series into a game. The app also unbundled each episode into a series of stats and re-edited it into a sequence of zombie kills that displayed the "aesthetics of efficiency" that Max Dawson argues characterizes television's digital shorts.[27] In this sense, the app promoted the series (through the inclusion of trailers), augmented the experience of watching the drama (through adding additional sensory layers and through 'gamification'[28]), and reconstituted the content of each episode (through transforming it into edited highlights or sequences of statistics).

In production terms, the creation of this hybrid piece of promotional transmedia content drew on three broad areas of professional expertise found within the promotional screen industries. First, the origins of the project lay in the strategic insight into consumer behavior that formed the basis of Red Bee's white papers and presentations on second screening. In developing the Walkers' Kill Count app, Red Bee analyzed the online activities of the series' viewers—including the volume and nature of tweets during each episode's broadcast, forum discussions, and fan videos—and combined this with knowledge of television to propose strategic responses to the emergence of dual screening. In this sense, the Walkers' Kill Count app accords with Ethan Tussey's observation that companion apps can be understood as a form of digital enclosure in which "emergent audience practices are identified and repackaged in ways that affirm the traditions of the entertainment industry rather than transforming them."[29] The ability to offer an analysis of audience behavior and recommendations on how to act on that insight is a key component of promotional work, whether located in the audience research and media planning departments of broadcasters and media agencies or the strategic planners of creative agencies. The strategic insight offered by promotional screen intermediaries, therefore, plays a central role in the television industry's attempts to discipline the disruptive potential of mobile technologies to television viewing habits.

The centrality of insight into consumer behavior to the work of the promotional screen industries ties to the second area of promotional expertise evident in the production of the Walkers' Kill Count app, and that is problem solving. Problem solving is fundamental to promotional labor, based as it is on devising strategies to capture and manage the attention of viewers and consumers. During our time with Red Bee, staff frequently referred to creative pitches in terms of the 'exam question' that the client was asking. The creative brief for the Walkers' Kill Count app laid this out as a series of questions that the campaign needed to address: What key business challenges do Fox and *The Walking Dead* face? Who is the campaign trying to engage and what competes for their attention? What is the role of the promotional communication? Where and when will that communication have most power? Meanwhile, the particular way Red Bee positioned itself through its 'Tomorrow Calling' research program was as a company that could offer solutions to the challenges of an uncertain future. As such, the thought leadership the promotional screen industries offered can be understood as a form of problem solving in the face of new market opportunities.

Finally, the production of the Walkers' Kill Count app demanded the combination of technological and creative expertise. For Red Bee Media in particular, the technological innovation within second screening made it a particularly strategic area of future business development because of the company's relatively unusual combination of technological and creative expertise. Red Bee's creative division includes a digital interactive team that combines staff with technological expertise in user experience with designers who have skills in interface design. For a project such as *The Walking Dead* app the technologist and designer worked together with the strategic planner and an account manager to create an initial concept to sell to the client. Once approved, the technology team created user journeys and a wire frame for the app that was passed to the design/creative team to overlay the front-end design. This development process points to the close interrelation between design and technology in the production of new media applications and platforms.

Not all companies within the promotional screen industries combine technological and creative expertise like Red Bee. However, it is common for promotional intermediaries to position themselves as experts in new media platforms. This includes the establishment of specialist digital and new media agencies, such as Endelman Digital, and a growing number of start-ups and digital companies focused specifically on creating second screen applications, such as Beamly, tvtag, and tweetTV.[30] At the same time, creative agencies and in-house marketing divisions have developed integrated digital divisions purporting to sell transmedia solutions adapted to the demands of a connected viewing era. This is not to overplay the ease with which the promotional screen industries are adapting to new technologies. Indeed, there is much debate within the promotional screen industries about the best way to manage the production demands of new media technologies.[31] However, such debates can be taken as indicative of the extent to which expertise in digital is central to this industry. Across our interviews with professionals within the promotional screen industries it was emphasized that promotion and marketing specialists need to position themselves as experts in new media forms and platforms.

The case of Red Bee reveals a shift in the broadcast television market for promotional expertise. In the early 2000s the BBC's subsidiaries were commercializing by selling expertise in television promotion and design to new broadcast clients, such as OnDigital. By 2012 within the broadcast market Red Bee was competing with a range of players that were attempting to position themselves as able to navigate broadcasters through the demands of 'connected viewing.' Beyond the global media conglomerates (Viacom, Time Warner, News International, and so on), online corporations (Amazon, Apple, and Netflix) and technological start-ups (Beamly and tweetTV) that Jennifer Holt and Kevin Sanson argue operate within the space of connected viewing, are promotional screen intermediaries with expertise hewn from backgrounds in advertising, broadcast promotion, and design.[32] Within this context, advertising, promotion, and design expertise is recast as strategic insight into new audience behaviors able to solve the 'problems' of a changing media landscape through the combination of creative and technological skills in the demands of new media design and an ingrained knowledge of television.

On-Brand TV

If the example of social television reveals an industrial shift in which the skills of television promotion and design are being recast in the production of new forms of audiovisual content for the broadcast market, then On-Brand TV illuminates a broader blurring between television and advertising. On-Brand TV is indicative of the ways advertisers are looking toward new means of engaging audiences through the production of content that consumers actively seek out, rather than through advertising that interrupts the content they are watching.[33] This stems from larger shifts in media engagement that have challenged the dominance of the thirty-second television spot ad, particularly through the rise of video-on-demand and personal video recorders that make ad-skipping easier for viewers. As with social television, On-Brand TV, or what is more broadly referred to as 'branded entertainment,'[34] is an area in which a range of companies are staking turf and competing for business. This extends from media and advertising agencies setting up content divisions, to independent production companies working directly with non-media brands, to digital and communications specialists, such as Red Bee.[35]

As with social television, Red Bee's On-Brand TV proposition is indicative of the need to stake territory that exists across the promotional screen industries. Indeed, 'Tomorrow Calling' included a white paper on 'The 8 principles of an effective content strategy for brands' that shared 'lessons from the world of broadcasting.'[36] The white paper argued that the digital media world "is becoming a more televisual place" that requires brands to make "TV-quality content that's shareable and consumable across any screen platform."[37] In suggesting that consumer brands would need to start behaving like media brands to communicate with audiences, Red Bee proposed that practices drawn from broadcasting could inform the use of online video as advertising. This included various lessons in televisual remediation: how to give video content dramatically gripping narrative structures; how to recognize the value of scheduling and the function of editorial calendars such as seasons; how to position and package the 'channel brand' through idents; and how to increase audience interactivity through live events and second screens.[38]

Red Bee's white paper gave the example of Bacardi's True Originals, which the company created for the drinks brand in 2011. Red Bee created a range of short videos offering advice, demos, and new recipes integrated into a Web site that aimed to function as a "trusted destination for the key bartender audience, building loyalty and advocacy" with one of Bacardi's most crucial brand advocates.[39] For Red Bee, the key difference between True Originals and traditional advertising was that the Web site and videos addressed the bartending community as an audience rather than as consumers. As Red Bee claimed of On-Brand TV more broadly, "It's no longer about the brand feeding something to someone (irrespective of whether they want it). It's about attracting, captivating and holding."[40] As with the Walkers' Kill Count app, True Originals blurred the boundaries between advertising and programming forms. The online videos, such as one in which a bartender describes the contents of his specialist kit, offer engaging short-form content that is not explicitly selling Bacardi. At the same time, however, the Web site does work to promote Bacardi through videos on the production process of the drink and cocktail recipes using Bacardi as a core ingredient. The site also promotes Bacardi in 'soft' ways by encouraging loyalty and goodwill through the construction of a bartending community around the brand.

The interest of non-media brands such as Bacardi in developing compelling online video material that audiences want to engage with offers a potential opportunity for companies with expertise in television promotion to expand their client base. As a broadcast communication and design company with roots at the BBC and with major clients from the television industry, Red Bee's On-Brand TV proposition aims to persuade non-media brands that its deep-rooted television know-how applies to Web video. Again Red Bee is not alone here. Independent production companies, such as Maverick, Endemol, and Twofour, are diversifying into the production of digital video content, games, apps, and branded events for the film, television, and advertising industries. What promotional experts such as Red Bee attempt to offer, however, is combined expertise in television, digital, *and* advertising. As its On-Brand TV white paper claims, "we have a foot in both camps: one in the territory of branding, advertising and design and the other in the realm of broadcasting and televisual technology."[41] Here, Red Bee's promotional expertise is recast as specialization "in the creation, promotion and distribution of video content across platforms."[42] In the early 2000s BBC MediaArc applied its skills in television design to the creation of television spots and print advertising in an attempt to break into the advertising market. By 2014, it was Red Bee's understanding of the ways television addresses its audience (through storytelling, scheduling, branding, and interactivity), combined with its expertise in advertising and online, that is being sold to non-media brands.

Conclusion

The case of Red Bee is indicative of the broader 'mess' that Caldwell argues characterizes the contemporary screen industries. New markets are emerging that demand the combination of a range of disciplinary skills from strategic planning to technology development and digital design. However, if this points to a larger conjunction between the industries of advertising, broadcasting, and digital design, it is one in which established players retain their dominance and disciplinary boundaries are still asserted. Advertising and media agencies keep their dominant position as the primary providers of advertising content for non-media brands and broadcasters still rely primarily on their in-house marketing departments for promotional content. At the same time, however, an examination of these new markets reveals the role that promotional screen intermediaries are playing in the production of audiovisual content beyond the trailers and idents traditionally associated with broadcast promotion. To understand the production cultures of the contemporary screen industries we need, therefore, to pay attention to the work of the promotional screen industries.

Notes

1 This work was based on research supported by the Arts and Humanities Research Council (grant number AH/J006475/1).

2 See Emily West and Matthew P. McAllister, eds., *The Routledge Companion to Advertising and Promotional Culture* (London and New York: Routledge, 2013); Helen Powell, ed., *Promotional Culture and Convergence: Markets, Methods, Media* (London and New York: Routledge, 2013); Aeron Davis, *Promotional Cultures* (Cambridge: Polity, 2013); and Jennifer Gillan, *Television Brandcasting: The Return of the Content-Promotion Hybrid* (New York: Routledge, 2014).

3 This chapter builds on the conceptualization of the promotional screen industries out-lined in Paul Grainge and Catherine Johnson, *Promotional Screen Industries* (London and New York: Routledge, 2015).

4 John T. Caldwell, "Para-Industry: Researching Hollywood's Backwaters." *Cinema Journal* 52, no. 3 (2013): 163.

5 See, for example, Petr Szczepanik and Patrick Vonderau, eds., *Behind the Screen: Inside European Production Cultures* (New York: Palgrave Macmillan, 2013); Andrew Dawson and Sean P. Holmes, eds., *Working in the Global Film and Television Industries: Creativity, Systems, Space, Patronage* (London and New York: Bloomsbury, 2012); and the books in the BFI's International Screen Industries series, edited by Michael Curtin and Paul McDonald.

6 See Georgina Born, *Uncertain Vision: Birt, Dyke and the Reinvention of the BBC* (London: Vintage, 2005) and Martin Harris and Victoria Wegg-Prosser, "Post Bureaucracy and the Politics of Forgetting: The Management of Change at the BBC, 1991–2002." *Journal of Organizational Change Management* 20, no. 3 (2007): 290–303.

7 BBC, *Annual Report and Accounts 2000–01*, June 11 (2001): 26. http://downloads.bbc.co.uk/annualreport/pdf/2000–01/bbcannualreport_200001.pdf; Barbara Marshall, "BBC MediaArc Completes Ads," *Broadcast*, October 5, 2001. www.broadcastnow.co.uk/bbc-mediaarc-completes-ads/1183268.article.

8 All London-based BBC MediaArc staff were integrated into BBC Broadcast, while its Bristol- and Birmingham-based staff remained part of the BBC's production subsidiary, BBC Resources.

9 Luke Satchell, "BBC Names Fourth Commercial Arm," *Broadcast*, November 7, 2001. www.broadcastnow.co.uk/bbc-names-fourth-commercial-arm/1185197.article.

10 Andy Bryant, interview with the authors, July 2, 2012.

11 Broadcasters typically have separate departments in media planning, scheduling, and research that would provide the kinds of expertise offered by strategic planners within advertising agencies.

12 In 2014, Red Bee's creative division retained these specialisms and this organization; see Grainge and Johnson, *Promotional Screen Industries*.

13 On May 12, 2014, Swedish communications technology giant Ericsson completed acquisition of Red Bee Media.

14 Anon., "BBC Broadcast Sells for £166m," *Broadcast*, June 30, 2005. www.broadcastnow.co.uk/bbc-broadcast-sells-for166m/1026664.article.

15 UKTV is a broadcaster with ten British digital channel brands, co-owned by BBC Worldwide (the BBC's commercial arm) and Scripps Network Interactive.

16 From 2016 the BBC will be taking its day-to-day, clip-based promotional work back in house and, in the meantime, will be reviewing its roster of suppliers for other creative marketing services. See George Bevir, "BBC to End Red Bee Promo Deal," *Broadcast*, July 22, 2014. www.broadcastnow.co.uk/techfacils/bbc-to-end-red-bee-promo-deal/5075462.article.

17 A wide range of literature explores these changes. See, for example, Amanda Lotz, *The Television Will Be Revolutionized* (New York: New York University Press, 2007); Catherine Johnson, *Branding Television* (London and New York: Routledge, 2012); William Boddy "'Is It TV Yet?' The Dislocated Screens of Television in a Mobile Digital Culture," in *Television as Digital Media*, edited by James Bennett and Niki Strange (Durham, NC: Duke University Press, 2011); and Henry Jenkins, Sam Ford, and Joshua Green,

Spreadable Media: Creating Value and Meaning in a Networked Culture (New York: New York University Press, 2013).

18 Gerrard Goggin, *New Technologies and the Media* (New York: Palgrave Macmillan, 2012), 89–90.

19 Ofcom, *International Communications Market Report 2012*, December 13, 2012. http:// stakeholders.ofcom.org.uk/binaries/research/cmr/cmr12/icmr/ICMR-2012.pdf.

20 Ofcom Web site, "The Communications Market Report: United Kingdom, the Reinvention of the 1950s Living Room." http://stakeholders.ofcom.org.uk/ market-data-research/market-data/communications-market-reports/cmr13/uk/.

21 Hye Jin Lee and Mark Andrejevic, "Second-Screen Theory: From the Democratic Surround to the Digital Enclosure," in *Connected Viewing: Selling, Streaming, and Sharing Media in the Digital Era*, edited by Jennifer Holt and Kevin Sanson (New York: Routledge, 2014), 41.

22 See, for example, the Media and Entertainment Services Alliance, which has established a Second Screen Society that holds regular conferences in the United States and Europe (www.2ndscreensociety.com/ces2014/about/).

23 "Red Bee Media: Tomorrow Calling." www.redbeemedia.com/insights/tomorrow-calling.

24 John T. Caldwell *Production Culture: Industrial Reflexivity and Critical Practice in Film and Television.* (Durham, NC: Duke University Press, 2008).

25 Red Bee Media, "Second Screen Series, Paper 1: Setting the Scene," September 2012. www.redbeemedia.com/system/files/private/second_screen_series_paper_1_white paper_red_bee_media.pdf, 2.

26 FX was FOX International Channel's UK entertainment channel. It was rebranded as FOX in 2013.

27 Max Dawson, "Television's Aesthetic of Efficiency: Convergence Television and the Digital Short," in *Television as Digital Media*, edited by James Bennett and Niki Strange (Durham, NC: Duke University Press, 2011).

28 Lee and Andrejevic, "Second-Screen Theory," 51.

29 Ethan Tussey, "Connected Viewing on the Second Screen: The Limitations of the Living Room," in *Connected Viewing: Selling, Streaming, and Sharing Media in the Digital Era*, edited by Jennifer Holt and Kevin Sanson (New York: Routledge, 2014), 204.

30 All three apps facilitate social media interaction around television and were founded by entrepreneurs with expertise in new media technologies.

31 See, for example, Anon., "The Changing Game," *Creativity*, August 1, 2008, 29, and Alex Farber, "The New Rules of Engagement," *Broadcast*, March 14, 2013. www. broadcastnow.co.uk/in-depth/the-new-rules-of-engagement/5052885.article.

32 Jennifer Holt and Kevin Sanson, "Introduction," in *Connected Viewing: Selling, Streaming, and Sharing Media in the Digital Era*, edited by Jennifer Holt and Kevin Sanson (New York: Routledge, 2014), 4.

33 Powell, *Promotional Culture and Convergence*, and West and McAllister, *Routledge Companion to Advertising*.

34 Scott Donaton, *Madison & Vine: Why the Entertainment and Advertising Industries Must Converge to Survive* (New York: McGraw-Hill, 2004) and Christina Spurgeon, *Advertising and New Media* (London: Routledge, 2008).

35 For a more detailed discussion of the development of branded entertainment since 2000 and the ways this has blurred the lines between advertising and film and television, see Grainge and Johnson, *Promotional Screen Industries*.

36 Red Bee Media, *On-Brand TV: Learning from Media Brands*. www.redbeemedia.com/insights/10-principles-effective-content-strategy-brands.

37 Red Bee Media, *On-Brand TV*.

38 Red Bee Media, *On-Brand TV*.

39 Red Bee Media, *Bacardi True Originals*. www.redbeemedia.com/work/bacardi-true-originals.

40 Red Bee Media, *On-Brand TV*.

41 Red Bee Media, *On-Brand TV*.

42 Red Bee Media, *On-Brand TV*.

6

POP STARS PERFORM 'GAY' FOR THE MALE GAZE

The Production of Fauxmosexuality in Female Popular Music Performances and Its Representational Implications

Kristin J. Lieb

Since the introduction of MTV, the level of sexual exhibitionism required of top-level global female popular music stars has intensified considerably.[1] In recent years, Katy Perry, Rihanna, Shakira, Miley Cyrus, Christina Aguilera, Britney Spears, and Nicki Minaj have all incorporated same-sex attraction and seduction into their acts, performing lesbianism, bisexuality, or heteroflexibility/bicuriosity in their lyrics, videos, and live performances.

These performances—costumed spectacles designed to stimulate the ever-increasing demands of the male gaze and fuel the acceptance of a "pornography of everyday life"—are a means for these celebrities, who all publicly identify as straight, to get what they want: commercial attention.[2] Once they get that, they generally deny their flirtation with women. This has created a new theme in popular music videos: fauxmosexuality. Meanwhile, representations of real sexual diversity, in the form of 'out' bi and lesbian musicians, remain practically invisible.

The term 'fauxmosexuality,' circulating in online dictionaries and gay-themed media texts since 2004, generally means a false portrayal of gay, bi, or bicurious/ heteroflexible behavior, enacted to reap a personal and/or commercial reward. In this study, I apply the term specifically to the construction and reception of music videos as I talk with music industry insiders about video performances in which straight-identified, globally successful female artists demonstrate fauxmosexuality.

My academic construction of the term 'fauxmosexuality' draws on the concepts of Gagnon and Simon's sexual scripting, Mulvey's male gaze, Judith Butler's gender performance, and Yoshino's bi invisibility/erasure.[3] Taken together, these ideas work to inform and explain the use of fauxmosexuality in music video productions. Under these layers of context, fauxmosexuality emerges as a strategic form of scripted gender performance in music video productions in which straight-identified artists enact heterosexist, stereotypical displays of sexual difference for attention and profit.

The music industry uses fauxmosexuality as a production strategy in which straight-identified female artists play gay, sometimes with a celebrity peer, in order to attract the male gaze and all that its validation enables. It is not, in any way, a celebration of sexual diversity or a challenge to gender and sexuality norms, as all of the stars who use it are highly feminine, gender normative, and constructed to please male audiences. Instead, fauxmosexuality cheaply appropriates sexual difference, incorporating it into a tidy, heterosexist frame for public consumption. This frame may look politically inclusive, but representationally, it further erases and stigmatizes bisexuality and lesbianism by depicting them as mere performances, not real identities.

The industry drivers behind the use of fauxmosexuality are clear—shock value, sales, and the relentless pursuit of the male gaze. My respondents discussed these factors and deconstructed fauxmosexuality's tenets as we viewed three videos during our interviews: Katy Perry's "I Kissed a Girl," Rihanna's "Can't Remember to Forget You" (featuring Shakira), and Lady Gaga's "Telephone" (featuring Beyoncé). We also discussed public comments by various pop stars about same-sex attraction, and Madonna's trend-setting kisses with Britney Spears and Christina Aguilera at MTV's 2003 Video Music Awards.

Between May 2014 and September 2014, I interviewed six music industry insiders in one- to two-hour initial interviews and several shorter follow-up interviews of thirty to sixty minutes each. Three initial interviews were conducted in person, and three were conducted over the phone. All follow-up interviews were completed by phone. The industry experts comprise: a major label performer, a radio programmer, a music supervisor for film and television advertising, an artist manager and director, a publicist, and an owner of a nonprofit music organization. All have been involved professionally with marketing and promoting artists. The group included five females and one male, ranging in age from twenty-three to sixty-six. Three identify as straight, one as bisexual, one as a bisexual who "fell in love with a woman, and has been in a committed relationship for 30 years," and one as lesbian. My sources had no professional involvement in the specific campaigns we discussed.

After viewing the videos, the experts identified numerous bisexual clichés and stereotypes operating within them. Namely, they saw the videos as illustrative of several misconceptions: that bisexuality is fictional; that it's a phase for most people; that it's simply a way for straight girls to tour an alternate sexuality; and that bisexuals are promiscuous. They also discussed how fauxmosexuality presents bisexuality as a production enacted for the pleasure of the spectator, not the participants.

Drawing on their music industry experience, they discussed how and why the artist handlers and video producers likely employed fauxmosexuality, and speculated about the implications of such practices on lesbian and bisexual performers and audiences.

She Kissed a Girl . . . or Did She?

Educator and activist Robyn Ochs defines bisexuality as the "potential to be attracted—romantically and sexually—to people from more than one sex and/or gender, not necessarily at the same time, not necessarily in the same way, and not necessarily to the same degree."[4]

Because Ochs's definition encompasses ideas like bicuriousity and heteroflexibility, it is difficult to know exactly how prevalent bisexuality is. In 2011, the San Francisco Human Rights Commission LGBT Advisory Committee declared bisexuals "'an invisible majority' in need of recognition, resources, and support."[5] A subsequent Pew Research Survey of GLBT Americans showed that 40 percent of respondents identified as bisexual, 36 percent identified as gay men, 19 percent identified as lesbian, and 5 percent identified as transgender.[6]

According to the 2013 Pew Report, "while 77% of gay men and 71% of lesbians say most or all of the important people in their lives know of their sexual orientation, just 28% of bisexuals say the same."[7] (Some may find staying in the closet preferable to being viewed as bisexual through contemporary cultural lenses. The lead entry for 'bisexuality' in *Urban Dictionary* is "the ability to reach down someone's pants and be satisfied with whatever you find.") Bisexual women reported they were less likely to be out than bisexual men (33% vs. 12% in the study). In certain contexts, such as female pop videos, it's safe to experiment with bisexuality, but unsafe to actually declare yourself bisexual in real life. My interviews with music industry experts explored how the producers of pop music exploit this dichotomy and manipulate the difference between 'straight' people feeling or acting on same-sex attraction, and the stigmatized 'others' who identify as bisexual, however privately.

Portrayals of female fauxmosexuality in pop music videos trade on the belief that bisexuality may not be real, but rather enacted for interested (male) audiences. Katy Perry's "I Kissed a Girl" video provides a telling example. The video opens with quick shots—a woman in fishnet stockings with a guitar, a handful of scantily clad women getting ready for a night out, and a slow pan up Perry's legs. Perry is revealed, in bed, wearing a negligee and stroking a cat. During the refrain, Perry dances amid five women of various races and ethnicities. She looks directly at the camera as she sings, inviting its gaze. She fans herself, as though this is all too hot to handle, but the women engage with the camera, rather than each other, save for an enthusiastic pillow fight toward the end.

Longtime artist manager and director/producer Jorge Hinojosa noted the inherent contradiction as Perry casts herself as both sexually curious and ultimately innocent:

> She's talking about having kissed a girl, but she doesn't kiss a girl once in this video. She's not even delivering on the lyric in the most minimal sense. It comes off as totally disingenuous and pathetic. It's like having a horror movie with no knife and no blood.

Veteran music industry publicist and MUSO Entertainment President Elizabeth Lang characterized the song's lyrics as the most "shocking" element of any of the songs and videos discussed in the study. She noted that despite the suggestive lyrics, the video retains a "cutesy pie" sensibility, in which Perry appears "flirtatious, not sexual." Lang speculated that the lack of sexuality exhibited in the video was likely an effort to "smooth over" any threat the lyrics posed. She also noted a narrative reversal at the video's conclusion, when Perry awakens from a dream alongside a man. Radio programmer and personality Kendall Stewart interpreted this shot as a reassurance to the audience: "Don't worry, Katy Perry is still straight." Audiences got the message, viewing the official video 60,261,434 times.[8]

My participants speculated that when straight-identified female pop stars play bisexual or bicurious/heteroflexible roles in videos, they are likely trying to add a bit of mystery, exoticism, or danger to their already hypersexualized images. Participant Holly Hung, a music supervisor for motion picture advertising, observed:

> It's cool to act bi in videos because it makes you look hypersexual and up for anything. You're free, wild, and fun. But it's not cool to actually be bi, because the reality is confusing to people. They don't know how to deal with it in real life because they only know it as a performance. They're hateful and dismissive of bis, like "pick a side."

Fauxmosexual performances enable the male gaze by encouraging its participation in the fantasy. Ann Hackler, executive director of the Institute for Musical Arts, a nonprofit dedicated to supporting women and girls in music, explained that the performance of bisexuality is critical in branding the pop star as simultaneously elusive and available:

> Bisexuality is sexy; homosexuality is not. Because with bisexuality, the artist has an out—the man watching's got a chance. If the artist is lesbian and not interested in men at all, men are like "so what?"

Industry experts report that brand managers, handlers, and video directors actively encourage pop stars to perform bisexual curiosity to garner attention and sales, but also acknowledge that portraying actual/more realistic lesbianism would not sell. Without exception, the pop stars flirting with women in videos are presented as conventionally 'feminine' and 'attractive' in look, dress, and behavior, which makes it more difficult for bi and lesbian women who don't look, dress, and act in this way to see themselves in such representations. Meanwhile, as audiences become conditioned to expect this feminized version of lesbianism/bisexuality, they may correspondingly become less likely to accept less heteronormatively produced constructions. Thus coming out as a lesbian performer is not actively encouraged for marketing purposes—such a disclosure is ironically thought to limit one's target market, not extend it. "To market an artist as being lesbian or bi would be a tremendous mistake unless their material specifically was aimed only at that audience," Hinojosa said. This may partially explain why no out lesbian performers exist at the top of the pop game now; Melissa Etheridge and k. d. lang, whose careers peaked in the 1990s, are the most famous.

Drivers of Fauxmosexuality: Sales and Shock Value

All of my experts said fauxmosexuality is an easy and effective way to drive traffic to videos, creating cachet and publicity for artists, and generating revenue for all involved. Fauxmosexuality also functions as a way of escalating already hypersexu-alized representations of female stars to new levels of objectification. Artists play along for various reasons, and their level of agency in decision making varies. But this so-called agency is bounded by the norms of the music industry and video production, which reproduce the same images of women, over and over again. So for female artists wanting to succeed, 'choosing' this path may well feel like a safer gamble than contradicting it.

June Millington, lead guitarist in Fanny, the first all-female rock band to release an album through a major label back in 1970, said the use of fauxmosexuality is likely encouraged by handlers. "None of these young women are making these decisions without entire departments vetting them," she said. "It's teamwork, and it's not like there's ethos behind this. Various parties coldly strategize about how to cater to the lowest common denominator and make money. . . . There are at least 30 people behind the stars planning those shots." Hackler observed: "It's men who control the industry—the money, the image, and the branding, for the most part—and it shows."

My other respondents agreed that many people besides the artist are involved in such productions, including record label execs, video promotion departments, artist managers, label and artist publicists, boyfriends and girlfriends, stylists, pro-ducers, directors, editors, video gatekeepers (such as MTV), lawyers, and broadcast standards and practices types. Lang explained that a provocative video could raise a pop star's value:

> You used to pay to make videos and get them on MTV. Videos used to be marketing tools, but now they're also revenue streams. Now you want to make videos provocative enough so people watch them repeatedly, and you make money from VEVO or whomever.

Sometimes artists may actually want to inhabit these performative fauxmosexual roles for a variety of complicated personal, industrial, and societal reasons (e.g., it feels transgressive, it has worked for others, it gets media attention), but if all paths lead to the same disingenuously hypersexualized representations, agency hardly matters. Hung alleged Shakira did it "because she's getting older, and being suggestively bisexual is a way of making her look younger. It's good PR." While such charades may keep Shakira's image contemporary and relevant, they don't do actual bisexuals any representational favors. When bisexuality is presented as a product of youthful curiosity, or a way of playing into a viewer's voyeuristic fantasy, rather than confirming an adult decision about one's own sexual orientation, it undermines and arguably prohibits more diverse or authentic representations of bisexuality.

Producing Fauxmosexuality in Megastar Pairings

Musical collaborations provide a popular way for one pop star to gain access to another pop star's target market in order to extend her brand. When no natural connection exists between the stars, they're encouraged to 'get sexy' together to manufacture chemistry and force the fit. Shakira offered a troubling explanation for her collaboration with Rihanna: She said her 'territorial' boyfriend would rather see her flirt with women than men.[9] Thus, the dynamic between the two is designed entirely for voyeuristic pleasure. Still, their inauthentic, awkward depiction of bicuriosity had generated almost 419 million views by the time this chapter went to press.

Lang explained the dynamics of filming two megastars, whose images are crafted and controlled at every stage, and who typically view each other as competition, not sex partners.

> Getting anything done with two stars of that magnitude is such a spectacular headache. It's so expensive, schedules are so demanding, and there is such posturing. No one can outshine the other, or have more screen time than the other, or look hotter than the other. When you're in that mode, there are so many obstacles that you just need to get it done.

Such extensive negotiations rarely leave room for any degree of passion, curiosity, or creativity. Lang cited the director's choice of "expensive location, lavish production, a lot of skin, and special effects" to mask the song's flaws. Hinojosa dismissed the song as "extremely bad." He charged producers with relying on sexuality and cheap tricks to gain traction.

> The song puts two international superstars together to try to make some magic. It's so contrived—it's like they've put everything that has worked in

the past together in one video to see if it will be twice as successful. . . . You would probably get the same number of views if you replaced them with Kim Kardashian and Megan Fox. . . . Video outlets just want videos that have people glued to their screens with or without the volume on.

For those reasons, the way such videos are positioned to the public plays a critical role in their reception by audiences. Lang noted: "['Can't Remember'] was leaked to the gossip onlines. . . . It was the super-sexy 'can you believe it' type story."

Producing Fauxmosexuality for the Intensifying Male Gaze

After interviews for this chapter were completed, two videos relying almost exclusively on generous booties and fauxmosexual conceits hit YouTube and various other telescreens: Nicki Minaj's "Anaconda," a modern spin on Sir Mix A Lot's "Baby Got Back"; and Jennifer Lopez featuring Iggy Azalea's "Booty," which makes its stars subservient to their own rear ends. (There are approximately ten booty shots before we see the stars' faces.) In fact, having big and desirable booties appears to be the motivation for their collaboration, as Azalea boasts: "The last time the world saw a booty this good was on Jenny from the Block."

These videos were similar to those discussed earlier in this chapter in that they follow the female pop star video playbook for 2014: show major booty, feign sexual interest in your costar, and get really wet with water or other lubricants. They diverge in their messaging to women. Both show women competing for men by using a single body part and a clear willingness to please them by any means possible. They also construct women with lesser booties as less desirable, and Minaj gets downright aggressive about this, betraying herself as antifeminist and misogynistic in the process: "I got a big fat ass. . . . Fuck the skinny bitches in the club." While "Booty" provides a celebration of ample derrieres, "Anaconda" serves more as an indictment of those too 'skinny' to possess one.

Narratively and visually, both songs feature stars using their booties in various ways (e.g., rubbing, spanking, grinding, twerking, and lap dancing) to attract and please men. "Booty" issues a direct come-on to those watching: "See everybody wanna get a taste/You know that we've got enough to share." "Anaconda," for its part, finds Minaj performing a lap dance on rapper/colleague Drake at the video's end, showing that her power resides, ultimately, in her ability to turn him on, with other girls or on her own.

Fauxmosexuality arises from "the pornography of everyday life" and the reality of the contemporary music industry, which increasingly relies on the objectification, pornification, and exhibitionism of its female performers.[10] In my 2013 book *Gender, Branding and the Modern Music Industry: The Social Construction of Female Popular Music Stars*, I showed how female pop stars today are coached and molded into hypersexualized representations of stereotypical female gender roles. Although these stars arguably become famous for being singers, their stardom and associated rewards derive mainly from what the industry views as their core assets—their bodies. Selling the pop star, her body, and her perceived sexual availability to any suitor, regardless of her sexuality, has become standard practice. Fauxmosexuality does nothing to challenge that sexist, reductive practice, and arguably reinforces and amplifies it. Now, rather than seeing one pop star parading around in increasingly pornified poses, we see two, in objectified collaboration. This provides new fantasy fodder for the audience, to be sure, but it's really designed to please the creators of music industry representations and video production—who are predominantly male.

"Men love to watch pornography with two women together," Lang said. "That's very acceptable. In clubs you'll see two girls dancing together provocatively just to get the attention of men." As on-demand, same-sex kissing becomes routine, the male gaze greedily demands multiples. "In videos, one girl is not enough anymore," Hung said. "Now you need three. They have to be black, white, and Asian." In "Can't Remember to Forget You," Shakira, who is Colombian, and Rihanna, who is Barbadian, roll around in bed, smoking cigars and stroking each other's bottoms.

Several participants noted that just as the artists began to sexually engage each other, the camera left the scene to focus on Shakira playing drums and guitar. "They had to stop the momentum of what was about to happen," Hung said. "Whoa, this is as far as we can go," Stewart said. "If they were to go farther than that, then they wouldn't need the man who's watching them." The lyrics fixate on male pleasure, as the stars insist they would "rob," "kill," and generally "do anything for that boy" . . . including each other, apparently.

"Are they implying that they would be with each other for this guy?" Stewart asked. "If so, that's disgusting." Hung, Hinojosa, and Stewart noted that there was more chemistry between each pop star and the walls than with each other. The lack of chemistry didn't faze viewers, who watched the official video 419,247,575 times, and the HD version 1,492,199 times.[11]

Fauxmosexuality and Gay-, Bi-, and Lesbian-Identified Audiences

Because fauxmosexuality is mostly a creation of heteronormative male cultural producers, it leaves little room for gay men and creates uncomfortable quandaries for bi and lesbian audiences. Framing bisexual activity under heterosexual scaffolding also serves the interest of those who wish to maintain control over representations of female pleasure. Hackler explained:

> You don't see "I kissed a boy" because it wouldn't turn on straight men. It's all about the hard-on and the fantasy. It's them controlling the fantasy of lesbian and bisexual women—making women act the way they want

women to act in the videos. It's one slant on female sexuality, and it's straight and male.

Four of my participants speculated that fauxmosexuality is meant to appeal to lesbian and bisexual audiences as well. Hackler observed:

> They're also courting the gay market, and that's where it hurts. For some viewers, it's the first time they see anything that looks like them or their impulses portrayed in the popular media. Then the artists themselves are like "haha-haha, we were just kidding!" which is a gay/lesbian/bi person's nightmare.

Kendall Stewart has identified as bisexual since high school. She interpreted the "I Kissed a Girl" video as infuriating and detrimental to public perceptions of bisexuality.

> I remember when that song came out because all of a sudden, girls in my high school were kissing each other at parties. And they were doing it because boys were cheering them on. When I would see it happen, I would be hiding in the corner hoping they wouldn't come to me next.

Bisexuals labor under the perception that bisexuality isn't real and that most are "on the way to gay."[12] The production of fauxmosexuality in pop music arguably perpetuates bi invisibility/erasure[13] and stereotypes about bisexuals being hypersexual and noncommittal.

The frivolous depiction of bisexuality, in which female pop stars can flirt through a four-minute video then deny it all with a giggle, makes it difficult for the small number of stars who publicly identify as bisexual to be taken seriously. In a 2009 interview with Barbara Walters, Lady Gaga said she is bisexual.[14] She is still questioned about it, presumably because she has not publicly dated women while in the spotlight, and because she built her brand on provocation. But Gaga has been emphatic. During a performance in Berlin, Germany in October 2013, Gaga said: "It's not a lie that I am bisexual and I like women, and anyone that wants to twist this into 'she says she's bisexual for marketing,' this is a fucking lie. This is who I am and who I have always been."[15]

The next month, Gaga said:

> I am bisexual, I've said it before, I'll say it again. . . . I'm sorry if this is a bit vulgar—but I don't need to eat pussy in front of the whole world for people to take me seriously.[16]

Lady Gaga's most public display of bisexuality came in her video for "Telephone," which featured Beyoncé. The video relies on some of the tropes of "I Kissed a Girl" and "Can't Remember to Forget You," but noteworthy differences may indicate genuine same-sex attraction. Stewart observed:

> Gaga makes out with a chick, and she enjoys it. The woman she makes out with is not a super-femme, girly-girl woman. That's not a turn-on for straight guys. They want to see two girls who look like straight girls making out. They don't want to see their stereotype of lesbian women making out.

"Telephone" also demonstrates a modicum of resistance to the male gaze. Stewart observed: "Gaga is eating a dick-shaped sandwich, which she shares with Beyoncé, until Beyoncé throws it out the window." Beyoncé also poisons a man who is disrespecting women. The end of the video finds the pair driving away in their "Pussy Wagon."

As this book went to press, Gaga became engaged to her male partner, Taylor Kinney, which might continue to generate skepticism over Gaga's attempts to identify as bisexual.[17]

Playing the Role Versus Living the Role

Confusing matters of identity versus representation even further, stars such as Nicki Minaj and Jessie J came out as bisexual, only to recant later. Minaj claims she lied to get attention, while Jessie J called her bisexuality "a phase."[18] Despite her flirtation with J. Lo in "Booty," Iggy Azalea has publicly criticized her peers' use of fauxmosexuality:

> I didn't want people to misconstrue that and think that I was being a fake lesbian. . . . I see it so much in songwriting and it's like, you're not even bi-curious! You've probably never even been with a girl in any capacity! But somebody's written this lyric for you and you think it's cool so you're saying it?[19]

Hinojosa drew a distinction between playing with fauxmosexuality in a video and lying about one's sexuality. "It's incredibly disrespectful to say you're gay when you're not," Hinojosa said. "The gay community suffers because their lifestyle is portrayed as something insignificant. . . . Anyone can portray being bisexual in a video but to live that life is a very different scenario with much larger stakes. Our culture universally celebrates great performances of characters who aren't like them, but in real life we are much more judgmental of each other."

Stars' willingness to manipulate the boundaries of sexual preference is shocking to an earlier generation of musicians who were encouraged to keep their sexuality under wraps. "When I was starting in the 1960s, sexuality was all implied. Now it's displayed as merchandise, like you're available to everyone," Millington said. "I couldn't even think about my sexuality internally, for fear of immediate backlash. Now people are pretending to be gay?"

While all of my participants found some fauxmosexual representations cheap, predictable, and somewhat damaging, Lang viewed "I Kissed a Girl" as potentially useful in building acceptance of same-sex attraction beyond gay or lesbian identification. Other participants disagreed, but Lang noted: "The lyrical content is true to how these kids think and how it is now. It's like 'Girls are pretty. I kissed her. I had to find out what that was about. . . . ' That video is made for teenage girls." Lang described the video's potential to change hearts and minds . . . in time:

> It's starting by mocking and teasing, and flirting with the topic. I think that's the first step to mainstreaming. It may look very one- or two-dimensional, but at least it's on the screen. The nuance happens over time.

Gerbner's cultivation theory indicates representation is indeed critically important, not only for the depicted group, which needs to see itself included in culture, but for others, who use media to become comfortable with 'othered' groups.[20] But Barnhurst, Diamond, and others complicate that notion, observing that problematic visibility perpetuates deleterious stereotypes, cementing them deeper into the public psyche.[21]

The stereotypes identified in these videos may have deeper ramifications for society, particularly in the ways we perceive bisexual or lesbian women. Because industry producers portray sexual difference as frivolous, fun, trendy, and sexy, these ideas become an accepted and repeated part of the production standard.

Such constructed depictions prove traumatic to some lesbians and bisexuals, who don't see themselves reflected accurately in their limited media representations. "The danger in all of this is that you're being trivialized for what is real and serious and true to you," Millington said. "It's not a party game. . . . Anybody who is pretending to be gay or bi has no idea what the reality is and how much it means. . . . And we don't want to laugh at this because we have to live these lives."

By promoting only selected, stereotypical, exoticized parts of lesbian or bisexual difference, and using fauxmosexuality to accessorize straight female pop performances, music industry producers repackage sexual diversity into a false frame for wide public consumption and likely make it more difficult for artists living those identities to succeed.

So why does the music industry keep producing fauxmosexuality despite potentially damaging social effects? Why can't artists who are actually gay or bi become 'out' pop stars? Why can't straight artists own their own sexuality more convincingly? "For female pop stars, this strategy's just a winner," Lang said. Hinojosa concurred: "It's hard to give up something that works in the hope of doing something that might work."

Notes

1   Kristin J. Lieb, *Gender, Branding, and the Modern Music Industry: The Social Construction of Female Popular Music Stars* (New York: Routledge, 2013).

2   Laura Mulvey, "Visual Pleasure and Narrative Cinema." *Screen* 16, no. 3 (1975): 6–18; Jane Caputi, "The Pornography of Everyday Life," in *Race, Class & Gender in the Media* (4th ed.), edited by Gail Dines and Jean Humez (Thousand Oaks, CA: Sage, 2014), 373–85.

3   John H. Gagnon and William Simon, *Sexual Conduct: The Social Sources of Human Sexuality* (Social Problems and Social Issues) (Chicago, IL: Aldine Publishing Company, 1973); Mulvey, "Visual Pleasure and Narrative Cinema"; Judith Butler, *Gender Trouble: Feminism and the Subversion of Identity* (London: Routledge, 1990); Kenji Yoshino, "The Epistemic Contract of Bisexual Erasure." *Stanford Law Review* 52, no. 2 (2000): 353–461.

4   Robyn Ochs and Sarah E. Rowley, eds., *Getting Bi: Voices of Bisexuals Around the World* (2nd edition) (Boston, MA: Bisexual Resource Center, 2009), 9.

5   LGBT Advisory Committee, "Bisexual Invisibility: Impacts and Recommendations" (San Francisco Human Rights Commission, 2011), 1. http://sf-hrc.org/sites/sfhrc.org/files/migrated/FileCenter/Documents/HRC_Publications/Articles/Bisexual_Invisiblity_Impacts_and_Recommendations_March_2011.pdf.

6   Pew Research Center, "A Survey of LGBT Americans," June 13, 2013. www.pewsocialtrends.org/2013/06/13/a-survey-of-lgbt-americans/.

7   Pew Research Center, "A Survey of LGBT Americans."

8   As of October 27, 2014.

9   Jason Lipshutz, "Shakira's Boyfriend No Longer Allows Her to Make Music Videos with Men," *Billboard*, March 7, 2014. www.billboard.com/articles/columns/latin-notas/5930263/shakira-boyfriend-gerard-pique-no-more-music-videos-with-men.

10   Caputi, "The Pornography of Everyday Life."

11   As of October 27, 2014.

12   Eliel Cruz, "Op-ed: Why 'Bi' Is so Tough to Say," *Advocate.com*, June 10, 2014. www.advocate.com/commentary/2014/06/10/op-ed-why-bi-so-tough-say.

13   Yoshino, "The Epistemic Contract of Bisexual Erasure," 3.

14   "Barbara Walters 10 Most Fascinating People (Truth About Gaga!)," 2009. www.youtube.com/watch?v=XnbhKQT78bw.

15   James Nichols, "Lady Gaga Defends Her Bisexuality, Says It's 'Not A Lie,'" *Huffington Post*, October 31, 2013. www.huffingtonpost.com/2013/10/31/lady-gaga-bisexuality_n_4182059.html#slide=2896281.

16   James Nichols, "Lady Gaga Discusses Bisexuality, Gay Icon Status in 'Attitude,'" *Huffington Post*, November 10, 2013. www.huffingtonpost.com/2013/11/10/lady-gaga-gay-icon_n_4241950.html.

17   Annie Martin, "Lady Gaga, Taylor Kinney Reportedly Held a Commitment Ceremony," *upi.com*, October 16, 2014. www.upi.com/Entertainment_News/2014/10/16/Lady-Gaga-Taylor-Kinney-reportedly-held-a-commitment-ceremony/6271413497386/. Historically, commitment ceremonies united two people not legally allowed to marry.

18   Diane Anderson-Minshall, "Nicki Minaj Admits She Lied about Being Bisexual," *Advocate.com*, 2012. www.advocate.com/arts-entertainment/music/2012/09/05/

nicki-minaj-admits-she-lied-about-being-bisexual; Trish Bendix, "Nicki Minaj Says She's Not Really Bisexual," *After Ellen*, 2010. www.afterellen.com/blogtrishbendix/ nicki-minaj-says-shes-not-bisexual; Andy Greene, "Nicki Minaj Opens Up on Childhood Abuse, Sexuality," *Rolling Stone*, December 1, 2010. www.rollingstone.com/ music/news/nicki-minaj-opens-up-on-childhood-abuse-sexuality-19691231; Cavan Sieczkowski, "Jessie J Denies Being Bisexual, Says It Was a Phase," *Huffington Post*, April 8, 2014. www.huffingtonpost.com/2014/04/08/jessie-j-bisexual_n_5111368. html?&ir=Celebrity&ncid=tweetlnkushpmg00000028.

19 James Nichols, "Iggy Azalea Opens Up about Her Sexuality," *Huffington Post*, April 23, 2014. www.huffingtonpost.com/2014/04/23/iggy-azalea-sexuality_n_5199658.html.

20 George Gerbner, "Cultivation Analysis: An Overview." *Mass Communication and Society*, 1, no. 3/4, (1998): 175–94; George Gerbner, Larry Gross, Michael Morgan, and Nancy Signorielli, "Growing Up with Television: The Cultivation Perspective," in *Media Effects: Advances in Theory and Research*, edited by Jennings Bryant and Dolf Zillman (Hillsdale, NJ: Lawrence Erlbaum Associates, 2002), 43–68.

21 Kevin G. Barnhurst, "Visibility as Paradox: Representation and Simultaneous Contrast," in *Media/Queered: Visibility and Its Discontents*, edited by Kevin G. Barnhurst (New York: Peter Lang Publishing, 2007), 1–19; Lisa M. Diamond, "I'm Straight but I Kissed a Girl: The Trouble with American Media Representations of Female-Female Sexuality." *Feminism and Psychology* 15, no. 1 (2005): 104–10.

III

PRODUCTION PEDAGOGIES

7

CRAFT, CREATIVITY, COLLABORATION, AND CONNECTIONS

Educating Talent for Danish Television Drama Series

Eva Novrup Redvall

"One of the secrets behind the recent success." That is how Piv Bernth, the head of the in-house production unit DR Fiction at the Danish Broadcasting Corporation (DR), refers to the public service broadcaster's collaboration on educating new television talent together with the National Film School of Denmark (NFSD).[1] Bernth stresses the importance of collaboration for understanding the quality and acclaim of DR series such as *Forbrydelsen/The Killing* (2007–10) and *Borgen* (2010–13). Her statement is one of several examples of how producers and executives at DR prioritize engagement in talent development when creating new series.

Since the late 1990s, DR and the NFSD have worked closely together on educating writers and producers, particularly for high-end television drama series. Since 2004, this collaboration has been institutionalized through the now established 'TV term,' where student writers and producers from the NFSD spend half a year developing a potential series for DR together with production designers from the School of Design at the Royal Danish Academy of Fine Arts. This term has often been highlighted as central to the emergence of a new generation of skilled television talent and of strong series with a huge domestic mainstream audience and enthusiastic niche viewers around the world. Almost all writers of series from DR are now alumni from the NFSD (including all writers of *The Killing* and *Arvingerne/The Legacy* (2014–) as well as all writers of *Borgen* except creator Adam Price). In a small country of 5.6 million inhabitants, this one institution is having a major impact on the TV drama output.

This chapter explores the rather unique collaboration between DR and the state-financed film school, which is the only official institution training screenwriters, directors, cinematographers, and other crew for film and television in

Denmark. Based on findings from a major research project on the production of drama series from DR,[2] I analyze how the NFSD has played a part in the recent rise of Danish television series through the TV term. This chapter traces the teaching of television back to the late 1990s, when the screenwriting department at the NFSD saw the emergence of new quality series from the United States and better job opportunities for writers in the field of television as reasons to include the writing of series to the School's curriculum (rather than focusing exclusively on film). This curricular turn came at an ideal time for the broadcaster. DR was experiencing a lack of talent for its new focus on long-running series and was keen to teach the students its ideas of how to create modern public service television drama.

With a qualitative case study of the TV term of 2012/13 at the core, this chapter analyzes the structure of the term and the film school conceptions of the skills needed for the industry. The main purpose of the term is to teach the students the craft of creating television series, but the term is also the only time at the School when writers work in teams. Based on observational studies of teaching sessions and of the final pitch of projects for DR as well as interviews with teachers, DR executives, and screenwriting alumni, this chapter discusses how to understand the interplay of craft and creativity within the context of collaboration that is designed to mirror television industry development.

The Education of Film and Television Talent

The education of new talent is a topic that has received limited attention in media industry studies despite the fact that many practitioners regard the formative years of training for a specific professional role as crucial to their work.[3] Seminal research on production cultures, on media work as creative labor, or on production processes in the new television economy has provided rich analysis of the professional lives and roles of both above-the-line and below-the-line workers, but does not focus on the topic of training or the educational 'food chains' that have traditionally not been central to film and media studies.[4] However, the past ten years have seen a new interest in issues of training specifically. Dana Polan's *Scenes of Instruction* chronicles the first U.S. classes on the art as well as the industry of cinema, and Lee Grieveson and Haidee Wasson's *Inventing Film Studies* offers insights into the history of film studies as an academic discipline in its own right.[5]

A milestone publication in the emerging scholarly literature on the training perspective is the two-volume anthology *The Education of the Filmmaker* edited by Mette Hjort.[6] The book addresses a wide range of approaches across the world and constructively widens the scope of thinking about film education to not only deal with the actual teachings in a particular pedagogical environment, but to also include issues of how the training of filmmakers has more far-reaching implications for other aspects of culture and society. Who is chosen to train for these roles? What kinds of stories do filmmakers tell? How do filmmakers perceive of their role in a specific society? As Hjort states, it is worthwhile investigating how a filmmaker becomes a filmmaker, but it is also important to explore how a film-maker becomes "a particular *kind* of filmmaker, where 'kind' encompasses skills, as well as narrative and aesthetic priorities, preferred modes of practice, and under-standings of what the ideal roles and *contributions* of film would be."[7] As Hjort demonstrates, different national and institutional contexts tend to encourage dif-ferent approaches, yet, in terms of what to teach, there are also many similarities across cultures and countries.

A crucial question in terms of all practice-based film education is the fun-damental issue of why to teach the making of film and television in the first place—with the ever-present tensions between art and commerce being an important part of this question. As analyzed by Duncan Petrie, most European film schools started out with a clear emphasis on teaching cinema as an art form and training their students as artists.[8] Focusing on the theory/practice divide and the British film conservatoire, Petrie has argued how this gradually changed with still more emphasis on the "industry approved vocational skills" needed to suc-ceed in the world of film and media today.[9] Most recently, Petrie and Rod Stone-man have discussed this "fetishization of instrumental skills" further in *Educating Film-Makers*,[10] which contains a history of film schools and case studies of Brit-ish institutions by Petrie combined with chapters by Stoneman defined as more polemical 'provocations.' Stoneman's chapters are intended as a starting point for debates about what the authors call "the shortcomings inherent in the current formation of film schools."[11] I will address some of their thoughts on film schools as more than mere training providers when discussing how to understand the TV term of the NFSD within an art school context.

The National Film School of Denmark

The NFSD was founded as an art school in 1966 and is financed by the Danish Ministry of Cultural Affairs. Currently, the School presents itself first and foremost as "an art school, which means that the teaching aims at developing and support-ing each student's unique talent."[12] However, the description of the school clarifies that it is also important "that our students learn the craft of filmmaking to ensure their future employment."[13] What can be regarded as an interplay between the creative talent of the student and learning a specific craft needed in the industry is thus at the core of the School's presentation of itself to the world.

The NFSD is a highly competitive school, accepting around six students for each program (e.g., writing, directing, producing, cinematography, sound) every second year. The state-financed school offers one of the most expensive educations in the country, but students pay no tuition. The chosen few are expected to have a main focus on filmmaking, and the teaching of television writing only became part of the otherwise film-oriented curriculum during the late 1990s—and, as illustrated in the quote cited earlier in this chapter about learning "the craft of filmmaking," television still hasn't made it into the official description of what students study at the School.

In the 2000s, the NFSD was generally regarded as a success story in the production of film. Danish scholars singled out constructive teaching strategies such as scaffolding and working with restraints[14] or the importance of creating a shared language of storytelling between professions.[15] International scholars highlighted the NFSD curriculum as part of the explanatory framework for how a number of prolific alumni created the Dogme95 manifesto[16] and for the rise of a "new Danish cinema,"[17] with Lars von Trier as its art house star. Meanwhile, national audiences have appreciated the domestic film output, securing the national films an impressive share of the domestic ticket sale (29 percent in 2012).

The NFSD has continuously been credited as an important reason for this interest in Danish cinema. But after many years of general enthusiasm, the 2010s saw criticism of the School emerge. The critical voices pointed to a lack of diversity in student films and called for changes in what some regarded as a standardizing approach to forming future filmmakers. During the hiring of a new head of the School in 2013, debates around the School became fiercer,[18] but it was remarkable how the teaching of television was not a part of these discussions. With alumni from the School playing a major part in now internationally renowned series such as *The Killing* and *Borgen*, everyone seemed to silently agree that all was well when teaching for the small rather than the big screen.

Building the Television Curriculum

The first course on television at the NFSD dates back to 1996. At that time, DR started focusing on long-running series and, according to then DR producer Sven Clausen, experienced "an acute lack of Danish episode writers with experience in writing for the medium and the genre—and an enthusiasm for the format."[19] The teaching at NFSD was seen as a method "to secure future deliveries by being visible—not the least as a source of inspiration—already at the level of education."[20] DR was thus very interested in collaborating with the School and took part when the first attempt to teach television was offered to writing students at the NFSD in 1996. The course led to making television writing an integrated part of the screenwriting curriculum.

Head of the screenwriting department Lars Detlefsen describes how the introduction of television writing was initially met with resistance at the School. He finds that one of the reasons this resistance gradually faded was a shared sense of remarkable changes in the nature of television series with a number of international 'quality series' becoming popular and well respected, making it more artistically legitimate to focus on television in an art school context.[21] Former students such as producer Christian Rank have described how the term was at first a revelation in creating a new awareness around television,[22] but quality TV series are now firmly established in the minds of the students. According to screenwriting teacher Hanna Lundblad, the current students are familiar with many television series and quite fluent in basic television storytelling terms and traditions.[23]

In 2004, the teaching of television found its current form as the so-called TV term, which is organized around groups of writers and producers from the NFSD and production designers from the School of Design spending four to five months developing a potential series for DR. Thus, there is no individual program for television; rather, it is integrated into the overall curriculum for the writers and producers, and the teaching is built around a set assignment for a specific broadcaster, rather than a free assignment, as is the case with the cinematic midterm or final films.

The TV term groups normally consist of two writers, two producers, and one or two production designers, who work together through the process of conceiving an idea from the beginning of the teaching in August to the delivery of the completed assignment before Christmas, which is then presented to DR during a two-day pitch in January. The students are expected to produce a presentation of a whole concept consisting of pitches for the first six episodes, full scripts for the first and last episodes, plus ideas for a second season as well as budgets, production plans, and presentations of the production design and visual identity of the series.

The term runs every two years and serves as the third term out of four for the writing students and third of eight for the producing students (who are at the School for four years).[24] The 2012 assignment was formulated by then head of DR Fiction Nadia Kløvedal Reich and head of drama Piv Bernth, who represented DR as commissioners in the process and were keen to get ideas from the students on a format that DR had abandoned for quite some years while focusing on the high-end drama fare. In the early years of the TV term, students came up with ideas for the prestigious one-hour DR drama slot for Sunday nights at 8 P.M. In the TV term of 2012, students developed a weeknight comedy or dramedy series of 28.5 minutes targeting younger audiences.

The NFSD offers no assignments that mirror the processes of writers' rooms or that force the students to enter someone else's creative vision as episode writers on an existing series. However, the TV term can be regarded as an attempt to teach the students about the gifts and hardships of creative collaboration through working on a small team with a clear goal, and where disagreements will inevitably arise. Based on observational studies of some of the teaching and the pitch of the 2012 TV term combined with qualitative interviews around the term, the following case study outlines the NFSD objectives for the term as an ideal structure for teaching the craft, encouraging creativity, facilitating collaborations, and creating connections.[25]

Teaching the Craft

Because none of the students have been working with television when they start this term, the School gives them a so-called inspirational box before the summer break. Detlefsen describes the box as a tool to "tune in to making television series" and emphasizes the value of forming groups before the summer to get initial ideas going before the actual teaching starts in the fall.[26] The inspirational box always consists of a number of TV series, the book *Successful Television Writing* by Lee Goldberg and William Rabkin, and scripts for national and international series. In 2012, the box contained the first seasons of *2 Broke Girls* (2011–), *Bored to Death* (2009–11), and *In Treatment* (2008–), as well as *Forbrydelsen II/The Killing II* (2009). The scripts were the first episodes of *Mad Men* (2007–) seasons one through five, the third episode of *Forbrydelsen II*, and the first episode of *Boss* (2011–12). The students are also given what Detlefsen terms "a dummy paper" or "a recipe" for a TV series concept, which lists a number of things to include when thinking about new series, ranging from considerations of genre, theme, premise, issues of characters, arenas, and storytelling strategies to presentations of casting and crew choices, budgets, mode of production, time slots, and target groups.[27]

The start of the TV term focuses on creating a shared sense of the specific nature of television drama among the writers, producers, and production designers from that year's class. During the term they all attend classes on TV series and since the first iteration of the TV term, screenwriter Hanna Lundblad has given all students an introduction to storytelling for television and to the specific demands for DR series. Over the three days, students analyze the major turning points in all scenes of individual characters in an episode or study classic season openings. The teaching also consists of discussions of good arenas or main characters. Lundblad encourages students to present interesting arenas or characters from their own lives, which are then mixed in attempts to create intriguing combinations.

The cross-disciplinary classes aim at facilitating a shared sense of the nature of creating television across the different professions involved, but there is also a focus on the specific needs of each profession; they all have unique tasks during the term while working on the mutual project. Each term thus has industry tutors attached for the different professions. For example, in 2012, former DR producer Sven Clausen and Zentropa studio producer Louise Vesth coached producers, screenwriters Hanna Lundblad and Karina Dam assisted writers, and *Borgen* production designer Knirke Madelung consulted with production designers. The industry tutors follow the projects as they develop and are also part of the final pitch when they provide feedback as a supplement to the opinions of the DR commissioners. The students thus have the opportunity to not only get feedback on the end result, but also on the work processes and the way projects and collaborations evolve along the way.

DR and the NFSD do not exchange money in the teaching of the TV term, but DR does allocate substantial time for engaging with the students. The 2012 semester included one week at DR when the students followed productions and talked to professionals at DR. Later in the process, the students also met the in-house media researchers. At the pitch of the final projects, several groups referred to having consulted the researchers on issues related to the main audiences of certain time slots and so forth, and in the eyes of DR the groups seemed to have the right sense of the potential audience for their suggested series in terms of gender, age, and background in relation to content and time slot.

As indicated by "the TV dummy paper," the term is not only based on students learning the craft of storytelling for television, but also on thinking about issues of financing and logistics, positioning projects, and getting an upper hand over competing series. However, while students are asked to take all these industry aspects into account when developing a unique product for a certain broadcaster, instructors encourage them to focus on their personal desires and original ideas in the process. This is based on the DR production concept of one vision. While the structure of the course is designed to encourage professionalism, the School places significant focus on the creative voice of each student, in particular that of the screenwriter.

The Issue of Creativity

Because DR Fiction reorganized its approach to television production in the late 1990s to focus on long-running flagship series, screenwriters are at the center of the production framework.[28] This is markedly different from the more auteur-oriented Danish film culture, which places directors in charge of a production. In the so-called production dogmas formulated in 2003 as guiding principles for in-house DR productions, the first dogma describes the concept of one vision, stating that the author is the one person who has the vision that drives the narrative fiction.[29] In the DR production framework, this notion of one vision is regarded as crucial to ensure that writers feel ownership of series and that original ideas are developed from the ground up based on the desire of the creative people in charge. Even in the instance of adapting existing material for television or having executives commission certain kinds of stories, writers' visions are primary. However, there are limits. Writers' ideas have to fit within the public service obligations of DR. The second dogma calls for series with 'double storytelling,' meaning that stories should not only be entertaining but also contain ethical and social layers.[30] The DR series are targeted at the mainstream national audiences, but the aim is to provide dramatic content, which can spark wider conversations and reflections about important issues in society. Accordingly, when developing a specific series for DR, students are asked to keep the dogmas in mind and focus on the ideas of one vision and double storytelling, which create a specific DR framework for the process.

In the scholarly literature on creative processes, most definitions of creativity highlight the importance of creators developing something original, of high quality, and appropriate to the task at hand.[31] In terms of the TV term, the DR commissioners determine what is regarded as creative. Here the strict framework emphasizes creativity within industry constraints: on creating series acceptable to the industry gatekeepers rather than developing more eclectic or artistic ideas. That said, the final pitches from 2012 clearly presented the personal drive and interest behind proposed series. The one vision concept balances this DR framework, encouraging students to follow their individual desires within the industry structure.

The concept of one vision was continuously highlighted as important in the research interviews about the term, and yet the difficult development processes of certain groups showed how a concept focusing on one person having one vision for a project that demands a collaborative process (with two writers involved) presents quite a challenge. Whereas the professional roles of head writer and episode writers are more clear in an industry context, trying to maintain a shared vision as two writers with equal footing within the collaborative school context can be a complicated task. Different groups handled this in unique ways. For example, one group had the writers splitting up work midway through the term. At the final pitch, the project of one of the writers splitting up found praise for the consistency in the way all aspects supported the main idea of the individual writer. As a contrast, the DR evaluation of another project was met with concerns that the group process had created confusion about the core of the idea. The DR commissioners found that the premise for the series of this group was centered on romance, but all A-plotlines for episodes dealt with professional conflicts while the B-plotlines were about romance. The DR commissioners argued that this muddled the premise, and in the following discussions the students commented on the challenges of wanting to take the project in different directions along the way and maybe sometimes settling on compromises rather than having one clear vision.

As illustrated in this example, the TV term is marked by constant negotiations between individual and collective creativity. While the mission of the NFSD as an art school is to nurture each student's unique talent, the more industrial context of the TV term creates a controlled framework for a specific kind of process. According to Detlefsen, the creative process of each student is important, but the TV term is first and foremost "a course on collaborating."[32] This can be challenging when students have to negotiate their personal ideas and desires with those of the other members of the group, while developing a series that will be considered original, of high quality, and appropriate by the DR commissioners.

The Gifts and Hardships of Collaborations

The TV term is the only coursework where students within the writing track are asked to work in pairs. For Detlefsen this term is designed to teach about much more than just developing a TV series. Detlefsen argues that important lessons relate to collaborating with writing colleagues as well as with other professional groups because collaboration is crucial to bringing ideas to fruition. When to compromise or not and what sacrifices might be needed when working with other creative people are lessons that are critical to the program's goals of teaching students how to become writers that not only know their craft but are also able to get work in the industry.[33]

Where traditionally the NFSD offers little teaching on collaboration,[34] the TV term is unique in its focus on instrumental lessons regarding the risks and rewards of collaboration not only between NFSD students, but also with design students from another institution. In 2012, creativity coach Thea Mikkelsen was attached as an advisor for the students, but Detlefsen argues that the students should not be nursed too much in terms of their collaborations because they have to learn the way back to the work after things have gone wrong. Accordingly, he tries to allow for some processes to go off track because students learn more from their "mistakes and disasters than from being guided through so that everything is smooth and fine."[35]

The mutual classes on TV series encourage the sense of being a team by creating a shared set of references and a common way of talking about storytelling or stylistic choices. According to several alumni, there is a great value in getting everyone on the same page from the outset, and alumni such as screenwriter Jeppe Gjervig Gram have emphasized how learning a certain way to talk about series has had a significant impact on their later work. Shortly after graduating, he became part of writing *Borgen* together with fellow alumnus Tobias Lindholm. The series was created by Adam Price who is not from the NFSD, and according to Gram it took a while "to learn how to speak with him," while this "is different with people from the school; we have the same point of view from the beginning."[36] While the TV term places strong emphasis on learning how to collaborate on a specific project, it may be as much about creating a shared language of communication as it is about learning to collaborate on ideas.

Industry reports on European TV drama practices point to how writers often work alone,[37] and scholarly studies have highlighted the traditional skepticism toward team writing in many European production cultures.[38] The TV term allows for gaining educational experiences of collaborative writing as well as working with other professions from the outset of an idea, and the current number of screenwriting alumni working at DR as head writers and episode writers points to how the graduates from the school now provide the television writers that DR desperately called for in the 1990s and to a television industry where writing teams have become an established mode of production.[39]

The Importance of Connections

While the TV term provides training in collaboration—an important skill for future employment—the term also provides an opportunity to learn networking skills and to build students' connections with specific broadcasters. During the term, students meet real-life commissioners—and commissioners use the term as a place to scout for talent. Over the term, instructors introduce the core values of DR as an example of a specific broadcaster, well before the students ever enter the industry.

The screenwriting alumni now working at DR place great emphasis on the fact that the term is built around pitching to actual decision makers at DR.[40] Jeppe Gjervig Gram argues that the term is the time at the School that mirrors what he calls "virtual reality" the most because students have an assignment that might actually be real and allows them to meet the industry commissioners, whom they want to impress.[41] This does not only happen at the final pitch, but also at a midterm so-called paramount meeting, where students pitch their initial ideas to the DR commissioners, followed by an evaluation the next day. The paramount meeting mirrors the in-house production structures at DR, where the meeting is regarded as crucial for ensuring that the creative team and the drama executives are on the same page regarding the overall concept for a series.[42] In this way, the DR commissioners not only meet the final projects, but are involved in the process. This provides the opportunity to sense how a project has evolved along the way and how the students deal with feedback, mirroring what, for instance, Caldwell has described as the often challenging industry process of note giving.[43]

The TV term offers DR the opportunity to scout for talented writers and producers as well as production designers. Particularly the amount of NFSD writers now working at DR has received attention because the domestic film industry has repeatedly complained about the broadcaster using the term to swallow up the best writers before they have even entered the job market.[44] It is hard for the film industry to compete for talent with DR, given the precarious and time-consuming nature of developing and financing film projects. DR can offer attractive work conditions with longer and more secure terms of employment.

So far, none of the series pitched for DR over the years have made it to the screen, but according to Piv Bernth some ideas are still in play.[45] The lack of produced projects illustrates how the TV term is more about working with a set assignment and about students pitching their interests and skills to a broadcaster than about selling a finished concept. The students sign contracts at the beginning of the term in case any projects should be picked up by DR, but according to Detlefsen the aim of the term is not to sell a perfect project; from the NFSD perspective, he argues, the term should be regarded as a school assignment with an overall educational purpose.[46]

In an industry where jobs are rarely advertised and the flexible labor market is based on professionals forming 'networks of interdependence'[47] or 'Screen Idea Work Groups,'[48] students building the right connections is a major part of securing a successful career. The TV term is a platform for the School to give students the opportunity to meet influential industry players as more than fleeting guest lecturers.

Conclusions and Cliffhangers

The TV term is an example of how a national broadcaster and a film school have established a collaboration, which they both regard as highly successful. I agree with Mette Hjort, who argues that "there can be no one-to-one correspondence between the profile of a given school, on the one hand, and the priorities and values of its graduates, on the other. After all, film schools are subject to the full range of complexities that characterize institutional life."[49] Students from the NFSD do not share the same priorities and values, but the TV term has hugely impacted a small national production culture. As an example, the School's emphasis on one vision and 'double storytelling' has helped graduate industry-ready television makers with an acute awareness of certain DR concepts for creating new series.

The broadcaster perspective of the TV term gives the teaching an explicit focus on the vocational skills needed in the industry. On paper, the main creative task is to develop a series that will find the acceptance of the DR commissioners, but—as Detlefsen argues—one can also regard the term as fundamentally about the nature of collaboration in an industry-like context; a context where one might learn more from failing than from succeeding while still in the rather safe surroundings of an educational institution.

As U.S. quality television and Danish series gained more respect during the 2000s, the School's teaching became less about selling the idea that television can also be an interesting medium to work in and more about creating strong series for a specific context. This happens in a work process that aims at teaching students not only about the craft of television writing, but also about the creative process of trying to negotiate one's artistic vision in a highly collaborative production framework. However, the term is not primarily about expressing the unique talent of each student—as stated in the School's definition of its art-oriented agenda—and the term's industry context does stand out in comparison with the other terms focused on filmmaking.

In their book on film schools, Petrie and Stoneman argue that from a historical perspective, "rather than being primarily a site of innovation and new thinking, film schools gradually began to adopt a more overtly professional role, dictated by the needs of industry, which has served to reproduce commercial forms and arguably discourage genuine creativity."[50] Thinking along these lines, the TV term has been instrumental in providing much-needed talent for DR. The focus on high-end drama and the DR dogmas has encouraged students to build on existing forms and norms, and the years of teaching television have offered little opportunity to approach television drama in completely new ways.

The 2013 conference organized by the International Association of Film and Television Schools (CILECT)—under the title 'From Education to Business—The Connection between National Film Schools and Broadcasters'—pointed to how European film schools are now discussing the need for students to learn more about working in new formats for new platforms rather than only learning to develop expensive drama for traditional broadcasters. However, the NFSD approach to television writing was repeatedly referred to as an example of best practice, and both NFSD and DR representatives were invited to explain the virtues of this particular collaboration. The conference illustrated how several new television training grounds are being established, making it highly relevant to keep asking the core questions of not only how to best teach television writing, but also of why it is being taught in the first place.

The TV term appears to have found a successful recipe for educating talent for the established DR framework. Maybe the coming years will also allow for playing around with other kinds of TV fiction. As Petrie and Stoneman discuss—and as the title of the CILECT conference indicates—there is much talk of 'the industry' and 'business' in film schools today. Petrie and Stoneman argue that this has implications on schools' tending not to recognize "the possibility of moving image practitioners as curious and critical thinkers, or of how the cultivation of ideas could serve the successful propagation of creative, vibrant and socially relevant film and television industries."[51] While the close links to the industry offer great 'virtual reality' and calling card opportunities, television education in an art school context might need to look back at its origins. New strategies seem necessary to find the right balance between educating curious, creative artists *and* skilled, industry-oriented professionals—between teaching the existing ideas of best practice *and* encouraging innovation—for a rapidly changing television landscape.

Notes

1 Piv Bernth in Annika Pham, "DR's Queens of Drama Give the Ingredients to Their Winning Recipe," News from Nordisk Film and TV Fond, May 11, 2012. www.nordiskfilmogtvfond.com/index.php/news/stories/drs-queens-drama-give-ingredients-their-winning-recipe/.

2 Eva N. Redvall, *Writing and Producing Television Drama in Denmark: From the Kingdom to the Killing* (Basingstoke: Palgrave Macmillan, 2013).

3 See John Boorman, Fraser MacDonald, and Walter Donohue, eds., *Projections 12: Film-Makers on Film Schools* (London: Faber and Faber, 2002). For opinions of the NFSD, see three interview books with Danish feature film and documentary directors: Mette Hjort and Ib Bondebjerg, *The Danish Directors: Dialogues on a Contemporary National Cinema* (Bristol: Intellect Press, 2003); Mette Hjort, Eva Jørholt, and Eva N. Redvall, *The Danish Directors 2: Dialogues on the New Danish Fiction Cinema* (Bristol: Intellect Press, 2010); Mette Hjort, Ib Bondebjerg, and Eva N. Redvall, *The Danish Directors 3: Dialogues on the New Danish Documentary Cinema* (Bristol: Intellect Press, 2014).

4 John T. Caldwell, *Production Culture: Industrial Reflexivity and Critical Practice in Film and Television* (Durham, NC: Duke University Press, 2008); David Hesmondhalgh and Sarah Baker, *Creative Labour: Media Work in the Cultural Industries* (New York and

Abingdon: Routledge, 2011);Vicki Mayer, *Below the Line: Producers and Production Studies in the New Television Economy* (Durham, NC and London: Duke University Press, 2011).

5 Dana Polan, *Scenes of Instruction:The Beginnings of the U.S. Study of Film* (Berkeley: University of California Press, 2007); Lee Grieveson and Haidee Wasson, *Inventing Film Studies* (Durham, NC: Duke University Press, 2008).

6 Mette Hjort, *The Education of the Filmmaker in Europe,Australia, and Asia*, vol. 1 (Basingstoke: Palgrave Macmillan, 2013); Mette Hjort, *The Education of the Filmmaker in Africa, the Middle East, and the Americas*, vol. 2 (Basingstoke: Palgrave Macmillan, 2013).

7 Hjort, *The Education of the Filmmaker in Europe,Australia, and Asia*, 1.

8 Duncan Petrie, "Theory, Practice and the Significance of Film Schools." *Scandia* 76 (2010): 31–46.

9 Duncan Petrie,"Theory/Practice and the British Film Conservatoire." *Journal of Media Practice* 12 (2011): 125–38.

10 Duncan Petrie and Rod Stoneman, *Educating Film-Makers: Past, Present and Future* (Bristol: Intellect Press, 2014), 9.

11 Petrie and Stoneman, *Educating Film-Makers*, 10.

12 Filmskolen.dk.

13 Filmskolen.dk.

14 Heidi Philipsen, "Dansk films nye bølge: Afsæt og aftryk fra Den Danske Filmskole," PhD diss., University of Southern Denmark, 2005.

15 Eva N. Redvall, "Teaching Screenwriting in a Time of Storytelling Blindness: The Meeting of the Auteur and the Screenwriting Tradition in Danish Film-Making."*Journal of Screenwriting* 1 (2010): 57–79.

16 Mette Hjort and Scott MacKenzie, *Purity and Provocation: Dogme '95* (London: British Film Institute, 2003).

17 Mette Hjort, *Small Nation, Global Cinema:The New Danish Cinema* (Minneapolis: University of Minnesota Press, 2005).

18 E.g., Kjeld Hybel, "Filmbranchen: Den Danske Filmskole trænger til et los i røven," *Politiken*, November 21, 2013.

19 Sven Clausen, personal e-mail communication with Redvall, September 15, 2012.

20 Clausen, personal e-mail, 2012.

21 Lars Detlefsen, interview with the author, December 11, 2012.

22 Christian Rank, interview with the author, November 22, 2012.

23 Hanna Lundblad, interview with the author, September 3, 2012.

24 This is likely to change in the future because the NFSD screenwriting students will also have a four-year education from 2015.

25 The interviews are referred to with the last names of the respondents and the year of the interviews.

26 Detlefsen, interview, 2012.

27 An 'arena' refers to the main setting for a series, sometimes called a 'precinct.'

28 Redvall, *Writing and Producing Television Drama in Denmark*.

29 Redvall, *Writing and Producing Television Drama in Denmark*, 69.

30 Redvall, *Writing and Producing Television Drama in Denmark*, 69.

31 E.g., Robert J. Sternberg and Todd I. Lubart, "The Concept of Creativity: Prospects and Paradigms," in *Handbook of Creativity*, edited by Robert J. Sternberg (Cambridge: Cambridge University Press, 1999), 3–31.

32 Detlefsen, interview, 2012.

33 Detlefsen, interview, 2012.

34 Redvall, "Teaching Screenwriting in a Time of Storytelling Blindness."

35 Detlefsen, interview, 2012.

36 Jeppe G. Gram, Presentation at the conference "From Education to Business—The Connection between National Film Schools and Broadcasters" (a GEECT/CILECT conference) at the National Film School of Denmark, November 28–9, 2013.

37 E.g., Eva N. Redvall, *European TV Drama Series Lab: Summary of Module 1* (Berlin: Erich Pommer Institut, 2012).

38 Georgina Born, *Uncertain Vision: Birt, Dyke and the Reinvention of the BBC* (London: Vintage, 2005).

39 Redvall, *Writing and Producing Television Drama in Denmark*.

40 E.g., Maya Ilsøe, interview with the author, November 13, 2013.

41 Jeppe G. Gram, interview with the author, November 9, 2012.

42 Ingolf Gabold, interview with the author, May 17, 2013.

43 Caldwell, *Production Culture*, 221.

44 Redvall, *Writing and Producing Television Drama in Denmark*.

45 Piv Bernth, interview with the author, October 1, 2014.

46 Detlefsen, interview, 2012.

47 Helen Blair, "Winning and Losing in Flexible Labour Markets: The Formation and Operation of Networks of Interdependence in the UK Film Industry." *Sociology* 37 (2003): 677–94.

48 Ian W. Macdonald, "' . . . So It's Not Surprising I'm Neurotic': The Screenwriter and the Screen Idea Work Group." *Journal of Screenwriting* 1 (2010): 45–58.

49 Hjort, *The Education of the Filmmaker in Europe, Australia, and Asia*, 4.

50 Petrie and Stoneman, *Educating Film-Makers*, 106.

51 Petrie and Stoneman, *Educating Film-Makers*, 8.

8

CHARITY APPEALS AS 'POVERTY PORN'?

Production Ethics in Representing Suffering Children and Typhoon Haiyan Beneficiaries in the Philippines

Jonathan Corpus Ong

Production studies has much to contribute to current literature in media ethics, particularly to debates about documentary and news media's representation of suffering. Within the recent moral turn in media studies is a significant reconstructing of 'first principles' and 'virtues' in the normative critique of media practice—from hospitality,[1] to justice,[2] to accuracy, sincerity, and care.[3] These principles are typically applied to the ethical critique of the mediation of 'peak moments' of tragedy and natural disaster, and the ways specific narratives within the genres of news and charity advertising make different moral claims on Western publics. Whether 'distant sufferers' appear as passive, needy victims in stereotypical 'poverty porn' imagery or as active agents given both voice and historical context is a production choice assumed to have far-reaching moral consequences. Media narratives are generally assumed to create either positions of maximal distance that cause only "compassion fatigue"[4] or a productive "proper distance" that cultivates relationships premised on mutual understanding and empathy.[5]

But the dominance of these philosophical and text-centered approaches to studying audiences and producers lacks almost any ethnographic method of empirical study. In relation to audiences, we know very little about the correspondence between theorists' elaborate moral positions about the most 'proper' representational practices and ordinary people's diverse and unpredictable patterns of engagement and meaning making in relation to them,[6] although recent contributions suggest a determined effort to address this blind spot.[7] With a few honorable exceptions,[8] what is even more lacking are production studies approaches that illustrate ethics not just as principles but as *process*.

Production studies contributes a more expansive consideration of ethics in the mediation of suffering in its attentiveness to everyday practices and dilemmas of creative professionals and the particular local and institutional vocabularies of good and bad work used in media production.[9] This approach is particularly important as the current literature on mediated suffering has a tendency to analyze disparate moments of "peak tragedies" or the distinct "textual games" of each fundraising charity ad,[10] with less to say about the development of creative practices in relation to national cultures or organizational norms. The concern of production studies to explain media production as "creativity within constraints" in nuanced relation with producers' identities offers up an analysis of mediated suffering in the context of the "messy stuff" of institutional ecologies and regulatory conditions under which generic narratives are produced.[11]

I locate producers' ethics in the recruitment and treatment of vulnerable groups in relation to their everyday interactions, decision making, and application of institutional codes. Within this optic, the ethics of representing sufferers with agency, voice, and "proper distance" becomes subsumed by what Georgina Born calls an *ethics of translation*.[12] Born's call for an anthropological ethics of media analysis must attend to the connections and disconnections of broad ethical principles, institutional norms, and media producers' own personal intentions across three different scales of media ethics. This is what she calls:

> the normative, institutional ethics, and the practical ethics—where it is the last, practical ethics, that ultimately bears responsibility for the alchemical translation of the media-normative into the only form in which it can be publicly metabolized (by audiences and users): in the guise of specific genres of mediatized cultural experience, replete as they are with ethical and aesthetic potentials—potentials that are of course variably and imperfectly realized.[13]

In this chapter, I consider the producers of television network charity appeals as *agents of ethical translation*. This work is based on interviews and observations with fifteen television producers of charity appeals from 2009 to 2014 in Manila, Philippines. In studying these producers, I locate the aspect of their work as ethical translators who make everyday articulations of 'right' and 'wrong' in media practice, within the messy 'practical ethics' of balancing between their project deadlines and duties of care toward subjects, managing their emotions in the wake of tragedy, and justifying their work outputs in the face of public criticism. I begin by reviewing the current media ethics literature and its critique of humanitarian and charity appeals and then provide an account of local debates in the Philippine context. I also give a background to the peculiar role of Filipino television as a charitable social institution in the most "disaster-prone country in the world"—a remit that animates the production and reception of the local genre of the charity appeal.[14]

Inspired by production studies work on the interaction between producers and working-class 'ordinary people' participants,[15] this chapter offers *translation models* that exemplify producers' strategies of compliance and resistance as regards local media conventions of representing suffering. These translation models aim to account for producers' vitality and ambition for good work amid social and institutional pressures that, when in conflict, produce moral dilemmas in production.

Charity Appeals as "Poverty Porn"?

In the media ethics literature, the genre of the humanitarian appeal has been approached as a diverse and contested communicative space. Some media scholars regard charity appeals as enactments of ethical discourse that may activate emotional regimes of pity or indignation among audiences and publics.[16] For instance, Lilie Chouliaraki's pathbreaking work maps out a useful typology of different techniques in Western humanitarian advertising from 1) 'shock effect' campaigning to 2) positive imagery to 3) 'post-humanitarian' irony. Chouliaraki analyzes different campaigns' aesthetics, suggesting an evolution of styles and laying open each campaign's ethical claims. She criticizes 'shock effect' campaigns for their dehumanization of non-Western others: "captured on camera, these body parts, passively sitting in a row as they are, become fetishized: they do not reflect real human bodies but curiosities of the flesh that mobilize a pornographic spectatorial imagination between disgust and desire."[17] In contrast, positive imagery campaigns involve narrative techniques of personalizing sufferers and singularizing donors, where the presence of the benefactor becomes "instrumental in summoning up the emotional regime of empathy."[18] Nevertheless she admits that such campaigns may have the inadvertent effect of glossing over asymmetries of power and increase social denial to act on suffering "on the grounds that it may be unnecessary" because of the televised presence of benefactors.[19] The last and most contemporary technique of charity appeals eschews the factual and photorealistic representation of suffering altogether and instead relies on cartoon animation, computer-generated imagery, the hiring of paid actors, and the foregrounding of the corporate brand while erasing sufferers from the picture altogether. While each is rife with drawbacks, Chouliaraki is most anxious about this present-day, 'post-humanitarian' technique for its self-centered and consumerist sensibilities, ultimately failing to push audiences beyond their comfort zone.

It must be noted that the literature is not wholly negative about 'shock effect' campaigning. Karen Wells, for one, argues that melodramatic styles in children-centered charity ads effectively activate compassion and identification for suffering children who "unambiguously signify virtue" to potential donors.[20] With its exaggerated and high-emotion narrative, melodramatic campaigning can offer, in her view, "a critique of the worst excesses of economic inequality."[21] Stan Cohen supports this as well, arguing that representing suffering "at its worst" can motivate political action and challenge social denial.[22]

In the Philippines, charity appeals are popularly identified as productions of both the charity subsidiaries and the corporate communication arms of privately owned top-rated television networks. Appeals produced by the charity subsidiaries lean toward the 'shock effect' style of campaigning and employ a documentary mode of filmmaking. These appeals, which air at the end of primetime newscasts and during commercial breaks throughout the day, usually relate to charitable projects of the TV network charity foundations, which include feeding programs for the poor and fundraising for victims of natural disaster. The most common of these appeals are individual case studies of children suffering from a physical deformity—with the most 'iconic' image of these appeals being a child with hydrocephalus, which causes an abnormal body enlargement. The mise-en-scène of such an appeal is the everyday, the home and domestic spaces that children and their families inhabit. Following Chouliaraki's description of Western styles of 'shock effect' campaigns, there is also a "curiosity of the flesh," with lingering, close-up shots of poor children to authenticate their helplessness and deservedness of television viewers' attention and donation.[23] The appeal also includes testimonials from mothers who are individualized and personalized. Typically, mothers display an excess of emotion in the camera, which is assumed to evoke pity from viewers who can identify with being mothers or children themselves. The appeal closes with a number flashed on the screen, and an invitation for audiences to donate to the network, which mediates, in both symbolic and material terms, the collection of money and awards this televisually to the suffering subjects.

The charity appeal is just one of the services that exemplify the peculiarity of Philippine media as a space for gestural forms of economic redistribution and socially mediated recognition.[24] Although privately owned, Philippine television network stations are venues that people visit not only for live entertainment but also to access various public services such as legal advice, medical assistance, moneylending, and referrals to NGOs and government offices. One particular subgenre of charity appeals involves televising disaster relief efforts that seek donations from viewers at home, at the same time flagging the corporate brand in the effort to cultivate viewers' loyalty and trust within a highly competitive media environment. During events of natural calamity, representatives from media charities travel alongside their journalist colleagues to the site of disaster. After the journalist delivers a news report, representatives and journalists stand side by side in handing out relief goods to victims.

A justification of such practices, certainly one preferred by the television networks, is that media fill the gap left by corrupt and bureaucratic public institutions—not to mention the absence of welfare state provisions. In such a context of intervention, cultural critic Conrado De Quiros has described Filipino media as "acting as the government." When a major typhoon hit the capital of Metro Manila in September 2009, De Quiros observed:

In fact the monumental thing that happened last Saturday was the complete absence of government. The only government there was were the media, notably [privately owned television networks] ABS-CBN and GMA-7. You can forgive both for advertising their wares, or relief efforts, under the extenuating circumstances. They were the government. They were the central authority apprising the public of the situation. They were the central authority coming to the aid of victims. They were running the country.[25]

As both GMA network news anchor and head of its media charity arm, Kapuso Foundation, Mel Tiangco explains, their role is not just as the first reporters on a scene but also often as first responders:

The reason why Kapuso Foundation is tied to the news is because, from our news desk, we learn days beforehand of the possibility of, say, a typhoon, and therefore we are able to prepare and help the victims. Why, who arrives on the site first anyway? It's always us. And it's just irresponsible if we arrive and do nothing but just cover, when people are actually dying, or buried in [rubble]. . . . But when Red Cross and the government and the other charities arrive, then we [Kapuso Foundation] would pull out. But Kapuso Foundation is always there as the first to respond.[26]

This representation of news networks as benevolent charities does not tell the whole story. Television networks' 'spirit of service' to the poor and disaster victims in particular is subject to criticisms of exploitation and the perpetuation of 'bad values.'[27] Elite cultural critics and academics identify that media's charitable practices extend from the political economy of local television, which functions according to a 'sachet economics' business model where the spending (and voting) power of the *masa* (masses) is what generates profit and wins elections. As well, the targeting of the *masa* in television content and services is criticized as purely instrumental for television owners given the proportion of the lower class (two-thirds of the population) in comparison to the middle and upper classes.[28] Overrepresentation and 'redistributing' to the poor are pessimistically viewed by these critics as sinister strategies merely used to survive in the heated television 'ratings wars.'[29]

In addition, local commentators regard media practices of overrepresenting the poor in charity appeals and cash-distributing game shows as perpetuating a "culture of mendicancy" or a "mendicant society."[30] For example, the enormously popular but now defunct game show *Wowowee* supposedly conditions Filipinos to depend on "easy money,"[31] instead of "providing them the tools to navigate in a harsh and complex world."[32]

These multiple and contradictory discourses about the role of private media in a context of widespread poverty and frequent disaster inform the production of charity appeals. The media have historically positioned themselves as responsible agents who fill the gap of weak government, yet are surveilled by cultural elites for their conflation of public service with business strategy. The media act as truth-tellers to local realities of suffering in news reports and documentary-style shock appeals, yet they actively employ branding and loyalty strategies into the production of television content and dispensing of services.

Understanding Producers: Strategies of Compliance versus Risk and Resistance

The following section maps out strategies of translation work in the production of charity appeals. Following Georgina Born's call to trace the practical ethics in media work,[33] I relate how producers translate television networks' diffuse ethical commitments of public service into particular cultural forms. I present translation models that reflect the producers' strategies of either 1) *compliance*, where the producer follows institutional interests and established procedural codes, or 2) translation with greater *risk* and *resistance*. This second mode situates a producer with a stronger imperative to transmute personal (although socially shaped) moralities of care that directly challenge norms of production.

The following analysis is based on participant observations and in-depth interviews of fifteen producers of charity appeals created for privately owned television networks. These producers are generally in charge of the network's public service arm; some are actively involved in engaging with beneficiaries while others are tasked with the actual production of fundraising videos. To give focus to the discussion, I relate two portraits of individuals supervising production of two different types of charity appeals.[34] While these producers share similar socio-economic backgrounds and occupy similar middle-range positions within the institutional hierarchy, these two individuals exemplify different agentic practices of ethical translation: the first is an example of translation with a tendency toward compliance with institutional interests and established procedural codes, and the second is an example of translation with greater risk and resistance and a stronger imperative to transmute personal moralities of care (themselves socially shaped) that challenge norms of media production.

What emerges is that producers of child-centered appeals (usually of sick, disfigured children) generally comply with established procedures of recruitment and filming. In comparison, producers of disaster appeals are more ambivalent about the fusion of charitable aims with corporate interests—most especially in the context of Typhoon Haiyan's exceptional devastation. Here I argue that the divergent outcomes of producers' ethical translation work are a function of the different contexts of suffering that they encounter (children's suffering versus exceptional disaster) and the different styles of charity appeals they create (shock effect versus positive imagery/corporate branding).

Complicity in the Case of Child Subjects

In the case of producing child-centered charity appeals, producers often follow established codes and are very rarely experimental. What was evident from my interviews and observation is that producers are highly reflexive and cautious in relation to ethical criticism of and legal complaints about media's typical practices of 'acting as the government,' specifically as it relates to helping yet 'exploiting' poor and sick children. Producers then respond by articulating moral justifications of established codes and production techniques, but are also constrained by strict demands of production.

Thirty-four-year-old 'Bea' is a producer of charity appeals for one of the TV networks. She came from a lower middle-class background and has been employed in this institution since graduating from a polytechnic university in Manila. Bea leads a crew of two other people—a researcher and a cameraman—and is tasked to produce (plan, write, shoot, edit) fifteen thirty- to sixty-second appeals per week. These appeals air within various commercial gaps throughout the day and sometimes within the primetime news. They are also broadcasted in their network's satellite channel aimed at overseas Filipino audiences in the United States, Europe, and the Middle East (whom I learned from two directors of media charities are significant sources of donations). Networks strategically use these produced charity appeals as gap fillers within the flow of television,[35] such as during unexpected program interruptions or as a way of breaking the monotony of episodic promos and ads.

The most common subgenre of appeals that Bea shoots is what the team calls the *panawagan* plug (literally, 'calling out' or 'speaking into the air'), which, as discussed earlier, hearkens to shock effect campaigning, with the tearful testimonial of mother and lingering close-ups of a child's bodily deformities. Bea and her crew shared with me that they had just shot a *panawagan* plug about Angel, a nine-year-old child whose successful medical operation had corrected a physical abnormality. Angel was born without a hole in her anus and had part of her intestines sticking out from the side of her body, which facilitated bowel movement in the place of the malfunctioning anus. They had filmed Angel on her return to elementary school, where she used to be bullied by her classmates for always soiling her white school uniform.

For Bea, stories of charity recipients' 'personal transformations' crafted as 'thank you plugs' are the most personally gratifying stories to shoot. These are occasions when they meet again clients whom they had first met in pitiful contexts in happier conditions. For instance, Bea recalled nine-year-old Angel's intense embarrassment on camera when they had to shoot her mother changing her into new clothes in their home, never once smiling to her and her crew, but during their most recent shoot, this time a thank you plug, Angel finally broke into a shy smile.

The predominance of the *panawagan* subgenre of charity appeal over the thank you plug or general project appeal is a function of both material and time constraints. Because media charities open their doors several times a week for the 'screening' of sick and disfigured children, Bea and her team find subjects right outside their own offices. Children with cleft palates, heads enlarged from hydrocephalus, and blackened lumps on the body from meningitis queue with their mothers for a screening with Bea's colleagues at the network. Their social worker colleague is tasked to authenticate the children's documents (including a medical certificate from a doctor, a certificate of indigence from the town hall, and a breakdown of the cost of operation detailed by the public hospital). They then interview the families for possible recommendation to Bea for a *panawagan* charity appeal shoot.

My interview with Bea revealed that while she finds shooting thank you plugs personally gratifying, she considers the production of these *panawagans* her most important and sensitive task. The *panawagan*, as the most common form of appeal on television, is what fuels the everyday stream of fundraising income. Consistent with Orgad's findings in the UK context, where NGOs find that shock effect campaigns generate higher donations than positive imagery, Filipino media charities observe the same trend.[36]

Bea was defensive when I asked her about *panawagans* and whether she thinks this particular style is effective. I later learned through interviews with the corporate communication and advertising and promotions departments of the TV network that employees in the company are not unified in their support for shock effect campaigning. Bea is aware that her colleagues in these departments (from more elite backgrounds) have been commissioned to produce special videos directed toward high-profile investors, donors, and wealthy overseas Filipino organizations and that her coworkers employ more positive imagery in these videos that is more consistent with upper- to middle-class moralities of empowerment and dignity, not to mention Western discourses of development. It is not difficult to see that she takes this as a critique of her crew's work, as they are responsible for everyday fundraising and also the direct interactions with beneficiaries from whom her colleagues are, in her mind, comfortably detached. Nevertheless she justifies her good work by marshaling a discourse of authenticity:

> What is really important for us is the truth. We don't really direct them, "this is what we want you to say." Though we brief them what we're supposed to do, of course, we are asking for help from the public. And then we tell the parent, "Ma'am, whatever it is you're feeling, what your child's situation really is, we need that . . . whatever you're going through, you should tell the public." . . . And then we will do our best in our script to show what other people really need to see. For me, in what I write, I put myself as part of the audience. If I were the one watching, how could I be moved and be touched to offer help to a stranger? That's all.

Unlike their colleagues in other departments from private school backgrounds (or educated overseas), many of whom subscribe to broader public and academic criticism of shock-provoking 'poverty porn' imagery, Bea and her crew stand by the *panawagan* as a more authentic discourse of suffering designed to touch audiences through high-emotion narrative. Unlike the positive imagery and post-humanitarian campaigning aimed at affluent or even foreign audiences produced by other departments of the network, Bea as a lower middle-class person herself asserts proximity with the low-income *masa* from whom she believes her elite colleagues are distanced: she recognizes that the *masa* themselves are the main audiences of these *panawagans* she creates and thus uses high-emotion narrative techniques to relate to their personal conditions. The use of melodramatic and photorealistic imagery in local charity appeals is then rescued from the critique of pornographic spectatorship, but as an accountability mechanism for media's exercise of good faith and good judgment in a competitive "selection of unfortunates."[37]

Selecting disfigured children and their pitiful mothers authenticates the subjects' suffering and justifies their media-facilitated recognition and gestural redistribution over an imagined community of low-income people who may also see themselves as potential beneficiaries. At the same time, Bea relates during the interview that while their organization comes under critique for its shock effect imagery, she observes that critics neglect that it also produces thank you plugs that show beneficiaries in happier times. Indeed, charity appeals within broadcast media organizations take on a serial or episodic quality in the context of television flow, and afford a melodramatic quality of reception among loyal television viewers who see the story through.

My interview with Bea also revealed that her complicity with production guidelines laid out by upper management and legal consultants stems from the organization's anxieties and experiences with poor clients who have attempted to scam the organization. Authenticity mechanisms such as the collection and verification of clients' documents and medical certificates, as discussed earlier, are welcomed by Bea, as they ease the burden of selecting respondents. In other cases, adherence to production guidelines alleviates her fear of legal complaints from appeals' subjects.

In the specific case of charity appeals that focus on child victims of physical and sexual abuse, the recently established requirements of secrecy and anonymity are strictly followed by production crews in order to avoid litigation from affected parties. Charity appeal guidelines to solarize the face of rescued children and their abusive perpetrators are followed, in spite of Bea's own impulse to expose abusers' identities out of indignation:

BEA: You really want to show who the perpetrator is to make it at least known that this person is the one who abused the child.

ONG: It's like you want to show it?

BEA: Yes, you even want to strangle the guy . . . but you cannot reveal that because the child might be identified [by association]. So the one who'll get in trouble will be the child—especially if it's the father who is the perpetrator! So you really have to follow the guidelines.

Strict adherence to established procedures in the case of child rescues empowers producers to administer their duties in the morally grey context of media's "acting as the government," where government policies and industry self-regulation (historically confined to monitoring media content of sex and violence) are slow to catch up.[38]

Bea's compliance with traditional practices of representing suffering children is as agentic as it is practiced in the face of legal and moral surveillance from government, cultural critics, and even her own colleagues. While on one hand compliance can be seen as a passive translation of established codes, in Bea's case it is also a rejection of new trends of positive imagery or post-humanitarian campaigning. Bea's own proximity to harsh realities of poverty from her long professional involvement with the media charity and her own personal position of lower middle-class precarity orient her to reproduce the discourse of authenticity embedded in supposedly shocking 'poverty porn' appeals. As a person who has experienced hardship, Bea easily sympathizes with potential beneficiaries of media-assisted charity and rejects inauthentic middle-class discourses of development that are reflected in the positive imagery appeals. Therefore, her adherence to procedural codes is a further evidence of how producer Bea sees the value of the *panawagans* as well as the other, more suffering-oriented charity appeals.

Risk and Resistance in the Context of Natural Disaster

In the event of exceptional tragedy, producers embrace as primary their roles as charity employees over that of media producers. Their work becomes an occasion of tactical resistance against established procedural codes and regulatory constraints. The producers whom I interviewed who follow a translation model of risk and resistance had all filmed charity appeals for the communities affected by Typhoon Haiyan.

At the time of my interview with Raul, he had just flown in from Tacloban, a city in central Philippines that recorded over 5,000 casualties from the devastation of Typhoon Haiyan in November 2013. The month of our interview, May 2014, Tacloban was marking the six-month anniversary of Typhoon Haiyan, and it was crucial that their organization continued with relief distribution to the homeless and jobless people living as refugees in tent cities in Tacloban and neighboring cities. Raul described his job as disaster response manager as *bugbog sa field*, or "fatigued from the field." In 2013—a year marked by armed conflict, typhoons, and a 7.2 magnitude earthquake—Raul and his colleague Erlinda had barely spent any time in their Manila office. Instead, they had flown directly from one disaster zone to another.

> ERLINDA: The 2013 experience was really devastating. . . . It was nonstop. With God's mercy we were guided. Of course you've come from a war zone, then you go to an earthquake, then a fire, then a typhoon.
>
> ONG: There must be some trauma . . .
>
> ERLINDA: You're right, of course. We have no stress debriefing. . . . We miss out on it, but yeah, we carry on.
>
> RAUL: Sometimes we arrive in Manila; two days later we fly out again. They need this, they need that.
>
> ERLINDA: That's how life is. Sometimes it's fun.

The day after Typhoon Haiyan hit, Raul was in Tacloban along with the Philippine military's first response team. Prior to Haiyan's landfall, Raul had arranged for relief goods to be devolved to Tacloban from an existing stockpile in Cebu, originally intended for earthquake-affected populations. Raul's plan in Tacloban was to meet up with his journalist colleagues from the network (who had lost communication with Manila headquarters), to distribute food to his colleagues, then to facilitate relief distribution with local populations that would be televised for charity appeals. Raul recounted how he and his colleagues subsisted in the first few days by opening up their network's relief packs, which contained canned sardines and rice, unfortunately made soggy by the flooding caused by Haiyan's storm surge. He also proudly recalled being the first organization to coordinate relief distribution, even leading government efforts. Locals in Tacloban thanked him, and he remembered that even the national social welfare secretary commended him for the crew's efficient first response. "'Oh, hello, Raul, you've made it again before me,' she said to me. I got embarrassed." Raul recognizes that this part of his job, as charity worker and coordinator, extends from his company's longtime ambition to cultivate loyalty from audiences by fostering an image of an institution that audiences can turn to in times of need (*may matatakbuhan*). *May matatakbuhan* is arguably substantiated by surveys that indicate that television networks are some of the most trusted institutions in the country.[39]

As discussed earlier, producers' practical translation of Philippine media's 'spirit of service' is also shaped by codified regulations and industry agreements.[40] According to Raul, networks learned from previous disasters that systematic coordination with local government units is important in ensuring accountability. In the context of disaster response, a memorandum of agreement between media charities and the military was made in 2013 that allowed media personnel access to military resources in transporting relief goods and camera equipment. In turn, the military had discretion over their selection of media beneficiaries.

During our interview, Raul related an important moment of moral dilemma in Tacloban when he and his staff were tasked to plan the filming of relief distribution with television network celebrities. While it was standard practice to involve stars of current soap operas in charity appeal productions as part of tactical cross-platform promotions (to increase TV ratings) and corporate image building among audiences and stakeholders, Raul found this particularly difficult to implement in Tacloban, where there has been aggressive looting, presumably from desperate and hungry typhoon-affected communities. Raul and Erlinda challenged their network bosses' mandate of bringing celebrities to Tacloban:

> RAUL: As much as we want, we really don't want [a celebrity photo op] televised.
>
> ERLINDA: We don't want it. We don't want to be accompanied [by a celebrity] (laughing).
>
> RAUL: Of course, that's an added burden for us. . . . Already the Warays [an ethnic group that includes Tacloban locals] are a misbehaving lot. Of all the people I have helped, these are the ones who don't like to queue, who don't listen to you. Then you add the burden of taking care of a celebrity there. You know, that's a celebrity. That's a big boss. So really, as much as we want, we don't want that photo op. Because public service is not about showing off for the celebrity. So at times, for us, it's awkward. But we can't do anything, we're in a television network!

Raul also recounted the time when celebrities ignored their instruction of handing out one relief pack per individual during distribution, as the celebrity was too moved by the destitute appearance of a person on the queue that the celebrity unfairly handed out two sacks of relief. As this has become common during celebrity-led distributions, Raul adamantly shared with us his insistence to intervene and enforce protocol, even if it meant causing offense to a potentially sensitive celebrity.

Many times during our interview, Raul expressed disapproval of the televising of relief operations. Although aware that decisions should always come from their boss, Raul was proud in recalling how he consistently tries to fight for what he believes is the right thing to do on the ground, such as when his team decided not to shoot a charity appeal on the first day of relief distribution after Typhoon Haiyan:

> It's outside of the ratings, it's already outside of everything. It's about public service. Because we also don't want to show people, "Look how charitable we are." It's like we glorify ourselves too much that we're the first, then we need to shoot a video and stuff.

While typically compliant with network strategies of using natural disasters as opportunities for corporate branding and loyalty building through the filming of charitable activities, Raul's firsthand encounter with the exceptional tragedy of Haiyan compelled him to set priorities and make hard decisions. Choosing to conduct only relief distribution rather than filming appeals during the first day of Haiyan suggests a splitting of his duties as a charity worker and a media employee, where his personal moral commitment to care for typhoon-affected communities overpowered his concerns as producer. His 'sabotage' of the production of charity appeals indicates his crew's freedom to conduct operations in the disaster zone. Because they enter disaster zones as relief workers-cum-media personnel, they can conduct operations far from senior network executives' surveillance and therefore manage their priorities more independently.

The difficult labor conditions these producers endure and justify to themselves structure their experience of their own ethical translation work. Compared to Western contexts, the social distance between the producer and the sufferer in the Filipino case is not vast at all, given that the creative laborers themselves articulate stories of their own economic hardship and limited mobility. Within the course of our interview, Raul and Erlinda confided that their low income (scaled according to a charity scale rather than the corporate scale of their colleagues in broadcast network; with no access to company bonuses enjoyed by other employees) does not compensate for the Christmas that they missed because of Typhoon Haiyan and the trauma triggered every time they hear the whirl of helicopters, a sound that takes them back to living in fear within the war zone of Zamboanga. Nevertheless, Raul expressed during our interview personal justifications for his continued work, which he also described as not a job but a "service." He did see some status and symbol of justification by being seen on TV during relief distributions by his admiring and media-obsessed family and friends. Ultimately though, it is the sense of fulfillment of being able to help resolve the suffering of many Filipinos that motivates Raul—and other producers like Erlinda and Bea—to continue their work in producing media charity programs.

Toward Ethical Media Ecologies?

Representing suffering is a moral dilemma that producers reflect on, justify, and occasionally challenge as part of ordinary routine and exceptional tragedy. Compliance with and resistance to established procedural codes vary depending on producers' own social backgrounds and professional positions that orient them toward particular moral justifications or rejections of shock effect 'poverty porn' techniques that prevail in a local context of widespread poverty and frequent disaster.

While this chapter seeks to make a contribution to understanding why trite techniques of representing suffering endure in the face of widespread public criticism of 'poverty porn,' it also imagines ways we can combine that criticism of mediated suffering with a sensitive advocacy for more ethical ecologies for the media laborers behind these productions. As it applies to the Philippine context, this call to both study and advocate for media workers is not a demonization of media companies. Rather, it unpacks the contradictions in organizations' strategic benevolence to the Filipino underprivileged and their marginalization of their own charity subsidiary employees within the professional hierarchy. If we are to lament media's failure to break new expressive ground about suffering and its resolution through gestural charity, our concern should start not from first principle, but the 'messy stuff' of practice and how we can nurture and support its agents toward creative invention and experimentation, and toward the organic extension and mediation of care.

Notes

Acknowledgments: The author would like to thank Pamela Combinido for her contributions as research assistant for this chapter.

Declaration of Funding: The project is partly funded by a UK ESRC grant for the Humanitarian Technologies Project (ES/M001288/1), www.esrc.ac.uk/my-esrc/grants/ES.M001288.1/read.

1   Roger Silverstone, *Media and Morality: On the Rise of the Mediapolis* (Cambridge: Polity, 2007).
2   Daniel Dayan, "On Morality, Distance and the Other: Roger Silverstone's *Media and Morality*." *International Journal of Communication* (2007): 113–22.
3   Nick Couldry, *Media Society World: Social Theory in a Digital Age* (Cambridge: Polity, 2012).
4   Susan Moeller, *Compassion Fatigue: How the Media Sell Disease, Famine, War and Death* (London and New York: Routledge, 1999).
5   Lilie Chouliaraki and Shani Orgad, "Proper Distance: Mediation, Ethics, Otherness." *International Journal of Cultural Studies* 14 (2011): 341–45; Silverstone, *Media and Morality*.
6   For a review, see Jonathan Corpus Ong, "'Witnessing' or 'Mediating' Distant Suffering? Ethical Questions across Moments of Text, Production, and Reception." *Television & New Media* 15 (2014): 179–96.
7   See, for example, Martin Scott, "The Mediation of Distant Suffering: An Empirical Contribution beyond Television News Texts." *Media, Culture & Society* 36 (2014): 3–19.
8   See Shani Orgad, "Visualizers of Solidarity: Organizational Politics in Humanitarian and International Development NGOs." *Visual Communication* 12 (3), 295–314.
9   David Hesmondhalgh and Sarah Baker, *Creative Labour: Media Work in Three Cultural Industries* (Abingdon, Oxon: Routledge, 2011).
10 Lilie Chouliaraki, "Post-humanitarianism: Humanitarian Communication beyond a Politics of Pity." *International Journal of Cultural Studies* 13 (2010): 117.

11 Vicki Mayer, Miranda Banks, and John T. Caldwell, "Production Studies: Roots and Routes," in *Production Studies: Cultural Studies of Media Industries,* edited by Vicki Mayer, Miranda Banks, and John T. Caldwell (London and New York: Routledge, 2009), 1–12.

12 Georgina Born, "The Normative, Institutional and Practical Ethics: For an Anthropological Ethics of Media" (paper presented at the Ethics Media Conference, University of Cambridge, April 2008).

13 Born, "The Normative, Institutional and Practical Ethics," 2–3.

14 Greg Bankoff, "Dangers to Going It Alone: Social Capital and the Origins of Community Resilience in the Philippines." *Continuity and Change* 22 (2007): 327–55.

15 Laura Grindstaff, "Self-Serve Celebrity: The Production of Ordinariness and the Ordinariness of Production in Reality Television," in *Production Studies*, edited by Vicki Mayer, Miranda Banks, and John T. Caldwell (London and New York: Routledge, 2008), 71–86; H. Wood and Beverly Skeggs, "Spectacular Morality," in *The Media and Social Theory*, edited by D. Hesmondhalgh and J. Toynbee (London and New York: Routledge, 2009).

16 Chouliaraki, "Post-humanitarianism: Humanitarian Communication"; K. Wells, "The Melodrama of Being a Child: NGO Representations of Poverty." *Visual Communication* 12 (2013): 277–93.

17 Chouliaraki, "Post-humanitarianism: Humanitarian Communication," 110.

18 Chouliaraki, "Post-humanitarianism: Humanitarian Communication," 112.

19 Chouliaraki, "Post-humanitarianism: Humanitarian Communication," 114.

20 Wells, "The Melodrama of Being a Child," 287.

21 Wells, "The Melodrama of Being a Child," 287.

22 Stan Cohen, *States of Denial: Knowing about Atrocities and Suffering* (London: Polity, 2001), 183.

23 Chouliaraki, "Post-humanitarianism: Humanitarian Communication," 110.

24 Nancy Fraser and Axel Honneth, *Redistribution or Recognition?* (London: Verso, 2003).

25 Conrado De Quiros, "Three," *Inquirer.net*, September 30, 2009. http://opinion.inquirer.net/inquireropinion/columns/view/20090930-227605/Three.

26 Quoted from Jonathan Corpus Ong, "The Mediation of Suffering: Classed Moralities of Television Audiences in the Philippines," PhD diss., University of Cambridge, 2011, 63.

27 Raul Rodrigo, *Kapitan: Geny Lopez and the Making of ABS-CBN* (Quezon City: ABS-CBN Publishing, 2006).

28 Roland Tolentino, "Kabataang Katawan, Mall, at Syudad: Gitnang Uring Karanasan at Neoliberalismo" (paper presented at the Space, Empire, and the Postcolonial Imagination Conference, Ateneo de Manila University, Quezon City, Philippines, 2011).

29 Luz Rimban, "The Empire Strikes Back," in *From Loren to Marimar: Philippine Media in the 1990s*, edited by Shiele Coronel (Quezon City: Philippine Center for Investigative Journalism, 1999).

30 One of the responses in the comment section in Shiela Coronel, "*Wowowee*: A Filipino Tragedy," *The Daily PCIJ*, February 4, 2006. www.pcij.org/blog/?p=584; J. Gutierrez, "Philippine TV Stations Bring Out Trash," *The Jakarta Globe*, April 14, 2011. http://jakartaglobe.beritasatu.com/archive/philippine-tv-stations-bring-out-the-trash/.

31 Rina Jimenez-David, "They Were Invited," *Inquirer.net*, February 7, 2007.

32 Shiela Coronel, "*Wowowee*: Television and the Perils of Peddling Dreams," *The Daily PCIJ*, February 9, 2006. www.pcij.org/blog/?p=593.

33 Born, "The Normative, Institutional and Practical Ethics."

34 Interviewees were assured anonymity; thus, in the analysis observations in the presentation and analysis of this chapter, the real names of the interviewees were not disclosed.

35 Raymond Williams, *Television: Technology and Cultural Form* (London: Routledge, 1979).

36 Orgad, "Visualizers of Solidarity."

37 Luc Boltanski, *Distant Suffering: Morality, Media and Politics* (Cambridge: Cambridge University Press, 1999), 183.

38 De Quiros, "Three."

39 Carmela Fonbuena, "Pinoys Trust the Church more than the Gov't," *Rappler*, February 27, 2013. www.rappler.com/nation/22718-pinoys-trust-the-church-more-than-government.

40 Rodrigo, *Kapitan.*

9

GROUP WRITING FOR POST-SOCIALIST TELEVISION

Eva Pjajčíková and Petr Szczepanik

The melodramatic historical crime drama *The First Republic* (*První republika*, 2014–)[1] provides a lens to examine how the development and production of Czech television series have changed since the mid-2000s, first within the private sector and later through the public service network, Česká Televize (hereafter ČT). Something of a turning point for the post-socialist ČT, *The First Republic* exemplifies a recent Czech tendency to coproduce programs with independent partners, thus blurring the distinction between private and public interests. The series exemplifies a shift away from the long-standing Czech tradition of having one or two writers pen six- or thirteen-part screenplays as one whole in favor of having a writing team collaborate on dozens of screenplays. *The First Republic* also illustrates the emergence of family entertainment as a ČT programming slot to compete with private companies for the primetime soap opera audience, as well as a greater effort to follow trends in American and, to some extent, European quality television.[2]

Although it retains a high level of cultural cache and a significant market share—capturing about 30 percent of adults—the ČT lags behind private networks and struggles to compete with their popular soaps. It has responded to this situation by introducing recurring series, including public service versions of primetime soaps. Among their more popular series was *Wonderful Times*, a nostalgic family saga set against Czech(oslovak) political history of the late twentieth and twenty-first centuries. The commercial success of this series prompted Dramedy to propose a second coproduction with ČT; another period family saga, albeit one with loftier cultural ambitions and higher production values. The resultant series, *The First Republic*, boasted a mixture of melodrama, crime, and the supernatural, starting after the First World War and concluding in 1945.

This chapter focuses on the differing expectations and authorial subjectivities of the agents and institutions involved in the production of *The First Republic*. The initial conception of the series posited a complex, gritty historical drama, but this idea gave way to what many critics saw as a high-end soap. Shifts in power between ČT, its independent production partners (together with the series' director), and head writer were symptoms of the changing position of public service television on the Czech market and ČT's relationships with private producers.

The expectations and subjectivities of these parties fell into four categories: the ČT producer and his 'dramaturg's' (or script supervisor/editor's) focus on the literary traditions of single-authored Czech serials, the series' writers' idealization and defense of Anglo-American quality television, the private producer's commercial objectives, and the series directors' vision of a public service primetime soap. These overlapping positions represent stages in a process, whereby conditions of production shaped the content of a cultural product.

This chapter sheds light on the social logic that drove this collaborative effort. It focuses on two-way 'mediation' at different stages and sites of the production process; on the institutional frameworks, social relations, and aesthetic conditions that mediated the text during its development; and, to some extent, how the text mediated social relations between those involved in its production.[3] Research for this chapter is based on Eva Pjajčíková's experience as a writer intern on *The First Republic*, her nine-month participant observation of the writing team, and interviews both authors conducted with participants in the series.

Historical Background: Collaboration as Paradigmatic Change

Czech serial screenwriting dates back to the 1960s. From 1968, the state used television series as soft propaganda intended to legitimate hard-line policies dubbed 'normalization,' by embedding Communist Party positions into the lives of characters appearing in ostensibly apolitical tales of everyday folk. However, screenwriting did not simply concern this "domestication of politics";[4] it also involved quality storytelling that drew on nineteenth-century literary traditions. For example, the family saga *Sňatky z rozumu* (1968), which centered on two entrepreneur families in nineteenth-century Prague, was inspired by the BBC's *The Forsyte Saga* (1967). This local tradition of quality television would later be a point of reference for the authors of *The First Republic*. They too fashioned a tale of a provincial entrepreneurial family relocating to the Czech capital to witness its transformation into the modern industrial center of a new state—subject matter pitched to viewers as allegorizing the country's post-1989 transformation.

Historically, in the Czech Republic, the tradition of six- or thirteen-part screenplays crafted as a single piece by one or two writers was disrupted by the advent of recurring primetime soaps on the two dominant private television networks around 2005. This method of groups scripting dozens of episodes concurrent to shooting, and a more precise and hierarchically organized division of labor, bore similarities to the American writers' room model. A typical primetime soap writing team now consisted of the main author, sometimes working with two or three outline writers, around five dialogue writers, a rewriter, and several script editors, who meet about once a week.[5] In the process, development, approval, and production become more complex, open-ended, and contingent to external forces such as the availability of talent, management changes, and audience preferences.

It took several years for such collaborative practices to be incorporated into the organizational structures of private television production, and it is still far from standardized there. In ČT, this shift started half a decade later on a limited scale, with *Wonderful Times* (*Vyprávěj*, 2009–13) and then *The First Republic*. Because this type of collaborative writing could not exist in house because of the absence at ČT of a standardized organizational model, both series were coproduced by the private company Dramedy. Moreover, the production of television series requires dozens of scripts to be written concurrent to shooting, which makes it difficult to keep projects on budget and prevents casts and crews from exceeding ČT union regulations on working hours. It is therefore unsurprising that such a shift came from a private enterprise afforded a measure of budgetary and creative freedom during production. This new type of coproduction also changed the power dynamics between writers, producers, and directors. Previously, ČT writers typically exerted significant control over screenwriting, as it was usually completed prior to production. But after *Wonderful Times* and *The First Republic*, nonlinear continuous group writing, together with the strong position of the independent producer, limited the power of the head writer.

The First Republic also marked a growing sense that makers of public service serial dramas might learn from Anglo-American series, especially those of U.S. cable provider HBO. Initially, Dramedy's CEO and series producer Filip Bobiński hired unknown screenwriter Jan Gardner, who had worked on the third season of *Wonderful Times*. Gardner was a supporter of complex narration, having spent ten years in low-level creative jobs in the United States. Gardner and Bobiński developed the initial concept approved by ČT's Program Board, and assembled a writing team for the series' first season. Before their scripts were complete, casting and shooting began under the supervision of *Wonderful Times* director Biser Arichtev. Over time, though, Gardner, as the series' head writer, was stripped of creative control. At this point, Gardner, who continued to work on the first season, felt that the original story idea had been compromised, as a different product to the one he had envisaged took shape. There follows a description of the four institutional frameworks that mediated this shift, starting with ČT.

Literary Traditions of Single-Authored Czech Serials

ČT still bears the traces of its state-socialist predecessor. It is a large institution comprising 3,000 permanent staff members, most of whom are high school-educated, middle-aged people who started their careers under communism. It is controlled by 'council members' elected by the Czech parliament, and continues to produce most programming in house.

In 2012, ČT was reorganized and partially decentralized: an 'editorial office' system of program development was replaced by a series of 'creative producers' units,' which specialize in specific genres and compete to have projects approved by the Program Board. This new unit-structured system is seen to have provided public service television an opportunity to reinvent itself, by attracting new talent, diversifying output, and appealing to younger audiences. One such unit, 'the unit for series and cyclical dramas,' headed by veteran TV producer Jan Štern, supervised the development and production of *The First Republic*—the top-rated program of Friday primetime on the local TV market between January and June 2014.

ČT represents an institutional framework in which historically 'situated aesthetics' and 'ethics' related to Czech serial television collided with the contemporary practices and tastes undergirding the production of *The First Republic*.[6] It needs stressing that ČT is not a monolithic institution. Rather, it is characterized by struggles between individuals holding competing cultural values, themselves examples of broader taste formations, such as the criticism some intellectuals leveled at ČT for compromising its public service mandate or the neoliberal imperative to downsize to better compete with private networks. With respect to serial drama, there exists, on one hand, a tradition of depicting everyday folk in relation to social issues and national history, an approach that has enabled ČT to compete against the private companies' long-running series with its own soaps, crime series, and medical dramas. On the other hand, a recent tendency for newly appointed producers to collaborate with respected external talent has led to the production of comparatively progressive series derived from the Anglo-American quality television model, such as the sitcom *čtvrtá hvězda* and the crime drama *Cirkus Bukowsky* (both 2013). *The First Republic* represents a meeting point of these tendencies, and mediates their struggle insofar as it is a public service equivalent of the primetime soap and—in terms of the original ambitions of its writers—the gritty historical drama.

Having outsourced production, ČT did not control *The First Republic* through direct creative decision making or during shooting, but via its execution of supervision and approval procedures during development and preproduction (especially casting). Before its approval, ČT's Program Board called for the series' budget to be cut and its production schedule tightened. As for creative influence at that time, the head of development and its unit head met repeatedly with Dramedy to express their concerns about *The First Republic*'s complex narrative structure and dark look, and asked for its supernatural underpinnings to be reduced. Head writer Gardner later encapsulated this sentiment by irreverently inverting HBO's promotional tag line as "We are not HBO, we are television."[7] After the Program Board greenlighted the series, and in the absence of an established procedure to systematically oversee independent producers, creative producer Jan Štern and dramaturg (or script supervisor/editor) Helena Slavíková were placed in charge of policing ČT's "aesthetic boundaries."[8] Interviews with the two reveal their perspectives on this creative process and their values.

Štern said he was drawn to Gardner's script by its combination of family-oriented primetime soap and rich drama; this was exactly what he wanted for the Friday evening timeslot traditionally devoted to family entertainment. He also supported Dramedy producing the series, as he recognized that the overburdened ČT would have struggled to produce this series in house, and Dramedy's *Wonderful Times* had enjoyed a five-year run in the Friday evening slot *The First Republic* was scheduled to fill. However, Štern expected *The First Republic* to deliver not only more complex narration and higher production values than *Wonderful Times*, but also stronger public service values—the latter by weaving a national history around its narrative structure and characters' motivations.

Štern also acknowledged that the interventions of the producer and director lightened Gardner's vision, especially in terms of characterization. Štern defended these changes, suggesting it gave the series an attractive look. "It's the kind of fast shooting where there is no time to work on individual scenes. You have to have a director that shoots fast without thinking too much about it," he explained. "If you had a director aiming for high quality, he would have done only half of it."[9] Claiming he had no direct influence on the production process after casting, Štern suggested the producer and director had taken charge, and that making changes to content after test screenings would have been prohibitively expensive. Štern's supervision after the start of the shooting therefore amounted to providing notes about upcoming episodes rather than calling for reshoots. Stern saw his main task as striking a balance between soap and drama, citing *The First Republic*'s viewing figures as evidence that he did not need to intervene any more than he already had. Štern passed on day-to-day supervision of script development to his closest collaborator, Slavíková.

Slavíková[10] had worked as a dramaturg in Czech serial screenwriting since the mid-1960s. What changed for her on *The First Republic* was not her working methods, but the conditions under which she worked. Instead of editing scripts for an entire season as one piece, she was supposed to work with draft outlines that would be drastically revised at a later date. Because *The First Republic* consisted of several complicated storylines, it was difficult to keep track of the dramatic arc, narrative logic, and character psychology. Consequently, she felt concerned that the narrative integrity of the series might be compromised. Slavíková worked on five episodes before she felt she had adapted to this approach and stopped demanding the definitive outlines she was used to receiving. "I realized it is better not to know what will come next in the story . . . and let myself be taken by surprise," she explained.

The value system that ČT applied to *The First Republic* was not brought out administratively. Rather, it was Slavíková's situated ethics and aesthetics, solidified during her long-term work in public service television, that were seen to provide a reliable litmus test. Slavíková acknowledged that working on *The First Republic* was an atypical experience, but one that largely met her standards. The series' public service remit "to let people remember what they forgot" was met by its historical content. Similarly, the series fulfilled its duty to entertain thanks to its crime, investigative, and supernatural elements. Her major concerns and most frequent calls for revisions centered on its romantic storyline, which she felt included love scenes so protracted and implausible as to render them kitsch.

Slavíková mostly interacted with head writer Jan Gardner. She admired his resourceful and imaginative approach to storytelling and his ability rapidly to devise narrative solutions to various problems. In one sense, she considered his approach somewhat foreign: American in its "discrepancy with the tradition" and lacking the kind of practical literary erudition, creative intuition, taste, and naturalized ability to make prompt judgments about narrative logic and realistic detail that she herself had acquired during a fifty-year career. She explained that:

> A certain level of taste is required. . . . I can feel it in my guts when things cross the line, when they are too much and don't fit . . . you can't make everything up so easily. And when I complain, he says: "It is like *Dexter.*" But I don't care if it's like *Dexter*; I need it to be *The First Republic.* . . . Anything is possible, but it needs to follow certain logic and order.

When Slavíková spots what she considers an overcomplicated or contrived narrative twist, such as a murderer investigating his own crimes, she argues against Gardner. For example, she revealed:

> He responds, "It will work." But what does it mean, "it will work"? He combines the narrative elements so that point 1 links up with point 53 and doesn't contradict it. . . . He can do this perfectly, and the dialogue will be good, too. But overall, the story will be far-fetched. Viewers might watch it breathless, but the question is, whether it is worth it; whether it's not better to give them something to think about.

Thus, the ČT's aesthetic boundaries were policed by Slavíková's localized judgments. These were based on a genre-specific aesthetic horizon naturalized while working in the state-socialist production system. They were pushed to their limits as she adapted to professional life in an outsourced, collective, time-pressured, open-ended, nonlinear system of writing. She was often forced to abandon her aesthetic and ethical values, which demanded numerous compromises. In this way, her situated ethics ("to let people remember," "to give them something to think about") and situated aesthetics (protracted love scenes are kitschy, a Dexter-like character is far-fetched) functioned as a mediation channel through which the transforming nature of the public service network—its internal dynamics and contradictions, cultural history meeting the new, market-driven developments such as the presence of an external commissioning for serial content—coalesced in the version of *The First Republic* that reached the screen.

Dramedy: The Commercial Strategy

Although it is a small company, Dramedy has become the leading supplier of fiction programming to the Czech public service sector since the success of *Wonderful Times*. Its corporate strategy is based on a long-term partnership with ČT and a gradual shift from low-budget fare to medium- and big-budget output boasting higher production values and a greater degree of cultural cache. *Wonderful Times* helped cement Dramedy's reputation as a reliable producer of inexpensive, public service, family-friendly television capable of competing with the private networks' primetime soaps.

Dramedy's marketing materials differentiated *The First Republic* from *Wonderful Times* by emphasizing the new series' heightened sense of drama and superior production values. Producer Filip Bobiński maintained that *The First Republic* was not merely another period piece about everyday family life, but an "internationally financed" "modern drama"; one that was "emotional, suspenseful, dynamic," and "visually attractive," and featured "expensive costumes."[11] Promotional rhetoric of this sort notwithstanding, these two Dramedy projects were similar in terms of their production, not least because they shared key crew members. Bobiński explains that *The First Republic* represented a natural progression for Dramedy inasmuch as it enabled the company to upgrade its product, offering relatively high production values at a lower price than in-house productions.[12] Realizing this objective involved using shorter shooting schedules, cheaper and more versatile sets, minimal location shooting, and adopting a more flexible development process that permitted a screenplay to be significantly redrafted during production. This model ultimately allowed Dramedy to move toward greater autonomy during development, to craft ever more complex narratives, to increase production values, and to pursue international sales, all without losing its competitive edge.

Bobiński's strategy was bound up with the dynamics of the Czech market. In this sense, it enabled Dramedy to differentiate its output from the basic narratives and low production values of the private networks' primetime soaps, and from public service broadcasters' old-fashioned, niche interest culture programs. He calls this approach "European mainstream" because it patterns its combination of commercial genres, higher production values, and cultural cache after Spanish family melodramas such as *Gran Hotel* (2011–13).

During development, Bobiński worked to ensure that *First Republic* featured a viable narrative and combination of genres, before making sure its high production values were secured through casting, sets, costumes, and other visual elements such as opening credits. The screenwriting process was largely overseen by the head writer. Bobiňski maintained that:

> I don't really care what individual episodes' scripts are about because I know the overall style, how we want to narrate, how fast or slow it should be. So, in the end, it is not important whether this or that happens: I leave it to the writers to decide. What I really care about is, first, the concept we create in the beginning; the feeling of what viewers are to expect. And that's a mix of all those things: the image of the program, rhythm, period, characters—all what is created in the first stage. And, second, during the physical production, I need to make sure it really looks this way, so again a lot of producers' work comes in.[13]

This collective writing process was therefore marked by two 'stand downs' by agents involved in the development process—something unusual for ČT's in-house productions. The first involved the public service network limiting its editorial supervision to allow a trusted partner to control production. The second saw the main producer and director concentrate on the look of *The First Republic*. The writers thus operated in what amounted to a void between two institutional frameworks, as they were left to envisage content that would fulfill the producers' expectations; content that would differ significantly from a compromised finished product, as markers of distinction gave way to lighter material reminiscent of primetime soaps.

Writers' Dreams of Post-Socialist Quality Television

The professional background of the head writer of *The First Republic*, Jan Gardner, distinguishes him from others working in the Czech Republic. After studying songwriting in Prague, and briefly writing for Czech public service television, Gardner moved to the United States in 1993 to learn screenwriting at UCLA. He worked stateside for a decade, as a script reader and production assistant to Roger Corman's head of development, where he became familiar with the dynamics of genre film production. Upon returning to Prague in 2002, Gardner grew frustrated with local production practices that differed from those he had encountered in the United States and in American screenwriting manuals. "[In the Czech Republic] people are used to writing *petit* characters and conflicts, kind of everyday anecdotes," he bemoaned. "I tended to write big stories, arc-plots, while people here write those mini-plots."[14] Gardner remains critical of what he sees as weak Czech screenwriting, especially when it comes to genre and characterization. It took him a further eight years to accept the professional culture of his homeland, when in 2010 he accepted a relatively prestigious writing position on *Wonderful Times*, a series that nevertheless exemplified the piecemeal storytelling he so disliked.

The initial idea for *The First Republic* that Bobiński and Gardner discussed was a contemporary ghost story. The project's distinct generic identity would become increasingly fractured, however, as crime and romance superseded supernatural elements. The series ultimately became a family drama set in the interwar years. Gardner rationalized that "a big drama of life and death, where characters really die, with tragic love, . . . was all made easier by the period setting."[15] Each episode featured a period attraction and a cliffhanger, and interwove three storylines—such as a love triangle, a murder investigation, and paranormal activity. Written as psychologically rounded and complex individuals who oscillated between moral and immoral behavior, the main characters were inspired by those in HBO-style quality dramas, as Gardner has admitted. In contrast to the highly pragmatic business models behind Spanish melodramas, which the Spanish-educated Bobiński brought to the process, and in contrast to the public service family entertainment supported by Štern, Gardner imagined that *The First Republic* would be heavily indebted to recent British and American quality dramas such as *Downton Abbey* (2010–) and *Boardwalk Empire* (2010–). Comparisons to these series were made repeatedly by members of the core writing team, and were foregrounded in publicity as a means of establishing an aesthetic basis for the series and of positioning it culturally.

For the first time in his career, Gardner was asked to assemble his own writing team and set its working protocol. The decision to use a group of writers rather than individuals was a result of the series' tight, nonlinear production schedule, and Dramedy's positive experiences of employing such an approach on *Wonderful Times*—the first ČT series produced in this fashion. *The First Republic* nevertheless departed from *Wonderful Times*, whose less structured and preplanned writing derived from the absence of a master synopsis and its use of omniscient voiceover narration instead of complex storytelling.

Gardner found it challenging to build a writing team because of the aforementioned institutional void and a general lack of Czech writers with experience working as a group on a sophisticated drama. Not until episode eight were his team and its working processes stabilized. Working practices were initially highly integrated, with meetings to discuss such matters as the main storyline involving three staff writers as well as two dramaturgs typically chosen by Gardner and Bobiński from *Wonderful Times* alumni. Gardner (and later Magda Buštová) synopsized the entire season and every episode,[16] leaving outlines and scripts to be developed by the three remaining writers. Usually dissatisfied with their outlines and scripts, Gardner routinely demanded two or three major revisions per manuscript. Pavel Gotthard, a PhD screenwriting student, and the only writer to remain on board for the full season, recalled:

> Jan Gardner had a very clear vision of what he wanted to happen in each
> episode. But the team didn't share his vision or he wasn't able to explain

it to them. . . . This made the collaboration very problematic and stressful for everybody involved, because they didn't know where the problem was—what they did wrong. . . . The final scripts were bad, but it wasn't clear why, if the problem lay in the dialogue, or in the structuring of the scenes, or the overall design of the episode, or in its place among other episodes. There was a whole pyramid of possibilities which diverged in multiple directions in a puzzling way. It was basically hell. Jan eventually started to dismiss individual writers one by one.[17]

Gotthard's perspective reveals that the staff writers had trouble understanding why the writing process was encountering problems. The head writer might have had a clear vision of how the series should look, but he was unable to convey this to his team or to make its members work well together. This epistemological uncertainty reflects in personal terms the ambiguities inherent in a production system undergoing a transition characterized by changing practices and values.

Between episodes four and eight, most members of *The First Republic*'s writing team, including all of those who had worked on *Wonderful Times*, were replaced, as Gardner assumed tighter control of a process that became increasingly one-directional and hierarchical in nature. The master synopsis and episode outlines, which included around forty-five scenes and some dialogue, were written by Magda Buštová and Gardner. The scripts were mainly penned, often out of running order, by Gotthard. This shift away from the writers' room concept and partly back toward a traditional Czech approach permitted Gardner better to communicate his vision to the dialogist, Gotthard, who in turn could better comprehend Gardner's conceptualization of the series and the limits of his own input. Helena Slavíková along with the coauthor of this chapter, Eva Pjajčíková, served as script editors. They polished each episode's script two or three times, with Gardner himself making any final revisions before passing it on to the producer and ČT.

Buštová, an experienced writer and dramaturg on the long-running Czech soap *Surgery in the Rose Garden* (2005–), helped Gardner with characterization and historical accuracy, and to realize his vision across each episode outline. Gardner valued Gotthard for the naturalistic dialogue inspired by *Boardwalk Empire*, praising the newcomer for an aesthetic taste and value horizon even more profoundly influenced by HBO quality drama than his own. "[Gotthard] has watched it all and feels it," mused Gardner.[18] With Gotthard's vision of *The First Republic* even grittier than that of Gardner, Gardner needed to mediate between his writers and producers, as he was more interested in the overall dramatic arc of the series. By contrast, Gotthard was less concerned with story structure than embellishing scripts with realistic details and conjuring what he described as a "morbid" tone. He summarized his vision of *The First Republic* thus:

a dark crime story with ghost motives: Gloomy Prague, diseases, . . . poverty. Laundrywomen coughing out their lungs onto clothes in the big dye works, children playing in dirty gutters, and so on. We wanted to show *The First Republic* as it really was, with all the misery and hypocrisy—rich against poor, and just a bit of romance. But then, this screenwriting vision met with that of the producer.[19]

Much to his disappointment, Gotthard's vision was tempered by the more pragmatic Gardner. "I gave them some lively dialogue, which they liked, and they, in return, forgave me when I occasionally crossed the line and came out with a rotting dead child," Gotthard conceded. "When it was too much, they cut it, but some of it remained—a milder version of my depressing tones."[20]

Following a period in which the series writers were effectively left to their own devices, institutional frameworks and ideologies came back into play during casting and shooting. Dramedy exerted its authority on the production process, lightening the tone of the series so it might fit neatly into a Friday evening programming slot traditionally filled by escapist, female-friendly fare, and mainstreaming it to facilitate pan-European sales. The competing visions of the writers and producers were spotlighted in notes Bobiński wrote about episode one (while writers were already working on episode sixteen), after the series had been cast. He called for darker material and dense drama to be diluted by the addition of family-oriented, visually attractive flourishes, many featuring children and their parents.

At a time when the remaining episodes were being written, rifts opened between head writer Gardner and main producer Bobiński when production started on *The First Republic*, revealing the true balance of power between the two. The writers were confronted with their contractually determined subordinate position when they started to notice significant disparities between their own visions for this series and those of the producers. Gardner remembered that "[a]t a certain moment, I realized we [Gardner and Bobiński] were doing a 'different series,' so I found myself struggling to adapt to the producer's vision." Gardner had discovered that his position was weaker than his American counterparts, who usually had the power to make production and casting decisions.

The transformation of the writers' ideas into a 'very different' product started with casting: a crucial point at which all the agents involved could air their concerns. Inspired by American quality drama, Gardner backed the casting of highly skilled, ordinary-looking actors—"like [Steve] Buscemi in *Boardwalk Empire*"—rather than glamorous celebrities. By contrast, main producer Bobiński, Štern as head of ČT's creative producers' unit, and director Biser Arichtev all felt that conventionally attractive television stars needed to play the main characters. Nowhere were these differences of opinion more apparent than in the casting of the principal protagonist, Vladimír: a legionnaire who returns from the Great War to rekindle an affair with his brother's wife and to investigate the murder of her parents. Gardner strongly disagreed with the casting of the handsome but wooden Slovakian actor Ján Koleník; a tabloid pinup that Gardner felt was incapable of playing a war-weary, psychologically ambiguous character.

The Director: Public Service Primetime

Even at this early stage, series director Biser Arichtev's commitment to the melodrama, tradition, and lightness of *Wonderful Times* was provoking a series of disagreements between the producer and the head writer, which would also characterize the shooting of *The First Republic*. His preferences for a glossy look and romance, which the producer encouraged, influenced shot composition, choices of locations, costumes, and props, and the simplification of character psychology. Gardner noted facetiously that the guiding principle of the series was now, under Arichtev, "to show beautiful people in beautiful places with a beautiful atmosphere." He even suggested that Arichtev's background in light entertainment left him ill equipped to shoot a complex drama,[21] that his failure to read scripts carefully left little room for discussions with the head writer, and that he shared little of Gotthard's predilection for realistic detail and dark atmosphere. For Gotthard, instead of evoking *Boardwalk Empire, The First Republic* had effectively become *Downtown Abbey* meets *Surgery in the Rose Garden*; less a Czech equivalent of HBO's quality dramas than a combination of European heritage series and local primetime soap opera.[22]

As a director, Arichtev sees himself as an efficient and flexible craftsman who delivers the best possible product under trying circumstances and considerable time pressure. While he did not influence the construction of *The First Republic*'s story directly, his long-time collaboration with Dramedy afforded him a significant advantage over Gardner in their power struggle, for it was he whom the producers trusted and he who shared their vision of the series. For Arichtev, the dramatic tenor of the original script was too "heavy," and dialogue and character actions were too histrionic; he admitted that this often brought him to laughter and that he was tempted "to make a parody of out of it." Arichtev felt compelled to make the story "lighter" and the aesthetics "cleaner" by dressing attractive actors in lavish costumes, deleting tragic dialogue, and eschewing "dirty, social, heavy, overfull" sets. Arichtev also claimed that he wanted to appeal to younger viewers by "refreshing" its historical subject matter and fashioning a "modern" visual style that updated the milieu and the language used there.[23] The growing mistrust between Gardner and Arichtev led Gardner to avoid the set and eschew face-to-face discussions about shooting.

The casting of *The First Republic* shifted the balance between individual storylines toward melodrama and romance, with the detective subplot and psychological complexity only resurfacing in the middle of the season. These changes caused frustration for the director and the cast, none of whom were informed about how the narrative progressed across the full series—a fairly uncommon scenario at ČT. They repeatedly complained they could not cope with characters' emotional changes and struggled to deliver particular lines, that the narrative was too dense and "dramatic," and that the characters were too complicated and ambiguous, especially for those who had mainly worked on primetime soaps. According to Gotthard, it was a "real duel, on multiple levels, beginning with casting. . . . There were two sides of a barricade, writers on one, the director and producers on the other."[24]

The writers of *The First Republic* soon came to accept their subordinate position in the production process. Feedback from the set, editing room, and test screenings alerted them to the fact that during production many of their psychological nuances and subtexts had been lost, and many of their tougher realistic details softened. They decided that, for the second season, it was necessary preemptively to 'flatten' the story. Instead of creating a hierarchical dramatic structure with a single dominant story line, around which unfolded a series of subplots, they needed move toward a more shallow, broader, continuous flow of loosely interconnected lines. Gardner realized there was little point in negotiating, explaining, or defending his concept to the producers. "They don't understand it and think we are just spoiling their beautiful images with our script," he lamented. The only solution to his conflict with the production team seemed to be to "write it in a way they will understand how to shoot it."[25] In strategic terms, the writers realized that they could also expect stricter supervision from both Dramedy and ČT when they started work on the second series. By the end of season one, it was clear that their grand experiment with quality television was over.

This confrontation of conflicting perspectives shows that it would be reductive to state that the head writer's ambitions, backed by his American background and approach to dramatic writing, were fully justified, and that they were destroyed by the producer's and the director's interventions. Gardner's vision was simply too far removed from the producer's initial assignment. The tensions between the two, as well as those between the head writer and the director, were likely to have been a product of inadequate communication between the principal agents involved, agents whose ambitions, as it turned out, would not have seemed all that incompatible had they operated in a more standardized production system and had they been discussed more thoroughly.

Conclusion

In the version of *The First Republic* that reached the screen, the struggles described earlier in this chapter reveal themselves as discrepancies in an otherwise coherent audiovisual package: inconsistent casting, sudden shifts in characterization, unexpectedly rough dialogue, incongruous glimpses of realistic violence or poverty, and a complex crime storyline at times overwhelmed by light melodrama. However, what at first glance appears to be little more than sloppy craftsmanship is in fact evidence of a struggle between producers and writers coming to terms with a production culture in transition.

Through an ethnographic study of day-to-day production processes, the significance of the apparent irregularities in the first series of *The First Republic* becomes clearer. Such an approach reveals an equally compelling behind-the-scenes drama. It casts a light on how compromises in the final product mediate social relations between key production personnel—ones characterized by different levels of decision-making power, and by competing situated aesthetics and ethics. It is only through ethnography that we can illuminate the writers' unrealized vision: a vision of Czech quality television that became a victim of the pragmatism of producers and a director as well as the inaction of a public service broadcaster concerned with protecting the traditional character of its Friday evening slot. And yet this series fared remarkably well in the ratings, suggesting that Czech audiences cared little about the impact of the drama unfolding behind the scenes. They instead responded positively to an attractive cast and the combination of romance and suspense.

When described from all the key agents' perspectives, the competing interests that marred the production process and that surface in the final product highlight the transformative state of Czech public service television and its place in the broadcast market. This post-socialist institution is struggling to retain its share of the market, by continuing to produce formulaic primetime soaps that differ little from the more popular and less costly examples of the genre produced by private networks. At the same time, public service television is becoming increasingly conscious of the need to match the standards of imported series, and of the demands of its media-savvy younger viewers. Some at ČT hope that the future of this institution will hinge on the specializations of its producer units and on granting its independent production partners greater autonomy. Yet, with no truly transparent policy of dealing with private producers currently in place, a trusted company like Dramedy has become a clear market leader. As the dominant player in this emerging sector, Dramedy has sought to protect its own interests—consolidating its national status and penetrating the pan-European television market. As the most commercially successful program of its kind, and as an example of this new production model, *The First Republic* stands as a striking emblem of a transforming production culture.

Notes

The authors would like to thank all of the interviewees for their generosity, and Richard Nowell for his editing assistance.

  1 *Manor House* is at present the international distribution title of this series.

2 This chapter uses the term 'quality' in line with the Anglo-American critical discussion that started in the 1990s with Robert J. Thompson's concept of the 'second golden age' of American television. However, it also acknowledges that there are different traditions of quality television (even if they are not labeled as such) on individual non-American markets, which both compete with and imitate the U.S. precedent. See Milly Buonanno, "The Transatlantic Romance of Television Studies and the 'Tradition of Quality' in Italian TV Drama." *Journal of Popular Television* 1, no. 2 (2013): 175–89.

3 See Georgina Born's concept of the "sociological hermeneutics": Born, "The Social and the Aesthetic: For a Post-Bourdieuian Theory of Cultural Production." *Cultural Sociology*, no. 2 (2010): 171–208.

4 Paulina Bren, *The Greengrocer and His TV: The Culture of Communism after the 1968 Prague Spring* (Ithaca, NY: Cornell University Press, 2010), 147.

5 Interview with Magda Buštová, December 9, 2011.

6 The concepts of situated aesthetics and ethics—rooted in historical discourses of specific genres—are adopted from Georgina Born, "Reflexivity and Ambivalence: Culture, Creativity and Government in the BBC." *Cultural Values* 6, nos. 1 & 2 (2002): 65–90.

7 Field diary, 2013.

8 Born, "The Social and the Aesthetic."

9 Interview with Jan Štern, March 20, 2014.

10 The following section is based on two semi-structured interviews with Helena Slavíková, conducted in Prague on December 5, 2013 and February 7, 2014.

11 A promotional interview with Filip Bobiňski on ČT's home page of *The First Republic*: www.ceskatelevize.cz/porady/10532695142-prvni-republika/7161-filip-bobinski.

12 Interview with Filip Bobiňski, February 7, 2014.

13 Interview with Filip Bobiňski, February 7, 2014.

14 Interview with Jan Gardner, December 13, 2013.

15 Interview with Jan Gardner, February 6, 2014.

16 The master synopsis covered the main story of the whole season, condensed into basic storylines according to characters and topics, each of which boasted its own story arc. According to this document, storylines and story arcs were then outlined in the synopsis of each episode.

17 Interview with Pavel Gotthard, March 9, 2014.

18 Interview with Jan Gardner, December 13, 2013.

19 Interview with Pavel Gotthard, March 9, 2014.

20 Interview with Pavel Gotthard, March 9, 2014.

21 Interview with Jan Gardner, February 6, 2014.

22 Interview with Pavel Gotthard, March 9, 2014.

23 Interview with Biser Arichtev, April 9, 2014.

24 Interview with Pavel Gotthard, March 9, 2014.

25 Field diary, November 5, 2013.

IV

Putting the Public Back in Public Service

10

PUBLIC SERVICE AS PRODUCTION CULTURES

A Contingent, Conjunctural Compact

James Bennett

"I am an innately public service creature."

(BBC Producer, IV48)[1]

"I feel really passionately that I want to work for a media company that I believe in."
(Channel 4 Senior Executive, IV85)

"A lot of our stuff is PSB (public service broadcasting); it's what we get out of bed in the morning for."

(Managing Director, Television Company, IV12)

"[Our company] absolutely believes in public service."

(Managing Director, Digital Agency, IV24)

"I went into filmmaking partly, or largely, because of public service. I mean public service runs through my veins."

(Freelance Producer, IV79)

This chapter examines the ways producers within the United Kingdom's television and digital media factual production sector understand public service media (PSM), the extent to which public service motivates the kinds of content that they make, and the ways they work. How workers understand public service underpins what ends up on viewers' screens as PSM. As producers seek to balance their commitment to the purposes and characteristics of PSM against the economic demands of their production modes, a 'compact' is formed across the diverse production cultures involved in the creation of PSM.

As these opening quotes suggest, public service can act as an important inspiration to an array of workers involved in PSM production: from in-house BBC producers to Channel 4 commissioners, from independent television and digital company directors to freelancers. Because PSM is not only produced by the main public service broadcasters—the BBC and Channel 4—but also by an array of independent production companies, a production culture of PSM is therefore invariably shaped by a network of different actors. Independents are responsible for supplying 100 percent of Channel 4's non-news, UK-originated content and as much as 50 percent of the BBC's.[2] Thus, while Georgina Born's study of the BBC found that public service might situate the ethics and aesthetics of in-house producers working for the Corporation, taking a wider view of the public service production ecology suggests that not only may the notion of public service be more diffuse, but it may also be shaped by both competing and collaborative aims.[3] In particular, we must understand how it is shaped as much by the production modes and agendas of the commercial, independent sector as it is by the concerns of in-house BBC producers. David Lee's study of independent television production usefully turns our attention to such matters by finding a "neo-Reithian" ethic among television producers—whereby producers "care about the product that they are working on . . . because they want to inform, educate, and have a positive impact on society."[4] However, the concern in Lee's study remains with television production. In a multiplatform digital landscape, a production culture of PSM must be analyzed across the BBC's license fee–funded production of content, Channel 4's not-for-profit corporate status, as well as the commercially driven production strategies of independent television and digital production companies. Finally, any production culture of PSM must be understood as invariably contingent, shaped by an array of what Graeme Turner terms "conjunctural forces" in play within the given historical context of study, including the wider social, cultural, political, technological, and industrial conditions.[5]

The production culture of PSM studied here, therefore, is one that is contingent—shaped by not only an array of conjunctural forces, but also the research methodology. This chapter emerges from a two-year study of BBC in-house, independent television and digital producers, as well as commissioners at Channel 4 and the BBC, of 'multiplatform' PSM, undertaken between 2010 and 2012. 'Multiplatform' is understood here as a specific strategic response by broadcasters to the changing technological and social terrain of digital television, involving the commissioning and production of content, services, and applications interlinked across different platforms, including television, rather than simply video-on-demand service. The project took place at a moment in UK television industry especially marked by flux, particularly in terms of the BBC and its position within, and strategy toward, this emerging digital television landscape. In 2010, thanks to a combination of low ratings for multiplatform content and public service cuts, the BBC had effectively withdrawn from its 2006 strategy to reimagine the broadcaster as a 360° multiplatform organization.

In contrast, while Channel 4 had experienced similar economic pressures as a result of a reduction in its advertising revenues caused by the global recession, the broadcaster had reinvigorated its multiplatform strategy. At the start of 2010 it had appointed a new head of online, Richard Davidson-Houston, and recruited a team of multiplatform commissioners across a range of genres. This new structure of the online division immediately set about creating a range of initiatives to encourage and develop multiplatform production in the independent sector. Despite the contrasting impetuses toward multiplatform at both broadcasters, as Andrew Chitty notes, multiplatform had moved away from its earlier phases of innovation and experimentation toward a more hard-nosed approach that required multiplatform "to deliver for the core business" of the public service broadcasters.[6]

These changing approaches to multiplatform at both the BBC and Channel 4 took place against the backdrop of relatively recent shifts (2003) in the structure of intellectual property ownership laws in television, which enabled independent producers to retain the IP of the programs they created.[7] Importantly, however, this was not a situation that extended to multiplatform production, where digital applications, services, and content remained predominantly funded by the broadcaster who, in turn, retained the associated rights in most cases. Nevertheless, as production, commissioning, financing, and revenues remained largely television-led during this period,[8] the change in IP ownership saw a corresponding reduction in the level of funding the public service broadcasters were prepared to invest in content creation. And yet, finally, the independent sector remained largely *dependent* on the BBC and Channel 4 for the majority of its work and income: approximately 80–85 percent of independents' new commissions came from the United Kingdom's public service broadcasters during this period.

This brief overview of the conjunctural factors in play indicates not only that PSB was in flux, as it almost always is, but also that a range of vested interests was at stake during the interview work conducted for this research. Attempting to account for this led to two broad strategies in how our research team approached interview work.[9] First, we conducted 105 interviews to capture as wide a cross-section of the production ecology as possible: from in-house BBC and Channel 4 staff members to workers in a range of different-sized independent television and digital media companies. Second, bearing in mind John Caldwell's 'inverse credibility law,' we interviewed people working at a variety of levels across the sector.[10] Thus interviewees ranged from the BBC's director general at the time, Mark Thompson, and a range of company managing directors, down to producers, directors, coders, developers, designers, assistant producers, and those occupying a range of freelance and junior positions.

Caldwell's 'law' is a useful one to bear in mind when conducting interviews as part of any production study. Certainly managerial discourse, both in interviews and in strategic documents, tends to espouse strong statements about PSM and what it might mean to that organization: for example, the digital and television companies' managing directors quoted at the head of this chapter felt able to speak on behalf of the entire workforce. Closer study of the workers involved, however, often revealed more ambivalent relations to the concept.[11] Moreover, such above-the-line discourse often highlights individual programs as exemplars of PSM, tending to invoke current programming in which the interviewee has had a direct input. As such, these responses frequently avoided any consideration of historical trends or change: television production is, after all, characterized by the continual call to the present and by the demands of what comes next in the schedule. Moreover, the cultural function of these stories is often geared toward "professional legitimacy and accumulation of career capital."[12] There is, therefore, a strong predisposition toward retrofitting accounts of how public service production values resulted in particularly prominent pieces of television or multiplatform.

However, taking the 'inverse credibility law' as Caldwell recommends it to us—as law—can also be too totalizing an account of how hierarchies within institutions shape disclosure. Equally important can be the range of conjunctural factors I have outlined here. For example, the majority of interviews conducted with BBC multiplatform producers was undertaken at a time when the Corporation was culling its multiplatform staff, and this colored producers' perspectives on the possibilities for multiplatform PSM. Moreover, one should not treat below-the-line accounts as inherently more truthful than their more senior counterparts. Thus, while long-term, below-the-line workers were more likely to reflect on historical shifts in the sector and programming form, rose-tinted glasses or embitterment about the failure to win commissions for their favored type of programming often inflected such accounts. Here, particularly in the field of documentary and factual production, there was a significant number of long-term producers who perceived all current factual television as entertainment led and, in turn, inherently inferior to the 'hard' programming of the British social realist tradition in documentary. The methodology employed throughout the research project was therefore to test both above- and below-the-line discourse across a number of discursive layers and sites, ranging across the 'deep texts' of industry, through to official strategy documents and the texts of multiplatform production themselves.

Beyond the sheer volume of data that such an approach yielded, it also produces an understanding of PSM as both contingent and dispersed. That is, a public service production culture must be understood as a network of interlinked and overlapping production cultures, operating inside and outside of the broadcasters, and across diverse production modes: from TV's linear plan, shoot, edit, broadcast, to digital's more iterative modes of production, whereby the finished product is always open to further change. Within that digital mode of production, there is also a plethora of more specific cultures of coding, gaming, software engineering, and designing. The production cultures of public service are therefore best understood as networked. People move across the networks and spheres of production I set out earlier: those who worked within the BBC or Channel 4 often go on to have successful careers in the indie sector—or vice versa.

Moreover, these cultural relationships suggest how the production cultures of public service are entwined and entangled with different aesthetic concerns and, perhaps more important, economic structures. In what follows, I explore the aesthetics of PSM production cultures in relationship to questions of quality and risk as well as the economics of production in relation to the different financial imperatives of the not-for-profit public service broadcasters and the for-profit commercial, independent sector. This chapter sets out an understanding of public service production cultures that is invariably contingent, networked, and conjunctural, shaped by an array of factors in play at any given moment of study. But it is also a set of cultures that share common values and dilemmas, which I term the 'public service compact.' As the term 'compact' suggests, the production cultures of PSM involve a mutual agreement or understanding to do, or to forbear to do, something. Overall, public service emerges as a culture that seeks to balance creativity, remit, and the forbearance of economic reward as highest priority in the production, economic, and textual practices of the sector. It is also, in an era of neoliberalism, a culture increasingly under threat, making the public service compact a fragile one.

Diverse: Risk and Quality in Television and Digital Production

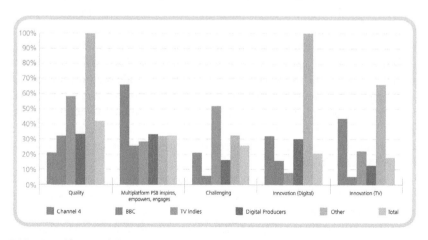

Table 10.1 Characteristic as percentage

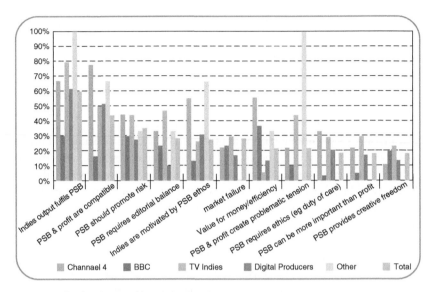

Table 10.2 Production modes as percentage

We began all interviews by asking what PSM meant to the interviewee. We supplied no preset definitions, and instead coded responses as they emerged, using Ofcom's regulatory definition of PSB to categorize answers in terms of how interviewees described the purpose, the characteristics of the programs produced, and the ways public service affected production.[13] The result was over fifty different articulations of what PSM meant to interviewees. In this section I concentrate on characteristics and production modes, represented by Tables 10.1 and 10.2, in order to examine the diverse nature of the role public service played in the different production cultures of the sector. Here the predominant understanding of public service content was that which was of high quality, produced in a mode that encouraged and facilitated risk. This understanding was largely shared between those working inside the broadcasters and those working in the independent sector. However, what risk and quality meant differed significantly between digital and television producers—with the question of who was at fault for changing attitudes to risk and quality revealing the way conjunctural factors influenced the place of public service across these different work cultures.

Despite the diversity of opinion as to what constitutes public service that these responses revealed, there was a clear interest in the topic across the sector. The prevalence of such discourses of PSM should, in fact, not be surprising given the role it has in the funding structures and economic livelihood of all who work in the sector. As Elana Levine's study of 'Canadianness' suggests, "funding structures, regulatory policy and industrial and critical discourses" can often echo one another when producers are given a strong incentive to claim their programs fulfill particular ideals and remits, which also underpin the economics of production. Just as her study found that "the discourse of national identity has a powerful place in the Canadian television industry," we found public service an equally influential discourse within the UK multiplatform production ecology.[14] However, whereas Levine found that beyond recalling the importance of national identity, producers in her study could only bring "vagueness and ambivalence" to any discussion of the meaning and role of Canadianness in production, the majority of our interviewees spoke passionately and informatively about PSM.[15] Indeed, one interviewee spoke uninterrupted on the question of public service for over an hour.

However, it was also clear that significant differences emerged between how interviewees in different production cultures across the sector understood PSM. To turn first to the question of production modes, beyond the issue of profit and public service that I shall return to later, the most important understanding of how PSM influences production is in the promotion of risk (Table 10.2). Thirty-five percent of all interviewees suggested that PSM production should involve risk taking. However, there was significant divergence between how producers in digital companies understood risk in comparison to their television counterparts. Thus while the former emphasized the notion of technological risk, the latter were concerned with editorial risk.

To digital producers, technological risk meant experimentation in form and content without fear of economic failure. As one interviewee described it, in digital, "risk taking is not only the norm, it's the thrill . . . because the cost of things is so much lower that you can try something, . . . see how it will do, learn from your mistakes" (IV17). As another opined, digital production has "a kind of openness, the feeling of iteration, [the business philosophy of] you release early, release often, fail fast, all that kind of stuff," which is "totally alien to TV" (IV85). Undoubtedly the vastly different sizes in budgets had a strong impact on the emphasis placed on economic risk in digital companies who, in terms of multiplatform production, were operating on budgets a fraction of the size of their television counterparts'. For example, Channel 4 spent thirty-seven times more money on television commissions than digital in 2011/12.[16]

But alongside, and to a certain extent consequent upon, the different economic scales at stake in promoting a culture of risk in digital PSM production there was also a work culture of play evident in digital companies. Andrew Ross and others have noted that a playful culture often permeates the digital workplaces, making them more 'humane' at the same time as they blur the boundaries between work and play, waged and free time.[17] While more recent work on the moral economies of media production has called into question the overarching narrative of neoliberalism and self-exploitation found in such post-Foucauldian studies,[18] the digital companies we studied had a clear concern to promote an atmosphere of creative play in their workplaces: video game machines, table football, shared music, and social spaces were all hallmarks of these production spaces that made work "fun" (IV53). Here risk is facilitated through a production mode that is both playful and iterative, learning from mistakes as content, services, and applications are tested and re-versioned. However, the emphasis placed on PSM as a space to undertake risk was also clearly motivated by the range of conjunctural factors in play: most particularly, digital companies' less advantageous position in the economics of multiplatform production. At a point in time when the global recession had made public sources of funding increasingly crucial to the commercial survival of digital agencies (IV46), there was concern among many producers about the financial implications of the BBC's withdrawal from multiplatform. Read in this light, the emphasis on technological risk, with its corresponding implication of putting bigger budgets at stake, can be understood as much as a form of industrial posturing as an investment in public service as a production culture.

In contrast to the weight placed on technological risk by digital producers, television workers understood risk as creative and editorial freedom to tackle difficult and challenging topics, without fear of poor ratings. Again, producers' investment in a culture of PSM also functioned as a form of industrial posturing, with interviewees in independents often complaining of a lack of risk in the commissioning processes of the broadcasters. Much of this concern centered on the importance placed on ratings and legal compliance, which "complianced risk to death" (IV76) and emphasized editorial policy over ambition. One interviewee, citing the rise in prominence of editorial policy, often shortened to 'Ed. Pol.,' criticized a BBC culture in which "you have to go through Ed Pol. I thought Ed Pol was an actual person when I first started. . . . And Ed Pol, I can tell you, knows nothing" (IV78).

In such a view, public service was inevitably a culture in decline, the blame for which lay at the door of the BBC and Channel 4, who were seeking to compete in a multichannel, multiplatform environment. However, such rhetoric also served to mask independents' concern to demonstrate that the shift in IP ownership rules and growing pressure to produce returnable and exploitable formats had not been at the expense of their own ability to produce challenging or experimental programming. The place of public service within independents' production cultures can therefore be understood, to an extent, as a concern to position the sector as a key source of public service values at a time when PSM was under threat and indies remained dependent on the broadcasters for commissions. Nevertheless, such posturing also underscored the importance of the PSM compact to both broadcasters and independents, who are almost inexorably tied to one another: what cultures and values they shared, therefore, remain of prime importance to what PSM is produced.

Tied to questions of editorial risk for television producers was the issue of quality. What quality means differed significantly between television and digital producers and companies, although these cultures share an interest in quality as a marker of the caliber of ideas and of production values. In television production, quality aligned high production values with particular, middle-class taste codes in terms of aesthetics, research, and the desire to tackle 'challenging' topics. In contrast, the understanding of quality for digital producers was more "nebulous" (IV89). Thus while television producers might talk about quality programming as "'Beautifully shot' . . . if you call a website beautiful, you can't think of any other compliment to make about it. There's no value to beauty there" (IV89). While this may be true, it was also clear that many digital producers had concerns with aesthetics in multiplatform productions, but these were often understood in relationship to questions of usability and robustness. 'Usability' referred to both interface design and planning of user journeys, where "one click is good, two clicks is bad," in terms of delivering users to the content or experiences they desired. This concern with the user experience extended the discourse of quality to ensuring the technological builds were "robust and scaleable" (IV64) in order to ensure the platform where content and services were hosted was ready for the deluge of users who might respond to a broadcast program's "call to action" (IV10).[19] Failure to adhere to these standards of quality often meant that Web sites "fell over" (IV29), such as the BBC's *Virtual Revolution* (2010) site or Channel 4's *Seven Days* 'Chat nav' application (2010), which crashed because of high user demand. The disjuncture between different production cultures' understanding of quality, therefore, had a profound impact on how viewers and users experienced PSM.

Equally, however, where understandings of public service aligned across production cultures, examples of good multiplatform PSM content and services were produced, such as the award-winning *Embarrassing Bodies* or *Fish Fight* series that combined robust and useable multiplatform experiences with challenging programming that risked, in the case of the former, offending viewers with the grotesque, and in the case of the latter, alienating viewers from a primetime series about European fishery laws.[20] Such successful examples of multiplatform were those that were not only underpinned by a public service desire to 'make a difference,' but that also negotiated the tension between profit and public service. How these demands are balanced is crucial to the PSM compact.

The PSM Compact: Contingent and Pragmatic

"I thought I was going to make films about the developing world. I rapidly discovered that my child would starve if I tried to do that."

(IV57)

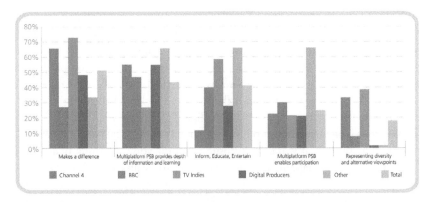

Table 10.3 Purposes as percentage

Table 10.3 represents how interviewees understood the purposes of PSM. Read in conjunction with Table 10.2 regarding production modes, it was clear that PSM was content, services, or applications that 'made a difference,' while also balancing the tension between profit and public service. Here we find an ideal of public service that remains tied to the origins of UK broadcasting and the Reithian edict of "inform, educate, entertain": but one that must increasingly balance the competing demands of commerce. Barry Dornfeld's study of U.S. public television during the 1990s aptly describes the tensions inherent in such a situation:

> The opposing imperatives of education and commerce, embedded in the structure of public television itself and as an outgrowth of its complex institutional history, pull public television in two directions simultaneously.[21]

This pull between public service and profit is one that was constantly negotiated by producers who often found compromise, as with so many producers of independent media, an inevitable outcome.[22] The existence of the compact, however, meant that this compromise did not always place commercial imperatives ahead of public service. Moreover, as the quote at the top of this section suggests, the requirement to make a profit is not necessarily always at the behest of multinational conglomerates—with the desire to make public service content often involving profound ethical dilemmas for producers. The notion of the compact helps us understand that commerce and public service are not inherently antithetical—indeed, finding points of alignment is vital to the future of PSM production and the cultures that thrive around it. In this section I set out how a commitment to public service, understood as a desire to produce content that 'made a difference,' brought together shared PSM production cultures, enabling the compact to exist across the competing demands of public service and profit, television and digital production, independent and broadcast cultures.

Producers' drive toward making PSM came from their dual position as viewers and producers. However, producers articulated a particular understanding of their position as viewers that was informed by a notion of citizenship:

> Public service motivates me in two ways. One is as a citizen, one feels that we could have a television model like the American model that is the lowest common denominator.... As an individual I think it's a critical part of our body politic. And [the other is] as a producer too. For this company, the value for us is that [PSB] does inform our skill set: how to conduct difficult interviews, [deal with] difficult issues ... that sort of thing.
>
> (IV18)

For this producer, public service was a concern motivated by higher ideals as well as pragmatic business decisions. These higher ideals were articulated across the sector as an attempt to 'make a difference' to society by educating and inspiring people with content, applications, and services that might affect social change or individual betterment: whether that be documentaries about alcoholism or interactive mapping services about antisocial behavior, through to multiplatform campaigns to change European or UK law. As another producer explained, "It's great to win an award or to get a good audience, all those things are satisfying; but much more satisfying is to bring about change, to actually affect the world outside the television box.... And it's also kind of addictive as well" (IV41).

Such statements may read as the kind of retrofitted accounts of PSM I highlighted in my introduction, or as high-minded ideals that, as in the case of the producer who felt his children would starve if he followed them, invariably produce incompatible drives in terms of risk, quality, or the kinds of content producers sought to make. However, producers at all levels spoke of how they found ways to align the drive toward public service with the need to make profit. For example, quality was a crucial marker of public service, as well as independents' business models: as one interviewee put it, "it's a good business strategy. Because the opposite of making good stuff is don't make good stuff, and that's a suicidal business strategy" (IV40). This alignment of business models with public service extended to the digital sector, with one company director talking about how working with the BBC had produced an approach that "wouldn't work with a commercial broadcaster ... they have a particular kind of DNA which is very British and very much aimed at entertaining and informing an audience" (IV25). In effect, just as the creation of Channel 4 had done in the early 1980s for television, the BBC's and Channel 4's investment in multiplatform production throughout the 2000s had incubated a number of digital agencies that had a strong alignment between their commitment to, and understanding of, PSM and their business models.

In turn, this influenced the staff they employed, the culture of the workplace, and the DNA of the company (IV104), producing a belief in "digital public service" that posited "Public purposes [as] best delivered online because of their participatory nature and personalization" (IV1).

However, this commitment to public service often involved forbearance of profit. As one long-term producer and managing director of a small independent television company suggested:

> There is a strong cultural imperative behind [what we do]. We make it without subsidy as an SME that is a private limited company. . . . That's not a comfortable and not a particularly remunerative place to be, but it's been possible to do that with ups and downs for more than twenty-five years.
>
> (IV4)

The compact is, thus, built on the balancing of these competing tensions that is underpinned by a notion of service.

As Paddy Scannell has noted, the ideal of service was profoundly influential in shaping the origins of British broadcasting. It remains apparent in the way producers understood their role as citizen-viewers and creators. Such a perspective, however, is not entirely unproblematic given it owes much to the "the Victorian reforming ideal . . . [which] was animated by a sense of moral purpose and of social duty on behalf of the community aimed particularly at those most in need of reform—the lower class." Given our interviewees were almost entirely middle-class, white, and predominantly male, therefore, it is worth noting that while such an ideal might espouse "a genuinely humane concern to alleviate the harsh consequences" of industrial, and perhaps even postindustrial, life, Scannell and Raymond Williams provide a compelling critique of this notion of public service as doing "nothing to change the balance of power in society."[23] As some interviewees recognized, one could "get into quite difficult territory when you start to talk about making a difference" (IV68), in terms of the complexity of proving such change and in whose name, values, and beliefs change was 'made.' Moreover, in a multiplatform landscape where audiences were increasingly empowered, there was a concern that such an approach was overly paternalistic and outdated.

Conclusion

The compact we found, therefore, is already on the move—but one that continues to tie together the diverse production cultures discussed here via not only a commitment to shared values and beliefs, but also economic demands and necessities. The existence of this production culture within the wider frame of neoliberalism therefore points to not only the movement of the compact, but also its fragility.

As competition in the television marketplace has grown and funding is cut from public service broadcasters at the same time as independents' entrepreneurialism has been fostered through intellectual property ownership, the forbearance of profit in public service production has been harder to maintain. Such conjunctures have influenced the business strategies of companies in television and digital media, as well as the working conditions and cultural commitments to public service of those across the sectors. For digital agencies the BBC's change in multiplatform strategy had led companies to turn their "attention elsewhere and a bit more commercial, because a lot of those public service projects don't exist anymore" (IV46). Equally, in television, the perceived lack of risk brought about by the emphasis on returnable and exportable formats and the need for the broadcasters to chase ratings meant that challenging documentaries that sought to make a difference "just don't exist anymore" (IV90), while another reflected that "it would be commercial suicide" to orientate a business around such programming (IV91).

As companies shift away from traditional areas of public service production, or away from the BBC and Channel 4 altogether, in order to compete in the global television marketplace, there was a concern about independents continuing investment in public service as a culture and production value. As Mayer, Banks, and Caldwell note in the prequel to the first volume of *Production Studies*, production cultures "shape and refashion their identities in the process of making their careers in industries undergoing political transitions and economic reorganizations."[24] For younger workers, entering a sector in which PSM may no longer be such a dominant production mode, there was a concern that a diminished commitment to public service was inevitable. As one managing director who had been in television for over twenty-five years commented: "I'm not sure whether Indies that have effectively grown on a very commercial culture, [will have] public service values" (IV13). Moreover, the shift to more freelance labor—both inside and outside the broadcasters—had brought about more contingent relationships to the values and ideals of PSM. As one young producer, who had worked inside and outside broadcasters, relayed: "I don't know much about [public service] . . . it's something that was drummed into me when I was a student, but then I never had to professionally pay much attention to it" (IV100).

To an extent this chapter's key argument is obvious: PSM only exists to the degree to which those who produce it believe in it, understand it, and share some sense of value. Clearly the PSM compact is increasingly under threat and fragile. But understanding PSM as a compact between contingent and conjunctural production cultures should also give us hope for its renewal and move the debate beyond binaries of public service and profit. In particular, the mixture of continuing strong cultural commitment from long-term television producers, broadcasters, and companies alongside an emergent and playful approach to public service in the digital sector offers the possibility for profoundly innovative and hybrid forms of public service to emerge in the future.

Notes

1 Unless express permission was given to use individuals' names, interviewees are designated by the abbreviation IV and the number of their interview, 1–105.

2 The BBC must commission at least 25 percent of its UK-originated, non-news content from independents and make a further 25 percent contestable between in-house and independent production under the Window of Creative Competition (WOCC), introduced in 2007.

3 Georgina Born, *Uncertain Vision: Birt, Dyke and the Reinvention of the BBC* (London: Vintage, 2005), 74.

4 David Lee, "The Ethics of Insecurity: Risk, Individualization and Value in British Independent Television Production." *Television & New Media* 13, no. 6 (2012): 487.

5 Graeme Turner, "Convergence and Divergence: The International Experience of Digital Television," in *Television as Digital Media*, edited by James Bennett and Niki Strange (Durham, NC: Duke University Press, 2011), 31–51.

6 Andrew Chitty, "How Multiplatform PSB Stopped Trying to Change the World and Grew Up (But Got Smaller)." *Critical Studies in Television* 8, no. 1 (2013): 127.

7 This was a result of the 2003 Communications Act.

8 See James Bennett and Niki Strange, "Linear Legacies: Managing the Multiplatform Production Process," in *Making Media Work: Cultures of Management in the Entertainment Industries*, edited by Derek Kompare, Derek Johnson, and Avi Santo (New York: New York University Press, 2014).

9 The research was conducted with Niki Strange, Paul Kerr, and Andrea Medrado. For a more detailed discussion of methodology and description of interviews undertaken, see: James Bennett, Niki Strange, Paul Kerr, and Andrea Medrado, *Multiplatforming Public Service Broadcasting: The Economic and Cultural Role of UK Digital and TV Independents* (London: University of London Press, 2012).

10 John T. Caldwell, *Production Culture* (Durham, NC: Duke University Press, 2008), 3.

11 See Andrea Medrado, "'Do You Get It?': Narrative and Production Complexity and the Making of a Multiplatform Project for Channel 4," Paper presented at *Contemporary Screen Narratives: Storytelling's Digital and Industrial Contexts*. Department of Culture, Film and Media, University of Nottingham, May 17, 2012.

12 Medrado, "Do You Get It?" 38.

13 Ofcom, *Second Review of Public Service Broadcasting: Putting Viewers First* (2009).

14 Elana Levine, "Crossing the Border: Studying Canadian Television Production," in *Production Studies: Cultural Studies of Media Industries*, edited by Mayer et al. (New York: Routledge, 2009), 158.

15 Levine, "Crossing the Border," 155.

16 Channel 4, *Annual Report 2012*.

17 Andrew Ross, *No Collar: The Humane Workplace and Its Hidden Costs* (Philadelphia, PA: Temple University Press, 2003). See also Trebor Scholz, ed., *Digital Labor: The Internet as Playground and Factory* (New York: Routledge, 2013).

18 See James Bennett et al., "A Moral Economy of Independent Work? Creative Freedom and Public Service in UK Digital Agencies," in *Media Independence: Working with Freedom or Working for Free*, edited by James Bennett and Niki Strange (New York: Routledge, 2014).

19 Niki Strange, "Multiplatforming Public Service: The BBC's 'Bundled Project,'" in *Television as Digital Media*, edited by James Bennett and Niki Strange (Durham, NC: Duke University Press, 2011), 132–57.

20 James Bennett and Andrea Medrado, "The Business of Multiplatform Public Service: Online and at a Profit." *Media International Australia* no. 146 (2013), 103–13.
21 Barry Dornfeld, *Producing Public Television: Producing Public Culture* (Princeton, NJ: Princeton University Press, 1998), 180–1.
22 James Bennett, "The Utopia of Independent Media," in *Media Independence: Working with Freedom or Working for Free*, edited by James Bennett and Niki Strange (New York: Routledge, 2014), 1–39.
23 Paddy Scannell, "Public Service Broadcasting: The History of a Concept," in *British Television: A Reader*, edited by Edward Buscombe (Oxford: Oxford University Press, 2001), 55–6.
24 Vicki Mayer, Miranda J. Banks, and John T. Caldwell, "Production Studies: Roots and Routes," in *Production Studies: Cultural Studies of Media Industries*, edited by Mayer et al. (New York: Routledge, 2009), 2.

11

INVISIBLE WORKERS IN AN INVISIBLE MEDIUM

An Ethnographic Approach to Italian Public and Private Freelance Radio Producers

Tiziano Bonini and Alessandro Gandini

Production studies represents a well-established interdisciplinary approach to the cultural studies of media industries. Within this approach, film, television,[1] print media,[2] the music industry,[3] and the digital game industry[4] have been considered and dissected extensively. In contrast, radio production cultures and practices have been substantially under investigated.[5] Although radio still represents one of the most important mass media in the Western world, its audiences are growing in each of the BRIC countries.[6] As Lewis and Booth claim, radio has been for a long time "the invisible medium."[7] In this chapter, we investigate these 'invisible workers' in this invisible medium.

Public service media in Europe—both television and radio—employ thousands of workers (around 18,000 in the United Kingdom, 12,000 in Italy, 15,000 in France).[8] Public service media were employing 127,000 persons in the European Union in 2010, which represented 16 percent of the employment of the EU audiovisual market.[9] However, nonstandard forms of employment within this sector quickly spread to become common practice. Over the past few decades, employment in the radio sector has become increasingly fragmented and insecure mainly because of a combination of the global economic crisis, the rise of digital media, and transformations at the level of the political economy of traditional media. In the past decade, European public service media have faced increasing budget cuts, together with a constant decrease in advertising revenues.[10] Meanwhile, thousands of communications and humanities graduates dreaming of working in the creative industries, radio included, frequently encounter unfulfilled expectations of employment when they attempt to access the labor market. This young and over skilled labor force represents, in Marxian terms, a huge 'reserve labor army' undergoing new and unprecedented forms of exploitation and polarization of work.[11]

This chapter investigates the experiences and emotional responses of Italian radio industry employees when discussing their working conditions. Grounded within critical approaches of creative and cultural industries,[12] this study is based on an ethnographic investigation—a mix of in-depth interviews and participant observation—of work practices within the radio production industry, undertaken between November 2013 and March 2014. This consented to describe the usual working conditions of precarious and freelance workers at four Italian national radio stations as well as common experiences of insecurity, uncertainty, socializing, networking, and isolation. This chapter examines the distinct roles workers play in the daily production flows of radio stations; what happens when someone is made redundant; to what extent the precarious status of their work affects workers' everyday life and how they cope with it; if they rely on social capital when and if their contract is interrupted; if they make plans for their professional future, or feel stranded in the present.

Italy can be considered a classic example. The Italian radio sector has followed the same declining path as that of the European sector more generally, in terms of employment conditions, with fragmentation highly significant across creative industries, as well as in relation to production organization. Italian radio has had to cope with a decrease in advertising revenues similar to those that have affected television and the print media industry. As a consequence, both business models and employment strategies have been affected by downsizing and nonstandard forms of contracting and freelancing are particularly common.

Methodology

This study is based on an ethnographic investigation of freelance and precarious workers' conditions within the radio production industry. We conducted participant observation between November 2013 and March 2014 at national public and private radio stations, combined with semi-structured, in-depth interviews with twenty people, fourteen women and six men, aged between twenty-six and forty-seven, working in Milan or Rome (the main cities where radio jobs are concentrated) for: RAI Radio 2 (the light entertainment public service channel, with 3.3 million daily listeners); RAI Radio 3 (the public service channel dedicated to culture, drama, intelligent speech, jazz, and classical music, with 1.4 million daily listeners); Radio 24 (a private talk and news channel with a special focus on economics and politics, with 2 million daily listeners); Radio 101 (a contemporary hit music station, with 1.8 million daily listeners); Radio Popolare (a private talk and news listener-supported channel, with a leftist perspective and 190,000 daily listeners[13]). Eighteen of them hold a university degree in humanities, and two have not finished their university studies. Sixteen of them started working in radio through an internship.

The producers we met and interviewed for our study largely perform freelance jobs in terms of tasks and daily routine. However, in terms of employment regimes, we can essentially divide workers into two types. A large majority of people was employed under the regime known as 'partita IVA' (the Italian name for the VAT number), which essentially represents the registration code to formally operate as self-employed. Some of those employed with partita IVA also have the possibility to obtain a share of the royalties paid by SIAE, the Italian institution that regulates authors' rights and earnings. This is to be taken effectively as a consistent benefit as it represents a fixed share, paid according to the overall amount of royalties that pertain to a single radio program in the year considered, and is paid over twelve months, thus enabling a consistent form of revenue on a fixed basis. This, however, is often a form of bogus self-employment as the workers are strongly discouraged—when not explicitly forbidden—to work for other national radio stations or programs and therefore have to cope with income gaps when the program is not running. On the other hand, a minority of the workers involved in this study was employed with a temporary, atypical contract of a project-based or collaborative nature, with a formally recognized status as an employee, in other words as dependent workers who do not have a partita IVA.

In all these cases, however, and independent from the type of contract or employment, workers are treated largely as standard employees, although with no sick pay or paid holidays, having to comply with timing, schedules, and office-like hours with no significant autonomy, self-organization, or independence. The average net income is substantially comparable for the two groups, ranging between 1,200 and 1,600 euros per month or 12,000 and 20,000 euros per year.

Background: Creative Labor in Italian Radio

Creative industries, variously defined, are significant components of advanced economies. The term was introduced by the British Department of Culture, Media and Sport in 1998.[14] This definition, however, fails to include activities connected to cultural heritage (galleries, museums, libraries, and archives), education, and sports. Many definitions of these industries exist, from both the administrative and academic worlds, and scholars have still not come to an agreement. John Hartley has contributed to greater clarification in his description of the boundaries of this new term, defining creative industries as "the conceptual and practical convergence of the creative arts (individual talent) with Cultural Industries (mass scale) in the context of new media technologies (ICTs) within a new knowledge economy, for the use of newly interactive citizen-consumers."[15] According to Hartley, creative industries include copyright industries, content industries, cultural industries, and digital content industries.

International creative workers should be taken as "a vast multinational workforce of talented people applying their individual creativity in design, production, performance and writing. They range from fashion designers in Milan to shoe-factory operatives in Indonesia. They do the work of combining creativity and value, being an increasingly casual, part-time, freelance workforce often embarked on a 'portfolio' career with many jobs from different employers."[16] Specifically, the evolution of creative industries in recent years resulted in the expansion of a project-based creative labor market increasingly leaning on *freelance work*.[17] The term 'freelance' signifies a form of contract-based, self-organized work, not subject to a formally stable and continuous dependent relationship with a single firm or employer.[18]

Here we will focus on one of the most crucial issues concerning this sector of the creative industries, that of work and labor. We are particularly interested in media-based industries, primarily radio but also television, print and ICTs, advertising, public relations, communication, and design. All these are constitutive of a creative labor market made up of knowledge workers employed at all levels with different degrees of experience, independence, and autonomy.

In Italy, the most popular definition of the creative industries was provided by economist Walter Santagata.[19] Santagata's definition is very broad and includes sectors such as gastronomy (the production of protected food products) as well as a focus on historical-artistic heritage that the English definition did not provide. This very broad definition presents the creative industries in Italy as employers of approximately 2.5 million people, 11.79 percent of all working Italians, and producers of wealth equal to 9.31 percent of the Italian GDP.[20] The 2008 economic crisis hit the sector hard, but no overall data exist that are more recent than Santagata's. Instead, data can be drawn from Italy's 2011 ISTAT census.

Milan is the city with the highest number of employees in the creative industries in relation to the total number of those employed. According to the latest ISTAT data, approximately 250,000 people work in this sector, approximately 15 percent of the active population of Milan's metropolitan area. The leading sectors are fashion and software, but Milan is also the city with the highest percentage of employees in design, advertising, radio, and television production and publishing. Among these sectors, publishing has suffered the most from the economic crisis. Between 2001 and 2011, the number of employees in publishing dropped from 16,199 workers to 14,865.[21] The radio-television sector went from 5,055 employees in 2001 to 9,734 in 2011,[22] while in Italy over the same period the sector increased its employees from 27,047 to 31,048. Therefore, 31.35 percent of those employed by the radio-television sector are concentrated in Milan. In particular, Milan's radio industry employs 582 workers, out of a total of 3,803 in Italy,[23] so 15 percent of all those employed in the sector. Milan is home to eight of the seventeen national private radio stations, fourteen local commercial radio stations, and a local branch of RAI, the Italian public service broadcasting company, where some radio programs are produced and broadcast. RAI employs 12,136 workers, of whom 1,660 hold a fixed-term contract.[24] The company's headquarters are in Rome, where most of its employees work. Radio RAI, the radio sector of the Italian public service, employs 750 people with permanent contracts and 48 with fixed-term contracts, for a total of 798 people (6.57% of all RAI workers), to which 250–300 workers with temporary labor relations may be added, according to internal sources at Radio RAI.[25]

This data connects with the specific labor market structure that defines the Italian media work, and the labor market in general. Italy's total amount of independent and freelance work is higher than the average figures in Europe[26] and works in conjunction with a labor legislation that de facto incentivizes the recourse to so-called atypical contracts. These are a set of nonstandard employment arrangements that differ in name and status among each other, from 'project work' to 'collaboration,' but nevertheless are often used interchangeably in employment practices and substantially lead to precarious work or 'bogus' freelancing. The term 'bogus' associated with 'self-employment' indicates 'false' forms of independent professions that cover for a dependent job.[27] The findings presented here document the different dimensions and tensions attached to the working conditions of Italian radio producers.

Findings: Being an Invisible Worker in Radio

The majority of the workers we interviewed and shadowed all perform seasonal labor. Their contract is linked to one or more programs, which are seasonal in duration. Therefore, as Subject A explains, when the program is not being aired, for example during the summer, they find themselves without a contract:

> There's a big difference between TV and radio: TV has a shorter season, with better pay—you work two or three months on a program or project, then you have a break in your contract, and three months later you start again on another program. In radio, the seasons work like school: you begin in September and end in June, so you actually work 200 or more days per year. It's hard to say that if you work 200 days a year you cannot be equated with a full-time employee.
>
> (Subject A, female, 45 years old)

An important question therefore becomes how they make ends meet in the months when they are unemployed. Alternative forms of income generation include renting houses to tourists, translation work, newspaper writing, or even working in advertising, such as Subject B: "I'm the copywriter in an agency that creates Web sites, so I also work there on specific projects; it's always changing . . . then I work in radio, and I also correct drafts for a magazine on African issues" (Subject B, female, 25 years old).

If the program they are working for is not renewed or is cancelled at the beginning of the new season, workers lose their jobs and hope to be offered a new contract for another program with the same radio station soon after. Even when a program has a long history and does not seem at risk of closure, the certainty of a contract renewal only comes just a few days before the start of the new season. This uncertainty generates anxiety and fear, together with a sense of powerlessness, as Subject C explains:

> It's not only fear . . . it's more like Chinese water torture . . . a needle in your brain . . . you call them, but they tell you, "Well, I don't know yet, I'll let you know . . . "; you call and in the end you think you're bothering them, but you can do nothing about it, because they'll call you, they'll have to call you . . . or so you tell yourself. It's clear that in this kind of system . . . if you insist . . . you weaken your position, because you're the annoying one . . . the one that complains.
>
> (Subject C, male, 47 years old)

But this uncertainty also persists for the duration of one's contract because this kind of employment does not allow for sick pay or paid holidays. The precarity of labor demands that all time lost must be made up, as Subject D explains:

> Last year I was at work and had a fever, so they told me to go home; since I don't have sick pay, the only way to make up the days I had missed was to work extra days, up to six days a week, for maybe four or five weeks if you stay at home four or five days.
>
> (Subject D, female, 36 years old)

All those who work for either public or private radio have to face the instability of their positions and the irregularity of their incomes. For those who live in cities with high costs of renting such as Milan or Rome, the wages earned from a radio job are often insufficient, and it is sometimes necessary for them to seek other sources of income, just like Subject D, who lives in Milan, did: "This year I had to find another collaboration because I couldn't make ends meet. . . . Consider that our hourly wage is 5.30 as per the contract" (Subject E, female, 28 years old).

All of our subjects work in the newsrooms of four national radios, as producers or as assistant producers. According to David Hendy, producers are the "all-encompassing *program makers* of radio. They generate and research ideas, plan running orders, record and edit material, and very often direct studio operations during transmissions. They must have ideas—ideas for programs, or items, people to interview, pieces of music or subjects for discussion."[28] Among the producers interviewed, some worked more as 'content researchers,' others worked more on programs' sound design. Their work requires specific technical skills (knowledge of audio editing software, use of social media, ability to create a sound interview, etc.), a combination of humanities background and social skills, and—as Subject F explained—this involves developing a great sensitivity for listening: "I think you have to like it . . . you have to be passionate, and most of all you need the ability to listen to what goes on air . . . and to analyze what goes on air in order to improve it . . . I don't think everyone can do it" (Subject F, male, 32 years old). We saw the producers we shadowed doing a great variety of tasks: recording and editing audio interviews, finding the guests for a program, finding new and fresh content, preparing news for the host, writing scripts, choosing and editing music, selecting user-generated content, filtering phone calls for the host, mastering programs' social media accounts, replying to e-mails sent to programs by listeners, organizing the production workflow, and even looking after the host, comforting him or her when required. Their tasks involve 'passionate work' that requires emotional labor, consisting in a complicated combination of personal human feelings and social skills.

As a result, according to our subjects, a key requirement of their job is that of knowing how to manage the personal relationship with the host. The majority of our interviewees say that their work is mostly social and based on personal contact. Much depends on emotional intelligence, as Subject E explains when elaborating on the relationships among hosts and workers:

> The relationship with the host is the nucleus of all our work, because he/
> she can become your friend, your boss . . . it's too many things in one single
> figure. With some you can build a friendship, with others it's based on pure
> terror or subjection, and power play, with others there are symbiotic rela-
> tionships . . . so it's hard to manage, because it's an informal relationship,
> there are no regulations, but it is a professional relationship, you have work
> constraints . . . the host often asks you to go beyond the job description
> written in your contract, so you have to decide whether to satisfy his/her
> requests or not, and think about your colleagues as well, because if you say
> yes to something, you could cause problems for someone else.
>
> (Subject E, female, 28 years old)

All this work is invisible to listeners' eyes and ears, who are used to associating a program with the voice that distinguishes it: the radio personality. Freelance and precarious workers work opposite the radio hosts and personalities, whose work is visible (audible) and whose value is determined by the audience they can aggregate around their voices. The invisible radio producers work for them behind the scenes but are rarely acknowledged for their crucial roles in the production value chain.

The producer's work is an invisible job in and of itself, for those who work behind the scenes, but even more so because many of the producer's skills are not recognized by his/her contract. Our interviewees were often authors of programs, independently choosing content to go on air (news, music, phone callers, guests), being authors of (often) significant parts of the program, and sometimes using their own voice; nevertheless, their contracts do not generally or automatically recognize their authorship role, with the exception of the SIAE share, which, indeed, comes from an informal agreement with the hosts or the rest of the news-room, not as a decision of the station management. Producers working for public service radio can be rewarded with a certain amount of the SIAE share, but this is a decision usually taken only by the hosts, not by the station managers. Their labor as producers and authors is only noticed by the host, who works side by side with his/her producers. Much of this is invisible labor, the public credit of which is left to the willingness of the host to publicly state this, often at the end of the program, as Subject G describes:

> When I work and create an informational program, I find the person, I do the pre-interview, I communicate all the useful information for the host who has to have the basic information, especially if this person has never been interviewed at the national level . . . consequently, I do two-thirds of the interview. So much so that at the end of the broadcast, the host says that I wrote the program along with him, but it's something that our radio sta-tion doesn't want them to say, because I'm not employed as an author.
>
> (Subject G, female, 30 years old)

During our ethnography, we saw producers work up to ten to eleven hours a day and leave their offices very late. But this 'extra' work goes unacknowledged and unsupported financially because, as Subject H, a 'nighttime worker' in a major radio station noted, this does not explicitly make part of their contracts. Still, it is an implicitly mandatory requirement:

> I work until midnight, but I obviously don't have night pay or overtime, and I work Saturdays and Sundays, and that isn't recognized either, so even if I work Christmas or New Year's, it's still a regular Thursday.
>
> (Subject H, female, 39 years old)

The quality of a producer's work is difficult for radio directors to evaluate. The only evaluation system is the number of listeners, which is easily associated with—and often depends on—the host or radio personality's popularity.

Furthermore, the very low pay and the recurrent budget cuts in the public sec-tor risk negatively influencing the work's quality, and contribute to the symbolic and material decline of the value of their work. A job with low pay tends to be considered trivial. Subject H offers a description of how this decrease in financial remuneration easily transforms into lower-quality production:

> These types of contracts, with VAT numbers and atypical workers, have an important effect on the quality of the work in general. The progressive reductions in pay (we're talking about cuts between 5% and 10%) that have

hit hosts, directors and editorial staff in the last three or four years, elicit a natural disaffection to the work, often producing an inevitable drop in quality. . . . In my case, for example, I repeatedly end up being the only one that deals with audio editing, and often I can't physically find the time to do all the work as I would like to.

(Subject H, female, 39 years old)

The precarious workers of Italian radio are also invisible to the companies that hire them. While their peers hired with permanent contracts have a permanent badge for entering the office, the freelancers and precarious employees must get a guest badge to enter the office, every day. Symbolically, the company considers them guests, people who come to visit the company every day, but who are not a part of it.

The difference between permanent and precarious employees is also emphasized in the newsrooms. In Rome, one of our subjects told us how her colleagues with permanent contracts expected the freelancers to work as they did, even though their precarious contracts entitled them to some degree of flexibility with their schedules. But those who took advantage of the flexibility of their freelance status were ironically called 'vacationers,' or tourists, those who did whatever they wanted to, who came and went as they pleased. Subject D explains this practice well: "In the newsroom, they talked about people who had worked there before me, who came in late or left early, and they called them 'vacationers' . . . last summer they were looking for a producer, and one of these 'vacationers' was not called because of this" (Subject D, female, 36 years old). The precarious producers work as standard employees, even though their contracts should allow them more flexibility with their schedules. When they behave as freelancers, they feel their colleagues are watching them. Only those who have slightly more important roles, or who have managed to obtain greater contractual power over time, can take advantage of the freedom set forth by their contracts.

Conclusions

This study has unveiled the problematic working conditions of freelance radio producers and shown the many contradictory dimensions attached to a job connoted with highly symbolic rewards that provide for a good degree of job satisfaction and that doesn't necessarily require the forms of personal branding often associated with creative jobs.

We found no substantial differences between the precarious workers' experiences working for public service radio and for private commercial radio. Both perform the same kind of work, with the difference being that in public service the producers are linked to one program, while in the private sector a producer works simultaneously for many different programs; this explains why public service programs require more research for content. The one big difference lies in the type of contract they are employed with: at RAI, everyone must have a VAT number, which means that they must be self-employed as entrepreneurs, while private radio more frequently adopts the atypical forms of project-based precarious contracts. But fighting for justice when you know no other system does not come naturally to those in a precarious position. This becomes accepted as the status quo, as Subject I clearly says:

> I have never experienced anything else, anything that was different. . . . I have never had the experience of a permanent contract . . . it's my life; it's normal. I'm not calm, because I don't know what will come next, but I'm not anxious, I'm not afraid, it's my life, this is how I work, I have always worked this way. It's like asking a doctor what he would do if he had no patients tomorrow, I don't know.
>
> (Subject I, female, 31 years old)

This persistent precariousness, in which one's personal career depends exclusively on oneself (and on the help of one's peers), induces a transformation in one's self-perception. The self-entrepreneurship ethos seems to have been incorporated into the everyday life of our interviewees.

The culture pioneered by dot.com companies and popularized by the social media era—a culture based on entrepreneurial labor models, creativity, self-actualization through work—has spread to the old creative industry of radio as well. But this narration only holds up in a system where work is abundant and the pay is high. Only radio personalities are truly self-employed entrepreneurs in Italy, and are therefore able to develop genuine personal brands, being able to benefit from their popularity and visibility.

Radio producers, although they are forced to perceive themselves as entrepreneurs, instead represent an entrepreneurial workforce unable to elevate their labor power to a valuable status on the market—indeed, a "very complicated version of freedom."[29] Their voices are desperate to be heard.

Notes

1 Gillian Ursell, "Labour Flexibility in the UK Commercial Television Sector." *Media, Culture & Society* 20, no. 1 (1998): 129–53; Gillian Ursell, "Television Production: Issues of Exploitation, Commodification and Subjectivity in UK Television Labour Markets." *Media, Culture & Society* 22, no. 6 (2000): 805–25; Helen Blair, "'You're Only as Good as Your Last Job': The Labour Process and Labour Market in the British Film Industry." *Work, Employment & Society* 15 no. 1 (2001): 149–69; David Hesmondhalgh and Sarah Baker, "Creative Work and Emotional Labour in the Television Industry." *Theory, Culture & Society* 25, no. 7–8 (2008): 97–118.

2 Tiziana Terranova, "Free Labor: Producing Culture for the Digital Economy." *Social Text* 18, no. 2 (2000): 33–58; Angela McRobbie, "Clubs to Companies: Notes on the Decline of Political Culture in Speeded up Creative Worlds." *Cultural Studies* 16, no. 4 (2002): 516–31; Angela McRobbie, "Everyone Is Creative: Artists as Pioneers of the New Economy," in *Contemporary Culture and Everyday Life*, edited by Elizabeth B. Silva and Tony Bennett (Durham, UK: Sociologypress, 2004), 186–99; John Storey, Graeme Salaman, and Kerry Platman, "Living with Enterprise in an Enterprise Economy: Freelance and Contract Workers in the Media." *Human Relations* 58, no. 8 (2005): 1033–54; Annette Henninger and Karin Gottschall, "Freelancers in Germany's Old and New Media Industry: Beyond Standard Patterns of Work and Life?" *Critical Sociology* 33, no. 1–2 (2007): 43–71.

3 David Hesmondhalgh, "Flexibility, Post-Fordism and the Music Industries." *Media, Culture & Society* 18, no. 3 (1996): 469–88.

4 Julian Kücklich, "Precarious Playbour: Modders and the Digital Games Industry." *Fibreculture* 5 (2005). http://five.fibreculturejournal.org/fcj-025-precarious-playbour-modders-and-the-digital-games-industry/.

5 For important exceptions, see: Rosalind Gill, "Justifying Injustice: Broadcasters' Accounts of Inequality in Radio," in *Discourse Analytic Research: Readings and Repertoires of Texts in Action*, edited by Erica Burman and Ian Parker (London: Routledge, 1993), 75–93; Rosalind Gill, "Ideology, Gender and Popular Radio: A Discourse Analytic Approach." *Innovation: The European Journal of Social Science Research* 6, no. 3 (1993): 323–39; Caroline Mitchell, ed., *Women and Radio: Airing Differences* (Oxon: Psychology Press, 2000); Peter Lewis, "Opening and Closing Doors: Radio Drama in the BBC." *Radio Journal: International Studies in Broadcast & Audio Media* 1, no. 3 (2004): 161–76; Tiziano Bonini and Belén Monclus, eds., *Radio Audiences and Participation in the Age of Network Society* (London: Routledge, 2015).

6 BRIC stands for Brazil, Russia, India, and China. Ofcom, "International Communications Market Report—Radio and Audio, 2011." http://stakeholders.ofcom.org.uk/market-data-research/market-data/communications-market-reports/cmr12/international/.

7 Peter Lewis and Jerry Booth, *The Invisible Medium: Public, Commercial, and Community* (London: McMillan, 1989).

8 EBU, *EBU Report: Funding of Public Service Media* (Geneve: Ebu Press, 2011).

9 EBU, *EBU Visions 2020. Annex 3: Media Markets, Media Distribution & Production Technologies* (Geneve: Ebu Press, 2014).

10 EBU, *EBU Report*.

11 Alan McKinlay and Chris Smith, eds., *Creative Labour: Working in the Creative Industries* (New York: Palgrave Macmillan, 2009); David Hesmondhalgh and Sarah Baker, *Creative Labour: Media Work in Three Cultural Industries* (Abingdon, Oxon, 2011).

12 Ursell, "Labour Flexibility"; Richard Paterson, "Work Histories in Television." *Media, Culture & Society* 23, no. 4 (2001): 495–520; McRobbie, "Clubs to Companies"; Ursula Huws, "The Spark in the Engine: Creative Workers in a Global Economy." *Work Organisation, Labour & Globalisation* 1, no. 1 (2006): 1–12; Hesmondhalgh and Baker, "Creative Work and Emotional Labour in the Television Industry"; Hesmondhalgh and Baker, *Creative Labour*.

13 For a history of Radio Popolare, see Sergio Ferrentino, Luca Gattuso, and Tiziano Bonini, eds., *Vedi alla Voce Radio Popolare* (Milano: Garzanti editore, 2006).

14 DCMS, Creative Industries Mapping Document, London (1998).

15 John Hartley, *Creative Industries* (Oxford: Blackwell Publishing, 2005), 5.

16 Hartley, *Creative Industries*, 29.

17 Susan Christopherson, "Project Work in Context: Regulatory Change and the New Geography of Media." *Environment and Planning A* 34, no. 11 (2002): 2003–15; Susan Christopherson, "Beyond the Self-Expressive Creative Worker: An Industry Perspective on Entertainment Media." *Theory, Culture & Society* 25, no. 7–8 (2008): 73–95; Brett Neilson and Ned Rossiter, "From Precarity to Precariousness and Back Again: Labour, Life and Unstable Networks." *Fibreculture* 5. http://journal.fibreculture.org/issue5/neilson_rossiter.html; Stephen R. Barley and Gideon Kunda, "Contracting: A New Form of Professional Practice." *The Academy of Management Perspectives* 20, no. 1 (2006): 45–66; McKinlay and Smith, *Creative Labour*; David Lee, "Networks, Cultural Capital and Creative Labour in the British Independent Television Industry." *Media, Culture & Society* 33, no. 4 (2011): 549–65; Irena Grugulis and Dimitrinka Stoyanova, "The Missing Middle: Communities of Practice in a Freelance Labour Market." *Work, Employment & Society* 25 no. 2 (2011): 342–51; Irena Grugulis and Dimitrinka Stoyanova, "Social Capital and Networks in Film and TV: Jobs for the Boys?" *Organization Studies* 33, no. 10 (2012): 1311–31.

18 Christopherson, "Project Work in Context" and "Beyond the Self-Expressive Creative Worker."

19 Walter Santagata, *La fabbrica della cultura: ritrovare la creatività per aiutare lo sviluppo del paese* (Bologna: Il mulino, 2007); Walter Santagata, *Libro bianco sulla creatività. Per un modello italiano di sviluppo* (Milano: Egea, 2009).

20 Santagata, *La fabbrica della cultura.*

21 ISTAT, *Censimento industria e servizi 2001.* www.istat.it/it/censimento-industria-e-servizi/industria-e-servizi-2001; ISTAT, *Censimento industria e servizi 2011.* http://dati-censimentoindustriaeservizi.istat.it/#.

22 ISTAT, *Censimento industria e servizi 2001* and ISTAT, *Censimento industria e servizi 2011.*

23 ISTAT, *Censimento industria e servizi 2011.*

24 RAI, *Bilancio RAI 2012*, 73. www.rai.it/dl/bilancio2012/ita/dwl/pdf/Bilancio_Rai_2012.pdf.

25 RAI doesn't publish figures about the exact number of its precarious workers. The figures reported in this chapter come from a source internal to RAI who wants to remain anonymous.

26 Richard Arum and Walter Müller, eds., *The Reemergence of Self-Employment: A Comparative Study of Self-Employment Dynamics and Social Inequality* (Princeton, NJ: Princeton University Press, 2004); Costanzo Ranci, ed., *Partite Iva. Il lavoro autonomo nella crisi italiana* (Bologna: Il Mulino, 2012).

27 The term is taken from the literature on self-employment in the construction industry; see Geoff Briscoe, Andrew Dainty, and Sarah Millett, "The Impact of the Tax System on Self-Employment in the British Construction Industry." *International Journal of Manpower* 21.8 (2000): 596–614. See also European Construction Industry Federation. www.fiec.eu/en/themes-72/self-employment-and-bogus-self-employment.aspx.

28 David Hendy, *Radio in the Global Age* (Cambridge: Polity, 2000), 71.

29 David Hesmondhalgh and Sarah Baker, "'A Very Complicated Version of Freedom': Conditions and Experiences of Creative Labour in Three Cultural Industries." *Poetics* 38, no. 1 (2010): 34.

12

DETACHMENT, PRIDE, CRITIQUE

Professional Identity in Independent Factual Television Production in Great Britain and Germany

Anna Zoellner

In principle, independent television producers have the power to select specific content for mass media exposure and to offer a public platform for specific contributors and issues. However, to bring this content to screen, they depend on the cooperation of commissioning editors at broadcasting networks. Independents suggest program ideas, but it is the broadcasters who make the final decisions about whether a project idea is realized. This power imbalance in the broadcaster–independent relationship submits the latter to significant economic and editorial dependency. As a result, independents primarily develop program ideas that meet the general and specific preferences and requirements of a particular broadcasting slot and the responsible commissioner to further their chances for a commission. In this process they systematically prioritize project ideas that conform to broadcasters' preferences. This commercially motivated compliance with broadcaster demands and the resulting self-restriction limit producers' creative autonomy, which is arguably one of the main attractions of television work and a significant aspect of the self-actualization many media workers seek. This practice is justified with reference to economic necessity, especially by practitioners in high-level positions (CEOs, executives, company owners, etc.) who combine artistic and managerial roles. Even so, this is not an unproblematic process.

This chapter explores the role professional identity plays in the negotiation of tensions between culture and commerce that result from this uneven power relationship between broadcasters and independent production companies. In particular, I focus on independents who specialize in serious factual and documentary programs.[1] The arguments presented here stem from an ethnographic study that combined participant observation and interviewing with document analysis. My observation focused on the team of practitioners involved in program development,[2] where new program ideas are developed and proposed to broadcasters for commission. This stage of production determines the subject and approach of a program. It is particularly sensitive to commercial pressures and occurs under opaque, even secretive conditions. To be less obtrusive in the production office and to secure access to ongoing internal project-related discussions, I entered the field as a participant observer in the role of development researcher. Fieldwork was undertaken in two independent production companies in Great Britain and Germany[3] over a period of five months. For reasons of confidentiality the identities of workers and companies have been anonymized. In both countries, the observed practices and values were strikingly similar. The overwhelming parallels I have found can be explained to some extent with reference to practicalities and organizational logic of television production processes. More important, there is a high degree of similarity in systemic conditions including the relationship between independents and broadcasters, the commercial pressures they experience, and the professional discourses in circulation that are the subject of this chapter. There is, however, a difference in degree with a slightly greater intensity of commercialization in the British system, which results in a more flexible interpretation of professional genre values in response to commercial pressures, as this chapter will illustrate.

Commercial Compliance and Professional Identity

In their attempt to please commissioning editors, independent producers[4] exclude all those program ideas from the start that they consider to have limited chances for commission. Despite a general acceptance of the industrial and commercial nature of their work, this orientation can come into direct conflict with their personal preferences and opinions. Such creative self-restriction clearly became evident in the observation, for instance, during brainstorming meetings of the development teams. In those meetings reasons for the internal rejection of a suggested idea included (aside from practicalities of realization) the requirements of a particular broadcasting slot, the potential to raise audience interest, cultural sensitivities that might lead to lower audience ratings, as well as the personal interests and likes of individual commissioning editors. Project ideas that centered, for example, on issues such as transgender identity or pedophile rehabilitation were rejected straightaway on the grounds that they were known to 'rate badly' or were too 'risky' or too 'dark' when it came to attracting the attention of an audience.

The CEO of the German company argued accordingly that:

> [I]n development it's completely idiotic to say, "Well, I think this topic is interesting, I want to make a film about it." Total idiocy, one shouldn't even think like that. You have to think about what broadcaster, what slot, what fits into that slot and we try to develop something that fits.

She summed up the general attitude toward independent production as follows:

> [F]irst of all, it's a business and one has to try to sort of serve his business partners as well as possible; and that is something one needs to be able to do to begin with. That's an art in itself, I'd say. What I am interested in personally, that's an altogether different matter.

The head of development in the British case study similarly considered it his job "to come up with ideas that commissioning editors want, knowing and trying to second-guess what they want." These statements illustrate how independent producers see their roles (especially in project development) primarily as service providers who need to satisfy their broadcaster clients. Moreover, they indicate the positive interpretation the practitioners assign to this function. Rather than presenting it as a manifestation of constraint, they portray it as a skill, an 'art' that requires expertise and carries connotations of meeting some form of quality standard. This process is not alleged to be conflict-free, but tensions are dismissed as producers claim the separation of their own interests and preferences from the projects they develop. Nonetheless, the observation revealed that the nature of broadcaster requirements repeatedly opposes the values, intentions, and judgments of practitioners, leading to frustration in everyday production. Development workers have to cope with intense and repeated rejection of their work. They need to be able to handle rejection and criticism and are advised by colleagues to not take it personally. But this can be difficult, especially when workers feel high personal investment or attachment to a topic, for example, when the idea is their own brainchild or when they are convinced of the value or worthiness of the program. One development researcher had invested a lot of work in a program idea about surrogacy. The development had gone on for some time, a broadcaster had expressed interest, and more in-depth research had been carried out. Personally, the researcher was highly convinced of the quality and worthiness of the project idea but was aware that it was also becoming a problem for her, as she was really keen on seeing this project realized: "I am really getting my hopes up; I really want it to be commissioned."

Broadcasters' focus on commercial success in an industry where demand is notoriously uncertain[5] leads to risk-averse commissioning strategies that favor familiar, formatted, and extreme content that has previously proven to have potential for audience success.[6] This climate does not prioritize textual experimentation and innovation that television producers value but instead requires them to think inside the box and develop projects along familiar lines and to demand. This suggests a potential "disjunction between the heroes and ideals of an occupation and the reality of the work situation"[7] and raises questions about how practitioners respond to this situation. During the investigation of how producers experience and act within this production culture, their professional identity and the application and reproduction of discourses of professionalism emerged as defining variables. Furthermore, it became apparent that this professional identity was based on inconsistent perceptions of self that were related to conflicting professional values. This result parallels Dover's[8] findings of contrasting values between the 'practitioner community' of British documentary makers she studied and the broadcasting culture they operated in. She noted that the shared values of creativity and craftsmanship among documentary makers can come into conflict with the demands of a commodified television culture. I observed similarly conflicting values but contend that Dover's binary of 'good' artistic documentary culture versus 'bad' commercial broadcasting culture polarizes and simplifies this relationship. Rather, I suggest we need to understand documentary (and other television genres for that matter) as one constitutive part of commercial and public service broadcasting cultures whose production is marked by ambivalent influences with regard to creativity and commerce. Accordingly, I argue that practitioners are, on one hand, integrated into the television production culture and perceive themselves as television professionals operating in a particular commodified industrial setting. On the other hand, they are committed to a particular program genre. In this case, the practitioners perceived themselves also as documentary makers dedicated to genre-related values of production and representation. These two dimensions of professional identity—industry and genre—are grounded in various, at times competing, discourses of professionalism. They determine how practitioners reflect on and evaluate their work and ultimately shape their actions and decisions. The remainder of this chapter discusses how such discourses manifest themselves with regard to independents' economic dependency and consequent editorial compliance.

Pride and Detachment: Independents as Television Professionals

Compliance with broadcaster preferences is not only structurally determined by independents' position in the broadcasting system as outlined earlier in this chapter. It is further encouraged by industry-specific perceptions of professionalism and craftsmanship, some of which are formalized and documented in broadcasting regulation and the codes of practice issued by broadcasters and media regulators such as Ofcom in the United Kingdom and the Landesmedienanstalten in Germany. Others are based on more informal knowledge, agreements, and practiced traditions developed over time. Practitioners can find it difficult to express these clearly; according to the British head of development, "they are the things that you just know." The participatory method proved useful to illuminate the informal and vague nature of such standards. The immersion in the field over a longer period of time made it possible to identify what producers considered professional and how they used these perceptions to evaluate the production culture and their role in it.

During fieldwork it became apparent that the self-understanding of independents as skilled service providers—that justifies and elevates the commercial compliance described earlier in this chapter—was supported through the association with positive professional standards. The adherence to such standards was perceived as a demonstration of competence that increases the reputation and therefore the symbolic capital of independents. The latter may contribute to a potential shift in the power relationship with broadcasters in the long term, but primarily this perception of professionalism supports commercially conformist behavior through its emphasis on professional service and execution.

To offer a professional service refers to the successful collaboration with broadcasters. This includes the delivery of completed programs within time and budget limitations, the adherence to technical specifications, legal and ethical obligations, and meeting promises and expectations with regard to program content and form. The better this collaboration is experienced by broadcasters, the greater an independent's professional reputation and the higher the chances for future commissions. The following quote illustrates the importance of and pride in delivering "without a problem," making a company an attractive partner for broadcasters:

> I don't want to sound like I'm blowing our own trumpet too much, but I think we make life easy [for commissioners]. I think, when a lot of companies deliver that kind of volume there are lots of teething problems, there're lots of problems to get the format right, or there're technical problems or legal problems or whatever. And I think what we sort of have really worked hard on doing is just delivering without a problem and really some high quality.
>
> (Executive Producer, UK)

The term 'quality' refers here to values of professional execution that concern the production value and aesthetic qualities of the created texts. For factual producers these include, among other things, investment in research and technical craftsmanship (including direction, camera, sound, and editing) that lead to programs being "nicely shot and edited" and "visually interesting" with contributors who are not just "statement givers" but rather "people who have something to tell." At first glance, this seems to ensure high-quality work that is indifferent to its commercialized setting. However, the financial pressure of budgeting constrains the extent of producers' investment in these values. Furthermore, the focus on the technical execution of a production implies an overemphasis on form that dominates over social and political values concerning the content of the produced programs. The following quote by a British executive illustrates how practitioners refer to industrial values when assessing the quality of a program they are involved in. He refers to a recent commission for a weekly factual magazine program the company had received that presented a departure from their usual focus on documentary films and series:

> Alright, people might say, "Well that's not the coolest slot on earth." Actually, we're gonna do a really good program, it's gonna have lots of proper documentary in it, it's gonna have interesting people in it—it's one of the relatively few places in British broadcasting now where you get an hour of TV every week to yourself. And that's fantastic for us.

The tone of the statement and its reference to "proper documentary" and "interesting people" reflect a sense of defensive justification for the commissioned program against accusations of a lack of social relevance. It is legitimized with reference to production values and the broadcasting economy. By focusing on a professional execution, responsibility for a lack of social relevance and impact of a project idea can be disclaimed and it still makes a "good program."

Such a focus on professional execution and service as a demonstration of competence legitimizes creative compromise and helps producers, on an individual level, to displace or dissolve aesthetic or ethical conflicts between culture and commerce by referring to seemingly objective professional and production values of the television industry. These results confirm Elliott's suggestion that by relying on professional standards, practices, and values, media producers "may distance themselves from the content and disclaim responsibility for the message."[9] This provides producers with the opportunity to emotionally detach themselves to some degree from the cultural product they create[10] and to disperse conflicts between commercial objectives and genre-related cultural and social values. In this process, the producers' identity as television professionals, materialized in perceptions of professional service and execution, reinforces and reproduces the status quo. It encourages practitioners not only to comply with broadcaster requests but also to develop a sense of pride in doing this well and according to industry-specific (technical) standards. At the same time, it enables producers to emphasize form over content and thus to ignore creative compromise with regard to the latter.

Informal Critique: Independents as Documentary Makers

Discourses of professionalism in television production do not only facilitate distancing and detachment from program content. They also contribute to the contestation of the conformity to broadcaster preferences, thus illustrating their ambivalence in determining independent practitioners' response to creativity-commerce tensions. A professional identity associated with genre as a program category—in this case documentary and serious factual programming—emerged as particularly influential in this context. While objectives of professional service and execution tend to overlap with broadcasters and independents' commercial interests, genre values emerged more frequently as opposing commercial priorities. Documentary and serious factual programming primarily aims to inform and educate and for this reason (among others) it has become a stable constituent of public service broadcasting in both studied countries, while commercial broadcasters without public service remit are much less committed to this form.[11] Although documentaries can be entertaining and attract high audience numbers, overall they are neither as popular nor as cost-effective as other forms of factual programming such as reality TV and factual entertainment. They are consequently not a program priority from a commercial perspective. As a result, producers in both case study companies developed programs predominantly for broadcasters with public service remits. In the British case this included especially the BBC and Channel 4, and to a lesser degree ITV and Channel 5, and the German company developed programs predominantly for the ARD stations and ZDF as well as transnational broadcasters 3Sat and Arte. However, commercial imperatives dominated the objectives of commissioning editors even at these stations, both with regard to cost saving and presumed audience popularity.

Although accepted as part of their identity as television professionals who operate within a commodified industry, such commercial priorities are starkly contrasted by the priorities of the observed practitioners in their identity as professional documentary makers. The role of the genre values that emerged during the fieldwork reiterates Dover's observations about the 'documentary culture' of program makers mentioned earlier in this chapter.[12] Their relevance for the producers' evaluation of their production culture relates to what Born describes in her long-term study of media production at the BBC as "reflexivities of genre," which are "characterized by particular aesthetics and ethics" and linked to the historical trajectory of program genres.[13] All of the observed workers shared the view that the potential for social impact by providing new insights and alternative perspectives of social reality is a strength of this particular genre that makes their products 'worthwhile.' This view originates in traditions that reach back to Griersons' social documentary in Great Britain and the educational *Kulturfilm* in Germany and are linked to the idea of making a contribution to the public good, more specifically, raising awareness about the state of our society. It is further supported by a broadcasting culture shaped by a strong public service mandate in both countries, which includes values that can also be found in the documentary genre. The practitioners assign special importance to the fact that their programs have a direct link to social reality—a "real-life connectedness"[14]—which, according to a British development producer, "can't be faked" and, therefore, has greater social significance: "Actually, I think it means more, because you can make anything up, can't you?" The producers value social critique and disclosure in textual representation, and giving voice to the ordinary and marginalized. The thought of "changing people's perception" and "making people think" provides the practitioners in both countries with work satisfaction and the feeling of "making a difference." Such objectives act as goals and motivating factors that constitute a defining part of their professional identity.

However, according to the program makers, commissioners are allegedly known for not wanting to be 'too political' (and program schedules seem to confirm this), which relates to the generally risk-averse commissioning culture in both countries. Social critique and activism are not particularly encouraged in the contemporary commissioning culture as it is presumed to deter television audiences. Some documentary strands dedicated to the traditional forms of the genre and its social functions[15] still exist, but their number has been substantially reduced in the past two decades. The producers lament that opportunities to produce consciousness-raising programs are increasingly rare in a more commercialized production climate. The following statement by a British executive producer with more than twenty years of experience in factual TV production illustrates this point:

> I've made films in the past that I think were worthwhile. Proper worthwhile. People would have watched them and thought, "I've seen the world differently." . . . [Y]ou know, in terms of social, economically differently but there are not many of those around these days.

The German HoD expressed similar concerns but also emphasized the fact that the passion for documentary and its generic values motivates producers to proceed in this area of production, even if this involves compliance with commercial imperatives and battling severe economic pressure:

> The aspect that one is working on press freedom, I still think that is a great thing and I think it is sad that ultimately the projects that are exciting are happening once in a blue moon. We are doing one right now, the history of the Russian mafia, where we are coproducers. These are the projects that really excite me and where I say, this is the reason for me not to leave this field.

The practitioners frequently voiced informal criticism in conversations with colleagues about broadcasters' preferences and decisions as well as the commercial motivation behind them; for instance over lunch, while making tea, in e-mail communication, and at meetings. Often, such critique was expressed in humorous form, serving to disguise and dissolve creative frustration. It became clear that practitioners are not only acutely aware but also highly critical of commercialism and its influence on broadcaster preferences. Ironic and sarcastic comments in reference to the formalized and populist orientations and preferences of broadcasters are a common feature in development work. For example, during a development meeting the British team was brainstorming ideas for an observational series for

Channel Five. After discussing various ideas, one development producer comments on the restrictive properties of the channel's preferences. To the amusement of the rest of the team, he sums up what the channel wants as "How can you cross Wildlife with Homes and make it boysy?" Criticisms about a lack of social significance in program content became evident when the British workers discussed a recent shoot for an observational documentary series about animal rescue workers in their lunch break.

> One of the stories they followed involved an elderly lady whose dog had been stolen. The team was able to witness and film when the dog was found and reunited with his owner. The emotional value of this storyline will resonate well with viewers and the producer/director therefore refers to this story ironically as "TV gold." His assistant producer joins in and remarks in a mockingly overenthusiastic tone: "We produced award-winning television, I'm telling you, award-winning television."
>
> (Field notes, UK)

A similar attitude toward their own programs was evident in the German company, for example when a producer responded to critical comments with pretended offense: "Don't be so mean about our beautiful program." The German HoD referred to the "mediocracy of television" as the main frustration of working in this industry. She blamed the "sluggish" and risk-averse attitude of commissioning editors combined with the influence of financial constraints and audience preferences. Producers in both countries expressed explicit critique of broadcasters' preferences especially when their program ideas were rejected on grounds they found hard to agree with. Such disagreement was predominantly rooted in genre values of documentary as visible in the following example:

> The British company had been approached by the BBC to develop a season of single documentaries about body image. When the commissioning editor's feedback arrived by e-mail several days later, the head of development shared its contents with the rest of the team who were keen to hear the results. All the ideas the development team considered more interesting and innovative were rejected while their program suggestions about "skinny young men" and anorexic old people, essentially a new angle to a very familiar topic, were chosen for further development by the commissioner. The workers criticized the decision on the grounds that it lacked the originality and innovation television documentary should offer—which are qualities that are not only valued by the practitioners but also by broadcasters who request original and innovative programming from independent program proposals. After several minutes of discussion and mutual disagreement with

the decision, the HoD eventually ended the conversation with the words, "She is a commissioning editor and she can say what she wants."

(Field notes, UK)

This example also highlights producers' awareness and sense of futility with regard to the disproportionate power of commissioning editors. The producers in both countries blamed broadcasters' commercial focus on ratings success and their consequent risk-averse preference for familiar patterns and light entertainment as well as the decline in social engagement and ambition in contemporary television documentary. In this context, the genre dimension of their professional identity fuels a critique that acts as a counter discourse to the justification of independents as professional service providers. This counter discourse of commercially constrained creativity emphasizes feelings of powerlessness among television workers. However, it also creates a sense of unity among the workers in an independent company based on a sense of 'us' (independents) against 'them' (broadcasters).

Managing Tensions: Reinterpretation of Genre

As I discussed earlier, professional identity in television production can justify and encourage as well as criticize commercial compliance. Critical counter discourses are subordinate to the discourse of commercial enterprise and success that encourages compliance. They rarely inspire direct action from independent producers against commercial demands. Nevertheless, the frustration about the increasingly rare opportunity to meet genre expectations in their own work compared to the dominance of commercial influences and considerations can create a dilemma for practitioners between "using one's talents for a purpose and having them used for none except the survival or commercial success of the organization for which the work is done."[16] This in turn raises the question of how producers deal with the contradictory dimensions of their professional identity. I found that in order to balance conflicting values and to reduce the resulting emotional and rational dilemma, producers performed a nuanced reinterpretation with regard to the program genre that reduces tensions between the different dimensions of their professional identity.

While industrial structures are difficult to alter on an individual level, genre interpretations have a distinct subjective quality that makes them susceptible to shifts and change. Genre theory in media scholarship does acknowledge the importance of context for textual readings, but it largely focuses on textual representation rather than on how genre relates to the production of these texts.[17] Bruun draws attention to this deficit and argues for the value of investigating genre in production studies research in order to better understand "the connections and causalities between the conditions of production and the actual products offered."[18] Fieldwork showed how practitioners respond to changes in the

broadcasting system, namely the intensified commercial prioritization in program production and development, and the resulting potential conflict, through
an adjustment of their genre interpretation. This adjustment concerns especially
those areas where reflexivities of genre are at risk of coming into conflict with
broadcaster requirements.

For example, the idea of social impact and critique as a constitutive value of
documentary remains central for program makers; however, its interpretation is
shifting gradually from the political to the personal and its extent is somewhat
toned down. The following example by a British executive producer illustrates
the changed conceptualization but continuing importance of social relevance and
impact for documentary makers in a commercialized broadcasting culture:

> One of the first films I made at First Tuesday[19] was . . . at the time of the
> South Africa Apartheid era. South Africa was hanging more people than
> anywhere in the world, sometimes seven at a time. And we went out and
> filmed secretly in South Africa with the families of those who were being
> hanged that week. What I hoped for was that it would show people, bring to
> life the human tragedies behind it rather than just a blank line in a newspaper
> or report. And I think the South African government was embarrassed by
> that; they froze the death penalty the week that that [program] went out.[20]
> . . . [Today's] equivalent in a way would be a very different film—but we
> went to make a film about a family who were in the newspapers branded as
> Britain's weirdest family, yeah, sex-changed men who were bringing up this
> little girl. . . . Far from being a kind of a condemnation of Britain's weirdest
> family [it] turned into a plea for tolerance and understanding for her family
> and I thought that is what TV should do. I was very proud of that because
> it turns expectations on its head, I guess.

As this example shows, the opportunity to represent what they consider relevant
content motivates many factual producers but the extent of their ambitions seems
reduced compared to traditional social objectives of most auteur documentaries.
First and foremost, producers perceive themselves as service providers for broadcasters rather than as authors, and dissociation from auteur and advocate filmmakers became apparent in several conversations with the research participants.
This attitude is more prominent in the British production culture, where the
commercial pressures and emphasis on television as a business are more intense.
It contributes to a shift of their professional identity to that of 'factual producers,'
which is based on a broader genre definition in contrast to being a 'documentary
maker.' The latter perception, with its emphasis on authorship and social critique,
remains stronger in the German context—for now. On the other hand, German
producers perceive British productions as more innovative but they also highlight
that these are exceptional programs within a culture that they perceive as driven

by more intense economic competition and formulaic confrontational reality television than the relatively cozy German broadcasting industry.

The reinterpretation of the social aspects and objectives of documentary and serious factual programming allows workers to integrate the different sets of values outlined earlier in this chapter and to dissolve or at least reduce the potential tension between them. It decreases producers' emotional investment and the nature of their expectations with regard to textual representation and facilitates creative compromise. But it also raises the question of whether genre values become less meaningful in the process. For example, there is a risk that social impact becomes an empty or at least vague or soft value, replaced with a pseudo-meaningfulness regarding the value of producers' work. On the other hand, one may consider this merely part of the constant evolution of genre. Independent from how we may evaluate this development, it is important to note that as producers adjust their genre interpretation, this impacts the texts they create and ultimately reinforces their amended genre schema.

Conclusion

Elliott argues that "adopting a professional identity has an impact on thought and behaviour through the development of distinct professional ideologies."[21] Professional ideologies in this context can be understood as the "belief systems developed within the profession through which the practitioners make sense of their work experience."[22] Exploring these belief systems within particular occupational contexts accordingly helps to better understand media producers' attitudes, actions, and their impact on the products they create. Using factual television production as an example, this chapter has shown how exploring professional identity can increase our understanding of media production, especially with regard to the relationship between structure and agency. It can explain how workers perceive themselves and their work, how they create and manage their occupational identities in response to industrial conditions.

Not only did the research results demonstrate the importance of professionalism discourses for the formation of media producers' professional identity. They further draw attention to the fact that this construction is not straightforward and uncontested, but instead the result of multiple competing and ambivalent discourses and their respective ideological perspectives. With regard to the compliance with commercialized broadcaster priorities and preferences, for example, professionalism, on one hand, preempts managerial control as they encourage media producers to govern themselves through mechanisms of self-control and motivation. Producers' agency in this context helps to reproduce and implement structural constraints and priorities. On the other hand, professional identity also feeds counter discourses that oppose existing structures, as the following statement illustrates:

Right from the start we filter out ideas where we think: this is a nice story, it's a great thing, but completely impossible to place here or there for various reasons. You could try, but the probability is relatively low, and why should we spend so much time on it? So you'd rather leave it, and it's a shame about the story in a sense. And maybe it could get made—that has happened—because another producer invests the time and the nerves or whatever and keeps on trying.

(Director/Company Partner, Germany)

The resulting critical reflexivity describes in itself a form of agency that may lead to a more subtle or indirect impact on creative decisions and even compensate if not alter the structural imbalance of the broadcaster–independent relationship. Therefore, a sufficient exploration of professional identities in media production should not only focus on how they support existing power structures but also on how they might contribute to a bottom-up change—if not in action, then at least in attitude.

Notes

1 When referring to 'factual television' in this chapter, I mean programs that rely on the observation of social reality with none or few elements of construction and scripting, and that are rooted in genre traditions of documentary and investigative journalism. Therefore, I exclude, first, news production, and, second, forms of factual entertainment, such as quiz, game, and talent shows or the recently popular trend of scripted reality series. They can be diverse in content and form, including one-off programs as well as serial forms, but are usually longer forms with each episode or a program lasting at least a commercial hour.

2 Development teams of researchers, producers, and assistant producers (AP) are led by the head of development (HoD), who coordinates and guides the activities of the team, in conference with the companies' executive producers. The size of project development teams varies even among middle-sized companies; it can range from a single person to whole teams in single or even double figures per company, and in some cases workers switch within a company between development and production. In my case studies the size of the team fluctuated slightly during the fieldwork period between three to five people.

3 Both countries have a large television market with similar structures including a large and competitive independent production sector and a strong presence of public service broadcasters that are decisive for the production of serious factual programming and documentaries as discussed here.

4 In the following, I apply the general term 'producer' to refer broadly to all of the practitioners in the studied development teams rather than to the occupational job title. The specific work roles of individual team members are indicated where necessary. Although the degree and nature of their involvement in program production differ, they could all be considered what David Hesmondhalgh (*The Cultural Industries*, 3rd ed., London: Sage, 2013) refers to as primary creative personnel, meaning those workers directly involved in textual production.

5 See Hesmondhalgh, *The Cultural Industries.*

6 See Anna Zoellner, "Professional Ideology and Programme Conventions: Documentary Development in Independent British Television Production." *Mass Communication and Society* 12, no. 4 (2009): 503–56.

7 Philip Elliott, "Media Organizations and Occupations: An Overview," in *Mass Communication and Society*, edited by James Curran, Michael Gurevitch, and Janet Woollacott (Beverly Hills, CA: Sage, 1977), 148.

8 Caroline Dover, "British Documentary Television Production: Tradition, Change and 'Crisis' in a Practitioner Community," PhD thesis, Goldsmiths College, University of London, 2001, unpublished.

9 Elliott, "Media Organizations and Occupations," 151.

10 Stuart Hall, "Culture, the Media and the 'Ideological Effect.'" in *Mass Communication and Society*, edited by James Curran, Michael Gurevitch, and Janet Woollacott (Beverly Hills, CA: Sage, 1977), 344.

11 The importance of this remit as market correction became highly visible after public service obligations were reduced for the commercial broadcasters ITV and Channel 5 in the United Kingdom in 2011. This led directly (and swiftly) to a reduction of documentary programming and the closure of regional production arms.

12 Dover, "British Documentary Television Production."

13 Georgina Born, "Reflexivity and Ambivalence: Culture, Creativity and Government in the BBC." *Journal for Cultural Research* 6, no. 1 (2002): 83.

14 Richard Kilborn, "Playing the Reality Card: Factual TV Programming for a New Broadcasting Age." *Zeitschrift für Anglistik und Amerikanistik* 56, no. 2 (2008): 143.

15 See John Corner for a distinction of social functions of documentary ("Performing the Real: Documentary Diversions." *Television and New Media* 3, no. 3 (2002): 255–69).

16 Elliott, "Media Organizations and Occupations," 148.

17 See, for example, Stephen Neale, *Genre* (London: British Film Institute, 1980) and *Genre and Hollywood* (London: Routledge, 1999) or the *TV Genres Series* edited by Deborah Jermyn and Su Holmes, including, for example, Misha Kavka, *Reality TV* (Edinburgh: Edinburgh University Press, 2012).

18 Hanne Bruun, "Genre and Interpretation in Production: A Theoretical Approach." *Media Culture & Society* 32, no. 5 (2010): 734.

19 *First Tuesday* was a monthly documentary strand at the British channel ITV that focused on social issues and current affairs. The strand ran from 1983 to 1993 and was broadcast on the first Tuesday of the month.

20 This is most certainly an overestimation of the program's impact, but this perception is a good example of the high impact potential documentary makers might assign to the genre.

21 Philip Elliott, *The Sociology of the Professions* (London: Macmillan, 1972), 132.

22 Elliott, *The Sociology of the Professions.*

13

CBC ARTSPOTS AND THE ACTIVATION OF CREATIVE CITIZENSHIP

Mary Elizabeth Luka

Creative citizenship proposes that creative workers in media and the arts who focus on narrowcast audiences—particularly in public broadcasting and public service—activate a fluid blend of civic and artistic approaches and tools to generate cultural media production that can be presented across a range of media platforms and venues. This chapter presents *CBC ArtSpots*—an extensive Canadian digital media, television, and exhibition project produced between 1997 and 2008—as an exemplar of the transition to a multimodal, co-creative media production and broadcasting system. *ArtSpots* was a forerunner among the prolific number and types of cultural forms that generated artist and audience innovations via digital creative works and storytelling—and although presented on a national stage, its roots were regional and its reach was international. From the archives comes evidence that *ArtSpots* aspired to conduct itself from its first days in three interlocked ways: as a value-based media production to connect the Canadian Broadcasting Corporation (CBC) *with* the culture sector, deeply invested in public cultural identity; as a collaborative, community-centered art intervention *on* public broadcasting; and as a media program drawing on traditional and emerging business practices in the field, including narrowcast citizen participation. Probing the labor involved in the *ArtSpots* television and Internet project—including my own involvement as artist-in-residence, founder, and producer—helps to foreground the relationship of art and artists to public broadcasting in the twenty-first century.

Reflections on a richly networked assemblage of insider information focus on how a decade-long, groundbreaking, 'platform-agnostic' program operated, evolved, and died, establishing a framework for creative citizenship itself. These show that the creative uptake of technology in public service institutions is crucial at a transformative moment, helping to make space for those implicated in actualizing new cultural production practices. *ArtSpots*' goals sought to create conditions for representatives from the broadcasting sector to work successfully with members of what was then emerging as a broader creative labor force, as Stuart Cunningham and Vicki Mayer suggest.[1] The residue of linked collaborations, creative interventions, skill-sharing initiatives, leveraged partnerships, and embodied memories of *ArtSpots* combines to specify the potential of activating creative citizenship. *ArtSpots* as a program staked out a space on the World Wide Web for media producers and broadcasters, culture curators, and the institutional partners involved, but exceptionally, for artists during the transition from analog to digital broadcasting.

This chapter addresses two time spans. The first is the *ArtSpots* 'era,' incorporating its genesis and production, from 1997–2008. The second time period spans 2010–14, including reflective interviews involving former participants. During the original *ArtSpots* production period, approximately 300 interviews were conducted with Canadian artists across the country to develop content for television, digital, or exhibition purposes. During 2010–14, a number of original *ArtSpots* interviews and materials were accessed. I also conducted new interviews and discussion groups between 2010 and 2012 with thirty-two participants, including twenty-five with previous *ArtSpots* experience. Interview material from both eras was used to generate themes and insights through traditional and emerging qualitative methodologies including archival document and transcript analysis, video editing, and multimodal reflections for publication online. Digital software was mobilized to help generate subthemes arising from the emerging concept of creative citizenship. My research places equity concerns shaped by a feminist stance in a central position, including identity politics, social activism, civic engagement, and public broadcasting as a public service.

Production Methods and Interventions

The remnants of *ArtSpots* that can be seen on TV, in the archival documentation, and on the Internet shimmer brightly as suggestive indicators of a large, vibrant network of over 1,000 artists, curators, and arts-related producers, commenters, and presenters that took place using public broadcasting resources in a ten-year period. The networked relationships between local and national production and distribution nodes of activity were crucially shaped by policy commitments to equity and to sharing knowledge. The public broadcast mandate called for regional and cultural reflection and *ArtSpots* sought to activate the mandate by developing a hybrid consultative model for artist selection through its volunteer expert curatorial advisory groups and shared creative control with the artists involved. My interest in examining the *ArtSpots* case stems from recognition that my involvement in the regional operation of public television made me privy to distinctive creative media production practices. This was not limited to the *ArtSpots* project, but was shaped by it, and contextualized by my extensive work with CBC's Atlantic region program development. I facilitated the collaborative development and production of programs in a number of genres, each telling stories and developing talent in different ways, for regional and national audiences. The innovative professional and creative practices that came to be known as *ArtSpots* were generated by a combination of systemic conditions, individual agency, ongoing negotiations, and creative work. Despite its positioning as a professional media program, *ArtSpots*' beginnings during an artist residency raise interesting considerations about intellectual property and creative media production at the public broadcaster at the time. It is clear from archived notes from the fall of 1997 that my artist residency was the core development phase for the project, including the articulation of a pluralistic mandate, value statements, and artist selection criteria, and the formation of the first advisory group. Actual production first took place while I was a temporary employee for CBC in 1998, under a standard contract giving CBC copyright in the media materials produced, so the concept for the project remains my intellectual property, while the program material is CBC's.

That first phase of production early in 1998 set the tone for how to mobilize the creative resources and practices available at the public broadcaster. Multiyear plans held in the formal archives and the 2010–14 research interviews confirm the temporary, often part-time nature of the work of those involved as employees and freelance personnel, as well as the knowledge-sharing practices at play. Key personnel such as local producer-directors and crew members were hired as freelance employees or assigned on a piecework basis to produce the television and Internet content required. My archived notebooks—from the unpaid months of development work in 1997 through the next seven years of often short-term renewable contracts and the last three years of 'permanent' employment at CBC—illustrate how the industry shifted during that time period. On average, I was employed on *ArtSpots*-related work for about half the time most years, except for a three-year period around 2001–4, when several full-time contracts were signed almost back to back, mostly to work on *ArtSpots*. The amount of content generated and shared across several platforms during each of these time periods reflects the variable levels of employment commitments to all the individuals involved.

Initially, *ArtSpots* took the form of thirty-second interstitial 'spots' played during unused commercial breaks on television. These were the only regional broadcast times available in the late 1990s on an irregular but generous basis. They made possible the creation of a marginal space within which creative media producers and artists could intervene consistently in television programming, and experiment with the presentation of artwork on the World Wide Web. My initial idea to blend regional broadcast programming structured like PSAs with the history of video art intrusions into regular broadcast programming was meant to tell visual stories about art and artists. In hindsight, the precarious nature of this marginal scheduling commitment also contained the seeds of its demise: without a regular timeslot, it was difficult to gain a regular television following, despite its heavy use on the Internet. But that a group of individuals involved was able, in the fall of 1997, to seize this opportunity and fill a creative, productive space with it for so long, warrants further discussion. Each spot featured artwork selected by a particular artist, and each artist's work was featured on three or more thirty-second items. Artists were identified and prioritized for selection by expert curators who volunteered for regional advisory groups. They were provided with a nominal license fee for the use of their artworks, creative input throughout production, and a veto over the media material produced. Local arts producers were hired or assigned to work co-creatively with the artists, mobilizing regional CBC production crews to generate material for television and Internet broadcast. Within *ArtSpots'* first year, the CBC.ca/ArtSpots Web site was in development to highlight video, text, and still images at a time when few artists had their own Web sites, and few Web sites featured video. By 1999, *ArtSpots* began producing short profiles of artists (two to five minutes), full-length documentaries, and archival and exhibition content used by galleries, schools, and other artists, as well as on CBC.ca/ArtSpots, eventually involving more than 300 artists. It also participated in institutional partnerships involving specific audiences interested in cultural content. As production ceased in 2008, almost none of the video links work on the Web site, but a multitude of other fragments remains, sometimes appearing sporadically on late-night CBC television. The last of the explicitly arts-centric 'mandate' programs of the time, the project's final act was the formation of a fulsome archive. Although inaccessible except by contracted agreement, 700 field tapes, a sixty-five-tape master set of all the edited *ArtSpots* materials, several boxes of documentation, and two backup drives live on at CBC's corporate archives in Toronto. Numerous additional original master tapes and a copy of *ArtSpots* field tapes are held in the CBC Halifax program library as current and historical programming.

ArtSpots was seen as an important center for galvanizing an otherwise factory-like environment of television production by bringing artistically trained professionals into contact with it. Fred Mattocks, then regional director of TV at CBC Maritimes, notes:

> I asked [a] question when you arrived: How do we explore the question of the intersection of the art world with this factory that we run here. And given the medium that is television, how do we connect aesthetically based expression with this in a way that an audience will enjoy. . . . And you identified very early on, that one core value. . . . The whole notion of curation. And it turned out to be very powerful.
>
> (Personal interview, February 7, 2012)

Comments like these during the 2010–14 research suggest the iterative and pliable nature of creativity through direct artist involvements with television. These comments are consistent with Lynn Spigel's history of artists' interventions in television design and hosting in North America, and Mayer's broadening of creative resistance in production to include those building devices required to view the content (e.g., TV factory workers in Brazil) and the motivation of aspirational amateurs (e.g., soft pornography videographers in New Orleans).[2] As both scholars suggest, strategic emplacement of artists and creative workers in disruptive or developmental positions in industrial media production environments has long been associated with changes in production approaches.

Observations about the *ArtSpots* chronology also emerged through the process of sifting my own narrative of intervention *as an artist* in the television environment in Canada. In a recent multimedia interview, I reflect on the creative business practices involved in the ten-year trajectory of the *ArtSpots* production period.[3] From 1997 when work began on the concept, to early 1998 when the first pieces were produced, to mid-1999 when the Web site became operational, there was a clear transition from analog to digital production. By 2000, *ArtSpots* was officially a national program with a home more or less in the Arts and Entertainment Department, but even that ebbed and flowed over time. Annual regional contributions of editing and camera equipment (and often personnel) meant *ArtSpots* could maintain production levels at higher levels than that possible with resources from Arts and Entertainment alone, even though it was a lot of work to negotiate up to a dozen internal resource providers each year. By 2004–5, the multimodal project was as big as it was going to get, with production in about eight regional centers a year. And then a series of cutbacks that happened to the arts at CBC between 2005 and 2008 squeezed *ArtSpots* into nonexistence.

Narratives of Knowledge Sharing and Collaboration

Strategies of content development, content sharing, and knowledge sharing as elements of creative citizenship clearly articulate how *ArtSpots* built toward co-creation in the media industry. Piecing together the history of the *ArtSpots* show bible and later 'how to' manuals through visits to the archives was augmented by interview discussions about skill sharing during 2010–14. Written in 1998, the show bible was circulated in hardcopy form and on the CBC's intranet (the internal-use-only Web site). The bible documented the creative and logistical processes used to create relationships with the cultural community, internal CBC constituents, and the artists involved. It provided examples of administrative forms including waivers and contracts. Every second year, a strategy conference held for the Web and TV content producer-directors reviewed audience research, creative approaches, and logistical challenges, influencing later editions of the bible. Later, material drawn from the bible was made public on the *ArtSpots* Web site through the 'How To' feature (including seven videos) and a feature celebrating projects involving students in Alberta and Nova Scotia.[4] Part media literacy, part artistic training, and part team-building exercises, these educational initiatives served as outreach and audience engagement, emerging from public service elements of the broadcast mandate. The 'democratizing' of knowledge that *ArtSpots*' text and video instructions provide on the Internet is consistent with its foundations in shared creative control, and precursors of the massive growth of 'how to' videos that populate YouTube, DIY specialty Web sites, and digital device software applications now. Reflecting an attempt to spark what Axel Bruns was then starting to name 'produsage,' the uploading of material created by students outside the CBC was a crucial developmental moment in *ArtSpots* production, which activated students as narrowcast audiences and co-creators.[5]

ArtSpots is often compared to the Public Broadcasting Services (PBS) program *Art in the 21st Century* or *Art21* in the United States, a television project founded in 2001 featuring visual artists in their studios.[6] *ArtSpots* participants from both time periods (1997–2008 and 2010–14) remarked on *Art21*'s superior profile in the North American art education system compared to *ArtSpots*, including a group of students interviewed at NSCAD University in 2012. Interestingly, to match *ArtSpots*' output on a population basis, *Art21* would need to feature the work of 3,000 artists rather than the 100 they involved. I draw attention to this project to contrast it with the relative accomplishments of the creative citizenship-based efforts of *ArtSpots*. The NSCAD students' assumptions about being able to work in collaborative media production environments is reinforced by *ArtSpots* and *Art21*, precursors to the uploading of co-creative work to YouTube, Vimeo, Tumblr, and other social media networks. The present-day global availability of content about artist production processes and material outcomes means that these students cannot readily conceive of a time when programs such as *ArtSpots* and *Art21* would have been seen as sorely needed.

In 2007, *ArtSpots* programming was installed as part of the international NeoCraft scholar/practitioner conference held in Halifax at NSCAD University. An *ArtSpots* experimental production documented artists and curators affiliated with the conference, incorporating walkthroughs of exhibitions and a one-day turnaround of content uploaded to the *ArtSpots* Web site. This simulation of user-generated content, still employing professional producers and camera operators, held promise for future user-generated content for the then-imminent *ArtSpots* database. In combination with student-based 'how to' projects, this production initiative implied the increasing potential for sharing knowledge and skills with independent creative producer-directors and digital media practitioners. So did *ArtSpots*' decade of licensing shared intellectual property management with artists, and Creative Commons–like agreements between narrowcasters and artists. This scenario suggests a potentially more positive outcome in the middle ground between John Caldwell's concept of worker-generated content (i.e., piecework content experienced professionals deliver for low fees in increasingly precarious conditions), Bruns' concept of the aspirational producer making user-generated content for free, and Mayer's amateur-to-professional soft pornography videographers to producer-directors.[7]

A closer look at the creative process involved in generating *ArtSpots* helps to 'know the material' through narratives of innovative collaboration, providing insights about the production of art in Canada, then and now. Facilitated sessions with volunteer expert advisory groups provided curatorial insights into trends and practices in each region, establishing priorities (e.g., genres, demographics, emerging, and established, etc.) and identifying lists of artists who addressed these concerns. Artists were contacted well in advance of shoot days, selected the work, weighed in on concepts and notes, participated in shoots, and had a veto over the final edited items. Building toward what would become theories of co-creation in the emerging Internet era, including those of William Uricchio, James Hay, and Nick Couldry, the co-management of creative control by the individual artists/subjects and production crews reflects the limits of the time in broadcasting, and the increasing precarity of the creative workers involved.[8] While Uricchio focuses on producer/consumer relations in his exploration of co-creation and cultural citizenship, and Hay and Couldry highlight the relationship of imperfect democratic practices to the employment of convergence theory as an analytical tool concerning power relations, my analysis of *ArtSpots* emphasizes the direct relationships to the content produced and distributed in the activation of creative citizenship as well as the increasingly nuanced precarity of creative workers evident in the networked relations and practices among *ArtSpots* artists, curators, producers, and narrowcast audiences.

The advertisement-length 'spots' unlocked the door to everything else that *ArtSpots* became involved in, while the short interview profiles documented a dialogue about the arts in Canada that found further purchase in more complex documentary and exhibition projects for broadcast and gallery exhibitions, as well as a digital home on a Web site featuring substantial quantities of curated videos. The commitment to regional and national reflection through localized experiences of working with the public broadcaster was seen to contribute to ethical identification, selection, and production practices at *ArtSpots*. As I argue elsewhere, for artists, technicians, and producer-directors alike, *ArtSpots* became a site for a specific set of flows (professional relations) advancing the arts discourse of the time.[9] Mattocks reiterates the importance of instigating a collaborative approach by emphasizing connections with key narrowcast audiences through *ArtSpots*:

> We renovated, in one year, the CBC's relationship with the arts community. And we had entrée into rooms at The Canada Council [for the Arts] and other places that we'd just simply never had before . . . what they saw was a broadcaster engaging on an artistic and aesthetic level, and that's something they never imagined that they would see.
>
> (Personal interview, February 7, 2012)

Although such endorsements concerning *ArtSpots*' impact are characteristic of many of the former participants in the project, it wasn't an entirely open innovation experience at *ArtSpots*, nor did the approaches used always work collaboratively. The difficulties of finding a permanent TV timeslot proved an important limitation, as did the lack of a database for the growing amount of Web-based materials. There were also limits on how production work could involve artists inside the CBC buildings, including the use of studios or artists attending edit sessions. This was particularly pronounced in Montreal and Toronto, the two largest production centers with the greatest resources and the most complicated operating protocols:

> There were limits to what you could do, and I think that disappointed some of the artists. Well, first of all, budgetary constraints, and the fact that you couldn't be more spontaneous or improvise. The crew that had to come in nine to five, they had to have a one-hour lunch break. It was hard to execute the more challenging ideas.
>
> (Karina Garcia Casanova, personal interview, February 12, 2012)

The complex budgeting and resource management process at *ArtSpots* included a staffing structure marked by the use of freelance and temporary workers both inside and outside CBC, presenting growing challenges for building a cohesive, consistent work unit over time. These findings are synchronous with Caldwell's observations about 'worker-generated content' based on an increasingly precarious, piecemeal position within the media industry, as well as CBC's most recent budget and staffing cuts.[10]

Conclusion

The creative content development and knowledge-sharing practices developed within *ArtSpots* are an example of creative citizenship in action. An evaluation of these practices at *ArtSpots* offers insights into engagements in production and distribution through co-creation, often with narrowcast audiences. Growing a networked base of creative workers' social and professional relationships had produced a great deal of content. Iterations varied from platform to venue, including long-form documentaries, Web projects, and gallery exhibitions, on top of the core material of thirty-second spots and two-to-five-minute interview profiles. When things were working well, the expansion of forms of creative content connected *ArtSpots* to histories of television and visual arts and their interactive and distribution practices, as well as to emerging practices involving audiences. The linked nature of the audiences involved was supported by the discrete set of collegial professional relationships among individual artists, advisory groups, production crews, the *ArtSpots* producer-directors themselves, and a distinctive set of institutional relationships, inside and outside CBC. Budget and maintenance decision making at CBC since *ArtSpots* ceased production in 2008 has resulted in broken links or the actual removal of content from CBC servers developed for use in perpetuity as part of the public service offering based on the broadcasting mandate of the time. Probing *ArtSpots* as a dynamic hub of networked activity in the broader cultural community over an extended period suggests how broad the scope was at the time for discourses about civic engagement in creativity and the production of visual culture-based meaning in Canada. Finally, *ArtSpots* helped bridge visual arts and broadcasting in Canada and advance forms of co-creative digital media production and dissemination, indicating the deeply engaged position of CBC at the time as a proponent of experimental work in the production of creative citizenship. A Social Sciences and Humanities Research Council Vanier Canada Graduate Scholarship supported this research.

Notes

1 Stuart Cunningham, *Hidden Innovation: Policy, Industry and the Creative Sector* (Brisbane: Queensland University Press, 2013); Vicki Mayer, *Below the Line: Producers and Production Studies in the New Television Economy* (Durham, NC and London: Duke University Press, 2011).

2 Lynn Spigel, *TV by Design: Modern Art and the Rise of Network Television* (Chicago, IL and London: University of Chicago Press, 2008); Mayer, *Below the Line*.

3 Mél Hogan and Mary Elizabeth Luka, "Archiving *ArtSpots* with Mary Elizabeth Luka." *No More Potlucks* 25 (2013). http://nomorepotlucks.org/site/archiving-ArtSpots-with-mary-elizabeth-luka-mel-hogan/.

4 CBC.ca/ArtSpots Web site. www.cbc.ca/artspots/html/features/how_to/ and http://www.cbc.ca/artspots/html/features/highschoolproject/.

5 Axel Bruns, *Blogs, Wikipedia, Second Life, and Beyond (Digital Formations)* (New York: Peter Lang Publishing Inc., 2008).

6 Art21 Web site. www.pbs.org/art21/.

7 John T. Caldwell, "Worker Blowback: User-Generated, Worker-Generated and Producer-Generated Content with Collapsing Production Workflows," in *Television as Digital Media*, edited by James Bennett and Nikki Strange (Durham, NC and London: Duke University Press, 2011), 283–310; Bruns, *Blogs, Wikipedia, Second Life, and Beyond*; Mayer, *Below the Line*.

8 James Hay and Nick Couldry, "Rethinking Convergence/Culture." *Cultural Studies* 25, no. 4–5 (2011): 473–86; William Uricchio, "Beyond the Great Divide: Collaborative Networks and the Challenge to the Dominant Conceptions of Creative Industries." *International Journal of Cultural Studies* 7, no. 1 (2004): 79–90. http://ics.sagepub.com.

9 Mary Elizabeth Luka, "Mapping *CBC ArtSpots*," in *Diverse Spaces: Examining Identity, Heritage and Community within Canadian Public Culture*, edited by Susan Ashley (Newcastle upon Tyne: Cambridge Scholars Publishing, 2013), 124–47.

10 James Bradshaw, "CBC Plans Massive Staff Cuts as It Shifts to Mobile-First Strategy," *The Globe and Mail*, June 26, 2014. www.theglobeandmail.com.

V
TRANSNATIONAL CIRCUITS

14

AVENUES OF PARTICIPATION AND STRATEGIES OF CONTROL

Video Film Production and Social Mobility in Ethiopia and Southern Nigeria

Alessandro Jedlowski

The introduction of VHS technologies in the late 1970s and the early 1980s radically transformed the landscape of media production, distribution, and consumption throughout sub-Saharan Africa. Within this context, film production emerged as an affordable and attractive economic activity for an increasingly larger section of the local population, and myriad low-budget video film production ventures saw the light all over the continent. Besides the cases of Nigeria and Ghana, which have been the objects of numerous studies,[1] this phenomenon developed in many less investigated contexts, such as Tanzania, Kenya, Ethiopia, Cameroon, and Uganda, just to mention the most relevant cases. As for the introduction of other new media technologies such as mobile phones and the Internet, the emergence of video film production generated a wave of both academic and journalistic enthusiasm. This was connected to the idea that, in societies considered (from a Western point of view) as generally lacking freedom of expression, the introduction of these technologies would provoke an acceleration in processes of democratic transformation and an increase in the chances for upward social mobility.[2] But, as Monica Chibita among others has emphasized, "linguistic minorities, the poor and women continue to be excluded either at the level of ownership, or due to lack of the material and symbolic resources to participate fully in the new media bonanza."[3]

While much debate on the penetration of new media technologies does not ignore the ambiguous position they occupy in relation to power and politics, within the context of the scholarship on African video film production, the recurrent use of concepts such as 'African popular culture' and 'informality' has often hidden the complex intertwining between the opportunities for democratic participation that this emerging production has created, and the forms of political control and economic marginalization that it has equally helped in consolidating. Both concepts are the object of complex and controversial debates within the field of African studies whose discussion goes beyond the scope of this chapter. In general terms, however, it is possible to say that they are both implicitly grounded on hard-to-define attributes such as horizontality and openness that risk masking existing forms of exclusion, particularly in relation to access to the means of production. As Ramon Lobato pointed out, the International Labour Organization's (ILO) definition of informality considers 'ease of entry' as one of its defining features.[4] Within this context, informality is often "hailed as an act of free speech."[5] When applied to the study of film production in Africa, this definition creates a problematic confusion between the increase in possibilities of accessing media content that the introduction of new technologies fostered, and the transformation in the accessibility to media production processes that these same technologies have provoked. As Fredric Cooper suggested in his article on Karin Barber's seminal work on African popular arts, "just as economists' labelling certain activities as the informal sector has all too often led them away from analysing the highly structured patterns of behaviour that go on within such a domain, the label 'popular arts' can serve to obscure the particularity of the processes by which art is produced and meanings conveyed."[6] The 'African popular culture' concept, even when attentively and thoroughly scrutinized, is hardly able to avoid hiding some of the social, political, and economic processes of differentiation and exclusion that define the specificity of cultural production in contemporary sub-Saharan Africa. Furthermore, in many cases, African film producers seem to have appropriated, not without a certain degree of legitimacy, the generally optimistic perspective about the potential held by the recent explosion in video film production all over the continent for the 'liberation' of African people from neocolonial and postcolonial forms of oppression.[7]

In relation to this context, by applying an ethnographic approach to the study of film production, this chapter examines specific examples of "production cultures"[8] that highlight the ambiguous position digital film production occupies in Africa between, on one hand, the creation of new avenues of economic and social mobility, and, on the other, the emergence of strategies of exclusion and control. With a few exceptions,[9] the emerging field of production studies has dealt mainly with the analysis of Western film industries, thus leaving out of its radar the wide range of experiences that has developed over the past few years around the African continent. This chapter intends, then, to address this gap by making an attempt to look at the growing African digital film production industries through the lens of production studies, and by pointing out the specificities of the production cultures that have emerged within this context. This is done through the analysis of two specific case studies, Ethiopia and southern Nigeria, where I conducted fieldwork between 2009 and 2014.

My focus is twofold. On one hand, I look at the way film industries' professionals in Addis Ababa and Lagos construct themselves as a self-confined, elitist group through a set of "media rituals" such as film premieres and award ceremonies.[10] These rituals, which serve both marketing objectives and self-celebratory intentions, are based on specific rules of inclusion and exclusion that highlight the increasingly gated nature of the video film business community in these contexts. On the other hand, I analyze the way these video film industries, often celebrated for having emerged beyond or despite governmental intervention, entertain ambiguous relationships with forms of political patronage, in some cases directly connected to, in other cases less overtly related to, the central government's regulatory activity. The work presented here implicitly responds to the call for an interdisciplinary approach to the study of media production that characterizes much scholarship in production studies. Accordingly, the analysis it presents is based on a variety of data that includes interviews with key industry players, participant observation during production processes and professional gatherings, archival materials, and more general economic and industrial analysis.[11]

Film Premieres, Award Ceremonies, and the "Gating" of the Film Production Community

In both Nigeria and Ethiopia, the emergence of marketing events such as film premieres and award ceremonies has paralleled the development of the local film production sector. While antecedents of this kind of event were organized in both countries in relation to the success of the theatre and music industries, and in connection to previous forms of celluloid film production, the contemporary film premiere format emerged only recently thanks to the birth and growth of the video film phenomenon. According to Jonathan Haynes and Onokoome Okome, the release of Amaka Igwe's *Violated* (1995) marked one of the first appearances of the film premiere strategy in relation to Nollywood: "the venue for the opening was the MUSON Centre, the most prestigious and exclusive performance hall in Lagos. Opening night was by invitation only, the invitations being addressed to the elite of Victoria Island and Ikoyi."[12] In Ethiopia, the trend emerged more recently, with one of the first and most glamorous of such events being the release of Theodros Teshome's *Abay vs Vegas* (2009). The film was premiered at the Addis Ababa National Theatre, and simultaneously screened (for the entire day) in all cinema theatres around the country, with the red carpet ceremony screened live on national television for one hour.[13] A similar historical itinerary applies to the emergence of award ceremonies, an event format that also has various antecedents connected to other art forms in both countries, and that has established itself as a major ritual of Nigerian and Ethiopian filmmaking business communities over the past few years. If the African Movie Academy Awards (AMAA)[14] are surely the most internationally visible among these kinds of events around the continent,

Figure 14.1 Red carpet session during the premiere of *Tsenu Kala* (2014). Photo by Adriano Marzi.

countless similar award ceremonies have seen the light in both Nigeria and Ethiopia over the past few years.

During my research I assisted at many such events, but it is in Ethiopia that I participated in the most glamorous of them all, the premiere of Thomas Getachew's most recent production, *Tsenu Kala* (2014). The event took place in the Sheraton Addis, the most reputed and expensive hotel in Ethiopia, and Getachew, one of the most visible and successful Ethiopian film producers, organized it carefully. A VIP reception room was available, in which recognized members of the filmmaking community could gather, chat, and have a drink before the beginning of the film. While the event was scheduled to start at 5 P.M., most VIPs started arriving around 6:30 P.M., only to move directly to the VIP room, while invited members of the audience (admission was invitation only) sat in the screening room. Around 8 P.M., the stars (including reputed actors, directors, and producers) began to leave the VIP room to reach the screening venue, but only after going through the red carpet while being filmed and interviewed on a live TV program created for the event (Figure 14.1). The process took around one and a half hours, and the film screening started around 9:30 P.M., that is, almost five hours after the first audience members had begun to take their seats in the screening room. The venue was separated into two parts, the front one accessible only to stars and authorized journalists, and the back one for the rest of the audience, composed of aspiring filmmakers and industry practitioners, and members of the audience invited to the premiere. As a matter of fact, both the temporal and the spatial separation between the inner industry circle and its outskirts were clearly marked throughout the duration of the event.

While the premiere's structure does not differ much from that of other events of this kind around the world, what makes it relevant to this analysis is its radical contrast with the everyday life of most members of both the filmmaking community and the audience. If a few film professionals have achieved a significant level of economic success, most still belong to the Ethiopian middle and lower middle classes, which live on an average income of between 50 and 200 USD a month.[15] The premiere experience, in this sense, is a strongly decontextualized ritual that serves the purpose of making the difference between the inside and the outside of the industry visible, within a context in which such a boundary is still largely invisible in both social and economic terms. Through premiere events of this kind, a 'young' filmmaking community such as the Ethiopian (and to a lesser extent the Nigerian) one shies away from the average populace that looks at the film industry not just as a fan would, but also with a mixture of jealousy and frustration, something like 'I, rather than you, should be there!' As John Sullivan underlines discussing Leo Rosten's depiction of early Hollywood, in the industry's early years "those who were successful ... were perceived to be there because of their luck rather than because of some talent or tenacity."[16] In such a situation, beyond pursuing marketing objectives, attentively crafted rituals such as the premieres also function as strategies of differentiation through which film professionals belonging to an industry still in search of full economic, social, and political legitimization operate a form of self-objectification. Through this process, the industry's elite consciously "promote [its] own celebrity through extravagant spending"[17] and these highly public performances implicitly isolate (in social and economic terms) the film production community from the people who hope, one day, to become part of it, as well as from its audiences.

A similar analysis could be applied to the film premieres and award ceremonies I attended in Nigeria. A brief example from this context can develop the discussion further. In February 2011, I had the chance to participate in an awards ceremony organized by the Nigerian entertainment newspaper *City People* to celebrate the fifteen-year career of highly successful Nigerian film producer Emem Isong. This ceremony, restricted only to invited members of the video film industry, took place at a time in which Nollywood was just beginning to recover from a production impasse that had forced many out of the business.[18] Within this context, Isong was seen as one of the most successful producers, one of the few to be able to survive the crisis. Many professionals were eager to work with her because her presence on a production project seemed to ensure commercial success. Because of this, rumors started spreading in the industry about some sort of 'Emem Isong clique,' a group of successful actors and directors who were considered associated with Isong on the basis of secret ties aimed at ousting other competitors from the business.[19] In particular, by having created her own distribution outlet, Isong had attracted mistrust and jealousy from the powerful 'marketers' who had ruled the industry's economy since its beginnings.[20] These marketers had recently been affected by the crisis and by attempts made by governmental bodies to reform the industry's economic structure.[21] Emem Isong's ceremony, with its carefully restricted access, functioned in this case as a ritual to consolidate a smaller elite within the larger Nigerian filmmaking environment, within a context in which, because of the crisis, commercial competition had become harder and nastier.

David Karnes detected "certain potentially subversive forces within the fantasy-reality dynamics of movie culture" that played out through 1920s Hollywood film premieres' "carnivalesque style,"[22] but in contemporary Ethiopia and Nigeria, the film premieres and award ceremonies discussed here seem to serve a different objective. If they undoubtedly have the primary goal of making the industry visible to the public, and the film it promotes more attractive to audiences, they also play an implicit and strategic role in delimiting the boundaries of young industries that have yet to acquire full legitimacy. As Nick Couldry suggested, media rituals "do not so much express order, as naturalize it. They formalize categories, and the differences or boundaries between categories, in performances that help them seem natural, even legitimate."[23] In this sense, the rituals discussed here help legitimate who is in and who is out, who can rightly claim to be part of the film business and who cannot, thus actively participating in the "gating" of the filmmaking community while making this process look natural to the eyes of the people left at the margins of the industry.

Video Film Industries and the State: Autonomy, Control, Ruse, and Infiltration

As emphasized earlier, the development of video film production around the continent has generally been seen as disconnected from government intervention and control. This is partially true in both the Nigerian and the Ethiopian cases in the sense that neither of the two industries has received (at least in their early years) any substantial economic or infrastructural support from the state. But the answer changes if we look at the way governments have attempted to regulate the two industries and at how industry members have tried to manipulate or infiltrate regulatory efforts in order to gain a powerful position within the industry's economic environment, a position that could then help them define the rules of access to the filmmaking business. Before discussing specific examples from both contexts, it is important to underline the profound differences in the ways that state sovereignty is implemented in Nigeria and Ethiopia. Too numerous are the historical, political, and economic differences between the two countries to be meaningfully addressed here. It is enough to say that while both Nigeria and Ethiopia are federal states, central government control is generally much more strongly felt in Ethiopia than in Nigeria. If in Ethiopia the state seems to make an attempt to control every aspect of the social, economic, and political life of its subjects, in Nigeria it seems concerned mainly with the control (and exclusive exploitation) of existing economic resources (oil in particular), and tends to leave much larger space to the proliferation of all sorts of informal and autonomous economic and even political activities. In relation to video film production, these differences manifest themselves in various ways.

In Ethiopia, for instance, it is routine to find members of the ruling party in key industry positions. Both the president and the general manager of the powerful Ethiopian Audio-visual Producers Association, which brings together all audio-visual producers and distributors in the country, are long-time members of the ruling Ethiopian People's Revolutionary Democratic Front (EPRDF). While they are also directly involved in film production and distribution through their own private companies, they occupy a central position in the industry's structure and constitute two of the main interlocutors mediating between the industry and the government. A slightly different situation characterizes the position of the Ethiopian Producers Association's president. In fact, he is not only one of the biggest producers in the country. He also owns the largest number of private cinema halls in Ethiopia, thus playing a particularly influential role in defining the success or failure of a new release within the context of a distribution system that, unlike the straight-to-video model developed by Nollywood and other African video film industries, gets most of its revenues from theatrical release.[24] This powerful position, together with the quite explicitly nationalistic contents of some of the films he has produced, such as *Qey Sihtet* (2006) and *Abay vs Vegas* (2009), generated rumors, both within and outside the industry, about his connection with government officials.[25] Similar rumors circulate in relation to other powerful players in the filmmaking business, creating within the industry the general perception that the more you align yourself with the government's agenda, the easier and more successful your job as a producer will become, the stronger your ability to define the boundaries of the filmmaking business will be.

In Nigeria, things have evolved in a slightly different way. In the industry's initial years, the government did not make particular efforts to regulate or infiltrate video film production. Beyond the creation of the National Film and Video Censors Board, no other regulatory body was put in place, and no influential connections between film producers and the government could meaningfully be identified.[26] But crucially, things changed in the following years. While, on one hand, film professionals organized themselves into a number of guilds representing different industry professionals (marketers, producers, directors, actors, and so on), the government increasingly attempted to regulate (and limit) the guilds' power in order to acquire a key role as the industry's regulator. According to many film professionals, within this framework, the guilds have transformed themselves into gatekeepers that define the rules and the standards for newcomers to the

Figure 14.2 Idumota film market in Lagos, Nigeria, in October 2010. Photo by Anouk Batard.

business while implicitly protecting the privileged position of those who entered the industry first. As an aspiring Nigerian filmmaker I interviewed during my research underlined, "if you want your film to be accepted for distribution, they ask you to become a member of a number of guilds [in his case as a director, producer, and distributor], and it will cost you a lot of money, and it will waste a lot of your time . . . if you don't pay, or if you don't have any influential friend inside the industry, there are no chances for your film to see the light."[27]

This dynamic has reached a particularly critical level in relation to the marketers' guilds, which have played a controversial role in the negotiation of the enforcement of a new distribution framework by the National Film and Video Censors Board (NFVCB).[28] As much literature about Nollywood underlines, marketers have occupied a pivotal role in the emergence and extraordinary growth of the Nigerian video film industry. They were in fact those who first invested in production and those who, thanks to their experience with the distribution of pirated content, could already count on effective networks for the circulation of VHSs, and later VCDs and DVDs, around the country (Figure 14.2).[29] Their economic and political power within the industry (and particularly that of the main guild representing them, the Film and Video Producers and Marketers Association of Nigeria—FVPMAN) grew exponentially over the years and today the marketers "who began Nollywood also control it, as their control over distribution through informal and opaque networks gives them a level of power that is difficult to penetrate and even more difficult to usurp."[30] When, in the second half of the 2000s, the government made an attempt to regulate film distribution and limit marketers' influence, it faced major resistance. After a long and difficult negotiation, which brought the two main parties (NFVCB and FVPMAN) to court against each other, the marketers' guild managed to water down the governmental intervention, and progressively transformed it into an institutional mechanism to (at least partially) legitimate the marketers' dominant position as industry gate-keepers.[31] The Motion Picture Council of Nigeria (MOPICON) bill, a new bill drafted over the past few years by the government with the support (and active involvement) of key industry practitioners, and close to its final approval at the time this chapter was being written, further confirms this trend. The bill is supposed to establish an industry council whose explicit function would be that of regulating, through a licensing system, the entry to the filmmaking sector on the basis of a set of principles defined by the same elite that rules the industry today. While some, both within and outside the industry, welcomed the initiative and saw it as corrective to the excesses of unprofessionalism and adventurism existing in the industry,[32] others considered it a dangerous attempt to further restrict access to the filmmaking business, "legitimizing an elite and depriving the industry of the creativity that fresh talent can bring."[33]

Toward the "Gentrification" of Video Film Production in Nigeria and Ethiopia

As the examples discussed throughout this chapter highlight, and contrary to how video film production in sub-Saharan Africa is generally portrayed, in both Nigeria and Ethiopia, access to the local production environment is becoming increasingly exclusive. This is not to deny that some degree of openness exists, or that filmmaking in these countries can offer possibilities for upward social mobility. Rather, what this chapter has shown is that strategies toward the creation of more rigid entry points and more recognizable boundaries are being elaborated in a bid to affirm and protect economic and social privileges acquired over the years by a restricted elite of film practitioners. In most cases (but not always), this elite corresponds to the group of people who initiated the video film business in the country. These boundary-making processes are somehow similar to those identified by scholars in media studies and production studies but they are the result of specific local factors that need to be considered. Over the past few years, the Nigerian and Ethiopian video film industries have been able to achieve great economic success within contexts affected, throughout most of the 1980s and 1990s, by a severe economic crisis and a general increase in youth unemployment. As a result, the film sector and all the professional categories connected to it have come to represent new figures of economic and social success.[34] While film stars and well-known directors occupy the first pages of Nigerian and Ethiopian newspapers, they are only the tip of the iceberg of this phenomenon. A much larger group of people has found work in the film production sector over the past few years in both countries and, even if often working in conditions much less attractive than those portrayed by fanzines and entertainment magazines, they have managed to make a living.[35] It is then within a context marked by increasing competition for job opportunities and a relatively low number of opportunities available for jobseekers that the strengthening of the industry's boundaries is taking place.

While mirroring (or mimicking) processes that have characterized the consolidation of film industries elsewhere in the world, the application of these boundary-making strategies is the result of the particular position the video film industries occupy within the larger economic landscape of the countries in which they have emerged. If, in order to revive and expand its popular success (and its economy with it), Hollywood today masks its rigid boundaries through "360-degree promotional surround that *invites* former 'outsiders' 'in' [through] (s)ocial media, viral marketing, prosumer production, and the constant Twitter chatter to fans and critics from 'behind-the-scenes,'"[36] the Nigerian and Ethiopian industries are currently undergoing an opposite process, oriented toward making boundaries more visible and institutionally acceptable. This move is considered vital for an economic sector that many local professionals consider too weak and unstructured to maintain the openness that initially characterized it. In this sense, this phenomenon is part of a more general process driving the video film phenomenon in both Ethiopia and Nigeria toward forms of economic 'gentrification' that touch on all aspects of film production, distribution, and consumption.[37] In both countries, this process marks the progressive migration of the video film business from the rather 'popular' milieu within which it took its first steps toward higher strata of the local social and economic pyramid. In Ethiopia, this is more of a mimetic move because many of the industry's members do (still) belong to the middle and lower classes of Ethiopian society, and over time, try to set themselves apart from the social and economic contexts from which they have emerged through media rituals that explicitly sanction the existence of boundaries in places where no substantial, social, and economic boundaries are yet visible. In other cases, such as in Nigeria, this is a more politically and economically grounded move. This is demonstrated by the negotiation that took place between the marketers and the government, a negotiation through which an established professional elite tried to defend its privileges by partially infiltrating state-driven reforms of the filmmaking sector. In both cases, these are strategies of boundary-making that are destined to have a long-lasting impact on the way these industries work and on the way they will be locally and globally perceived.

Notes

1 Jonathan Haynes, "A Bibliography of Academic Work on Nigerian and Ghanaian Video Films." *Journal of African Cinemas* 4, no. 1 (2012), 99–133.

2 Cf. Herman Wasserman, ed., *Popular Media, Democracy and Development in Africa* (New York: Routledge, 2011).

3 Monica Chibita, "Policing Popular Media in Africa," in Wasserman, *Popular Media*, 274.

4 Ramon Lobato, *Shadow Economies of Cinema, Mapping Informal Film Distribution* (London: British Film Institute, 2012), 40.

5 Lobato, *Shadow Economies of Cinema*, 47.

6 Frederick Cooper, "Who Is the Populist?" *African Studies Review* 30, no. 3 (1987), 102. See also Karin Barber, "Popular Arts in Africa." *African Studies Review* 30, no. 3 (1987), 1–78.

7 According to Nigerian producer and director Lancelot Imasuen (personal interview), for example, Nollywood "has managed to create a niche for [Africans] to express [themselves], to speech for the speechless." 'Nollywood' is the term generally used to define the southern Nigerian video film industry.

8 John T. Caldwell, *Production Culture: Industrial Reflexivity and Critical Practice in Film and Television* (Durham, NC: Duke University Press, 2008).

9 See, for instance, Tejaswini Ganti, *Producing Bollywood: Inside the Contemporary Hindi Film Industry* (Durham, NC: Duke University Press, 2012).

10 Nick Couldry, *Media Rituals: A Critical Approach* (London: Routledge, 2003).

11 Cf. Caldwell, *Production Culture*, 4; Ganti, *Producing Bollywood*, 25–6.

12 Jonathan Haynes and Onokoome Okome, "Evolving Popular Media: Nigerian Video Films." *Research in African Literatures* 29, no. 3 (1998), 117.

13 It might be useful here to underline that, while Nollywood is generally considered as having emerged between the end of the 1980s and the early 1990s (Haynes and Okome, "Evolving Popular Media"), the Ethiopian video film industry saw the light in the early 2000s (Alessandro Jedlowski, "Screening Ethiopia: A Preliminary Study of Ethiopian Film Production's History and Contemporary Developments." *Journal of African Cinemas*, forthcoming).

14 The African Movie Academy Awards (AMAA) is a pan-African (but Nollywood-centered) award ceremony designed on the Oscar model that takes place in the south-eastern Nigerian city of Yenagoa (Bayelsa State) since 2005.

15 Cf. "Urgent: The Need to Revise the Income Tax Rate, Threshold in the Country." *Ethiopian Business Review* 10 (December 2013), 29–31.

16 John L. Sullivan, "Leo C. Rosten's Hollywood: Power, Status, and the Primacy of Economic and Social Networks in Cultural Production," in *Production Studies: Cultural Studies of Media Industries*, edited by Vicki Mayer, Miranda J. Banks, and John T. Caldwell (London: Routledge, 2009), 44.

17 Vicki Mayer, "Bringing the Social Back In: Studies of Production Culture and Social Theory," in Mayer, Banks, and Caldwell, *Production Studies*, 17.

18 Cf. Alessandro Jedlowski, "From Nollywood to Nollyworld: Processes of Transnationalization in the Nigerian Video Film Industry," in *Global Nollywood: Transnational Dimensions of an African Video Film Industry*, edited by Matthias Krings and Onokoome Okome (Bloomington: Indiana University Press, 2013), 25–45.

19 Some of these rumors were reported in the Nigerian magazine *City People Extra* published for the event. See "Emem Isong: 'Why I Left Banking for Film Making,'" *City People Extra* (Lagos: City People Media Group, 2011), 2–3.

20 By the term 'marketer' industry practitioners in Nigeria generally mean the film distributor.

21 See the next section of this chapter.

22 David Karnes, "The Glamorous Crowd: Hollywood Movie Premieres between the Wars." *American Quarterly* 38, no. 4 (1986), 569, 570.

23 Couldry, *Media Rituals*, 27.

24 Cf. Jedlowski, "Screening Ethiopia."

25 I refer here and later to rumors reported to me by a number of Ethiopian informants working within the film industry who asked to keep their identities anonymous.

26 Before the explosion of video production (in the early 1990s), two other governmental institutions had been created to regulate and support film production and distribution in the country (the Nigerian Film Corporation and the Nigerian Copyright Commission), but they both had very limited influence on the development of the film business in the country (cf. Jade Miller, "The Globalization of Cultural Industries: Nollywood—the View from the South," PhD diss., University of Southern California, 2010, 98–104). A few decrees to regulate film production had also been promulgated, but with little effect on the present structure of the video film industry (cf. Ikechukwu Obiaya, "Restructuring the Nigerian Film Industry: Effects of the National Film and Video Censors Board Distribution Policy," PhD diss., University of Navarra, 2012, 203–7).

27 Vincent Omoigui, interview with the author, September 21, 2009, Turin.

28 Cf. Alexander Bud, "The End of Nollywood's Guilded Age? Marketers, the State and the Struggle for Distribution." *Critical African Studies* 6, no. 1 (2014), 91–121; Obiaya, "Restructuring the Nigerian Film Industry."

29 Emmanuel Isikaku, interview with the author, February 19, 2010, Lagos; cf. also Brian Larkin, "Degraded Images, Distorted Sounds: Nigerian Video and the Infrastructure of Piracy." *Public Culture* 16, no. 2 (2004): 289–314.

30 Jade Miller, "Global Nollywood: The Nigerian Movie Industry and Alternative Global Networks in Production and Distribution." *Global Media and Communication* 8, no. 2 (2012): 119.

31 See Bud, "The End of Nollywood's Guilded Age?"

32 Cf. Obiaya, "Restructuring the Nigerian Film Industry."

33 Miller, "The Globalization of Cultural Industries," 114.

34 Cf. Richard Banégas and Jean-Pierre Warnier, "Nouvelles figures de la réussite et du pouvoir: Introduction au thème." *Politique Africaine* 82 (2001), 5–21.

35 Cf. Obiaya, "Restructuring the Nigerian Film Industry," 186–92.

36 Patrick Vonderau, "Borderlands, Contact Zones, and Boundary Games: A Conversation with John T. Caldwell," in *Behind the Screen: Inside European Production Cultures*, edited by Petr Szczepanik and Patrick Vonderau (New York: Palgrave MacMillan, 2013), 18.

37 Cf. Ganti, *Producing Bollywood*. See also Alessandro Jedlowski, "Small Screen Cinema: Informality and Remediation in Nollywood." *Television and New Media* 13, no. 5 (2012), 431–46.

15

FROM EXPERIENCING LIFE TO LIFE EXPERIENCES

Location Shooting Practices in Chinese and Taiwanese New Wave Cinemas

Dennis Lo

Chinese and Taiwanese New Wave Cinemas emerged onto the world stage at the same time, during the 1980s, presenting international audiences with aesthetically audacious portraits of the everyday effects of political reform and economic modernization in the PRC and Taiwan. Often shot on location in rural and developing communities outside the studio backlot, these films' visual and narrative styles played a pivotal role in the social dynamics between the production units and community residents. However, scholarship on the politics and aesthetic practices of location shooting is scant, likely because of a wariness in Chinese film studies toward the use of top-down or culturally unspecific models for mapping the cultural symptoms of creative practices.[1] Drawing on eighteen months of fieldwork, this chapter investigates the language of industrial self-theorizing and authorship in accounts of location shooting collected from Chinese-language creative statements, essays by filmmakers, and one-on-one, semi-structured interviews I conducted with twelve Chinese and Taiwanese filmmakers between 2011 and 2012.[2] By examining the social performances and cultural rituals constituted by these production narratives and practices as deep texts of the Chinese-language film 'para-industries'—John Caldwell's term for the sociocultural interfaces between the film industry and the public—I revise existing views that Chinese film auteurs either resist or are complicit with state ideology, and propose instead that auteurs' national identities are fluid performances that constitute acts of cultural and institutional survival.[3]

According to Chinese and Taiwanese filmmakers, regulations for location shooting in rural locales are either nonexistent or only loosely enforced, making the process of production a largely self-regulated affair. Chinese and Taiwanese filmmakers, like their Hollywood counterparts, call attention to how such production environments can be 'mastered' through improvisational techniques honed by years of professional experience. However, it is also generally believed that one's instinct for location shooting is culturally derived, rather than trained. In fact, one of the most common discursive tactics auteurs use to demonstrate the embeddedness of Chinese cultural traits in their filmmaking techniques is juxtaposing their philosophy of production with Hollywood's industrial practices.[4] For instance, in Chinese-language interviews and master's-level classes on film production in the PRC and Taiwan, Taiwanese director Hou Hsiao Hsien contrasted his workflow with Hollywood's by drawing on essentialist notions of East–West cultural and philosophic difference.[5] Rather than mechanically following a series of prescribed steps in production, Hou sees location shooting as an opportunity to perceive the social and natural environments of the shooting locations through pan-Chinese phenomenological, ethical, and aesthetic frames. Similarly, other Taiwanese filmmakers including director Li Youning and cinematographer Lee Pingbin explained to me that knowledge regarding locations is not solely acquired during dedicated periods of location scouting, but is born out of one's *shenghuo jingyan*, or "life experiences."[6] Their comfort with location shooting issues, above all, from an intimate familiarity with place rooted in their childhood experiences of growing up in small-town communities. This notion that culturally authentic production practices must not rely on industrial modes of production is equally espoused by both Fourth and Fifth Generation Chinese directors like Xie Fei and Zhang Yimou.[7] In the following excerpt from an interview conducted by Zhang Huijun, the president of the Beijing Film Academy, Zhang Yimou paints a vivid portrait juxtaposing Hollywood and PRC production environments:[8]

> We Chinese are sincere like family. When we shoot we all live together, not like how [Hollywood filmmakers] all go home when they're done shooting. I really like the family-style production atmosphere. I don't like it when the camera stops running, when the shoot is over, everyone drives away and some even leave by helicopter.[9]

In contrast to these theories of production that oppose Hollywood's assembly-line ethos with celebrations of Chinese cultural intimacy, are self-effacing descriptions of production practices—usually voiced by directors who are less internationally renowned. Exemplifying this style are production narratives by Taiwan New Wave Cinema directors Wang Tong and Yi Zhiyan, who assured me that their stylistic choices were the result of neither their creative independence nor their desire to oppose the militarization of a location shoot.[10] As Wang and Yi explained, because Taiwan lacked a 'true film industry' with scientifically managed modes of production, location shoots were by necessity guerilla affairs. There was no 'school' of production practices, as their techniques had simply evolved out of the impoverished filming conditions in Taiwan. Yet, while clearly downplaying any notion of their creative genius, Wang and Yi's production stories also fully aligned them with a popular figure in the Taiwanese public consciousness—the unexceptional yet resourceful small-business entrepreneur. Their impoverished practices and production environments had led them to improvise on location, much as smaller Taiwanese businesses had creatively cut corners to survive Taiwan's stagnant economy and global economic downturns. I detected in their disclosures more than a hint of pride for performing this role of the Taiwanese underdog.

I argue, then, that despite apparent syntactic differences between heroic and self-effacing production narratives, both 'genres' betray a common value system. Rather than serving as a demonstration of one's proficiency with a standardized code of production, or constituting an exercise of one's creative freedoms, location shooting is perceived as an intensified mode of lived experience that is ultimately inseparable from one's everyday practices 'off location' within the overarching Chinese cultural milieu. Further, this cultural milieu is one where the East is either viewed resolutely as the West's cultural 'Other,' or is perceived as lagging behind the highest industrial standards epitomized by Hollywood. In theoretical terms, one might say that location shooting is believed to constitute a practice of cultural survival amid a postcolonial episteme. As the following discussion on the location shooting practices of Chinese Fourth and Fifth Generation production units demonstrates, the notion of creative labor as a mode of cultural survival is not limited to auteurist theories and accounts of production, but also plays a pivotal role in shaping the broader historical contours of Chinese film industrial development.

On rural location shoots prior to the early reform era, Chinese production units often engaged in a period of preproduction called *tiyan shenghuo*, or 'experiencing life.' To experience life, members of the production unit would live on location for several months, sometimes sharing residences with local farmers. Tasks were informally divided among the cast and crew—the director sought creative inspiration for the script from surrounding landscapes, while above-the-line labor scouted for locations and cast members familiarized themselves with local customs, dialects, and rituals. During nightly sessions of collaborative script planning and revision, sometimes likened by directors to a family reunion, veteran filmmakers might share past stories about experiencing life with novices. Production members from various parts of China were called to momentarily set aside their regional cultural differences to perform a common national and creative identity in a purifying cultural setting believed to be uncorrupted by urbanization and modernization. Together, these and other rituals redefined the practice of experiencing life from being merely a stage of preproduction within an industrial workflow to a collective lived experience where the boundaries between 'off' and 'on' location were blurred.

Despite these portrayals of rural production environments as egalitarian social spaces, comparisons between casts and crews' recollections of location shooting reveal how the practice of experiencing life often establishes and also relies on a social hierarchy within the production unit. As I examine more thoroughly through discourse analysis in my larger project, above-the-line crew members for the Fourth Generation film *In the Wild Mountains* (1984), including the art designer and cinematographer, each kept a critical distance from the rural residents by describing them as parts of the landscape. Director Yan Xueru took a step further to observe the cast and rural residents as ethnographic subjects whose actions and social practices were diligently examined and evaluated. By contrast, members of the cast wrote embodied and affective accounts that expressed a conflicted sense of identity during their participation in everyday life within the community. Cast members noted that as they gradually identified with the villagers, it felt increasingly challenging to maintain a critical distance. Greater self-discipline was thus needed to situate the rural mindsets they were called to emulate within 'proper' sociohistorical contexts. As a social practice, then, experiencing life constitutes the production unit's collective auto-ethnography of rural subjects, where the roles of ethnographic participation and observation are divided along the lines of a more conventional labor hierarchy.

The asymmetric politics of production extend further to the relationship between filmmakers and rural residents. Filmmakers clearly spoke for the 'natives' in accounts of experiencing life; rural villagers could serve in one paragraph as emblems of authentic and proper Chinese-ness whom intellectuals 'corrupted' by urban culture must emulate, to constituting 'simple, naïve, and ignorant' national subjects needing to be reformed and 'enlightened' in another. Most problematically, filmmakers made efforts to shield the community from any knowledge of the films' critical representations of the rural.[11]

Despite the overtly colonialist logic underlying these claims and practices, the cultural politics of location shooting is complicated by a trope found in nearly all accounts of experiencing life—the social debt filmmakers felt they owed to the rural communities. Filmmakers bemoaned the fact that while the eastern Chinese provinces were rapidly modernizing and urbanizing, isolated rural communities in the central and western Chinese provinces (e.g., Shaanxi, Shanxi, and Gansu) that once served as sites of origin for both the Chinese Communist Party and the premodern Chinese civilization, had been all but left to fend for themselves. Some veteran directors such as Wu Tianming even acknowledged that the rural residents' inability to reform was not due to their natural tendency toward social backwardness. Rather, intellectuals—a social class the filmmakers were members of—were to blame, having betrayed the promises socialist China made when abandoning the rural to address urban concerns.[12]

Significantly, filmmakers manifested their discontent in a highly strategic manner. Rather than placing the blame on the inadequacy of national policies and risk offending the authorities, they stressed their own lack of 'mature' social consciousness. In particular, they chastised their own failure to properly outline national progress with their films, a social expectation that Robin Visser calls the "moral mandate," or belief that public intellectuals engaging in cultural critique should not stop at mere description and deconstruction, but must also reconstruct cultural texts within ideologically proper frameworks.[13] Indeed, one could not carry out the moral mandate simply by presenting uplifting portraits of rural reform, as the so-called model play films of the Cultural Revolution unsuccessfully attempted. Rather, culturally savvy experiencing life narratives implied that the more familiar a filmmaker was with the immense social obstacles facing rural reform, the more one would realize that the debt owed to rural folk could never be fully repaid.[14]

In a broader institutional context, stories about experiencing life can be said to constitute collective performances that smoothed institutional tensions when the Chinese state film industry restructured from a fully centralized to partly decentralized system. During this period of industrial transition, studio heads wielded greater control over the interpretation and execution of state directives. Resource-poor studios in the central and western provinces, such as Xi'an, Guangxi, and Xinjiang Film Studios, set out not only to catch up to the level of industrial modernization of studios in the eastern provinces, but also proposed courses of development that would differentiate their institutional identities. Wu Tianming, who was newly appointed as the head of Xi'an Film Studios in 1983, addressed the studio's industrial lag by calling for the development of Chinese Westerns, a genre scholars now mostly associate with the works of Fourth and Fifth Generation directors. Inexpensive to produce and requiring a variety of rural, natural, and historic settings, the Chinese Western was a genre where Xi'an held a natural advantage over other studios based in more densely populated urban areas. Notably, this genre allowed greater room for aesthetic experimentation, which filmmakers hoped might result in the state film industry's first truly 'native' genre since the end of the Cultural Revolution.[15]

In spite of greater aesthetic allowances, tensions between Xi'an and state film authorities in Beijing were inevitable as long as Xi'an was still fully state owned.[16] In fact, the Fifth Generation's international acclaim only warranted greater scrutiny from state film authorities, who censured aesthetically avant-garde films such as *Yellow Earth* for grandstanding to Western audiences through exoticizing portraits of cultural ambivalence and rural poverty. To survive domestically, it was imperative for filmmakers to reaffirm their abidance to the moral mandate. Seeking a proper balance between aesthetic boldness and ideological correctness, scholars, filmmakers, and film critics openly debated theories of production and screenwriting in the studio's trade journal, *A New Era for Cinema* (*Dianying xing shidai*)—renamed *Western Cinema* (*Xibu dianying*) in 1985, further securing the studio's focus on the Chinese Western. Significantly, experiencing life stories were a staple in these trade journals, featured prominently in the introduction of a creative statement, following a treatise on a film's aesthetic and narrative style, or alongside articles denouncing the colonializing ideology of American Westerns.

Replicating the discourse of self-sacrifice most famously presented during Mao's 1942 "Talks at Yan'an," where creative workers were called to "go down to the countryside" to serve the proletariat masses, these stories cultivated the notion that visual style arose out of authentic and sincere interactions with rural residents, rather than serving as a vain showcase for one's creative exceptionalism or extravagance.[17] Filmmakers thus fashioned themselves after the heroes of Chinese Westerns, who, unlike 'imperialistic' cowboys, lived among the folk and made personal sacrifices for the betterment of rural society. One might say, then, that such narratives not only greatly reinforced the Xi'an brand by underscoring its social pedigree and moral exceptionalism at a time when other studios had already shifted to the increasingly popular *chengshi dianying*, or urban cinema, but also served as institutionally sanctioned alibis that provided legitimacy to otherwise excessive forms of aesthetic experimentation.

A seemingly all-purpose tool, the creative statement built on stories of experiencing life had become so prevalent that they began to be parodied or mocked by filmmakers and scholars in critical cartoons and essays in the late 1980s—sometimes published ironically within *Western Cinema* itself. Critics were well aware that such statements might more accurately reflect an auteur's careerist ambitions than indicate any real affection for rural communities. Chen Kaige provided perhaps the most searing critique in his own creative statement, "Thoughts from the Production of *King of Children*."[18] The essay begins with a reflexive and self-mocking claim that creative statements do more to alienate their authors from the filmed subjects than to strengthen their ties. As Chen attests, not only did such narratives fail to reveal the auteur's sincerity, but they were read only as 'documents' or 'proof' of the author's *mingzu jingshen*, or 'national spirit.' The national spirit is then denounced as a pernicious myth that fetishizes the film author's oneness with an imagined rural collective and devalues the individual artist's creative agency. The essay takes a more personal turn as Chen laments that in a desperate attempt to "prove that (he) was a member of this nation," he had once relied on creative statements to assert the political properness of *Yellow Earth*.[19] However, he would no longer pander to the critics with *King of Children*, a film about the senselessness of pursuing the national spirit for its own sake. In an attempt to be more sincere, Chen described seeking inspiration from new understandings of the self he had acquired while being 'sent down' to a Yunnan mountainous village during the Cultural Revolution, where he discovered that it was impossible to ameliorate cultural irreconcilabilities between himself and the local villagers.

In one swift move, Chen deconstructed the strategic historiographical and institutional functions served by creative statements. Rather than extending this critique to suggesting that all experiencing life stories served as career capital, however, Chen cleverly proposed that a more proper mode of national subjectivity should be based on the authority of one's life experiences. Chen thus staged a performance of his own auteurist origins on the textual ruins of less sophisticated experiencing life narratives, demonstrating his aptitude for fulfilling the moral mandate. As this and other examples indicate, experiencing life narratives set a foundation for emergent auteurist discourses at a time when Fifth Generation filmmakers were struggling to establish themselves in domestic film circles. Perhaps unsurprisingly, within a few short years as the Fifth Generation auteurs gained greater international prominence, experiencing life narratives fell out of popularity as it became more critical for filmmakers to woo international financiers than domestic censors. Their usefulness spent, experiencing life narratives were superseded by their equivalent in a new era of commercially driven transnational art cinema—the auteurist coming of age fable, or 'life experience' narrative.

In closing, I draw attention to a few broader theoretical implications of applying this type of 'grounded' cultural-industrial analysis in the Chinese and Taiwanese contexts. First, by examining what Caldwell has dubbed industry's "hermeneutical" practices, or the ways industry formulates, disseminates, and guards theories of its own corporate and aesthetic practices, it becomes clear that purely symptomatic readings of the cultural politics of filmic texts are ill equipped to capture the sociocultural complexities of production and may exaggerate the hegemonic forcefulness of the political economy at the expense of the film institutions and filmmakers' agency.[20] At the same time, this should not be taken as a call to read what filmmakers disclose literally. The self-promotional nature of Chen's retort is made even more potent through his keen awareness of the constructedness of discourse and should serve as a cautionary reminder of the profound degree to which the Chinese and Taiwanese film industries are textualized.

I myself began this project largely unaware that film para-industries such as trade journals, master's classes, and publicly disclosed interviews in the Chinese and Taiwanese industrial contexts are as sophisticated in their tactics of guarding the interior workings of the industry as their counterparts in Hollywood. Rather naïvely, I made it my initial objective to gain access to renowned auteurs in person, who I hoped would facilitate my efforts in sorting industrial fact from fiction. After conducting just a few interviews, however, I found to my dismay that the auteurs' responses contained significant portions that were highly scripted and rehearsed, while other segments were fine-tuned to my own performance as a border-crossing film scholar. It was not until I began to sift through this textual mess that my initial sources of frustration—inconsistencies and discursive excesses—became more illuminating than any underlying industrial truth. Rather than chiseling away at the paratextual walls in a futile effort to unveil the industrial treasures guarded within, I found it more satisfying to refocus my critical lens on the discursive textures that adorn these façades—and through an examination of the ways national and cultural subjectivities are inflected and refracted in separate institutional contexts, afford a glimpse into the tactics underlying the Chinese and Taiwanese film industries' layered constructions.

Notes

1   In Chinese film studies, location shooting is generally considered a technique used by auteurs to fashion distinctive visual styles. The few works that examine location shooting as a social practice are limited to the study of films shot in urban locales.

2   Caldwell argues that 'grounded' studies of social habitus and creative agency in Hollywood must take into consideration industrial self-theorizing, or how filmmakers perform, formulate, and regulate both personal and collective theories of creative labor as part of their professional practice. See John T. Caldwell, *Production Culture: Industrial Reflexivity and Critical Practice in Film and Television* (Durham, NC and London: Duke University Press, 2008).

3   John T. Caldwell, "Para-industry: Researching Hollywood's Blackwaters." *Cinema Journal* 52, no. 3 (2013).

4   These comparisons are found largely in Chinese-language interviews. Critiques of Hollywood and hints of cultural superiority are usually downplayed with non-Chinese interviewers.

5   Zhuo Buo Tang, ed., *Hou Xiaoxian dianying jiangzuo* [*Hou Hsiao-Hsien Film Lectures*] (Guilin, China: Guangxi Normal University Press, 2009).

6   Li Youning, interview with Dennis Lo, Taipei, November 23, 2011; Li Pingbin, interview with Dennis Lo, Taipei, September 23, 2012.

7   The *Fourth and Fifth Generations* refers to the first two classes of filmmakers who graduated from the Beijing Film Academy following the end of the Cultural Revolution.

8   By defining production practices along dualistic lines of cultural difference (East-West, or Third Cinema-Hollywood), these auteurs could navigate past the potentially treacherous waters of stylistic and cultural difference between the PRC's, Taiwan's, and Hong Kong's cinemas. During interviews with the Western press prior to the 2000s, PRC directors downplayed artistic influences from Taiwan, thus remaining 'politically correct' by protecting the notion of a Chinese national cinema bounded by territorial distinctions between the PRC and Taiwan. By contrast, Chinese auteurs acknowledged fluid exchanges with Taiwanese directors in Chinese-language interviews and portrayed such exchanges as a friendly competition happening 'within the family,' where the notion of Taiwan as a Chinese province was taken for granted.

9   My translation. Zhang Huijun, ed., *Xingshi zhuisu yu shijue chuangzuo: Zhang Yimou dianying chuangzuo yanjiu* [*The Pursuit of Form and Visual Production: Research on Zhang Yimou's Film Productions*] (Beijing: China Film Press, 2008), 18.

10   Wang Tong, interview with Dennis Lo, Taipei, November 25, 2012; Yi Zhiyan, interview with Dennis Lo, Taipei, December 1, 2011.

11   Zhang Yimou described that on various occasions hidden cameras were used during the location shoot of *The Story of Qiu Ju* (1992) to prevent residents from becoming self-conscious and for their "original flavor" to remain unadulterated.

12   Wu Tianming, "Laojing daoyan fangtanlu" ["Interview record with the director of Old Well,"] in *Huiwang chunzhen niandai: Zhongguo zhuming dianying daoyan fangtanlu* [*Looking Back at an Innocent Era: Interview Records with Prominent Chinese Film Directors*], edited by Luo Xueying (Beijing: Xueyuan chubanshe, 2008), 297–330.

13   Robin Visser, *Cities Surround the Countryside: Urban Aesthetics in Postsocialist China* (Durham, NC and London: Duke University Press, 2010), 91–2.

14   Some filmmakers like Wu Tianming even believed that it was necessary to engage in hard labor and other rural hardships to engender a more profound social consciousness. See Wu, "Laojing daoyan fangtanlu."

15 Li Xi, "Xian Dianying Zhipian Chang zaoqi chuangzuo yanjiu" ["Research on Xi'an Film Studio's Early Productions,"] master's thesis, Xibei Daxue, 2011.

16 Zhang Yingjin, *Chinese National Cinema* (New York and London: Routledge, 2004), 238–40.

17 Bonnie McDougall and Mao Zedong, *Mao Zedong's "Talks at the Yan'an Conference on Literature and Art": A Translation of the 1943 Text with Commentary* (Ann Arbor: University of Michigan, 1980).

18 Chen Kaige, "You Haizi Wang de chuangzuo suo xiangdao de" ["Thoughts from the Production of *King of Children*."] *Dangdai dianying* 6 (1987): 97–101.

19 Chen, "You Haizi Wang de chuangzuo suo xiangdao de," 98.

20 Caldwell, "Para-industry," 158.

16

THE CRUNCH HEARD 'ROUND THE WORLD

The Global Era of Digital Game Labor

John Vanderhoef and Michael Curtin

Electronic Arts (EA) is one of the world's leading producers and publishers of video games, renowned for such titles as *Madden NFL, FIFA,* and *The Sims.* Despite its success, the company has repeatedly come under fire for working conditions and compensation at its production facilities worldwide. Tensions escalated significantly in 2004 when 'EA Spouse' began posting anonymous online criticism regarding long hours, unpaid labor, and unreasonable expectations.[1] Worst of all, the anonymous spouse wrote, was 'crunch time,' the period leading up to the launch of a video game when workers were expected to put in twelve-to-eighteen-hour days, completing artwork, fixing game bugs, and making sure the final build was polished and ready for the heavily promoted launch date when eager fans were expected to snap up the company's latest release. Such complaints jibe with studies showing that developers are in crunch mode an average of ten weeks per year.[2] During these stretches, developers work seven days a week, leaving no time for family, friends, rest, or recreation. The EA Spouse postings created a stir among game developers, leading to a successful class action lawsuit against EA and a reshuffle of company management.[3]

In response to mounting criticism from consumers and the gaming community, EA executives pledged to clean up their act, but most observers contend that little has changed. Indeed, despite management claims that crunch time is being ameliorated, similar stories continue to circulate about grueling schedules leading up to the release of major titles.[4] These sweatshop conditions are a telling counterpoint to the common assumption among policy makers that the creative (or knowledge) industries offer the most promising prospects for job growth.[5] Although the number of game-related jobs is indeed growing, it is remarkable that tech-savvy programmers and talented visual artists—seemingly elite members of the global labor force—should find themselves in such circumstances. Having developed a rich and distinctive skill set, many of them soldier on despite adverse conditions, while others get burned out and leave the industry. Still others form their own small companies, hoping to realize the beguiling potential of online distribution. Some indies dream of producing a breakout hit while others target market niches the majors overlook. Yet independence carries its own price, with many start-ups failing and even successful companies finding that indie production can be exceptionally stressful and demanding. Consequently, the most plentiful and well-paying jobs in the video game industry continue to be those provided by major video game publishers either directly or indirectly. This chapter focuses on the challenges confronting game developers who work for the majors.

The very biggest companies develop, produce, and own the rights to their most popular titles, often contracting services from a network of suppliers. EA, for example, has studios and subsidiaries in more than a dozen countries and a network of suppliers that spans the globe. Overall, the industry and the workforce are huge. By 2017 video games are expected to generate over $100 billion in annual revenue, thanks largely to substantial growth in the mobile space and in emerging markets like East Asia.[6] Overall, the video game industry, along with other forms of software development, is one of the biggest drivers of economic growth worldwide, adding jobs in such cities as Warsaw, Bangalore, and Shanghai. In fact, many of the pressures that led to unrest among EA employees in the United States have been mitigated by the dispersion of tasks to a burgeoning transnational workforce, creating an elaborate global assembly line.

Yet despite this calculated globalization of production,[7] relatively little has been written about the impact it has on actual video game artists and programmers.[8] This seems especially odd when one considers that far more scholarly attention has been paid to the supposedly 'invisible' free labor gaming enthusiasts contribute.[9] Moreover, what little has been written about studio working conditions focuses almost exclusively on North America. Few have broadened their critique to examine the changing contours and increasing dispersion of big-budget game development, and the emergence of development clusters in such places as Eastern Europe, India, and China.[10] In this chapter, we connect the quotidian working conditions of game developers to the global structure of an industry oligopoly dominated by a handful of publishers.

Researchers have enumerated three historical stages to the globalization of labor, beginning with manufacturing (product assembly), service (back office operations), and most recently creative (media and design) labor.[11] Each of these stages has entailed a move from integrated mass production to 'flexible' modes of operation that depend on subcontracting and the casualization of labor.[12] The media industries have embraced these trends and today scour the globe for cost advantages, government subsidies, and cheap, compliant labor that can trim production costs on blockbuster feature films, television productions, and digital games. Miller and his colleagues say this has resulted in a New International Division of Cultural Labor (NICL) that pits various localities against one another as they angle to attract media production.[13] Consequently, NICL has had a devastating effect on unionized Hollywood craft and service workers, as well as technically sophisticated visual effects artists (VFX), and it results in a race-to-the-bottom competition between various cities such as Vancouver, London, and Hyderabad.[14] In this chapter, we examine these forces at work in the video game industry, paying particular attention to the respatialization of production, the increasing precarity of high-skilled labor, and the deteriorating working conditions that result from these interlinked phenomena.

At the center of these trends are the major game publishers—Activision Blizzard, Electronic Arts, Microsoft, and Sony—whose global reach and market dominance provide significant advantages over smaller companies that either succumb to competition or, if successful, become aligned with one of these titans. Consequently, most development shops are either owned by one of the big publishers or provide services on a contractual basis, which in turn means that the needs of the majors shape working conditions and creative practices. Although the International Game Developers Association (IGDA) and other advocacy groups have tried to draw attention to the dismal conditions of game labor, they lack the resources to engage, much less challenge, the dominant firms whose scale, reach, and mobility give them the upper hand over workers toiling long hours in isolated cubicles.

Through an analysis of trade and business publications, developer blogs, industry reports, and interviews with on-the-ground developers, this chapter examines the troubling relations of production in the video game industry. We describe the specific practices and protocols of the productive apparatus that feeds the major game publishers, demonstrating the impact on workers and labor organizing efforts. Tying together insights from political economy and production studies, this chapter offers a middle-range analysis that connects specific local labor conditions to the elaborate global production networks of the major game publishers.

Production in Dominant Regions

Historically, the dominant regions of digital game software production include Japan, Western Europe, and North America, with the latter arguably taking an industry-leading role in the twenty-first century, clustering in a handful of cities, including Vancouver, San Francisco, Los Angeles, and Montreal. Each has a healthy number of shops, allowing some game developers (depending on their skills and experience) to remain in one city while moving between studios as projects ebb and flow. Others find it necessary to migrate from city to city in search of work. Because most game production cycles last two to seven years, workers are almost constantly searching for new opportunities, even during stretches of stable employment. The globalization of game production has furthermore compounded the pressures to remain mobile because talented workers are often encouraged to move abroad to provide leadership and training in shops that are up-skilling their workforce in cities like Shanghai and Prague.

Game workers fall into several broad categories that include artists, programmers, quality assurance, designers, management, and promotion. According to data gathered in the 2014 IGDA Developer Satisfaction Survey, the majority of game developers are young men (30 to 35 years old) without families who work at large, publisher-owned or contracted studios.[15] Even in the leading studios, employees endure long hours (9–12-hour days) and mandatory (often unpaid) overtime, working sometimes in cramped conditions under intense pressure.[16] In fact, only 9 percent of developers get formal compensation for overtime during crunch periods. Even though many receive bonuses after the product launch, almost 60 percent say bonuses do not adequately compensate them for the additional labor.

Of course, conditions vary from studio to studio, but there is an alarming pattern of abuse and exploitation throughout the development cycle of each major title. For instance, most shops maintain a skeletal core staff during the preproduction phase of development when ideas are hashed out, prototypes built, and design documents written. These shops then hire more staff as development progresses, largely in the form of contract labor, who generally earn less than core staff members. Moreover, short-term employment and flawed crediting systems make it difficult for workers to earn recognition for their project contributions, which in turn undermines their chances for future employment.[17]

Despite such strenuous conditions, workers have historically been indifferent to unionization. Unlike craft workers who organized unions and guilds in the film, television, and publishing industries during the first half of the twentieth century, video game workers came of age during the dotcom boom. Educated, elite, and forever in demand, they participated in the spiraling fortunes of the digital economy around the turn of the century. Many were entranced by romantic notions of creative genius that permeated the countercultural politics of the online gift economy and the libertarian ideology of Silicon Valley.[18] Unions were disdained as remnants of an industrial past, which was in part why practices like unpaid overtime and crunch time have been largely unchallenged on a collective level. The lack of unionization also means that project-based employment contracts rarely provide health and retirement benefits.

Instability and insecurity are therefore the norm for most workers, and mass layoffs are standard practice following a product launch. For example, during a three-month span in early 2014, Sony Santa Monica, Disney Interactive, and Irrational Games let dozens, and in one case hundreds, of people go after they completed work on major titles.[19] Unfortunately, these high-profile layoffs represent just a small portion of the total layoffs that occurred in that same time period.[20]

Others were laid off because of 'restructuring' or 'consolidation,' both of which are recurring themes as some shops founder while others are bought up by the majors. As a result, the average time workers spend at any given job is just over three years.[21]

As suggested earlier, conditions are harsh in even the most celebrated shops. Take for example Irrational Games, developer of the critically acclaimed *BioShock* franchise. Even as critics celebrated *BioShock* for its originality and art direction, the project (2002 to 2007) was riddled with budgetary problems and personal strife. In the period leading up to the release date, the team endured a stressful stretch of crunch time that led to internal quarrels and the voluntary exit of many core staff after the project's completion.[22] Tensions continued with the team's next project, *BioShock Infinite*, which took even longer to develop and necessitated the hiring of management specialists to streamline development, amplifying the pressures on employees.[23] According to several team members, the studio was mired in competitiveness, perfectionism, and managerial intimidation, a stark contrast to the communal atmosphere the studio self-consciously tried to project via karaoke outings and social gatherings. Yet after completion of *Infinite* in 2013, more than a dozen permanent staff members left Irrational, as remaining staff members quickly turned their attention to downloadable content and another round of crunch, having received only a brief respite after the game's release. Despite its success, Irrational Games unexpectedly closed up shop in February 2014 following two dramatic rounds of layoffs that reflect the perpetual ebb and flow of so-called AAA development.[24]

Irrational's demise was no doubt due in part to managerial missteps, but structural factors were also at work. For example, unlike other forms of creative entertainment like films and television, video games do not have scripts or format bibles to follow. Most games have design documents prepared during preproduction, but as with the development of any new machine—and games are machines[25]—a number of prototypes need to be developed and tested, all of which takes time and resources, before a final design can be put into production. Furthermore, games are complex systems with many moving parts and sometimes problems don't become evident until those parts are brought together in late-stage builds, exacerbating the already complex process of development.

Besides the vicissitudes of digital game production, patterns of employee discrimination haunt the games industry as well. Long underrepresented in the digital game labor force, women now make up approximately 22 percent of the total industry.[26] Women get paid less than their male counterparts and tend to hold positions in marketing, public relations, or project management rather than working as programmers, artists, or creative directors.[27] Furthermore, discrimination and hardships escalate if a female employee decides to have a child because it is commonly argued that motherhood is incompatible with the demands of game development (fatherhood, not so much).[28] Highlighting gender problems at the core of game development, Nina B. Huntemann has also illuminated the systematic exploitation of women in digital game hardware production and game promotion at industry trade shows.[29] In November 2012, the full scope of this problem became public when women (and some men) across the games industry began to tweet about gender discrimination.[30] Marked by the hashtag *#1reasonwhy*, many wondered why women are underrepresented in the games industry, while others responded by pointing to inherent gender bias, harassment, and the masculinist work culture. Unfortunately, this public discussion did little to attend to the underlying structural problems embedded in gaming culture. In 2014 a disparate group of spurned gamers organized under the moniker 'Gamergate' to wage a vitriolic campaign targeting feminist and progressive critics, developers, and scholars engaged in critiques of the gaming industry and culture.[31]

Other forms of discrimination are also cause for concern. People of color and queer people have spoken about barriers to employment and hostility in the workplace that manifests itself both in the conditions of labor and in the output of the industry, which is subtly if not overtly tinged with misogyny, racism, homophobia, and transphobia. Current industry demographics based largely in North America, but indicative of other markets, reflect this problem, with an overwhelming 79 percent reporting as Caucasian and 86 percent as heterosexual.[32] However, these demographics are indicative of other markets. Moreover, industry events and networking opportunities skew toward heterosexual, white, young males, many of whom embrace their privilege as a seemingly necessary prop against the general adversity and insecurity that they sense in their working lives.

Overall, the structure and practices of the industry in the dominant production centers are characterized by exploitation, precarity, and a hiring system that privileges white men. Importantly, these structures are larger than any one individual or studio and as such have been slow to change despite growing concern. However, even as industry watchdogs grow more vigilant about conditions at core facilities, these same critics have paid little attention to the exportation of these abuses to emerging regions of digital game development.

Production in Emerging Regions

Confronted with the growing costs of AAA blockbuster games, the world's largest publishers have been establishing studios in emerging markets to take advantage of cheaper labor, tax incentives, and a growing base of consumers.[33] By 2006, 60 percent of game companies outsourced work to Eastern Europe and East Asia.[34] Three years later that figure jumped to 86 percent, reportedly because of the demand for high-definition visuals for seventh-generation consoles.[35] Now, in the eighth generation, outsourcing has become an industry standard.

Of course, transnational game publishers have been outsourcing work to cheaper parts of the world since at least the 1990s. Ubisoft was ahead of the curve in this respect, setting up its Shanghai offices in 1996 and up-skilling the resident workforce. Its investment sparked the growth of local creative capacity, as the employees trained by Ubisoft gradually migrated to other firms or splintered off to start their own game companies. After successfully producing components of franchise games, Ubisoft Shanghai was allowed to develop original IP for international audiences with 2008's *EndWar* and 2012's *I am Alive*.[36] Despite its success in both global and Chinese markets, and despite the fact that 90 percent of the staff is now Chinese, Ubisoft Shanghai is still a Western-focused company largely run by Western managers.[37] Thus, even as major publishers invest in local infrastructure and up-skilling, their corporate practices and priorities remain global.

Ubisoft reportedly employs over 9,000 game workers worldwide, from Montreal to Montpellier to Shanghai, in order to support its multi-nodal development apparatus.[38] As with most high-profile games, the *Assassin's Creed* (*AC*) franchise exemplifies this networked production structure, with ten studios across the world contributing to *AC: Unity*'s 2014 release.[39] Working conditions at these publisher-owned studios tend to be better than at independent shops working under contract. Ubisoft Singapore reportedly maintains eight-hour workdays at all times except during crunch, when workers receive overtime pay.[40] The studio employs 300 people from thirty-two countries and reportedly has good employee relations. This seeming contrast to EA-owned studios suggests either Ubisoft is more enlightened or, being a French company, its corporate culture may be more responsive to labor concerns, making it the exception rather than the rule. Consequently, jobs at the Singapore facility are highly prized, attracting a competitive slew of applications whenever positions are posted.

Eastern Europe has also been one of the prime destinations for outsourcing, especially the cities of Prague, Budapest, Kiev, and Warsaw. These cities are renowned for independent contract companies with educated employees willing to work at comparatively low wages. Although most companies started out porting and translating PC games in the 1990s, many have now transitioned to developing original products, typically for international publishing partners like EA or Deep Silver.

As these production clusters continue to expand, studios in these regions face the same pressures as those in more established locales. Long hours, crunch time, unpaid overtime, and insufficient crediting systems are compounded by low wages and a dependence on foreign financial support. Thus, while more and more work gets shipped to these emerging regions, employees are subject to the same sorts of precarity as their Western-based counterparts. Indeed, workers at 2K's Prague offices were forced to move their families 206 kilometers to Brno in early 2014 when 2K decided to relocate the studio, a move that also involved a downsizing of the workforce.[41]

Most international publishers do not even bother to inspect the often dire working conditions at contract studios, seen as sources of cheap, efficient labor, in this region. In May 2013, for instance, former THQ president Jason Rubin publicly commented on tough conditions at 4A Games (*Metro* series) in Kiev where workers spent long days crammed into tight quarters, perched intently on foldout chairs.[42] Rubin was surprised to discover that 4A employees had to bring power generators from home because the electrical grid at work was so unreliable. The creative director, Andrew Prokhorov, later confirmed Rubin's observations, adding that Rubin had been the only THQ president to visit the studio in ten years, a pattern of neglect only too common for Eastern European partners. Prokhorov also confirmed that wages and working conditions paled in comparison to those in Western Europe and North America.

The offshoring of game production became an industry standard with the releases of the seventh- and eighth-generation game consoles. Major publishers like EA and Ubisoft have led the way, setting up owned-and-operated studios around the world to produce their biggest franchise titles and establishing a network of independent studios to maintain a steady supply of cost-effective, niche product. Unfortunately, working conditions, pay rates, and facilities differ widely depending on location and a studio's relationship with its publisher. Although these conditions are slowly improving in some places, the globalization of management strategies continues to pose daunting challenges for game developers, whether located in Los Angeles or Prague.

Paths to Change

In 2006 Nick Dyer-Witheford and Greig de Peuter argued that reforms could be best affected by educating management and unionizing the workforce.[43] Today both options remain on the table, but little tangible progress has been made on either front. While nobody denies crunch time is bad for the health and morale of game workers, few studios have eliminated the practice entirely. Likewise, although some game developers recognize the benefits of unionization—and indeed the Animation Guild has expressed interest in organizing the workforce—such discussions are still held in private and with full awareness that many industry employees are suspicious of labor unions. Beyond unionization, the rise of indie development has offered another path for workers to escape the conditions of the dominant industry, although this option does not necessarily improve the quality of life for the developer, nor does it address larger structural issues in any meaningful way.

The industry's major trade organization, the IGDA, tends to act as the de facto global representative for game developers, despite the fact that it largely serves developers in North America and lacks any real authority. The association's major efforts include supporting young talent, organizing events, collecting industry demographic data, advocating for diversity and better working conditions, offering legal and business advice, helping with credit disputes, and fighting government attempts to censor or restrict game sales. However, as a volunteer-run association with no actual leverage over the major employers in the games industry, the IGDA lacks sufficient resources to mobilize its members and enact real and lasting changes regarding the worst workplace abuses. For instance, after its own 2004 data illustrated widespread injustices, it took three years for the IGDA to respond with plans for an Employment Contract Quality of Life Certification, a document designed to 'encourage' basic minimum standards at the major studios, most of which were promptly ignored.[44]

In the past several years, many industry trade groups (although not the IGDA) have promoted the adoption of tax rebates for game development studios in various countries, states, and cities. National and local governments, despite a competing host of budgetary priorities, often cave in to such pressure, believing that incentives will create good jobs in the information and technology sectors. For example, the Independent Game Developers Association (TIGA) partnered with UKIE, the leading UK industry trade group, to convince the British government to add a new incentive program for digital game production in 2013, even though the country's economy was in the doldrums and public services were being slashed.[45]

Likewise, in the United States, local governments are starting to compete to attract digital game development studios, a trend that backfired for Rhode Island when the state spent millions to lure 38 Studios from neighboring Massachusetts only to have the company go bankrupt before the state could benefit from its recruitment effort.[46] Even as incentives dictate the growth of digital game production clusters, they do little to change the management structures in place or the precarious conditions under which workers must toil. Quite the contrary, these incentives tend to uproot families, force them to move from state to state, and sometimes leave them jobless with freshly signed mortgages, as was the case with the workers at 38 Studios.

Despite the shortcomings of trade groups, the IGDA has over time come to recognize the need to take stronger action on behalf of workers. After the economic downturn in 2008, the IGDA established a health care program that offers pooled health and benefit plans for U.S. members.[47] The IGDA has also pushed for more diversity in hiring practices, for example, supporting the spin-off organization Women in Games International (WIGI). WIGI attempts to provide mentorship and safe spaces for women and men in the industry, yet so far the group's efforts mostly involve social mixers and its mentorship program. Moreover, its membership is largely located in North America, making the 'International' aspect more aspirational than descriptive.[48] While these efforts by the IGDA, its special interest groups, and spin-offs are admirable, the organization stops short of organizing campaigns that might encourage real diversity in the industry or establish genuine negotiating leverage on behalf of workers.

The unionization question therefore continues to haunt the games industry. Marie-Josée Legault and Johanna Weststar discuss strategies game developers use to fight back against poor labor conditions (quitting, sabotage, speaking with management, lawsuits), yet none of these offer long-lasting solutions by comparison to collective action and full-scale unionization. Unfortunately, the majority of game workers would not support a traditional shop-by-shop form of union organizing.[49] However, 55 percent of game workers have indicated they would support an industrywide union along the lines of the Writers Guild of America.[50] In addition to a general antiunion ethos, the high mobility of game workers deters traditional site-specific organizing techniques. These challenges are remarkably analogous to those found in the visual effects (VFX) industry, which also rose to prominence in the 1990s. Both industries suffer troubling labor conditions and yet both workforces express reservations about unions and collective organizing.[51]

Owing to these challenges, Legault and Weststar suggest that a global, "industry-wide, multi-employer certification and negotiation process" could address many of these obstacles to unionization.[52] This would eliminate the need to organize studio by studio and instead allow game workers to join a single union that represents the entire global industry and sets basic minimum agreements for salaries, hours, credits, and benefits. Yet if the obstacles to organizing a single studio seem intimidating, the obstacles to organizing a global campaign seem even more challenging. Such an organization would have to overcome competition between countries, and a diverse patchwork of national laws, regulations, and policies. Moreover, workers in different parts of the world have different perspectives on unions. For instance, people in the former Soviet Bloc of nations have a more fraught relationship with unions because for the better part of the twentieth century they were state-run entities. Moreover, a standard concern for workers everywhere is that those locations that lead the way in labor organizing could end up driving game development to other parts of the world with lax labor laws, tax incentives, and cheaper wage rates.

An alternative, if equally uncertain, response to the corporatization of game development and managerial manipulation of the workforce is the rise of independent developers. Even the dominant publishers have embraced the surge in indie game development, as can be seen by the prominent position they now occupy at the Game Developers Conference and E3.[53] Of course, the majors are maneuvering to benefit from this trend, seeing indie studios as incubators of innovation, allowing the larger studios to avoid the riskiest margins of the business. The indie option is therefore an ephemeral alternative because successful shops are quickly absorbed by their larger competitors.

Moreover, what indie developers gain in authority and autonomy by operating outside the traditional publisher-run models, they lose in financial security. Small studios are constantly in search of capital even in the era of crowdfunding and online marketplaces, which have proven a boon to only a select few. This is especially a problem on congested distribution platforms like Apple's AppStore. In other words, one shouldn't expect dramatic changes in working conditions to come from the indie sector because it presents major publishers with opportunities, not radical pressures to change. On the contrary, the discourses of creative authority and autonomy that circulate within and around the indie sector tend to reinforce exploitation and precarity. The dream of making your own hours and your own product helps to reproduce a cultural mythology that is skeptical of collective action, focused on personal ambition, and only dimly aware of the larger structural forces that drive the digital game industry.

Perhaps surprisingly, labor exploitation has if anything increased since the early 2000s, as game workers continue to toil under difficult conditions systematically orchestrated by major publishers that have agilely expanded their production networks and political connections around the globe. Although in some places conditions have improved and in others new opportunities have arisen, most shops are governed by wages, practices, and prejudices that undermine common assumptions about game development as an elite creative or IT career. Moreover, the possibility of reversing this overall trend is profoundly uncertain, given the challenges of building a reform movement in an industry where most workers are isolated in cubicles, anxious about job security, skeptical about organized labor, and susceptible to illusions that the indie sector might offer their best hope for deliverance.

Notes

1 ea_spouse, "EA: The Human Story," ea-spouse.livejournal.com/274.html.
2 Marie-Josée Legault and Johanna Weststar, "More than the Numbers: Independent Analysis of the IGDA 2009 Quality of Life Survey," *Gameqol.com*, 2012.
3 Nick Dyer-Witheford and Greig de Peuter, *Games of Empire: Global Capitalism and Video Games* (Minneapolis: University of Minnesota Press, 2009).
4 Indeed, frequent callbacks to EA Spouse occur every few years with new whistle-blowers. See Rockstar Spouse archive. http://gameqol.org/rockstar-spouse/; and 38 Studios Spouse archive. http://gameqol.org/38-studios-spouse/.
5 John Howkins, *The Creative Economy* (New York: Penguin, 2001); Richard Florida, *Cities and the Creative Class* (New York: Routledge, 2005).
6 James Brightman, "Mobile Gaming to Push Industry Above $100 Billion by 2017," *Games Industry.Biz*. www.gamesindustry.biz/articles/2014–01–14-mobile-gaming-to-push-industry-above-USD100-billion-by-2017.
7 See, for instance, Jennifer Johns, "Video Games Production Networks: Value Capture, Power Relations and Embeddedness." *Journal of Economic Geography* 6, no. 2 (2006): 151–80.
8 Peter Zackariasson and Timothy Wilson, eds., *Video Game Industry: Formation, Present State, and Future* (New York: Routledge, 2012); Nina B. Huntemann and Ben Aslinger, eds., *Gaming Globally: Production, Play, and Place* (New York: Palgrave Macmillan, 2013).
9 For example: Tiziana Terranova, "Free Labor: Producing Culture for the Digital Economy." *Social Text* 18, no. 2 (2000): 33–58.

10 Mia Consalvo, "Crunched by Passion: Women Game Developers and Workplace Challenges," in *Beyond Barbie and Mortal Kombat: New Perspectives on Gender and Gaming*, edited by J. Denner, C. Heeter, Y. B. Kafai, and J.Y. Sun (Cambridge: MIT Press, 2008), 177–93; Dyer-Witheford and de Peuter, *Games of Empire*.

11 David Harvey, *Spaces of Global Capitalism* (London: Verso, 2006).

12 Michael Piore and Charles Sabel, *The Second Industrial Divide* (New York: Basic Books, 1984).

13 Toby Miller, Nitin Govil, John McMurria, Ting Wang, and Richard Maxwell, eds., *Global Hollywood 2* (London: British Film Institute, 2005).

14 Michael Curtin and John Vanderhoef, "A Vanishing Piece of the Pi: The Globalization of Visual Effects Labor." *Television & New Media* 16, no. 2 (2015).

15 IGDA, "Developer Satisfaction Survey (DDS) 2014 Summary Report," *IGDA*, 2014.

16 Marie-Josée Legault and Johanna Weststar, "Are Game Developers Standing Up for Their Rights?" *Gamasutra*. www.gamasutra.com/view/feature/184504/are_game_developers_standing_up_.php?print=1.

17 Mike Rose, "Uncredited *LA Noire* Staff Allege 'Praise-Free' Working Conditions," *Gamasutra*. www.gamasutra.com/view/news/35364/Uncredited_LA_Noire_Staff_Allege_PraiseFree_Working_Conditions.php.

18 Thomas Streeter, *The Net Effect: Romanticism, Capitalism, and the Internet* (New York: New York University Press, 2010).

19 Brooks Barnes, "Interactive Unit at Disney Cuts a Quarter of Its Staff," *New York Times*, March 6, 2014. www.nytimes.com/2014/03/07/business/media/disneys-game-and-internet-division-cuts-one-quarter-of-its-workforce.html?_r=2; Dave Tach, "Sony Santa Monica Hit with Layoffs," *Polygon*, February 25, 2014. www.polygon.com/2014/2/25/5447306/sony-santa-monica-layoffs; Samit Sarkar, "Irrational Games Closure Led to 75 Layoffs, Job Fair Hosted 57 Studios," *Polygon*, February 28, 2014. www.polygon.com/2014/2/28/5458470/irrational-games-closure-layoffs-75-job-fair-57-studios.

20 Jessica Conditt, "Square Enix Shuts Down Its India Studio after One Year, No Games," *Joystiq*, April 4, 2014. www.joystiq.com/2014/04/14/square-enix-shuts-down-its-india-studio-after-one-year-no-games/; Leo Barraclough, "Sony Computer Entertainment Lays Off 'Numerous' Staff at U.K. Vidgame Studios," *Variety*, March 26, 2014. http://variety.com/2014/digital/games/sony-computer-entertainment-lays-off-numerous-staff-at-u-k-vidgame-studios-1201146662/; Brendan Sinclair, "Sega Cuts Staff at London Office," *Gamesindustry.Biz*, April 9, 2014. www.gamesindustry.biz/articles/2014–04–09-sega-cuts-staff-at-london-office.

21 Legault and Weststar, "More than the Numbers."

22 Simon Parkin, "Rapture Leaked: The True Story Behind the Making of Bio-Shock," *Eurogamer*, April 17, 2014. www.eurogamer.net/articles/2014–04–17-the-true-story-of-bioshock.

23 Chris Plante, "The Final Years of Irrational Games, According to Those Who Were There," *Polygon*, March 6, 2014. www.polygon.com/2014/3/6/5474722/why-did-irrational-close-bioshock-infinite.

24 Ken Levine, "A Message from Ken Levine," *Irrational Games*, February 18, 2014. http://irrationalgames.com/new-featured/a-message-from-ken-levine-2/.

25 Ian Bogost, "The Squalid Grace of Flappy Bird," *The Atlantic*, February 3, 2014. www.theatlantic.com/technology/archive/2014/02/the-squalid-grace-of-flappy-bird/283526/.

26 IGDA, DSS 2014.

27 "Salary Survey," *Game Developer Magazine*, April 2013. http://twvideo01.ubm-us.net/o1/vault/GD_Mag_Archives/GDM_April_2013.pdf.

28 Leigh Alexander, "Taking on the Challenges of Being a Mom in Game Development," *Gamasutra*, January 23, 2014. www.gamasutra.com/view/feature/209100/taking_on_the_challenges_of_being_.php?page=1.

29 Nina B. Huntemann, "Women in Video Games: The Case of Hardware Production and Promotion," in *Gaming Globally*, edited by Nina B. Huntemann and Ben Aslinger (New York: Palgrave Macmillan, 2013), 41–58.

30 Jennifer deWinter and Carly Kocurek, "#1reasonwhy Women in the Gaming Industry Matters," *Flow*, February 20, 2013. http://flowtv.org/2013/02/1-reason-why-women-in-the-gaming-industry-matters/.

31 Adrienne Shaw, Shira Chess, Mia Consalvo, Nina B. Huntemann, Carol Stabile, and Jenny Stromer-Galley, "GamerGate and Academia," ICA Newsletter. http://icanewsletter.com/2014/11/04/gamergate-and-academia/.

32 IGDA, DSS 2014.

33 Superannuation, "How Much Does it Cost to Make a Big Video Game?" *Kotaku*, January 15, 2014. http://kotaku.com/how-much-does-it-cost-to-make-a-big-video-game-1501413649. For more work on emerging production regions, see essays in Huntemann and Aslinger's edited collection *Gaming Globally*.

34 James Brightman, "Outsourcing: The Quiet Revolution," *Bloomberg Businessweek*, March 12, 2006. www.businessweek.com/stories/2006–03–12/outsourcing-the-quiet-revolution.

35 Staff, "Survey: Outsourcing in Game Industry Still on Increase," *Gamasutra*, April 2009. www.gamasutra.com/php-bin/news_index.php?story=23008.

36 Peichi Chung and Anthony Fung, "Internet Development and the Commercialization of Online Gaming in China," in *Gaming Globally*, edited by Nina B. Huntemann and Ben Aslinger (New York: Palgrave Macmillan, 2013), 244.

37 Mary-Anne Lee, "How Ubisoft Shanghai Went from Porting Games to Pretty Damn Awesome in Less than a Decade," *Games in Asia*, February 10, 2014. www.gamesinasia.com/how-ubisoft-shanghai-went-from-porting-games-to-pretty-damn-awesome-in-less-than-a-decade/.

38 Superannuation, "Ubisoft Has Over 9,000 Employees," *Kotaku*, April 18, 2014. http://kotaku.com/ubisoft-has-over-9–000-employees-1563003254.

39 Samit Sarkar, "Assassin's Creed Unity Being Developed by 10 Ubisoft Studios Worldwide," *Polygon*, May 15, 2014. www.polygon.com/2014/5/15/5721832/assassins-creed-unity-developers-10-ubisoft-studios.

40 Mary-Anne Lee, "What Goes on Behind Closed Doors at Ubisoft Singapore," *Games in Asia*, December 23, 2013. www.gamesinasia.com/what-goes-on-ubisoft-singapore/.

41 Kyle Hilliard, "2K Shutting Down Prague Offices and Relocating Mafia II Developer 2K Czech," *Game Informer*, January 10, 2014. www.gameinformer.com/b/news/archive/2014/01/10/report-2k-shutting-down-prague-offices-and-relocating-mafia-ii-developer-2k-czech.aspx.

42 Staff, "Jason Rubin: Metro: Last Light Is the 'Triumph of an Underdog,'" *Gamesindustry. Biz*, May 15, 2013. www.gamesindustry.biz/articles/2013–05–15-jason-rubin-metro-last-light-is-the-triumph-of-an-underdog.

43 Nick Dyer-Witheford and Greig de Peuter, "'EA Spouse' and the Crisis of Video Game Labour: Enjoyment, Exclusion, Exploitation, Exodus." *Canadian Journal of Communication* 31, no. 3 (2006).

44 Dyer-Witheford and de Peuter, *Games of Empire*, 35

45 Dan Pearson, "EU Approves UK Games Tax Relief Signalling £188m Windfall," *Gamesindustry.Biz*, March 27, 2014. www.gamesindustry.biz/articles/2014–03–27-eu-approves-uk-games-tax-relief-signalling-188m-windfall.

46 For information on Rhode Island and 38 Studios, see Brian Crecente, "Rhode Island's Reckoning: A Quick History of 38 Studios and Their Deal with Rhode Island," *Polygon*, May 18, 2012. www.polygon.com/gaming/2012/5/18/3028766/rhode-islands-reckoning.

47 IGDA, "The IGDA Starts Healthcare Program," International Game Developers Association, November 16, 2009. http://igdaboard.wordpress.com/2009/11/16/the-igda-starts-healthcare-program.

48 Sheri Graner Ray, interview with the author, May 2012.

49 IGDA, DSS 2014.

50 IGDA, DSS 2014.

51 Curtin and Vanderhoef, "A Vanishing Piece of the Pi."

52 Legault and Weststar, "Are Game Developers Standing Up for Their Rights?"

53 Chris Suellentrop, "Indies Grab the Controls at a Game Conference," *New York Times*, March 31, 2013. www.nytimes.com/2013/04/01/arts/video-games/game-developers-conference-celebrates-indie-creators.html?ref=technology&_r=0.

VI

REDEFINING THE INDUSTRY

17

"WHAT ACTUALLY MATTERS"

Identity, Individualization, and Aspiration in the Work of Glossy Magazine Production

Nicholas Boston and Brooke Erin Duffy

Over the past two decades, profound shifts in information technologies, economies, and markets have transformed the glossy magazine industry. Indeed, changes wrought by digitization have unsettled the very notion of what a magazine *is* and *does* materially. From a commercial standpoint, magazine publishers have had to contend with pressures to defend their authority as textual information providers against the encroachment of native new-media entities, such as blogs and online publications, as well as visual storytellers in the face of photo-based social media in the form of Pinterest and Instagram. In response to these and other sources of competition, most magazine companies have implemented sharp turns in strategy and corporate structuring. The organizational decisions that result from these negotiations are the signposts that industry watchers monitor to best predict outcomes in what remains a highly murky and speculative future, the relationship of print to digital production. However, the implications of these moves for individual workers and their professional identities demand closer attention.

There is a scarcity of scholarship that analyzes the effects of digitization on magazine company workforces. Discussion of these effects is commonly found in trade and mainstream media reports of corporate strategizing. It is worthwhile, therefore, to begin by briefly considering two of these reports as tangible examples.

In the summer of 2014, Condé Nast Publications and Hearst Publications, two industry-leading U.S. corporations, announced decisive shifts in their production practices. Both shifts were designed to intensify these corporations' competitiveness in an economy where deals once brokered in the impervious, brick-and-mortar chambers of print publishing are increasingly conducted on interactive digital platforms.

First, Condé Nast announced the merger of its digital direct-sales unit with its automated, or so-called programmatic, advertising sales initiatives as part of a large-scale partnership with Google. Across industries, the negotiation of ad rates and placement in the digital space has been moving away from classic methods, whereby ad reps try to woo prospective marketers with offers of premium placement and package discounts, to automated systems programmed to algorithmically conduct transactions. Trade press coverage of the Condé Nast–Google partnership speculated whether it was a sign that the publishing company was "one step closer to . . . handing severance packages to direct sales teams" to be replaced by "Google robots."[1] Alanna Gombert, Condé Nast's head of digital sales, who, significantly, had been hired from Google merely two months prior, refuted this claim. She praised programmatic sales technology for clearing time for the workforce to explore creative horizons beyond the day-to-day demands of direct selling. The sales team, she said, could now "focus on *what actually matters*. I'm having lots more phone calls about creative and how to tell the story to the consumer to accomplish the goals of the campaign."[2] While Gombert's own corporate storytelling articulates a standing corporate discourse that online and offline convergence is ultimately beneficial, it fails to acknowledge the consequences for individual workers trained for and professionally socialized in the analogue world.

A few weeks after the Condé Nast announcement, Hearst Publications went public with a new advertising-related digital strategy of its own. The company launched a content distribution platform to which it planned to migrate all of its eighteen magazines' Web sites. Cosmopolitan.com was the first to be moved, inaugurating a template that featured enhanced opportunities for native advertising and sponsored content, including "ads that appear seamlessly between videos of male models cuddling kittens and buzzy stories on celebrities."[3] Nodding toward the benefits of the template for advertisers and readers alike, Hearst reps explained that new features would simultaneously widen opportunities for marketers in the 'post-banner world' and make content more responsive and sharable for the expanding digital audience base. As for the platform's benefits to the workforce, Cosmopolitan.com editor in chief Amy O'Dell cited productivity and speed. "We could publish 20 percent more content a day," she said.[4] The question remained of how the corporation intended to adjust its infrastructure to support workers, keep pace with this acceleration, and increase in content production.

These are merely two ventures in a stream of implementations at major magazine corporations that are integrating e-commerce and digital distribution to the monthly print-based repertoire. Yet the significant shifts they either trigger or reflect in the culture and organization of contemporary magazine production have received scant attention to date.

This chapter thus takes a cultural sociological approach to examining the contemporary magazine industry's digital evolution and some of its implications for magazine workers. We look at developments at the three largest U.S. magazine publishing companies: Condé Nast, Hearst, and Time, Inc.[5] Our focus is on the glossy magazine sector of the industry, which is distinctive in the content and physical properties of its products and the cultural characteristics of its professional environment. Glossies come in a range of consumer genres—indeed, it was in this sector that publishers pioneered the practice of niche marketing—including lifestyle, fashion, sports and fitness, travel, bridal, and home and garden. The most numerous offerings fall under 'women's interest,' which makes glossy magazines highly consumed by women. Moreover, because the magazine publishing industry has historically been characterized as a welcoming career for women, it is a useful context in which to explore the gender-technology-media work nexus. In this vein, this chapter searches for definitions behind Gombert's assertions of 'what actually matters' in the work of digitized magazine production. In so doing, it responds to Mayer's call for "production studies that consider identity and identification as key factors in future labor struggles."[6]

Contextualizing Magazine Production Studies

Although contemporary studies of media industries have enriched our understanding of the creation, distribution, and marketing of film, TV, music, and advertising,[7] the glossy magazine sector has been underappreciated as a fertile site for critical analysis. Such neglect is indicative of a wider blind spot in the study of print and digital media convergence, wherein research has tended to privilege the production and delivery of hard news. Or, as David Abrahamson put it, "Magazines remain second-class citizens in the journalism academy."[8] Additionally, because much of the academic work on consumer magazines has been preoccupied with magazine *texts*,[9] questions of labor and organization have been marginal in magazine scholarship.

In the early 2000s, a spate of book-length studies of UK-based magazine production cultures was published that engaged more fully with magazine workers and their environments. Crewe's work approached popular men's magazines produced in the 1980s and 1990s by, in part, analyzing the motivations and dispositions of the publications' editors.[10] He argued that the editors' subjective tastes were important determinants of magazine content, which was noteworthy because the men's magazine genre in the timeframe and national context of Crewe's study was interpolating male youth identity, the so-named new lad. Similarly, Gough-Yates explored the ways editors at women's magazines discursively positioned their readers as subjects in a political economy that afforded greater lifestyle choices for women, creating a cultural milieu that celebrated the "new woman."[11] These and other editorial agendas interface with the commercial and representational forces of advertising, hence Nixon explored the professional relationships, both formal and casual, between the two industries. The study offered an account of how professional considerations of consumerism and marketing play a role in the reification of gendered identities.[12]

The insights of these studies require updating to take account of the challenges digitization is presenting the magazine industry. Magazine publishing outfits now compete for advertisers and audiences with Web sites, mobile apps, and social media sites. Audience categories are continually splintering, their tastes and identities demanding closer editorial scrutiny to address and satisfy. The 24/7 information cycle has increased work demands, at the same time that technological innovation, such as data analytical tools and platforms, has altered the character and composition of workforces. For one, companies have devised new systems for the design, production, and distribution of digital content, such as the Hearst platform discussed earlier. Magazine companies have also reconfigured their workforces by hiring workers with technological expertise and multimedia branding acumen, such as Condé Nast's Gombert and Hearst's O'Dell, who came to the company from the Internet native outfit BuzzFeed. Yet even staffers who hail exclusively from print backgrounds are encouraged to self-define as content producers for *brands* rather than individual print publications. In line with this adjustment in job title and description, magazines such as *Seventeen, Cosmopolitan, Elle*, and *GQ* have made inroads into the merchandising, radio, TV, and interactive media industries, respectively, by producing branded content and commodities across multiple platforms.

This branding rhetoric also structures the overt commercial logic of many twenty-first-century publishers. Not only are companies working with advertisers in more explicit ways (e.g., native advertising, sponsored content, ad-subsidized covers), but they are also visibly partnering with clients as they move more directly into the territory of marketing services. These initiatives dovetail with efforts to compile more granular data on magazine audiences by utilizing data-tracking and monitoring programs. Taken together, these challenges and responses urge a critical reinvestigation of glossy magazine production culture.

Method

Our account of production cultures in the glossy magazine industry brings together two independently produced projects. One involved more than thirty in-depth interviews, including those conducted for a book-length project on the women's magazine industry in the era of digital and social media.[13] Informants, who represented titles and divisions across Time, Condé Nast, and Hearst, included senior executives, editors-in-chief, junior writers, brand directors, developers, and former interns. The second study was an ethnographic exploration of Condé Nast that involved a fifteen-month participant-observation stint as a freelance blogger at one of the company's largest Web sites.[14] Additionally, formal interviews were conducted with company employees involved in both print and new media production, personnel at other magazine corporations such as Hearst and Time, independent industry consultants, and deans of graduate journalism schools. Both of these studies also entailed participant observation at industry events (e.g., Association of Magazine Editors, MPA, Association of Magazine Media, and the Magazine Innovation Summit), as well as systematic reviews of trade and mainstream presses that disseminate news and analysis of the magazine publishing industry.

We draw on this data here to reassess three issues that have been remarked on in the existing media production literature: identity politics; the individualization of creative and media work; and discourses of aspiration deployed toward the extraction of 'free' labor. These areas have been the primary battlefronts as digitization continues to transform the magazine publishing industry.

Worker Identity: Gender and Class

Feminist media scholars have long condemned glossy magazines, particularly women's fashion, beauty, and service titles, for perpetuating heteronormative ideals of domestic femininity. While these critiques implicitly define women's magazines as *magazines for* female audiences, we have argued elsewhere that these texts should also be understood as *magazines of*—or produced by—a predominantly female workforce.[15] Indeed, histories of the industry suggest it was one of the few employment sectors where women were granted access, even if their role was largely to connect with fellow readers in a commercial context. The movement of female editorial workers into magazine offices accelerated in the last decades of the twentieth century and, specifically, in the wake of second-wave feminists' singling out of women's magazines as places where women should have improved access to careers, income, and benefits.

More recently, and in light of the emancipatory discourse that has coincided with the rise of new media (e.g., the assumption that women are 'empowered' by technologies that enable them to work from home),[16] some may conclude that the industry is an even more inclusive work environment. In 2009, a leading female magazine executive declared publishing was a "great career [field] for women."[17]

However, our findings suggest that the movement from analogue to digital production cultures may reproduce—rather than challenge—social inequalities of gender. More specifically, assumptions about the technological proficiency of the male worker subject seemed to guide hiring and placement decisions. Most of the digital executives we spoke with were male; most of the editorial representatives were female. *Marie Claire's* former digital assets manager Emily Masamitsu Scadden was clearly an exception, making her assessment of the field especially noteworthy. Emily acknowledged discernible gender patterns in the workplace: "The reality of it is that a lot of men are into [technology]. . . . So I think a lot of times that can overshadow some of the participation by women or women's publications." Emily's acknowledgment of women's magazines being 'overshadowed' spoke to a more pervasive narrative about the women's magazine industry, namely that it doesn't do "serious journalism,"[18] or that the industry is akin to what another informant termed "the stiletto ghetto."

Participant observation conducted at a Condé Nast Web site revealed highly gendered dynamics between two groups of employees we dubbed the Glitterati and the Digerati. The former group was composed of female fashion print journalists, stylists, or marketers valued for their authority in the glossy magazine industry and hired to staff the Web site. The latter group, composed of men, arose from the new media workforce with expertise in digital and had been hired to manage the site. The two Digerati held most senior management positions at the site. About this situation, Jessica, a Glitterati, commented:

> They hired them more for their Internet experience, not for their experience in fashion. So, here are these straight men who are into, like, "the scene" and, you know, are kind of excited that they're at the "cool" place now. And clearly they had come from a place that was not fashion and they didn't really get it and didn't understand how fashion magazines are really put together or work. So, it was hard [for me] adjusting because they didn't necessarily structure it [the Web site] in the way that all fashion magazines are structured, so it was a big adjustment that way.

A bit of history is in order to unpack this quote. The recruitment of personnel at this Web site, one of Condé Nast's oldest and most heavily trafficked, reveals wider shifts in the media ecology. The burst of the dot.com bubble in 2001 produced widespread joblessness among Web developers and content producers.[19] These laid-off people were not only Web-trained professionals, but culturally oriented to the Internet. When the Internet reconstituted itself into what came to be known as Web 2.0, media companies began implementing new models for their online platforms. They turned to refugees from the first wave of online activity who were the best trained, most experienced, and, crucially, readily available professionals. At Condé Nast, these mostly male workers were the first hires in the group we define as the Digerati. These examples suggest we should approach narratives of technologically enabled meritocracy with a healthy degree of skepticism. In the magazine industry, at least, social hierarchies of gender may be reaffirmed—rather than challenged—by emergent production cultures and mandates.

Intensified Demands and the Individualization of Work

Creative workplaces have long been marked by long hours, temporary work arrangements, and the mindset that "you're only as good as your last [TV script, magazine article, commercial]."[20] Against this backdrop, it is perhaps not surprising that our informants were scrambling to keep abreast of technological change, particularly managerial directives or expectations that they 'think across various platforms.' At times, this cross-platform intelligence was facilitated by the company by, for instance, arranging skills-building retreats for staff such as one we attended in 2008, a stage of intensifying digital brand extension in the glossy magazine industry. More often, it was incumbent upon workers themselves to 'get up to speed' on such methods. Martha Nelson, who was editor in chief of Time Inc. at the time of our interview, remarked of the incorporation of tablet production mandates, "There were bumps along the road but generally it's really successful . . . [and editors] wanted to be involved when we were putting the magazine up. Because it's in their business and they know that." She added, "For their own career development, they need to know more about the iPad."

Many informants indicated that their added duties were not accompanied by adjustments in pay or time schedules. Sophie, a senior features editor at one of Condé Nast's premiere women's magazines, said in 2009:

> We are now required to edit for online. I am 36; I'm the youngest of the editors. So, you can imagine, none of us signed on to, or trained in, or really desire, to be frank, to work on the Net. Nothing against the Web, but that's not my thing. I don't want to do 200-word, fast, slap-it-on stories. But now each of us posts a couple times a week, partly because our pages in the magazine are down. [Editor in chief] is focused on the Web because she feels like it's a way to raise the profile of the magazine. So we now have online content that we have to produce. It's become an annoying part of my job, a fly buzzing around reminding me that "Oh, there's this post that I have to get up today." It's another couple of pieces to think about each week versus a monthly 2,000-word piece.

Others acknowledged how work responsibilities crept into non-work hours, symptomatic of what Melissa Gregg termed "presence bleed."[21] While *InStyle's* Lisa Arbetter explained that working across platforms had become "a juggling act of sorts," Chris Wilkes, vice president of the App Lab at Hearst Magazines, explained how about half of the staffers in the lab "had a day job in our company" but "moonlighted" in the App Lab. As he explained, "they have a primary focus that is not having to do with app lab but they've got skill sets that I've recruited . . . and I have them contributing or participating."

While digitization is creating new challenges for producers to 'think across platforms,' emergent platforms have also created opportunities for freelancers to write for blogs. However, they do so with the long-standing obligation to self-promote, commonly termed 'the hustle,' the never-ending quest to identify and secure the next or better gig. This quest was visible in a stable of bloggers that formed a virtually connected network although they were based in geographically disparate locations: New York, Los Angeles, London, Berlin, and Paris. Their professional training and educational backgrounds were also quite varied. Among them were a PhD student at an elite UK university, a columnist for an internationally renowned newspaper, a former editor at one of *Vogue*'s international editions, and a male socialite who self-fashioned as a latter-day Truman Capote auteur, socializing very closely with a well-heeled New York society crowd. This last blogger always wrote his posts in the first person—something none of the other bloggers was allowed to do. He was no doubt self-branding with a view toward striking out on his own media ventures, and because of his extensive social connections that facilitated his reporting, he was permitted to do so by editors.

Another way individualization manifested was as what scholars have termed 'compulsory sociality,' or networking that takes place in leisure time.[22] As a blogger, even when not on actual assignment, it was an informal, unspoken element of the job, un-facilitated and unfinanced by the company, to go out socially to 'check out the scene' and scout for bloggable material. Regular outings were done to make connections with people who would keep bloggers apprised of upcoming events and put their names on media or guest lists. There was a pervasive overtone of instrumentality in these social interactions: bloggers and other reporters seeking out stories, contacts, and 'ins'; entrepreneurs promoting their products or brands; and publicists of various stripes, while enjoying social time, keeping their professional antennae attuned to marketing possibilities or media opportunities for their clients. These instrumental dealings were not taken as expressions of insincerity, or even opportunism, unless they were carried out either by amateurs whose affective skills—their facility at schmoozing—were underdeveloped, or by individuals deemed to have nothing to offer in return on the terms set by the context: access to product, insider knowledge, career opportunity, or social capital.

The reward of the individualization of work we observed came in the form of a narrative that constructed those successful in mastering multiplatform competencies, adjusting to extended work hours, and absorbing additional expenses on their own cognizance and resourcefulness as 'right fits.' The cultivation of this technology of the self and discourse of individual agency, we found, in turn enabled the worker to advocate for less precarious work conditions.

Contingent Labor and Aspiration

Magazine companies have long maintained a contingent workforce of freelance creative workers on contract. While some companies boast of integrating these temporary workers into the corporate culture—an online editor for *InStyle* explained that freelance contributors are given office space within the organization to ensure a consistent editorial voice—the majority hold marginal standing within organizations. Blogging, as both a new technology and form of labor, disrupted this model.

While most pre-digital freelance workers were satellites in their professional universes, the blogger, given the spatial and social affordances of the Internet, was, at least initially, a far more independent and agentic worker who did not require, or even seek, the same measure of integration into the organization.

The practice of blogging intervened on established professional and organizational hierarchies. As Singer observes of newspaper industry dynamics, "Bloggers and others who have never set foot in a newsroom can and do legitimately claim some of the same occupational turf [as journalists]."[23] The blog introduced a channel through which aspiring or independent media professionals could pursue career or creative aspirations outside the mandates and platforms of corporate media. Initially, magazine publishing companies assumed a defensive stance on blogging, enabled by gatekeepers in related industries, such as fashion, where bloggers were denied official access to spaces such as Fashion Weeks, for media coverage. Condé Nast's peculiar organizational culture complicated this dynamic. As one Condé Nast online editor, who belonged to the Glitterati workforce, said:

> Condé Nast encourages unreasonable behavior [in its senior employees] because it kind of adds to the mystique of Condé Nast. A blog is not part of that mystique. It's not a beautiful, glossy magazine. It's the Web. And Condé Nast does not respect the Web.

This scenario began to change once industry insiders came to acknowledge blogs' economic and communicational potential. As noted in a 2006 *Wall Street Journal* report:

> Once snubbed by the insular fashion world . . . fashion bloggers are now attracting the attention of the fashion establishment. As blogs claim bigger followings, and advertisers shift more spending to them, designers see these independent Web publishers as a new marketing opportunity. Many small designers, in particular, now realize they can get valuable exposure on blogs that they might not get in mainstream media. This year, with 191 shows in New York, up 25% from five years ago, there aren't enough old-media critics to cover them all.[24]

In this climate, the stance of a magazine company like Condé Nast on bloggers and the blog platform shifted from defensiveness to what management theorist Daniel Isenberg has termed strategic opportunism: the organization integrated blogs into its own online editorial offerings.[25] Yet, as late as September 2008, when we began our research as freelance bloggers there, Condé Nast still regarded blogging practices as antithetical to its ethos, an organizational culture that operationalizes aspiration. In the words of a senior online director, a Digerati, who oversaw the Web site at which we worked:

We are an aspirational company, whether we're online or in the magazine space. I mean, that's the DNA of Condé Nast. It is upscale. If it's not that, then what is Condé Nast? I think that's important for the Web arm of the company, too. And, yes, so how do you translate that online? I think if you look at what we do, it's all really nicely designed. We're not *just a blog*. I shouldn't say, "just a blog," because blogs, in some ways, are the dominant way of presenting material on the Web and there are fabulous blogs and they're really successful, but, you know, I don't think that's quite right for us. We present these really nicely designed stories and I think that maintains the aspirational quality.

Internships were another form of contingent 'employment' for magazine companies in the midst of post-recession financial turmoil that instrumentalizes aspiration to extract free or low-cost labor. Bright-eyed college students and newly minted graduates eager to stand out among the inflated supply of creative workers willfully provide administrative and editorial support in exchange for a bit of padding on the résumé or the fleeting chance to schmooze with industry power players. One of our informants even bragged that her internship at Condé Nast gave her the distinct privilege of "carry[ing] Anna Wintour's dresses down to her limo." Of course, as Ross Perlin and others have noted, unpaid internships within the so-called glamour industries tend to exacerbate social hierarchies as young people whose families earn modest incomes can scarcely afford to forego monetary compensation.[26] Recent college graduate Kelly reflected rather favorably on her stint as an intern at *Teen Vogue* and "would not take back that experience for the world." However, she confessed that the unpaid position required her to commute back and forth between Philadelphia and New York (nearly 100 miles) at least three times a week. She continued:

> There were times when events were happening, and I wanted to be there so I'd end up staying a whole week. I would have to buy new outfits because I was staying extra days, and buy new bus tickets because I was staying extra days, brushing my teeth in a Starbucks. Like the weirdest things that I thought I would never be doing, I was doing for this job, and I wasn't getting paid to do it.

Others have faced quite grueling conditions, ranging from long hours and menial tasks to pejorative treatment and most staggeringly, a lack of recourse in sexual harassment suits. In October 2013, Condé Nast announced the shuttering of its coveted internship program. The decision came in the wake of a class action lawsuit filed by two former Condé Nast interns who alleged that the company violated federal and state labor laws by compensating them less than the minimum wage.

The close of Condé Nast's internship program (and the subsequent attention to internship conditions at competitors Hearst and Time) coupled with the dwindling of full-time employees may help to explain why magazine companies increasingly rely on digital content freely provided by consumers. From Instagram accounts that magazine readers are encouraged to 'follow' and 'like' to user-generated contests promoted on the Web sites, to opportunities to directly connect with editors and stylists, magazine companies are encouraging their fans to interact with publications and their staffers across brand platforms. Some digitally enabled initiatives seemingly address consumers' aspirations to break into the fashion or journalism industry. In 2014, for example, *Teen Vogue* launched the Instalist promotion that spotlighted ten young fashion enthusiasts with a substantial number of Instagram followers. As Publisher/Senior VP Jason Wagenheim explained to us, the initiative featured "up-and-com[ers] . . . that we would deputize, for lack of a better word, to work editorially and help us identify street style, and trends, and everything else."

Although these denizens of the new media world presumably enjoy the opportunity to gain followers to their own sites, they are lured to participate by the rhetoric of 'exposure,' a pipedream of rising above the din of the truly ordinary. In fact, in the *Teen Vogue* campaign, Wagenheim admitted that they don't pay Instalist-ers but, rather, are "helping them build their own brand through promotion in *Teen Vogue.*" This celebration of self-branding does little to obscure the value provided to the magazine and its sponsors who benefit from 'free' word of mouth. Commenting on the benefit for advertisers, Wagenheim added, "We had three editorial themes that the editors released on Instagram and then the Instalisters went and used those themes to tag advertisers and give a nice . . . swell to some of our advertising partners." Moreover, because these individuals fill their sites with personal information (e.g., habits, preferences)—and encourage their readership to do the same by leaving feedback or entering contests—they are enabling what Van Dijck and Nieborg describe as "tak[ing] the guesswork out of marketing by letting customers create online brand communities which then serve as marketing niches."[27]

While other companies have yet to suspend their internships, they continue to appeal to audiences' career aspirations, suggesting that by participating in a contest (e.g., *Glamour*'s "Young and Posh"), getting one's name emblazoned on a billboard screen (e.g., *Cosmopolitan*'s "Fun, Fearless, Female" promo), or being incorporated into a magazine-branded network (e.g., *Lucky*'s Style Collective for Bloggers), consumer-audiences can share the spotlight with magazine 'professionals.' Such forms of brand devotion encourage participants to align themselves with corporate sponsors while serving as brand ambassadors who work not for money, but for potential 'exposure.'

Conclusion

From the ever-revolving door of the C-suite to the flow of magazine brand content across social media platforms to savvy 'partnerships' with audiences and advertisers, the glossy magazine industry has changed dramatically in recent years. However, such transformations should not obscure some of the traditional work realities and tensions that have become more firmly ingrained in the culture of magazine production. For one, despite emancipatory discourses of female empowerment that frequently circulate in the new media sector, the gender distribution of workers in the digitized magazine space remains markedly disproportionate. Such social hierarchies are embedded in larger structural inequalities of the male-dominated tech sector. We find this imbalance particularly problematic within an industrial site where cultural products are primarily aimed at female consumers. It signals the continued relevance of an argument Liesbet van Zoonen put forward over a decade ago that "The political (new) economy of the internet thus tends to reconstruct the common gendered distinction between consumption and production, between entertainment and information."[28]

Demands on creative workers in the scene of magazine production are intensifying. Magazine editors are increasingly expected to work across magazine platforms and titles, often without commensurate remuneration. Meanwhile, for those trying to break into the industry—whether as freelance bloggers or interns—forms of compulsory sociality may prove a more reliable path than accomplishments listed on a résumé. The instrumentalization of social media platforms means that not only full-time and contract-based workers are contributing content; in an era where the power of the audience is valorized, magazine brands are encouraging consumers to contribute to the output of knowledge or content vis-à-vis interactive promotions, feedback spaces, and other incentives channeled through an aspirational prism. Aspiring media makers are enlistees in the reserve army of the unpaid, seduced by companies who promise to pay in 'exposure' rather than immediate income. That these participants—*Teen Vogue* Insta-listers, *Cosmopolitan* "Fun, Fearless, Female" entrants, *Lucky*-affiliated bloggers—are women may make these assurances particularly pernicious. As Sarah Banet-Weiser writes of the rise of such forms of post-feminist self-branding, "technologies of the self have vast and often contradictory implications for women in the 21st century, where 'putting oneself out there' and the ensuing quest for visibility, is an ever more normative practice."[29]

Taken together, these findings suggest that magazines are what historian Nancy Walker described as "revealing cultural artifacts" because of not only their nuanced *textual* messages, but also a *production* culture rife with contradiction and nuance. And it is because—rather than in spite—of such nuance that we urge more scholarly attention to the consumer magazine industry, particularly the glossies.

In this chapter, then, we have shown how magazine production research can shed new light on industrial transformations related to digitization, participatory culture, and the individualization of work. More significantly, we contend that the magazine industry's recent challenges and responses may presage larger shifts in creative labor in an era of digitally reconfigured circuits of media production and consumption.

Notes

1 Tim Peterson, "Condé Nast Teams with Google to Pitch Programmatic Ad Deals," *Ad Age*, May 22, 2014. http://adage.com/article/media/conde-nast-teams-google-pitch-programmatic-ad-deals/293366/.
2 Peterson, "Condé Nast Teams"; "Condé Nast's Digital Ad Army Is Not Being Replaced by Google Robots, Thank You!" *Media Wire Daily*, May 2014. www.mediawiredaily.com/2014/05/conde-nasts-digital-ad-army-is-not.html.
3 Alexandra Stiegard, "Cosmopolitan.com Gets a Makeover," WWD.com, July 8, 2014. www.wwd.com/media-news/fashion-memopad/cosmopolitancom-undressed-7787275.
4 Steigard, "Cosmopolitan.com Gets a Makeover."
5 The former two are privately held by family dynasties, while the latter is publicly traded. Condé Nast and Hearst produce so-called aspirational magazines with heavy advertising from luxury brands, particularly women's designer apparel companies, whereas Time's offerings are news- and service-oriented, with diversified advertising content.
6 Vicki Mayer, *Below the Line: Producers and Production Studies in the New Television Economy* (Durham, NC: Duke University Press, 2011), 3.
7 See, for instance, Vicki Mayer, Miranda Banks, and John T. Caldwell, eds., *Production Studies* (London and New York: Routledge, 2009); Mark Deuze, *Media Work* (Cambridge: Polity Press, 2007); David Hesmondhalgh, *The Cultural Industries* (London: Sage, 2012).
8 Quoted in Scott Fosdick, "The State of Magazine Research in 2008." *Journal of Magazine and New Media Research* 10, no. 1 (2008): 1–4.
9 See, for example, Ros Ballaster et al., *Women's Worlds: Ideology, Femininity and the Woman's Magazine* (New York: Macmillan, 1991); Bethan Benwell, ed., *Masculinity and Men's Lifestyle Magazines* (Oxford: Wiley Blackwell, 2003); Kenon Breazeale, "In Spite of Women: *Esquire* Magazine and the Construction of the Male Consumer." *Signs* 20 (1994): 1–22; David Gauntlett, *Media, Gender and Identity: An Introduction* (London and New York: Routledge, 2002); Angela McRobbie, *Feminism and Youth Culture: From "Jackie" to "Just Seventeen"* (London: Macmillan 1991; New York: Routledge, 2000); Janice Winship, *Inside Women's Magazines* (New York: Pandora Press, 1987).
10 Ben Crewe, *Representing Men: Cultural Production and Producers in the Men's Magazine Market* (Oxford: Berg, 2003).
11 Anna Gough-Yates, *Understanding Women's Magazines: Publishing, Markets and Readerships* (London and New York: Routledge, 2003).
12 Sean Nixon, *Advertising Cultures: Gender, Commerce, Creativity* (London: Sage, 2003).
13 Brooke Erin Duffy, *Remake, Remodel: Women's Magazines in the Digital Age* (Champaign: University of Illinois Press, 2013).

14 Nicholas Boston, "Digitizing 'Aspirationalism': Magazine-to-New_Media Work in the Mediatic *Mise en Abyme* at Condé Nast, Inc.," PhD. diss., University of Cambridge, 2013.

15 Duffy, *Remake, Remodel*.

16 Scholars like Rosalind Gill and Melissa Gregg have challenged these utopian claims. Rosalind Gill, "Cool, Creative and Egalitarian?: Exploring Gender in Project-Based New Media Work in Europe," *Information, Communication and Society* 5, no. 1 (2002): 70–89. Melissa Gregg, *Work's Intimacy* (London: Polity, 2011).

17 "Top Women in Magazine Publishing," *Publishing Executive*. www.pubexec.com/docs/top-women-publishing.

18 Jessica Grose, "Can Women's Magazines Do Serious Journalism? Some People Don't Think So," *New Republic*, June 17, 2013. www.newrepublic.com/article/113511/can-womens-magazines-do-serious-journalism.

19 Andrew Ross, *No-Collar: The Humane Workplace and Its Hidden Costs* (Philadelphia, PA: Temple University Press, 2004).

20 Helen Blair, "'You're Only as Good as Your Last Job': The Labour Process and Labour Market in the British Film Industry." *Work, Employment & Society* 15, no. 1 (2001): 149–69.

21 Gregg, *Work's Intimacy*.

22 See, for example, Rosalind Gill, "Life Is a Pitch: Managing the Self in New Media Work," in *Managing Media Work*, edited by Mark Deuze (Thousand Oaks, CA, London, India, Singapore: Sage, 2011), 249; Rosalind Gill and Andy Pratt, "In the Social Factory?" *Theory, Culture & Society* 25, no. 7–8 (2008): 1–30; Gregg, *Work's Intimacy*.

23 Jane B. Singer, "Journalism in a Network," in Deuze, *Media Work*, 161.

24 Rachel Dodes, "Bloggers Get under the Tent," *Wall Street Journal*, September 12, 2006. http://online.wsj.com/articles/SB115801727410860002.

25 Daniel Isenberg, "The Tactics of Strategic Opportunism," *Harvard Business Review*, May 2009, 92–7. This term was originally proposed with a different meaning by Barbara Hayes-Roth in "A Blackboard Model of Control," Heuristic Programming Project, Report HPP-83–38 (Stanford, CA: Stanford University, 1983).

26 Ross Perlin, *Intern Nation: How to Earn Nothing and Learn Little in the Brave New Economy* (New York: Verso, 2012).

27 José van Dijck and David Nieborg, "Wikinomics and Its Discontents: A Critical Analysis of Web 2.0 Business Manifestos." *New Media & Society* 11, no. 5 (2009): 855–74.

28 Liesbet van Zoonen, "Feminist Internet Studies." *Feminist Media Studies* 1, no. 1 (2001): 67–72.

29 Sarah Banet-Weiser, *Authentic™: The Politics of Ambivalence in a Brand Culture* (New York: New York University Press, 2012), 55.

18

THE TRICK OF THE TRADES

Media Industry Studies and the American Comic Book Industry

Alisa Perren

Media industry studies scholars rely on a variety of sources to conduct their research, including court proceedings, annual reports, press releases, archival records, third-party industry reports, policy documents, magazine features, and newspaper articles. Such sources can provide a rich understanding of issues like ownership patterns, business strategies, government-industry relations, and labor practices. However, these sources often cannot provide the type of thick description available to those using methods drawn from cultural studies of production such as interviews and observation. These methods better enable scholars to speak to the lived experiences, cultural values, and representational practices of those working for and interacting with the media industries.

The strengths of such production studies methodologies, as well as the limitations of one particular, heavily relied on resource of media industry researchers—trade publications (e.g., *Variety, Broadcasting & Cable, Publisher's Weekly*)—are illustrated in this chapter through a case study of a specific industry: the American comic book business. Indeed, production studies methods can variably complement, enrich, and complicate other types of media industry studies scholarship. Through interviews and observation, industry researchers have the potential to learn about stakeholders other than those regularly represented in press reports; they also might better understand the complicated ways that social, political, and cultural factors impact creative choices, institutional relationships, and structural conditions.

For example, while Hollywood's trade publications might focus primarily on major media conglomerates' growing dependence on and exploitation of comic book properties as a source of profit, my interviews with those 'in the trenches' shed light on the ramifications of these industrial shifts on workers' personal and professional identities. What is not evident in the pages of *Variety* or even in the industry-specific *Comic Book Resources* are the ways that those working in the comic book industry are engaged in complex struggles over definitions of identity—whether professional (e.g., fan vs. amateur vs. professional), spatial (e.g., New Yorker vs. Los Angeleno vs. Atlantan), medium-specific (e.g., film and TV-trained writer vs. comic book-trained writer), or role-based (e.g., inker vs. colorist vs. editor). Whether serving as historical context, foundational knowledge prior to conducting ethnographic research, or discursive sites of analysis, industry trade publications can be valuable resources for a variety of different types of media industry studies researchers. Yet especially in the contemporary moment, when the media industries—and the trades themselves—are so in flux, important issues must be considered when referring to them for information. The trades' limitations, in turn, underscore the distinctive insights that production studies methods might provide, and call our attention to different types of information, relationships, and industrial power dynamics.

Some Do's and Don'ts When Consulting the Trades

Trade publications such as *Variety, Hollywood Reporter, Broadcasting & Cable, Billboard, Comic Book Resources, Publisher's Weekly,* and *Advertising Age* are often the go-to sources for industry professionals, the means by which media workers keep up with the latest news about their business. Historically, the trades have been valuable resources for media industry researchers for a number of reasons. First, they typically cover crucial industrial issues, events, and players in far more detail and with greater regularity than do mainstream publications. Not only can researchers follow the latest news pertaining to a particular issue, but they can also see how discussions about that issue have developed over time. Second, trade publications provide researchers with vital background knowledge, helping them to fill in the blanks before they initiate interviews with industry practitioners. As problematic as trade publications often are (a point to be discussed further), the fact remains that they are relied on heavily by many of those working within the business of entertainment. Third, the trades provide a sense of the dominant discourses within the media industries. Different trades speak to different industrial sectors and have their own language (or "slanguage," as *Variety* calls it). By reading these publications, it is possible to get a snapshot of the mindset of 'the industry' in the broadest sense—the anxieties, priorities, and achievements of those in power. Political economists such as Robert McChesney and Jennifer Holt have used the trades productively to illustrate changing patterns of ownership and control; media historians such as Tino Balio and Michele Hilmes have turned to them to analyze dominant industry strategies and business practices at different historical moments.[1] The range of scholarship informed by the industry trades is expansive and impressive.

As helpful as the trades can be—especially for those lacking other resources or direct access to the media industries—scholars are well aware that they must be approached with caution. As John Caldwell argues, the trades frequently function as little more than the public relations arm for the media industries. What's more, he argues, they often perpetuate long-standing industrial myths. He warns against media industry studies scholars using what is presented in the trades as the truth or in taking their reports at face value. Indeed, Caldwell's detailed analysis of Hollywood's below-the-line workers in *Production Culture* presents a different vision of that industry than is on display in the trades.[2]

Although the trades are clearly problematic, they should not be rejected out of hand. Kenton T. Wilkinson and Patrick F. Merle previously have identified several benefits and drawbacks involved in relying on trade publications.[3] They underscore the stunning regularity with which the trades have been incorporated uncritically and with a lack of self-reflexivity into work undertaken by communication studies researchers. Several of the considerations that they address are incorporated in this chapter, albeit reframed in ways that speak more directly to the interests and objectives of media industry studies scholars.

Perhaps the overarching point that industry-oriented researchers should keep in mind is that the trades function *as part of* the media industries in general, and of the news business more specifically. As such, issues discussed extensively in the studies of the journalism—and issues facing journalists today—are pertinent to consider when approaching the trades. Those coming to the study of the media industries from more humanistic backgrounds in film and media studies, in particular, might not have read widely on the sociology of news (see Gans; Tuchman). Yet it is vital to do so in order to be cognizant of how institutional cultures constrain what journalists can do as well as how the pursuit of advertising dollars impacts what is covered.[4] The trades are especially dependent on advertising revenue from the specific industries they cover, and will do what they can to curry favor from the biggest players (and often heaviest advertisers) in that industry. This is especially apparent during awards seasons; the trades' coverage reflects their financial dependence on major studios, networks, and so forth. Further, trade reporters rely on the same types of sources that journalists rely on more generally—official sources, public relations spokespeople, press conferences, quarterly conference calls with investors, wire services, and so on.[5] These sources, of course, frame certain issues in particular ways. Reporters typically avoid being too critical of such sources both in the interest of 'journalistic objectivity' and in order to remain in favor with them, thereby continuing to gain access to vital players and events.

Beyond this general context, a couple other key issues are worth noting. First, the trades aren't what they used to be. These publications have been affected as much as the rest of the news business by digitization, conglomeration, and consolidation. Older trades have been gutted (e.g., *Variety*) or reformatted (e.g., *The Hollywood Reporter*) while newer publications have emerged as go-to sources (e.g., *Deadline Hollywood, The Wrap*). The quality of reporting as well as the attention to copy editing at these outlets is uneven at best. Fewer resources and smaller staffs have led trade reporters to rely even more on press releases than they had in the past. Such conditions have also led to larger gaps in what is covered. Such gaps can be partially filled by surveying a wider range of sources, as many formerly print-based journalists have now dispersed to a wide range of Web-based start-ups (e.g., *Buzzfeed, Huffington Post, Hitfix*, etc.). Researchers face additional challenges in turning to these new venues. While at times, they can provide substantive reporting and analysis unavailable in established trade publications, just as often, they turn to salacious topics likely to gain page views. In this context, industry researchers need to be especially attuned to which reporters can be relied on for accuracy. Even more troubling, as publications have turned primarily to the Web to publish content, their archives have proven unstable; links might change and articles might be altered with no prior notice.

Second, the trades are concerned primarily with the most prominent executives and top creative figures. Although they are, in a broad sense, targeted to those who work in the industry they cover, they are most explicitly speaking for and to those in positions of greater economic and cultural power. Smaller companies, lower-level managers, and below-the-line workers rarely merit coverage unless there is a controversy surrounding them in some fashion. Not only does this typically translate into a 'great white man' and 'great Western company' presentation of the industry, but it also diminishes the complicated network of relationships (both institutional and interpersonal) that exists within the media industries.

While these considerations must be kept in mind in approaching any of the trades that cover the media industries, these publications nonetheless have value, speaking to and for each industry sector in specific ways. Perhaps nowhere is this more apparent than with the modestly sized American comic book industry, an industry in which the trades often function (and are perceived by those within that industry) more as hybrid fansites-PR venues than as official, legitimate sources of business information. The distinctive relationship that this industry has to its audience, as well as to other media industries, makes it an especially revealing and instructive topic. The issues that come to the fore in analyzing the comics industry, in turn, can shed light on issues pertinent to other industrial sectors and other national/regional contexts. At the same time, the particular challenges that arise in studying the comics business reinforce how important it is for industry researchers to understand the culture, politics, and structural conditions of the *specific* industry sector(s) they are studying.

Two Tales of the American Comic Book Industry

The comic book industry serves as my object of analysis here for three key reasons. First, on the most basic level, it is the industry to which I have had the greatest personal access. During the past several years, I have had the opportunity to interview numerous comic book artists and writers, as well as observe their interactions on social media, at popular culture conventions across the United States, and in work contexts in Los Angeles, New York, San Diego, and Atlanta. Through these exchanges, I have gained a sense of the comics industry that is far different and more complex than the one depicted in *Variety* or the *Los Angeles Times*. Even a casual observer can see that comic book properties are all the rage—our screens are overwhelmed with images of characters ranging from Spider-Man to Hellboy to Scott Pilgrim. Although news stories trumpet Hollywood's growing dependence on comic book properties, they rarely convey the ways these changes are impacting comic book professionals directly. As the lines between comics and other media are renegotiated, these professionals are seeing their work roles and processes redefined, their ideas about career trajectories adjusted, their professional and personal identities altered, and their relationships with audiences, employers, and colleagues transformed. The meaning of a medium—and an industry—is shifting, and these pros are on the front lines of such shifts.

A second reason that the comics industry serves as a productive site of analysis is because it has received such limited attention either by comics studies scholars or by media industry studies scholars. Comics studies scholars have tended to focus on the formalist, ideological, and sociocultural dimensions of the medium; their emphasis has been largely on legitimating the study of comics within the context of literature and rhetoric programs.[6] Meanwhile, media industry scholars largely have viewed comics as a negligible extension of the publishing industry or as 'merely' intellectual property exploited by the filmed entertainment industries. Certainly the limited financial returns generated from the American comic book industry would lead many political economists to dismiss its relative economic worth: according to one industry report, the publishing component of this industry generated a modest $770 million in revenue and $125 million in profits in 2013.[7] This is in contrast to an estimated $37.6 billion in revenue and $1.6 billion in profits for the American broadcast industry in the same year.[8] Yet the comic book industry's perpetually marginal cultural status and uncertain economic value might be seen as advantageous from an analytical perspective. With so little scholarly literature on the comics industry readily available—and much of the industrially produced literature proving equally problematic methodologically, as discussed further later in this chapter—there arises the potential to rethink how we study the comics industry as well as other related industries. Indeed, an examination of the small, insular niche industry of comics might provide fresh ways for thinking about how industry studies are conducted across media.

This point connects to the third reason that the comics industry is a compelling site for analysis: namely, depending on the sources consulted and definitions used, this industry can be considered as a stand-alone business or it can be seen as a part of the magazine industry, the book industry, and/or the filmed entertainment business. The figures mentioned earlier define this modestly sized industry solely in terms of publishing output (graphic novels and comic books, including digital books). Certain third-party business reports as well as political economic analyses similarly isolate identifiable traits of the contemporary comic book industry. These traits include:

- A mature industry possessing a high degree of conglomeration and ownership concentration, with oligopoly at the level of production and near monopoly at the level of distribution;[9]
- A publishing sector dominated by 'The Big Two' (Marvel and DC Comics), which control close to 65 percent of the market and emphasize superhero tales over other types of stories; non-superhero tales tend to be released by imprints of the Big Two (e.g., Vertigo) or by smaller-scale 'independent' publishers (e.g., Image, Boom! Studios, and IDW);
- Physical distribution of periodicals primarily taking place through a direct-market sales system controlled by one company, Diamond;[10]
- Retail sales of physical copies occurring mainly through independently owned specialty stores and, to a lesser extent, bookstores chains (although online bookstores and digital sales represent a growing sector of the business in recent years);
- A production process in which only a handful of individuals are directly involved, including a writer, penciler, inker, colorist, and letterer as well as an editor who manages the workflow;[11]
- A freelance-based creative labor force lacking union or guild representation and typically taking on a work-for-hire role with the two mainstream publishers.[12]

This depiction of a stand-alone comics industry is in marked contrast to the portrayal of this industry provided by most mainstream journalistic accounts or in the corporate documents produced by media conglomerates such as Disney (owner of Marvel) and Time Warner (owner of DC Comics). For example, a cursory perusal of Time Warner's 2013 annual report reveals an industry valued almost exclusively for the potential of its intellectual property.[13] (Batman's shadow even appears on the report's cover.) In terms of Time Warner's corporate structure, the recently renamed DC Entertainment exists as a part of Warner Bros.' filmed entertainment division. The majority of the coverage of DC Comics in the report (i.e., all but a few paragraphs in a 146-page document) focuses on the value of the division's stable of characters. For Time Warner, superheroes such as Superman, The Arrow, Green Lantern, and Wonder Woman exist primarily for 'exploitation across multiple distribution platforms' including film, television, and video games. From this particular top-down position, then, comics function primarily as a resource, even an appendage; this division simply fuels the larger licensing and merchandising objectives of a global media corporation. In this sense, DC Comics' characters are no different than other Warner Bros.-licensed properties such as Bugs Bunny, Harry Potter, and Gandalf. Indeed, the current president of DC Entertainment, Diane Nelson, came to her current position after serving as an executive in charge of brand management at Time Warner. As is true with Hollywood accounting more generally, determining the economic value of these comic book properties is complicated, if not impossible—although the numerous ongoing lawsuits from the heirs of comic book creators such as Jerry Siegel and Joe Shuster indicate the extent that the metrics and worth of the comics business remain contested. (Details about these lawsuits comprise the other major discussion point regarding DC Comics in the 2013 annual report.)

Whereas conglomerates' annual reports as well as trade publications such as *Variety* and *Hollywood Reporter* depict comics as important only to the extent that they service the larger entertainment business, production studies' methodologies reinforce the unique industry and, especially, *culture* of comics. From professionals' perspective, the comics industry has its own distinctive organizational hierarchy, power dynamics, and network of personal relationships. However, the singular traits that these artists and writers have identified to me in their discussions of the comics industry differ markedly from the bulleted traits about the comics industry provided earlier. Significantly, I found that even those professionals who have produced content for other types of media—whether writing movie screenplays, drawing animation for television series, or designing characters for games—still carefully delineate how comics differ socially, politically, economically, and culturally from other industry sectors. Divisions and distinctions—sometimes subtle, sometimes not—were regularly made by professionals on the basis of criteria such as race, ethnicity, class, gender, sexuality, nation, region, age, experience, education, and corporate affiliation. Who one works for—Marvel or DC, this writer or that artist—is a source of constant judgment and discussion not only by fan communities but also by other professionals and executives. The lines between 'inside' and 'outside' the comics industry are continually patrolled, and decisions made by both executives and talent are regularly debated. Who qualifies as a professional—versus an amateur—also remains a subject of contentiousness for some.

Professionals often expressed particularly complicated feelings about fan communities. Many of the individuals I have interviewed viewed their own early identities as fans as motivating their entry into comics in the first place. Perhaps in part because of this, in interviews they often sought to regularly reinforce their position as professionals. Despite the commonplace rhetoric that this is the age of the empowered audience—especially in relation to comics—boundaries between professionals and fans are constantly asserted, whether in private message boards maintained by artists and writers, at dinners during conventions, or in comments sections of online publications. Repeatedly during interviews, professionals maintained that there was no 'trade publication' for comics workers—that every comics-based publication serviced fans first and foremost and functioned mainly as a means of promoting geek culture. This orientation didn't necessarily deter them from reading sites such as *Newsarama, Comic Book Resources,* and *The Beat*—many of my interviewees approached these online comics-oriented outlets simultaneously as professionals learning about their business and as fans debating the latest industry developments. Some pros, however, underscored their avoidance of such venues in the interest of 'just focusing on their work.' That I found so much disagreement over the value of trade-cum-fan sites by professionals is significant not only because it reveals the complexity of the industry-audience relationship in comics, but also because it reinforces the difficulty of using such Web sites and resources as a means of analyzing any sector of the media industries.[14]

To better illustrate what production studies methods might add to a study of the comics industry, it is helpful to briefly turn to a particular example: the move of DC Comics from New York City to Burbank. In 2009, Warner Bros. announced the formation of a new division, DC Entertainment, "to be charged with strategically integrating the DC Comics business, brand and characters deeply into Warner Bros. Entertainment and all its content and distribution businesses."[15] Beginning in 2010, the approximately 250 staff members not directly involved with the publishing side of the business were moved from DC Comics' headquarters in Manhattan to facilities near Warner Bros.' facilities in Burbank. At that time, the company maintained that those involved on the publishing side would remain on the East Coast. Yet this did not stop the rumors on the part of fans, journalists, and professionals. Speculation ran rampant for years regarding when the rest of the staff would move west, with the advantages and disadvantages of such a move debated both off and online.[16] Finally, in fall 2013, the other shoe dropped: DC announced that all remaining employees would relocate to Southern California or depart the company by 2015.

The broad strokes of such a transition merited a few paragraphs in articles in industry trade publications.[17] Business reports, whether internally or externally produced, certainly couldn't be concerned with such a small piece of news, especially because the development would have such a modest direct impact on the company's expenses or income. But this move deeply affected many of those working as artists, writers, and editors in the mainstream American comic book industry. For example, one middle-aged artist based in the Southeast, when asked if any recent industry developments stood out to him, observed:

> You know, [I despair] whenever the big corporations take a firmer hand in the little comic book companies they own—Warner Bros., Time Warner, Time Warner-whatever-they-are-called-this-week-AOL. . . . Only in the last few years have they sort of stepped in and said, "We want to streamline our pipeline. We want to have better communication between Warner Bros. and DC Comics." This is why DC Comics is leaving New York City and going to Burbank. Only time will tell [what this means for comics]. I'm not

a big fan of change when it's sideways change—when it's just an arbitrary "Hey, we're doing this because we don't want to commute from coast to coast!" But is this really good for comics? Is this really good for DC Comics?

Another middle-aged artist, based in the South, added:

> In a way, this is a move that started not in 2009 or 2015, but decades earlier as technology has steadily made it easier to live in places other than New York and still be able to freelance for a comic book company. But no matter where we all live, the big companies stayed in Manhattan and our drafting tables and laptops are all pointed toward it as we work, as if it were Mecca. But the thing to remember is that New York isn't just the traditional center of comic book publishing, but of American publishing itself. So what does it mean to the culture and identity of artists and writers whose craft is that of the printed page when our symbolic capital city shifts from one of publishing to the traditional town of American film? It's seismic to an insular group like us, and I think it's pretty easy for people who have done this for a while and invested our lives in it to get caught up in the question of whether we're seeing the death of what we love. But look, we've been dead before.

These statements connect to several themes that emerged through my analysis of artists, writers, and editors' discourse—themes that indicate the struggles over industrial boundaries and professional identities. To many, such a geographic relocation signaled a rethinking of who mattered for the company and why. Although freelancers working for DC Comics are located all over the world, New York City has long been perceived as the headquarters for comic book publishing. This has been the case since the 1930s, when DC Comics first developed its home base there as one of the first prominent comic book publishers in the industry. It was inconceivable to some that DC could reject its New York legacy so that its staff could better serve the IP objectives—and be subject to the greater interference—of Time Warner executives. Generations of comics professionals had worked in or located near New York City so that they could have ready access to both Marvel and DC. Now, unless they chose to move at their own expense, much of the talent situated near New York believed they would have far less of an influence on the types of stories told in comics and beyond. Instead, 'Hollywood talent'—that is, film and television writers, who had become increasingly interested in working in comics as their mainstream profile had grown in recent years—would have greater access to the company on a regular basis, potentially influencing how its stories were told and the ways its characters were developed. Significantly, in spite of the technologies (theoretically) enabling work to take place anywhere, space and place still mattered profoundly to those working in comics.

Not only did the move resonate in terms of its meaning for the historical legacy of DC Comics and the comics industry writ large, but it also served as a moment when professionals could demonstrate their social capital. This became a time when pros as well as engaged fans traded on their knowledge—or beliefs—regarding which staff members would relocate to California and which staff members would stay put. It became a point of pride to be among the first to know when a given editor would jump from DC to New York-based Marvel. Those artists and writers possessing strong working relationships with editors who made the transition from DC to Marvel stood to benefit in a number of ways—from gaining the chance to work on new projects to cultivating relationships with a different set of talent to working on a different set of characters. Of course, these creatives could also suffer from such a move by losing a contact at DC who championed their work.

For my purposes here, less important than the particular types of intra-industry conversations that circulated about DC Comics' move from New York to Burbank was that these discussions evoked ideas about regional identity, spatial relationships, generational values, and work cultures. Innumerable other cases might be drawn from to reveal different types of tensions and negotiations. A specific example such as this, however, reinforces how ideological changes are accompanied by material ones; it also underscores how cultural values shift along with corporate structures. The richness of a production studies approach comes from its ability to ground large-scale institutional and industrial transformations, revealing the ways that dramatic political, economic, cultural, and social changes impact workers—and how these workers, in turn, might contribute to larger transformations.

Notes

1 Please note that trade publications are just one of the types of sources that these authors effectively employ in the works cited. Robert McChesney, *The Problem of the Media: U.S. Communication Politics in the 21st Century* (New York: Monthly Review Press, 2004); Jennifer Holt, *Empires of Entertainment: Media Industries and the Politics of Deregulation, 1980–1996* (New Brunswick, NJ: Rutgers University Press, 2011); Tino Balio, *Hollywood in the New Millennium* (London: British Film Institute, 2013); Michele Hilmes, *Hollywood and Broadcasting: From Radio to Cable* (Urbana: University of Illinois Press, 1990).

2 John T. Caldwell, *Production Culture: Industrial Reflexivity and Critical Practice in Film and Television* (Durham, NC: Duke University Press, 2008).

3 Kenton T. Wilkinson and Patrick F. Merle, "The Merits and Challenges of Using Business Press and Trade Journal Reports in Academic Research on the Media Industries." *Communication, Culture & Critique* 6 (2013), 415–31.

4 Herbert J. Gans, *Deciding What's News: A Study of "CBS Evening News," "NBC Nightly News," "Newsweek," and "Time"* (New York: Vintage, 1979); Gaye Tuchman, *Making*

News: A Study in the Construction of Reality (New York: Free Press, 1978). Wilkinson and Merle point to how issues such as agenda setting, gatekeeping, the 'pack mentality,' and the demand of deadlines, in particular, impact trade reporting in important ways.

5 See Wilkinson and Merle, "Merits and Challenges of Using Business Press and Trade Journal Reports," 418–21, for an extended discussion of this.

6 For an overview of comics studies, see Gregory Steirer, "The State of Comics Scholarship: Comics Studies and Disciplinarity." *International Journal of Comic Art* (Fall 2011), 263–85.

7 This estimate only counts comics as a publishing industry and excludes licensing and merchandising. Figures from "Comic Book Publishing in the US: Market Research Report," *IBISWorld*. www.ibisworld.com/industry/comic-book-publishing.html.

8 Figures from "Television Broadcasting in the US: Market Research Report," *IBIS-World*. www.ibisworld.com/industry/default.aspx?indid=1261.

9 Information in bullet points culled from a variety of sources including ICV2. www.icv2.com/index.php; Matthew P. McAllister, "Ownership Concentration in the U.S. Comic Book Industry," in *Comics and Ideology*, edited by Matthew P. McAllister, Edward H. Sewell Jr., and Ian Gordon (New York: Peter Lang, 2001), 15–38; Randy Duncan and Matthew J. Smith, *The Power of Comics: History, Form and Culture* (New York: Continuum, 2009).

10 Different companies handle the distribution of trade paperbacks for different publishers. For example, Hachette distributes Marvel's graphic novels to bookstores while Random House handles DC Comics' books.

11 Some of these tasks may be shared by multiple people or one individual may take on multiple roles.

12 Gaining precise figures regarding employment in the comics industry is complicated not only by its freelance basis but also by the difficulty in ascribing clear boundaries to the business. Note that the Big Two will sometimes strike creator-owned deals with star talent, and independents frequently offer creator-owned deals instead of work-for-hire contracts.

13 Annual Reports, *Time Warner*. http://ir.timewarner.com/phoenix.zhtml?c=70972&p=irol-reportsannual.

14 For a discussion of the problems involved in using trade publications as sources for industry data, see Caldwell, *Production Culture*.

15 Nikki Finke, "TOLDJA! Warner Bros Creates DC Entertainment," *Deadline Hollywood*, September 9, 2009. www.deadline.com/2009/09/toldja-warner-bros-creates-dc-entertainment/.

16 For example, see Tom McLean and Michael Avila, "Op/Ed: DC Comics—New York City or Hollywood? A Debate," *Newsarama*, September 20, 2010. www.newsarama.com/6122-op-ed-dc-comics-new-york-city-or-hollywood-a-debate.html; Heidi MacDonald, "The End of the 'Big Two' Era as Diane Nelson Confirms DC Entertainment Relocation to West Coast," *The Beat*, October 29, 2013. http://comicsbeat.com/the-end-of-the-big-two-era-confirmed-as-diane-nelson-confirms-dc-entertainment-relocation-to-west-coast/.

17 For example, see Dave McNary, "Holy Relocation, Batman: DC Comics Moving Operations to Burbank in 2015," *Variety*, October 29, 2013. http://variety.com/2013/film/news/holy-relocation-batman-dc-comics-moving-operations-to-burbank-in-2015-1200776428/.

19

CO-PRODUCING CONTENT FOR PAN-ARAB CHILDREN'S TV

State, Business, and the Workplace

Naomi Sakr and Jeanette Steemers

When the ruling families of two oil-rich Arab emirates decided in the 2000s to put money into producing satellite television content for Arabic-speaking children, one of their first steps in the process was to hire foreign executives. Preparing in 2002 for the 2005 launch of Al-Jazeera Children's Channel (JCC), based in Qatar, Shaikha Moza bint Nasser al-Missned, head of the Qatar Foundation for Education, Science and Community Development and wife of the then emir, paid France's Lagardère Group to start the project. In time the channel's head turned to UK independents for consultancy and coproduction. Separately, the Abu Dhabi government, recruiting in 2007 for a new Arabic content creation and media support initiative known as twofour54, appointed two Britons and an Australian to the most senior roles. Twofour54's first foray into coproduction of preschool Arabic children's content in 2009 was with a UK production company, 3Line Media.

Although the intention in both cases was to provide children in the region with culturally relevant programming made especially for them, the two projects underline difficulties with the concept of 'local content.' Involving transnational collaborations, they blur any dichotomy between local and global, demonstrating that so-called local content needs to be "contextualised geographically, culturally and politically."[1] The transnational dimension opens the situation up to an 'industry lore' that may universalize ideas about childhood held by 'gatekeepers' of children's television who operate internationally.[2] The existence of shared assumptions within the industry is plausible in light of efforts over several decades to foster a worldwide professional network of 'creative leaders' of children's television.[3] At the same time, however, the rejection of 'inappropriate' content, stressed by JCC's backers at the time of its launch,[4] reminds us that coproductions with international professionals may necessitate cross-cultural negotiation to meet local and regional requirements.

Existing production studies demonstrate the need to scrutinize such collaborations in a way that investigates their "micro contexts and macro forces."[5] In the Gulf context, however, the multiplicity of macro and micro influences and ambitions extends beyond nationals of the host country to those of other Arab countries and countries further afield. This chapter investigates how these actors negotiated relationships in the case of JCC and how workplace interactions were shaped by wider political, economic, social, and cultural factors. Evidence for the analysis is drawn from a period of approximately five years in JCC's evolution, starting before a sweeping change of management in September 2011 and ending two years after it. This research is based on interviews, industry statements, and press archives, with the most credible local press source being the online *Doha News*. Because of particularities in its ownership and mission, the latter can risk covering sensitive items avoided by Qatari national media, which are nervous of contravening the country's vague and antiquated press law.[6] Overall, this chapter's selection and interpretation of data aims to amplify the production studies literature by tracing and contextualizing the exercise of power in transnational production collaborations at JCC.

Tracking Individual, Corporate, and Institutional Ambitions and Influences

The term 'transnational' here is taken to include the 'distinct' transnational system that Marwan Kraidy sees as characterizing contemporary Arab television, and which he believes offers a better perspective for understanding Arab regional media markets and media professionalization than a traditional approach based on nation-states.[7] Additionally, in this case, the 'transnational' also extends into the worldwide network of children's television professionals referred to earlier, with their alleged industry lore. Are transnational collaborations prone to deploy 'local' investment for projects that may ultimately attempt, knowingly or otherwise, to "repress or efface the local"?[8] Conversely, where media organizations hire cultural workers from abroad, how visible are the effects of those workers being fired? As Toby Miller and his coauthors point out, quoting a 2001 U.S. Department of Commerce report, ad hoc television production teams lack the cohesion or unified identity to attract national attention if production is stopped, but the job loss is no less serious.[9] Thus cultural workers are "disciplined by their access to labour markets" and are not well placed to publicize concerns.[10] In these circumstances, who will draw attention to any kind of transnational 'censorscape,' in which internal and external forces—financiers, local political authorities, potential buyers—coalesce to limit producers' editorial freedom?[11]

Beyond these considerations, the term 'transnational' in the present context resonates with arguments that situate the ruling families of Qatar, Abu Dhabi, and Dubai within a transnational capitalist class (TCC). Jerry Harris points out that Qatar and the United Arab Emirates, a federation that includes Abu Dhabi and Dubai, were "never nation-states" in the sense of a polity promising "national development based on democracy and inclusive citizenship."[12] Instead their rulers—active in global art and real estate markets, sponsors of urban mega-projects, hosts to world-class educational institutions—are "embedded into flows of global accumulation." Assessing their investments at home and abroad, Harris concludes that they have built an "economic and cultural home for the select few with whom they share so much," constructing it "at a transnational level in every area—finance, real estate, labour, education, legal structure, culture, leisure, governance, and business."[13] To the extent that children's television meshes in some way with most of these categories, any study of collaborative content production in Qatar should be alert to possible contradictions between projects that promote inclusive citizenship on one hand and legal structures and systems of governance that serve the select few on the other.

Researching this type of collaboration poses particular challenges. While the macro forces of television production can often be tracked through press and industry reports, the day-to-day contexts in which content is developed and produced, including individual relationships and the internal workings of organizations,[14] are much harder to follow. It is difficult to probe what Simon Cottle calls the meso level of institutional decision making, which affects "organisational cultures, corporate strategy and editorial policies,"[15] because this crucial area of development and preproduction is shrouded in commercial secrecy. Access is also often limited at the micro level, where individuals create content within a system of "everyday working practices" guided by "artistic and other cultural demands," as well as the "beliefs and actions of individuals and social groups."[16] In light of these constraints it is not surprising that there are few studies of children's television production,[17] and even fewer about production of children's content in the Arab world.[18]

Major Players and Macro Forces in the Evolution of JCC

It may be fair to say, following Bryant's terminology,[19] that children's TV communities had started to develop in several Arab countries before JCC was launched. One stimulus came from the New York-based Children's Television Workshop (CTW), later renamed Sesame Workshop (SW). Backed by U.S. funding, SW has collaborated with various Arab partners since 1979, when Kuwait produced a local version of the preschool program *Sesame Street* with input from across the Arab world. Handled by a predecessor of the six-country Gulf Cooperation Council Joint Programme Production Institution (GCCJPPI), it featured actors, producers, and scriptwriters from Bahrain, Iraq, Saudi Arabia, and Syria, as well as Kuwait.[20] Other *Sesame Street* coproductions followed with Egyptian, Palestinian, and Jordanian partners in the 1990s and 2000s, while *Al-Manaahil* (*The Sources*), inspired by CTW's school-age literacy show *Electric Company*, was made in Jordan in the 1980s and aired in at least eleven Arab countries.[21] Commercial programming in Arabic came later, with the launch of a satellite channel, Spacetoon TV, from Dubai in 2000. Owned by a Syrian, Fayez al-Sabbagh, and built on his business experience in toy retailing and dubbing Hollywood content, Spacetoon relied on foreign cartoons dubbed into Arabic and cut to suit Arab sensibilities, alongside a modicum of locally originated material. When the Saudi-owned children's satellite channel MBC3 launched from Dubai in 2004, it followed the practice of dubbing a large volume of imports.

Whatever communities were formed through these initiatives, they were not the ones from which JCC recruited its top personnel. The Qatar Foundation for Education, Science and Community Development (QF), which housed and funded JCC for its first eight years, was accustomed to relying on non-Arab experts in most of the areas encompassed in its title. By some accounts, QF and other ruling family projects constituted a "soft power empire intended to enhance Qatar's global profile,"[22] being aligned with Qatar's purchases of Western assets, its visibility through the Al-Jazeera Network of television channels, and its drive for national human resource development and economic diversification through the leveraging of its global presence. QF, briefly involved in foreign football club sponsorship in 2011–13, became simultaneously part of the "Qatar National Vision 2030" and efforts to boost the credibility of Qatar's bid to host the 2022 football World Cup. In 2003 QF commissioned Rand of the United States to research Qatar's publicly funded education system and reform it. In 2007, QF's head, Shaikha Moza, created the Doha Centre for Media Freedom and put a Frenchman, Robert Ménard of Reporters sans Frontières, in charge. QF's choice of Lagardère Active and its subsidiary, Lagardère Images International, to advise on JCC's program acquisition, supervise external productions and graphics, and design the channel's Web site meant, according to Lagardère's own press release in September 2005, that "[m]any other French experts, professionals and companies" would also be "involved in the new channel."

Senior Arabic-speaking managers hired for JCC did not have backgrounds in children's TV. Some may say this was evident in the early objective of creating a single channel, JCCTV, aimed at too broad an age group, from three years to fifteen. Mahmoud Bouneb, appointed as executive general manager in 2003, had moved to Doha in 1999, where he became adviser to the board of the Al-Jazeera news channel. A Sorbonne-educated Tunisian-Canadian, Bouneb had worked previously at the Arab League press office in Ottawa and with Swiss and Dutch radio, before spending seven years heading Swiss Radio International's Arabic Service.[23] Mazen Rifka, head of acquisitions and rights, ran a private television company in Syria. Malika Alouane, a Moroccan who later married Bouneb, joined JCC in 2004 as director of marketing and communications, taking up the belatedly created role of director of programs when JCC split a dedicated preschool channel, Baraem (Buds), off from JCCTV in 2009. Interviewed in 2010, Alouane echoed earlier publicity material by playing down the existence of any precedents for JCC or Baraem. She was quoted as saying that "JCC is the first ever children's channel in the Arab world," and that, as a preschool channel, "Baraem is a completely new concept to the Arabic-speaking audience worldwide."[24]

As became apparent at a conference on "Children's TV in the Arab World," hosted by the University of Westminster in June 2010, JCC management was prepared to go outside the Arab world not only to acquire readymade programs, but also to commission scripts from writers with no knowledge of Arabic language or even, in some cases, Arab culture. Question-and-answer sessions at the conference revealed issues about featuring pigs and dogs, which may be routine in content aimed at British children but is contentious on Arab TV screens. It emerged that scripts were being written for JCC in English, translated into Arabic by a translation agency, vetted by JCC language consultants, and then retranslated into English for their originators to keep track of changes. One UK producer admitted his colleagues were not used to having people outside the creative process checking dialogue, especially as it slowed things down. Another said her company would have liked to find Arab scriptwriters but "they didn't materialise."[25] However, if UK companies were prepared to navigate these difficulties, it was because UK market conditions were forcing them to look for work abroad. The arrival of JCC coincided with a severe downturn in UK domestic opportunities for producers.[26] This had started with the 2003 Communications Act, which removed statutory quotas for children's broadcasts and productions by commercial terrestrial broadcasters. ITV, the UK's largest commercial investor, took the opportunity to remove children's content from its terrestrial channel, regarding it as no longer economically viable in a multichannel environment. Between 2005 and 2008 ITV reduced spending on original children's content from £25m to an estimated £4m, leaving the BBC as the dominant commissioner. A junk food advertising ban around children's programming, introduced in 2007, further sapped ITV's interest in the children's sector.

With diminishing funding at home and market dynamics changing through the expansion of Disney, Cartoon Network, and Nickelodeon, JCC with its $100 million annual budget and declared intention to produce 40 percent of its own shows, became a serious contender as a coproduction partner. This was in stark contrast to MBC3 and Spacetoon. These and other commercial bodies saw no financial incentive to invest in originations aimed solely at the Arab market because of the region's low advertising spending and the general lack of government subsidies or support. These factors contributed to what Daoud Kuttab, a leading figure in the Palestinian coproduction of *Sesame Street*, described at the University of Westminster conference as a "famine of genuine original programming."[27] Thus JCC's corporate intentions came together with the expertise and underlying public service ethos of UK producers who needed to look beyond the United Kingdom.

That particular combination of external forces and internal strategies ended abruptly in late September 2011, when change behind the scenes at QF triggered an overnight purge of top staff at JCC. No sooner had Bouneb's budget for JCC's next five years been signed off than he was summarily sacked. Along with Alouane and Cost Control Manager Haitham Qudaih, a Palestinian, Bouneb was banned from travel and informed in October 2011 that the three would face charges of financial mismanagement. Formal charges were eventually filed in December 2012, even though two separate investigations by the Qatar National Audit Bureau and auditors Ernst and Young both concluded in 2012 that there were no grounds for criminal prosecutions.[28] At the time of Bouneb's removal, a total of some thirty JCC staff members left or lost their jobs with no reason given. More were let go in the next eighteen months. These Arab expatriates, many with families and school-aged children, lost their livelihoods at a moment of turmoil across the Arab region, when return to countries like Syria, Palestine, or Iraq was not a viable option. In the case of Bouneb, Alouane, and Qudaih, departure was anyway forbidden until early 2015 when the case against them was finally withdrawn.

Meanwhile, the same factors that pushed UK producers toward JCC were a deterrent to those same companies voicing any protest about the sackings. News of the purge took six weeks to emerge in the industry press[29] and foreign experts who had previously collaborated with Bouneb and his team assumed, initially at least, that the charge of financial irregularities must have had some basis. *Doha News* first covered the court cases when hearings began in February 2013, having been alerted to Bouneb's situation by a Canadian journalist.[30] One Arab former employee of JCC conjectured that Bouneb's Arab identity was the reason for a lack of Canadian diplomatic efforts on his behalf. Reluctance to jeopardize business with wealthy Qatar was another possible explanation. The most audible protests about Bouneb's treatment were from Tunisian journalists and Tunisian expatriates in Switzerland.

QF declined any comment on the JCC upheaval, except to announce the appointment of Qatari personnel to take over the vacant posts. But analysis of the macro forces behind the change of fortunes in JCC reveals two dimensions. One has to do with employment practices in Qatar, whereby unexplained summary sackings are not unusual.[31] The case of French footballer Zahir Belounis, told to drop a demand for unpaid Qatari wages in order to obtain an exit visa for himself and his family,[32] was one of several exposing the risks of Qatar's rules on employment sponsorship and exit visas, even before press investigations into the plight of foreign laborers on Qatar's World Cup football venues were published in 2013. The second has to do with the Qatar government's evolving vision for QF and Al-Jazeera Network. Qatarization of JCC management marked the start of a transfer of JCC from oversight by QF to oversight by Al-Jazeera, which had itself transferred the post of director-general from an Arab expatriate, Palestinian-born Wadah Khanfar, to a member of the Qatari ruling family in September 2011, shortly before the removal of Bouneb. QF had, by some accounts,[33] grown too unwieldy and was deemed to need rationalization.

At the meso level of institutional decision making, critical issues raised later by JCC's new Qatari managers implied concerns about viewership and the channel's market positioning in relation to its Saudi competitor, MBC3. Speaking to staff in 2012, Haya bint Khalifa Al Nassr, seconded from QF as acting head of JCC, announced that JCC was moving into a "commercial (profitable) phase," follow-ing administrative changes that had been "necessary to support the modernization and development process" and "cope with the fast-paced changes in the media industry."[34] One of the first decisions made after September 2011 was to halt a large number of programs. Saad Hudaifi, the QF Media Centre manager who took over as acting director of JCC channels, says he personally axed all but two of eighteen programs being produced.[35] Foreign coproducers received e-mails stating that their coproduction did "not meet or comply with JCC's artistic vision and strategic production plans for the future."[36] Eighteen months later, targeting both children and advertisers in Saudi Arabia,[37] JCC stole a march on MBC3 by signing a major licensing deal for Disney films and television shows. In Hudaifi's view, the "high quality" of Disney and BBC material acquired by JCC would help it to increase "viewership satisfaction."[38]

Values and Micro Contexts in JCC Coproductions

If 'local' refers to the particularities of a place or region, Bouneb's vision for JCC was local in stressing the needs of Arab children in terms of their being not only children but part of Arab society. He said he wanted to build a "new concept" in Arab television for children that would avoid "letting Western values be the only ones."[39] An official JCC launch statement in September 2005 said it would emphasize education through the "concept of 'edutainment,'" opening up "new avenues for Arab children to learn about different environments and cultures" while also helping them to "develop self-esteem, respect their traditions and val-ues, appreciate people around them and develop a passion for learning." Bouneb himself elaborated on this by reference to citizenship. He said:

> We will try to present something which is a balance between the need of a child to be part of a social tissue and the need of a child to be a child. This is our priority, a child is a child. But let's prepare him to be a good citizen and a constructive citizen and a positive citizen.[40]

On another occasion Bouneb declared that JCC had "planted the seed of hope for . . . a better Arab citizen."[41] The need to respect Arab "traditions and values" was reflected in acquisitions policy, whereby JCC, wanting to establish its "own identity," retained the right to cut material deemed to conflict with local mores.[42] Along with the concern for identity went creation of quality control and compliance units to check Arabic scripts and translations for correctness of language and to check content for dress codes, appropriateness of relationships, and other issues.[43]

This level of internal regulation reflected a realization among those in charge of day-to-day management at JCC that pan-Arab television lacked any effective system of regulating for children's benefit. Contrasting the situation in Arab countries with that in Europe, Alouane said in 2010 that people in the region should stop thinking of regulation as censorship because regulation was needed to provide "safe content for the younger age groups," who were starting to regard "bad content—in terms of junk food or . . . adverts as 'normal.'"[44] Given the constraints on all kinds of nongovernmental advocacy in the region[45] and a general lack of incentives for local innovation in children's content, JCC was more or less trying to build a children's television community on its own, without the pressure groups or private foundations that characterize such communities elsewhere. Bouneb was quoted as saying the Arab production sector was "immature," had "no experience of making kids' content for the Arab world," and was lacking in "means, ambition and projects."[46] Hence he saw a need for extensive consultancy and support from outside the Arab region. Individuals were brought in over extended periods to advise on writing commissioning briefs, scheduling, governance and finance, production management and budgeting, human resources and recruitment, market and audience research, outreach, building relationships with external partners, brand positioning, Web site development, and broadcast and production processes.

UK consultants in some of these roles, finding a difference in workplace culture, developed an industry lore that reinforced the notion of an "immature" sector, repeatedly identifying what they saw as an Arab skills deficit in commissioning content, time management, storytelling, directing, dubbing, and reliable audience research. Thus UK partners saw themselves as helping to 'professionalise' the workforce and build a production culture where there was 'no skills structure.'[47] Consultants on site were keen to communicate to UK producers that they needed to "put in budget lines for collaborating with local companies" because they would need local guidance on "this is the way we work in our part of the world." When Baraem launched, Alouane said children should feel that it "speaks to them" as a "channel of their homeland." For that reason, she said, JCC made clear to international producers that "[w]e will have to be involved from the very beginning, otherwise we can't get the version we want in the way that we have set our standards and benchmarks."[48]

By the time of the management change in 2011, UK companies had been, or were still involved in coproducing a number of shows that reflected values in tune with JCC's edutainment mission. Ceidiog's show for SC4 in Wales, *Baaas*, about an extended family of mixed-race, opera-singing sheep, was acquired even before the launch of Baraem because of its focus on "family, citizenship and harmonious relations"[49]; it became a coproduction with JCC in its second season. A press release on the second season of *Everything's Rosie*, made in Arabic with VSI Entertainment, said Alouane believed that Rosie's "amazing personality and individuality" made her a "great role model for young girls," adding that JCC had helped VSI with "fine-tuning the content to better meet and understand our viewers' cultural needs."[50] Fresh One, the television production company of celebrity chef Jamie Oliver, was commissioned in March 2010 to produce *Al-Tabaq al-Taer* (*Flying Saucer*), aimed at teaching children the importance of a healthy diet. Rival Media's team challenge game, *Power Struggle*, about energy use and conservation, whose Arabic title, *Maa al-Tayar* (*With the Current*), had somewhat different connotations from the English, was commissioned for a second series in 2011. Finally, Zodiak Media won a contract in 2011 to produce 115 half-hour episodes of *Burj al-Jaras* (*The Buzzer*), an action show designed to promote team spirit, physical fitness, and mental agility.

These were not the only coproductions under way in September 2011. *Nan and Lili* was being made for Baraem with Chocolate Moose Media of Canada, NHK was collaborating on a science show, and Malaysian companies were involved in making a feature film called *Seefood* and an animated adventure series called *Saladin*.[51] Indeed, not all UK pitches succeeded. Some British companies failed to grasp JCCTV's more didactic approach to 'educational' content, and its view of a child's place within the family. One UK producer who failed to get a proposal accepted conceded: "If I'm absolutely honest we didn't do our homework. We didn't do enough research as to the cultural needs. . . . It was arrogance, it was ignorance on our part. And we got caught out." Another said they had made the mistake of thinking they were pitching to the "BBC of the Middle East," not realizing that JCCTV's objectives were not about 'empowering the child,' which British producers may seek to do, but about addressing children's needs in another culture. There was concern about the use of classical Arabic, albeit in a simplified form, because it is not the vernacular of children and because of the time taken to resolve language issues. At the same time, however, there was some sympathy with JCC goals, which one consultant summarized as "to spread the [Arabic] language, halt American rubbish and keep Arab traditions."

September 2011 was not the end of the line for all UK-JCC coproductions. Agreement was reached in March 2013 on a third season of *Everything's Rosie*. JCCTV, rebranded as Jeem TV in 2013, showed interest in a new game show from Rival Media. But coproductions were overshadowed by JCC's decision to buy a 180-hour BBC package in November 2012[52] followed in February 2013 by what *Variety* called a "multi-year volume deal" with Disney for cartoon shows, films, and live action series,[53] plus another purchase from the BBC, this time for three series of *Dr Who*.[54] The shift in balance between local production and imports was accompanied by a shift in balance between education and entertainment. JeemTV presented itself on its Web site as a "lifestyle entertainment media platform for Arab children," while Haya bint Khalifa Al Nassr, as acting general manager, was quoted in all reports about the Disney deal as calling it the "start of an exciting content transformation." It was a transformation that went beyond content and rebranding. From being a wholly subsidized, nonprofit operation, JCC set itself on a path to commercial viability by opening up in late 2013 to advertising, licensing, and merchandising. An emphasis on sales was much in evidence at the Big Entertainment Show trade fair in Dubai in November 2013, where JCC was a joint sponsor.

Conclusion

This account shows how impossible it is to separate the micro, meso, and macro levels of analysis[55] in discussing coproduction involving Qatar's JCC. The JCC project owed its existence to wider Qatari policies for global visibility, regional influence, and national development, which in turn affected the evolving composition of JCC management and translated into day-to-day unpredictability and lack of continuity in program making during the period under review. Cross-border coproduction during that period was not a bilateral encounter of Qatari-backed commissioning and UK producers, but a multilateral interaction of Qatari interests with individual non-Qatari Arab staffers from many different countries, including some with Western passports, and UK production companies. However, as was evident when a large group of non-Qatari Arabs was pushed out of JCC at a time of intense instability across the Arab world, the interaction generated little practical solidarity between Arab and UK partners. With UK companies concerned about their own futures, given the commissioning downturn in the United Kingdom, Qatari capital was able to divide and discipline the creative workforce,[56] both Arab and non-Arab.

The workforce was disciplined also by the wall of silence that surrounded the management purge, court cases, and travel bans, with news emerging slowly and ineffectively only in specialist media circles. There is a stark contradiction between QF's lack of transparency about Bouneb and his colleagues, and Bouneb's idea in 2005 of teaching children to be good citizens. In light of the way Qataris taking over jobs from Arab expatriates opted to invest so heavily in imported content, it can be said that Qatari resources were used to prioritize the non-Arab over the Arab, thereby partly effacing the local.[57] Thus the transnational Arab media system[58] had the effect in this case of thwarting pan-Arab professionalization in the field of children's television. To the extent that Qatari ambitions are so strongly linked to global trends beyond the Arab region, the term 'local' is a less than satisfactory label for content produced through multilateral collaborations in JCC.

Notes

Part of the research presented here was funded by the United Kingdom's Arts and Humanities Research Council.

1 Katalin Lustyik and Ruth Zanker, "Digital Children's Channels: A Comparative Analysis of Three Locally Launched Services." *International Journal of Digital Television* 4, no. 2 (2013): 160.

2 Timothy Havens, "Universal Childhood: The Global Trade in Children's Television and Changing Ideals of Childhood." *Global Media Journal* 6, no. 10 (2007). http://lass.pur duecal.edu/cca/gmj/sp07/gmj-sp07-havens.htm.

3 David W. Kleeman, "PRIX JEUNESSE as a Force for Cultural Diversity," in *Handbook of Children and the Media*, edited by Dorothy G. Singer and Jerome L. Singer (Thousand Oaks, CA: Sage, 2001), 522.

4 Ed Waller, "Al Jazeera Launches Kids Channel," *C21*, September 9, 2005.

5 Vicki Mayer, "Bringing the Social Back In: Studies of Production Cultures and Social Theory," in *Production Studies: Cultural Studies of Media Industries*, edited by Vicki Mayer, Miranda J. Banks, and John T. Caldwell (London: Routledge, 2009), 15.

6 Richard Roth, "Awaiting a Modern Press Law in Qatar," *New York Times*, May 8, 2013. www.nytimes.com/2013/05/09/opinion/global/Awaiting-a-Modern-Press-Law-in-Qatar.html?_r=1.

7 Marwan Kraidy, "The Rise of Transnational Media Systems: Implications of Pan-Arab Media for Comparative Research," in *Comparing Media Systems beyond the Western World*, edited by Daniel Hallin and Paolo Mancini (Cambridge: Cambridge University Press, 2012), 178, 198.

8 Jane Landman, "'Not in Kansas Anymore': Transnational Collaboration in Television Science Fiction Production," in *Production Studies: Cultural Studies of Media Industries*, edited by Vicki Mayer, Miranda J. Banks, and John T. Caldwell (London: Routledge, 2009), 149.

9 Toby Miller et al., *Global Hollywood 2* (London: British Film Institute, 2005), 119–20.

10 Miller et al., *Global Hollywood*, 119–20.

11 Matt Sienkiewicz, "Just a Few Small Changes: The Limits of Televisual Palestinian Representation of Conflicts within the Transnational 'Censorscape,'" in *Narrating Conflict in the Middle East: Discourse, Image and Communication Practices in Lebanon and Palestine*, edited by Dina Matar and Zahera Harb (London: I B Tauris, 2013), 19.

12 Jerry Harris, "Desert Dreams in the Gulf: Transnational Crossroads for the Global Elite." *Race & Class* 54, no. 4 (2013): 98.

13 Harris, "Desert Dreams," 94, 98.

14 David Croteau and William Hoynes, *Media/Society*, 3rd edn. (Thousand Oaks, CA: Pine Forge Press, 2003), 23.

15 Simon Cottle, "Media Organisation and Production: Mapping the Field," in *Media Organization and Production*, edited by S. Cottle (London: Sage, 2003), 20.

16 Manuel Alvarado and Edward Buscombe, *Hazell: The Making of a Television Series* (London: British Film Institute, 1978), 3.

17 For a listing, see Jeanette Steemers, *Creating Preschool Television: A Story of Commerce, Creativity and Curriculum* (Basingstoke: Palgrave Macmillan, 2010), 7.

18 Edward L. Palmer, *Toward a Literate World: Television in Literacy Education—Lessons from the Arab Region* (Boulder CO: Westview Press, 1993); Lustyik and Zanker, "Digital Children's Channels."

19 J. Alison Bryant, ed., *The Children's Television Community* (Mahwah, NJ: Lawrence Erlbaum Publishers, 2007).

20 William Tracy, "Sesame Opens." *Saudi Aramco World* 30, no. 5 (September/October 1979): 8–17.

21 Palmer, *Toward a Literate World*, 1.

22 Bill Law, "Qatar Scales Back Ambitions amid Financial Constraints," *BBC News Online*, February 12, 2014. www.bbc.co.uk/news/world-middle-east-26140986.

23 See www9.qu.edu.qa/cedr/2nd_childhood_conference/bouneb.pdf.

24 Malika Alouane, interview with *The Channel*, 2 (2010): 34.

25 Authors' transcripts of conference proceedings, London, June 2010.

26 Steemers, *Creating Preschool Television*, 65–6.

27 Authors' transcripts of conference proceedings, June 4, 2010.

28 Human Rights Watch, "Qatar: Abolish Exit Visas for Migrant Workers," May 30, 2013. www.hrw.org/news/2013/05/30/qatar-abolish-exit-visas-migrant-workers.

29 DigitalTVEurope, "Jazeera Dismisses Kid's Channel Chief and Senior Staff," November 11, 2011. www.digitaltveurope.net/17567/al-jazeera-dismisses-kids-channel-chief-and-senior-staff/.

30 Data in this paragraph draw on interviews conducted by Sakr in Doha, November 23 and 24, 2013.

31 Jan Keulen, appointed to head the Doha Centre for Media Freedom in 2011, was fired by a letter dated November 27, 2013 that contained no explanation. See Shabina Khatri, "Qatar Fires Director of Doha Centre for Media Freedom," *Doha News*, December 2013.

32 Human Rights Watch, "Qatar."

33 E.g., Kristian Coates-Ulrichsen speaking on "Qatar and the Arab Spring" at the School of Oriental and African Studies, University of London, January 21, 2014. Sakr heard the same point during interviews in Doha in November 2013.

34 JCC, "JCC Celebrates Seven Years of Distinction." Press release. September 12, 2012.

35 Saad Hudaifi, interview with Naomi Sakr, Dubai, November 18, 2013.

36 DigitalTVEurope, "Jazeera Dismisses."

37 Hudaifi, interview with Sakr.

38 Hudaifi, interview with Sakr.

39 Mahmoud Bouneb, interview with Naomi Sakr, Doha, April 20, 2009.

40 Christian Henderson. "Aljazeera Launches Children's Channel," *Aljazeera online*, September 20, 2005. www.aljazeera.com/archive/2005/09/20084915548243588.html.

41 David Lepeska, "How Al Jazeera Children's Channel Grew Up," *The National*, January 8, 2010.

42 Mazen Rifka, interview with Naomi Sakr, Doha, April 20, 2009.

43 Rifka, interview with Sakr; JCC Compliance Unit, interview with Naomi Sakr, Doha, November 25, 2013.

44 Alouane, interview with *The Channel*, 35.

45 Francesco Cavatorta and Vincent Durac, *Civil Society and Democratization in the Arab World: The Dynamics of Activism* (Abingdon: Routledge, 2014).

46 Adam Benzine, "Al Jazeera: Arab Production 'Immature,'" *C21*, October 4, 2009.

47 Data in this and later paragraphs draw on interviews conducted by Steemers in the United Kingdom between February and June 2013.

48 Martin Buxton, "Meet the Buyers: Al Jazeera," *C21*, November 3, 2009.

49 Adam Sherwin, "A Family of Welsh Sheep—the New Stars of Al-Jazeera," *The Times*, April 3, 2006.

50 JCC-VSI, "Rosie Blossoms in Spring." Press release. April 27, 2010.

51 JCC, "Al Jazeera Children's Channel Launches New Grid as It Lights Its 5th Candle." Press release. September 27, 2010.

52 Andrew McDonald, "BBCWW Scores Big with Al Jazeera," *C21*, November 11, 2012.

53 Nick Vivarelli, "Deal Brings Toons, Pix to Middle East and North Africa," *Variety*, March 11, 2013.

54 "Al Jazeera Buys Dr Who," *doctorwhonews.net*, February 25, 2013. www.doctorwhonews.net.

55 Mayer, "Bringing the Social Back In," 15; Cottle, *Media Organisation and Production*, 20.

56 Cf. Miller et al., *Global Hollywood*, 119–20.

57 Cf. Landman, "'Not in Kansas Anymore,'" 149.

58 Kraidy, "The Rise of Transnational Media Systems," 180.

20

KEEP BIG GOVERNMENT OUT OF YOUR TELEVISION SET

The Rhetoric of Self-Regulation before the Television Code

Deborah L. Jaramillo

Regulatory Cultures and Production Studies

In the United States, broadcast television is subject to standards promulgated by different regulatory camps, which in turn abide by their respective missions, processes, and governance. The Federal Communications Commission (FCC) as government regulator does not produce content and technically cannot censor content, but it informs the production of content by erecting a legal schema of acceptability. Since 1934 the FCC has granted, renewed, or denied broadcasting licenses based partially on the relationship between broadcast programs and the public interest. Further, the FCC responds to complaints from viewers about those same programs. Television networks do not have licenses, so local broadcasters bear the burden of proving that their content (frequently supplied by the networks) meets FCC standards. Networks rely on local stations—affiliates—to air their programs and national advertisements, so the responsibilities of the all-important license, although shouldered by the station, necessarily extend to program producers and distributors.

As Congress has endowed the FCC with the power to regulate broadcasters, many commercial broadcasters have entrusted another entity—the National Association of Broadcasters (NAB)—with the power to protect them from, among other things, unfavorable government regulation. Historically, that protection has taken the form of self-regulation. Sometimes the NAB has worked with the FCC; sometimes the two have clashed. Their conflicting origins (public vs. private) and complementary interests (both have served the broadcast industry well) have resulted in complicated regulatory cultures.

The NAB has supported and regulated the commercial radio industry since the early 1920s and the commercial television industry since 1951 when it changed its name temporarily to the National Association of Radio and Television Broadcasters (NARTB). Eager to preserve the private, commercial backbone of television, the NAB has sought to reconcile the creative dimension of its trade with the demands of an advertiser-supported, government-regulated medium. This chapter examines the NAB's discourses of self-regulation leading up to the implementation of the 1952 Television Code, which attempted to answer television's vocal critics by constructing a paradigm for wholesome content. Feeling attacked by television reformers, the NAB's leaders framed the conversation about television content as a dire struggle between the democratic principles held by capitalists and the tyrannical intentions of a coercive government. The manner in which the NAB characterized its work privately and publicly during television's infancy illuminates crucial connections between the splintering of broadcast regulation, the interplay of regulatory cultures, and the resulting blueprints for television content.

Situated between the state and the industry—but steeped in both sets of practices—self-regulatory trade associations offer a unique lens through which to examine how social groups, unified by common jobs, negotiate relationships with public and private powerbrokers. The close analysis of archival documents, particularly those that reveal the public voice and the private, internal workings of institutions such as trade associations, encourages a more comprehensive interpretation of television production. Knowing who and what established the parameters of acceptable programs—and why—widens our critical field of vision to include an even longer list of non-creatives who attempted to steer creativity. With scholarly eyes constantly trained on advertisers and network executives, the trade association has received minimal attention. But as the documents show, the multiple roles of the NAB—protector of local stations, researcher, lawyer, lobbyist, and agitator—deserve attention, as they amounted to a culture of self-regulation that championed wholesome content for economic reasons.

The NAB and the FCC: A Strained Relationship

A pre-TV NAB publication poses the question, "What is NAB?" and answers it proudly: "A voluntary organization working to promote and defend, when challenged, the American System of privately owned, competitively operated radio. A self-governing organization comprising an overwhelming majority of American broadcasters whereby, through rational self-regulation, they give their answer to the cry for Government operation."[1] Formed in 1923 to negotiate the payment of royalties to the American Society of Composers, Artists, and Performers, the NAB's power grew as the radio industry did. And as is evident from the first two lines of its mission statement, the Association defined itself in overtly political and economic terms. Its enterprise was private, and its mission was to protect commercial broadcasting from a coercive government.

The NAB's propaganda consistently projects an image of a stable and antagonistic relationship with the government, but this belies the complexities of their day-to-day interactions. The NAB's self-conceptualization assumes new value when placed alongside evidence of internal inconsistencies. Long before the fight over television censorship emerged, Judge Justin Miller—then president of the NAB—set out to parse the NAB's relationship with the FCC. In a March 1949 memo, Miller asked the heads of all NAB departments to report back to him on how they had cooperated with the FCC and how they could improve on that cooperation.[2] The responses, which trickled in throughout March and April 1949, varied in tone and scope, revealing uneven relationships. Citing "a gratifying and daily growing spirit of close cooperation," the Engineering Department memo from R.V. Howard was positive and even effusive in its appreciation of its relationship with the FCC.[3] The head of the Research Department, Ken Baker, was more subdued in his response, stressing that philosophical differences prevented their relationship from being anything other than just satisfactory.[4] Maurice B. Mitchell of the Advertising Department was negative and even sarcastic.[5] Referring to the FCC's Blue Book as the "Lemon Book," Mitchell characterized the FCC's statements about commercial broadcasting as "clumsy" and misleading. He openly preferred a social relationship with the FCC to a professional one.

Social relationships seemed to be the forte of A. D. Willard, the executive vice president of the NAB (and soon-to-be head of the NAB's new TV department). Willard wrote about his numerous informal encounters with former FCC chairman Charles Denny and various commissioners; they would meet for lunch or golf outings.[6] Yet Willard advocated for an "arm's-length" professional relationship. Notably, Willard wrote that his attempts to set up monthly lunches with new FCC chair Wayne Coy were met with lukewarm responses. Coy would not prove the great friend of the NAB that Denny had been. Willard warned of compromising the NAB's "principles" by getting too close to the FCC; the Association had to be alert to any abuses of power.

For the Program Department those abuses amounted to anything having to do with content. The subject of censorship united the responses from both the Program Department and the Legal Department. Harold Fair, head of the Program Department, wrote "the FCC and programming are poles apart" in most cases.[7] Fair actually recommended *new* legislation to erect a distinct border between the FCC and the rights of station owners to operate without government interference. Likewise, Don Petty of the NAB's Legal Department wrote of the need to rein in a rogue FCC and educate its staff about censorship and the Constitution.[8]

The NAB–FCC relationship was philosophically fractured and socially awkward at the end of the 1940s. The data and technology-driven factions of the NAB had few complaints because they considered their fields objective and neutral, but the groups focused on content and legalities evinced a territorial and even prickly reaction to the thought of cooperating with the regulatory agency.

Convinced of a foundational disconnect with the FCC and its interpretations of the Communications Act of 1934, the NAB would move into the television age feeling burned by the FCC's attempts to regulate radio.

The Rhetoric of the NAB

Whereas internal NAB discussions about the FCC ranged from friendly and benign to sarcastic and belligerent, the NAB's public speeches were rife with animosity toward the government. A 1947 speech by Miller titled "Freedom of Communication" positioned the NAB as a canary in a coalmine, warning everyone of impending government censorship.[9] Evoking the country's forefathers and the freedoms they fought to secure, Miller connected everyday criticism of radio to a greater irresponsibility. When we criticize commercialism or genres like soap operas and demand that the government step in, he reasoned, we contribute to our own destruction. His appeal to self-regulation—"I hope the broadcasters of America will . . . eliminate all just causes of complaint and thus remove the temptation which incites to government control"—admitted some flaws in the private system, but, mentioning Hitler and Mussolini by name, he ultimately warned that the industry's failure to self-regulate would transform the FCC into a stateside Nazi propaganda machine.

By 1949, while hinting at the need for a Standards of Practice for television, Miller continued to vilify the government in public speeches. In a speech titled "Attacks on Freedom of Communication" in April 1949, he attributed nothing less than "lawless[ness]" to all administrative agencies.[10] He distanced the good intentions of private enterprise from the coercive strategies of government by encouraging all listeners to agree with "the proposition that it is government which has always threatened freedom, however much it may have disguised its actions and pretended they were for the common good." He further argued that Marxists had propagated the myth of a broadcast industry monopoly—a myth that would lead to government control and even worse, a system like the BBC.

Early in 1950 Miller stopped speaking in hypotheticals and began grappling with actual complaints about television. Viewer complaints about obscene necklines and profane language were pouring into the FCC and television stations around the country. The general manager of a radio station in Milwaukee wrote to Miller early in 1950 to assert that something needed to be done about television content. Miller replied in agreement, but other factors may have been at play.[11] Talk of government subsidies for broadcasting, which would have led to greater regulation, appeared in several of Miller's letters, so that, too, may have propelled Miller toward a more organized approach to the television problem.

Complaints about television content continued to mount in 1950, and they found their way to the NAB. In response to a *Christian Science Monitor* publication on children and television, Miller let loose a diatribe tinged with fear. He worried openly in his June 1950 letter to the publication that government involvement in content would stunt the medium and exacerbate the FCC's paternalism.[12] Referring to the government in all its forms as the "Great White Father," Miller's words sounded increasingly desperate.

In spite of the almost hyperbolically critical face that Miller displayed in his speeches, he turned a friendly face toward Chairman Coy after Coy spoke at the NAB's 1950 convention in Chicago. Miller wrote to Coy in May 1950, thanking him for attending and speaking, and sharing credit with him for improvements in broadcasting.[13] Still, Miller's strongly worded speeches painted the FCC as the oppressor and the NAB as the constant victim and crusader. The man who actually dealt with the government on a daily basis—Ralph Hardy, the director of government relations—managed to push Miller's rhetoric even further. In a June 1950 speech he described his experiences testifying before Congress and the FCC as "frightening" and as a "baptism by fire."[14] The man whose job it was to bridge the gap between government and the NAB viewed the men on the other side of that bridge as a "hideous three-headed monster of prosecutor, judge, and jury." For the NAB, escalating pressure to clean up television content meant that the walls protecting it from that monster could not be high enough.

Complaints about television content piled up as a major power grab solidified television's place in the NAB. After wresting television from the grip of the much smaller Television Broadcasters' Association, the NAB became the NARTB in March 1951, embracing television as a fully functional and autonomous branch of the association. Miller resigned as president, and the membership elected Harold Fellows to replace him in June 1951 (Miller stayed on as chairman of the board). The transition of power did not temper the antigovernment sentiment, however. By this time the NARTB was busy crafting a new self-regulatory document partially in an effort to stifle Senator William Benton's proposals to strengthen educational TV, promote a subscription alternative to commercial TV, and create a National Citizens Advisory Board, a nongovernmental body that would monitor radio and television broadcasts in the public interest. Approved in late 1951, the Television Code helped the NARTB rehabilitate the image of television and undermine multiple threats to the commercial paradigm. But in a December 1951 speech to the Television Association of Philadelphia, Fellows resisted this reading of the Code's adoption. He said, "I believe television broadcasters wrote and adopted a code because inherently . . . they are decent, self-respecting, God-fearing citizens. Television is going to be as good as you are . . . ; in your absence it's going to be as bad as the Government can make it—and that can be . . . pretty bad."[15] After celebrating the character of broadcasters he returned to the rhetoric that had served Miller so well for so long. "We adopted this Code before someone decided to adopt one for us," he said in a speech titled

"Television—The Shape of Things to Come" in March 1952, the month the Code formally went into effect.[16]

As Mark M. MacCarthy notes, "Industry codes sometimes have the public relations function of creating a favorable impression of a responsible industry policing itself."[17] The Code as a public relations document—a document that superficially showed the public the industry cared—lent a new dimension to Fellows's speeches; he gradually began to incorporate the public into his portrait of the Association and its battles with the government. A speech in May 1952 titled "Liberty—Let's Keep It" pit the government against the nation's citizens and cast the NARTB as the custodian of democracy. Fellows said, "judgment, program tastes, preferences, and economic decisions affecting broadcasting, under our American system, belong to the public—ALL of the people, and not to the government."[18] He went on to argue that by choosing which programs to watch, the people were exercising their freedoms. In a fiery speech in October 1952, Fellows extended this argument, claiming that all attempts to control television were offenses against the people.[19] The Television Code, which sought to control many aspects of television, was not implicated in these offenses.

Fellows's "Liberty" speech came just a few weeks after Miller commented in a letter about the maturation of broadcasters. He wrote in May 1952 that broadcasters' guilt over poor programming initially led them to seek out "government discipline" in spite of its invitation to "gradual government abridgment" of freedoms.[20] The Code signified a change; "broadcasters are beginning to 'grow up'" as the press did, according to Miller. The thrust of Miller's letter warned of a major consequence if self-regulation was perceived to fail: a constitutional amendment removing First Amendment protections from the broadcasting industry. His prediction leaped over Blue Book–style regulations and imagined an outcome so extreme yet perfectly in keeping with his indignant oratory. The "strength" of television, for Miller, was its pervasiveness and direct connection to the "family circle." Unfortunately, that made people forget that broadcasting was protected speech, so television's strength became its "weakness." Only the industry's "ability for self-government" had fended off the severe possibilities.

For Fellows, the Code was also proof that the industry was "grown up now," but he still referred to the NAB–government relationship as one of marked abuse in a November 1952 speech.[21] "Beyond the garden lies the woodshed," he said.

> That's where you get whipped! Over and over again—for thirty years—we've been constantly summoned to the woodshed by all kinds of people, for all kinds of reasons. By now we know too well where the woodshed is and who's in there. From here on when we're summoned there without cause . . . let's ask the gentleman with the birch branch in his hand to answer a question or two before we bend over to take it.

Conclusion

For all the ire it mustered and hurled at the government in anticipation of censorship that never materialized, the NARTB crafted a Code that some felt was particularly egregious. The ACLU protested the Code and called the document "stifling and illegal censorship."[22] In response, Miller, then chairman of the board of the NARTB, called the ACLU "a bunch of sneaking hypocrites" who were flirting with "communism, fascism, nazi-ism and all other forms of absolute totalitarian government."[23] The question of whether the Television Code actually carried the weight of state action has been explored by Netzhammer and others, but even the *suggestion* that the Code overstepped the bounds of self-regulation requires that we study the vitriol in Miller's and Fellows's words.[24]

While the NAB/NARTB may have argued against government censorship legitimately—the Communications Act of 1934 expressly forbade it—the association's leadership insisted on projecting an image of abject victimization at the hands of an oppressive regime. Did they really believe it? Internal documents reveal a much more complicated relationship with the government than the speeches articulated, but angry rhetoric allowed the association to conflate commercial prerogatives with democratic ones, eliding industrial goals. By 1950 the experiment of television prompted new concerns and new paths to government involvement in that experiment. Some reformers scrambled to fix problems before they got out of hand and before television became immoveable. Pay TV advocates hurriedly explored the potential of UHF and educational broadcasting. The industry needed a quick fix, so it sacrificed the creative side of its trade to save the commercial side, rewarding the strangling of stories, genres, and aesthetics with a seal of good practice.

Notes

1 National Association of Broadcasters, *What Is NAB?*, n.d., Folder 1, NAB Publications: General, Promotional, and Membership Materials, 1940–ca. 1970, Box 118, National Association of Broadcasters Papers (hereafter cited as NAB Papers), US MSS 156AF, Wisconsin Historical Society, Madison, Wisconsin (hereafter cited as WHS).

2 Justin Miller to NAB department heads, March 14, 1949, Folder 7 FCC, Box 102, NAB Papers, WHS.

3 R.V. Howard to Justin Miller, April 5, 1949, Folder 7 FCC, Box 102, NAB Papers, WHS.

4 Ken Baker to Justin Miller, March 14, 1949, Folder 7 FCC, Box 102, NAB Papers, WHS.

5 Maurice B. Mitchell to Justin Miller, March 21, 1949, Folder 7 FCC, Box 102, NAB Papers, WHS.

6 A. D. Willard to Justin Miller, April 5, 1949, Folder 7 FCC, Box 102, NAB Papers, WHS.

7 Harold Fair to Justin Miller, March 22, 1949, Folder 7 FCC, Box 102, NAB Papers, WHS.

8 Don Petty to Justin Miller, April 5, 1951, Folder 7 FCC, Box 102, NAB Papers, WHS.

9 "Freedom of Communication," speech by Justin Miller, May 23, 1947, Folder 6, Box 1, NAB Papers, WHS.

10 "Attacks on Freedom of Communication," speech by Justin Miller, April 23, 1949, Folder 7 Speeches, Justin Miller, 1948–59, Box 1, NAB Papers, WHS.

11 Justin Miller to Walter J. Damm, March 25, 1950, Folder 1 NAB, J. Miller, March 1950, Box 93, NAB Papers, WHS.

12 Justin Miller to *Christian Science Monitor*, June 9, 1950, Folder 2 NAB, J. Miller, April–May 1950, Box 93, NAB Papers, WHS.

13 Justin Miller to Wayne Coy, FCC Chairman, May 1, 1950, Folder 2 NAB J. Miller, April–May 1950, Box 93, NAB Papers, WHS.

14 Untitled speech by Ralph Hardy, June 23, 1950, Folder 14, Box 5A, NAB Papers, WHS.

15 Untitled speech by Harold E. Fellows, December 19, 1951, Folder 9 Speeches, Harold E. Fellows, Box 1, NAB Papers, WHS.

16 "Television—The Shape of Things to Come," speech by Harold E. Fellows, March 21, 1952, Folder 10 Harold E. Fellows Speeches, Box 1, NAB Papers, WHS.

17 Mark M. MacCarthy, "Broadcast Self-Regulation: The NAB Codes, Family Viewing Hour, and Television Violence." *Cardozo Arts & Entertainment Law Journal* 13 (1995): 673.

18 "Liberty—Let's Keep It," speech by Harold E. Fellows, May 27, 1952, Folder 11 Harold E. Fellows Speeches, Box 1, NAB Papers, WHS.

19 Untitled speech by Harold E. Fellows, October 9, 1952, Folder 13 Harold E. Fellows Speeches, Box 1, NAB Papers, WHS.

20 Justin Miller to Arthur L. Greene, May 7, 1952, Folder 3 NAB J. Miller, March–June 1952, Box 94, NAB Papers, WHS.

21 Untitled speech by Harold E. Fellows, November 24, 1952; Folder 15 Harold E. Fellows Speeches, Box 1, NAB Papers, WHS.

22 MacCarthy, "Broadcast Self-Regulation," 675.

23 Justin Miller to Bob Richards, September 26, 1952, Folder 4 NAB J. Miller, July–October 1952, Box 94, NAB Papers, WHS.

24 See Emile C. Netzhammer, "Self Regulation in Broadcasting: A Legal Analysis of the National Association of Broadcasters Television Code," master's thesis, University of Utah, 1984.

SELECT BIBLIOGRAPHY

Alvarado, Manuel and Edward Buscombe. *Hazell: The Making of a Television Series*. London: British Film Institute, 1978.

Andreae, Michael, Jinn-yuh Hsu, and Glen Norcliffe. "Performing the Trade Show: The Case of the Taipei International Cycle Show." *Geoforum* 49 (2013): 193–201.

Ballaster, Ros, Margaret Beetham, Elizabeth Frazerm, and Sandra Hebron. *Women's Worlds: Ideology, Femininity and the Woman's Magazine*. New York: Macmillan, 1991.

Banet-Weiser, Sarah. *Authentic™: The Politics of Ambivalence in a Brand Culture*. New York: New York University Press, 2012.

Banks, Mark, Rosalind Gill, and Stephanie Taylor, eds. *Theorizing Cultural Work: Labour, Continuity and Change in the Cultural and Creative Industries*. Abingdon: Routledge, 2013.

Banks, Miranda. *The Writers: A History of American Screenwriters and Their Guild*. New Brunswick, NJ: Rutgers University Press, 2015.

Barber, Karin, ed. *Readings in African Popular Culture*. Bloomington: Indiana University Press, 1997.

Barnhurst, Kevin G. "Visibility as Paradox: Representation and Simultaneous Contrast," in *Media/Queered: Visibility and Its Discontents*, ed. Kevin G. Barnhurst. New York: Peter Lang Publishing, 2007, 1–19.

Bennett, James and Niki Strange, eds. *Television as Digital Media*. Durham, NC: Duke University Press, 2011.

Bennett, James, Niki Strange, Paul Kerr and Andrea Medrado. *Multiplatforming Public Service Broadcasting: The Economic and Cultural Role of UK Digital and TV Independents*. London: University of London Press, 2012.

Benwell, Bethan, ed. *Masculinity and Men's Lifestyle Magazines*. Oxford: Wiley Blackwell, 2003.

Blair, Helen. "'You're Only as Good as Your Last Job': The Labour Process and Labour Market in the British Film Industry." *Work, Employment & Society* 15(1), 2001: 149–69.

Bonini, Tiziano and Belén Monclus, eds. *Radio Audiences and Participation in the Age of Network Society*. London: Routledge, 2015.

Born, Georgina. *Uncertain Vision: Birt, Dyke and the Reinvention of the BBC*. London: Vintage, 2005.

Born, Georgina. "The Social and the Aesthetic: For a Post-Bourdieuian Theory of Cultural Production." *Cultural Sociology* 4(2), 2010: 171–208.

Boston, Nicholas. "Digitizing 'Aspirationalism': Magazine-to-New Media Work in the Mediatic Mise en Abyme at Condé Nast, Inc." PhD diss., University of Cambridge, 2013.

Breazeale, Kenon. "In Spite of Women: *Esquire* Magazine and the Construction of the Male Consumer." *Signs* 20, 1994: 1–22.

Bren, Paulina. *The Greengrocer and His TV: The Culture of Communism after the 1968 Prague Spring*. Ithaca, NY: Cornell University Press, 2010.

Bruns, Axel. *Blogs, Wikipedia, Second Life, and Beyond (Digital Formations)*. New York: Peter Lang Publishing Inc., 2008.

Buonanno, Milly. "The Transatlantic Romance of Television Studies and the 'Tradition of Quality' in Italian TV Drama." *Journal of Popular Television* 1(2), 2013: 175–89.

Caldwell, John T. "Cultural Studies of Media Production: Critical Industrial Practices," in *Questions of Method in Cultural Studies*, eds. Mimi White and James Schwoch. London: Blackwell, 2004, 109–53.

Caldwell, John T. *Production Culture: Industrial Reflexivity and Critical Practice in Film and Television*. Durham, NC: Duke University Press, 2008.

Caldwell, John T. "Worker Blowback: User-Generated, Worker-Generated and Producer-Generated Content with Collapsing Production Workflows," in *Television as Digital Media*, eds. James Bennett and Nikki Strange. Durham, NC and London: Duke University Press, 2011, 283–310.

Caputi, Jane. "The Pornography of Everyday Life," in *Race, Class & Gender in the Media* (4th ed.), eds. Gail Dines and Jean Humez. Thousand Oaks, CA: Sage, 2014, 373–85.

Chouliaraki, Lilia. "Post-Humanitarianism: Humanitarian Communication beyond a Politics of Pity." *International Journal of Cultural Studies*, 13(2), 2010: 107–26.

Chung, Peichi and Anthony Fung. "Internet Development and the Commercialization of Online Gaming in China," in *Gaming Globally*, eds. Nina B. Huntemann and Ben Aslinger. New York: Palgrave Macmillan, 2013, 233–50.

Cohen, S. *States of Denial: Knowing about Atrocities and Suffering*. London: Polity, 2001.

Conor, Bridget. *Screenwriting: Creative Labour and Professional Practice*. Abingdon: Routledge, 2014.

Consalvo, Mia. "Crunched by Passion: Women Game Developers and Workplace Challenges," in *Beyond Barbie and Mortal Kombat: New Perspectives on Gender and Gaming*, eds. J. Denner, C. Heeter, Y. B. Kafai, and J.Y. Sun. Cambridge: MIT Press, 2008, 177–93.

Cormen, Thomas H., Charles E. Leiserson, Ronald L. Rivest, and Clifford Stein. *Introduction to Algorithms*. Vol. 2. Cambridge: MIT Press, 2001.

Cottle, Simon. "Media Organisation and Production: Mapping the Field," in *Media Organization and Production*, ed. S. Cottle. London: Sage, 2003, 3–24.

Couldry, Nick. *Media Society World: Social Theory in a Digital Age*. Cambridge: Polity, 2012.

Crewe, Ben. *Representing Men: Cultural Production and Producers in the Men's Magazine Market*. Oxford: Berg, 2003.

Croteau, David and William Hoynes. *Media/Society* (3rd edn.). Thousand Oaks, CA: Pine Forge Press, 2003.

Cunningham, Stuart. *Hidden Innovation: Policy, Industry and the Creative Sector*. Brisbane: Queensland University Press, 2013.

Currah, Andrew. "Hollywood, the Internet and the World: A Geography of Disruptive Innovation." *Industry and Innovation* 14(4), 2007: 359–84.

Curtin, Michael. *Playing to the World's Biggest Audience: The Globalization of Chinese Film and TV.* Berkeley: University of California Press, 2007.

Curtin, Michael, Jennifer Holt, and Kevin Sanson. *Distribution Revolution: Conversations about the Digital Future of Film and Television.* Berkeley: University of California Press, 2014.

Curtin, Michael and John Vanderhoef. "A Vanishing Piece of the Pi: The Globalization of Visual Effects Labor." *Television & New Media* 16(2), 2015.

Davila, Arlene. *Latinos Inc.: Marketing and the Making of a People.* Berkeley: University of California Press, 2001.

Davis, Aeron. *Promotional Cultures.* Cambridge: Polity, 2013.

Davis, Helen. *Understanding Stuart Hall.* London: Sage, 2004.

Deuze, Mark. *Media Work.* Cambridge: Polity Press, 2007.

Diamond, Lisa M. "I'm Straight but I Kissed a Girl: The Trouble with American Media Representations of Female-Female Sexuality." *Feminism and Psychology* 15(1), 2005: 104–10.

Duffy, Brooke Erin. *Remake, Remodel: Women's Magazines in the Digital Age.* Champaign: University of Illinois Press, 2013.

Dyer-Witheford, Nick and Greig de Peuter. *Games of Empire: Global Capitalism and Video Games.* Minneapolis: University of Minnesota Press, 2009.

Elliott, Philip. *The Sociology of the Professions.* London: Macmillan, 1972.

Elliott, Philip. "Media Organizations and Occupations: An Overview," in *Mass Communication and Society*, eds. James Curran, Michael Gurevitch, and Janet Woollacott. Beverly Hills, CA: Sage, 1977, 142–73.

Fosdick, Scott. "The State of Magazine Research in 2008." *Journal of Magazine and New Media Research* 10(1), 2008: 1–4.

Foucault, Michel. "What Is an Author?" in *The Foucault Reader*, ed. Paul Rabinow. New York: Pantheon, 1984, 101–20.

Fraser, Nancy and Axel Honneth. *Redistribution or Recognition?* London: Verso, 2003.

Ganti, Tejaswini. *Producing Bollywood: Inside the Contemporary Hindi Film Industry.* Durham, NC: Duke University Press, 2012.

Gauntlett, David. *Media, Gender and Identity: An Introduction.* London and New York: Routledge, 2002.

Geiger, Stuart. "The Lives of Bots," in *Critical Point of View: A Wikipedia Reader* edited by Geert Lovink and Nathaniel Tkacz. Amsterdam: Institute of Network Cultures, 2011, 78–93.

Gell, Alfred. *Art and Agency.* Oxford: Oxford University Press, 1998.

Gill, Rosalind. "Cool, Creative and Egalitarian? Exploring Gender in Project-Based New Media Work in Europe." *Information and Communication Studies* 5(1), 2002: 70–89.

Gill, Rosalind. "Life Is a Pitch: Managing the Self in the New Media Work," in *Managing Media Work*, ed. M. Deuze. London: Sage, 2011, 249–62.

Gill, Rosalind and Andy Pratt. "In the Social Factory?" *Theory, Culture & Society* 25 (7–8), 2008: 1–30.

Gillan, Jennifer. *Television Brandcasting: The Return of the Content-Promotion Hybrid.* New York: Routledge, 2014.

Ginsburg, Faye, Lila Abu Lughod, and Brian Larkin, eds. *Media Worlds: Anthropology on New Terrain.* Berkeley: University of California Press, 2002.

Gough-Yates, Anna. *Understanding Women's Magazines: Publishing, Markets and Readerships.* New York: Routledge, 2003.

Grainge, Paul and Catherine Johnson, *Promotional Screen Industries*. London and New York: Routledge, 2015.

Gregg, Melissa. *Work's Intimacy*. London: Polity, 2011.

Grindstaff, Laura. "Self-Serve Celebrity: The Production of Ordinariness and the Ordinariness of Production in Reality Television," in *Production Studies*, eds. V. Mayer, M. Banks, and J. Caldwell. London and New York: Routledge, 2008, 71–86.

Grugulis, Irena and Dimitrinka Stoyanova. "Social Capital and Networks in Film and TV: Jobs for the Boys?" *Organization Studies* 33(10), 2012: 1311–31.

Gutierrez, J. "Philippine TV Stations Bring Out Trash." *The Jakarta Globe*, April 14, 2011. http://jakartaglobe.beritasatu.com/archive/philippine-tv-stations-bring-out-the-trash/.

Havens, Timothy. *Global Television Marketplace*. London: British Film Institute, 2008.

Hay, James and Nick Couldry. "Rethinking Convergence/Culture." *Cultural Studies* 25(4–5), 2011: 473–86.

Haynes, Jonathan. "A Bibliography of Academic Work on Nigerian and Ghanaian Video Films." *Journal of African Cinemas* 4(1), 2012: 99–133.

Hennion, Antoine. "An Intermediary between Production and Consumption: The Producer of Popular Music." *Science, Technology & Human Values* 14(4), 1989: 400–24.

Hesmondhalgh, David and Sarah Baker. "Creative Work and Emotional Labour in the Television Industry." *Theory, Culture & Society* 25(7–8), 2008: 97–118.

Hesmondhalgh, David and Sarah Baker. *Creative Labour: Media Work in Three Cultural Industries*. Abingdon, Oxon: Routledge, 2011.

Holt, Jennifer and Kevin Sanson, eds. *Connected Viewing: Selling, Streaming, and Sharing Media in the Digital Era*. New York: Routledge, 2014.

Huntemann, Nina B. "Women in Video Games: The Case of Hardware Production and Promotion," in *Gaming Globally*, eds. Nina B. Huntemann and Ben Aslinger. New York: Palgrave Macmillan, 2013: 41–58.

Jimenez-David, R. "They Were Invited." *Inquirer.net*, February 7, 2006. http://getreal-philippines.com/blog/2011/03/filipino-tv-shows-like-willing-willie-make-filipinos-dumber/.

Kaige, Chen. "You Haizi Wang de chuangzuo suo xiangdao de." ["Thoughts from the Production of *King of Children*"], *Dangdai dianying* 6, 1987: 97–101.

Kohn, Nathaniel. *Pursuing Hollywood: Seduction, Obsession, Dread*. Lanham, MD and New York: Rowman & Littlefield, 2006.

Krings, Matthias and Onookome Okome, eds. *Global Nollywood: The Transnational Dimensions of an African Video Film Industry*. Bloomington: Indiana University Press, 2013.

Larkin, Brian. *Signal and Noise: Media, Infrastructure and Urban Culture in Northern Nigeria*. Durham, NC and London: Duke University Press, 2008.

Latour, Bruno. *Reassembling the Social: An Introduction to Actor-Network-Theory*. Oxford: Oxford University Press, 2005.

Lee, David. "Networks, Cultural Capital and Creative Labour in the British Independent Television Industry." *Media, Culture & Society* 33(4), 2011: 549–65.

Lieb, Kristin J. *Gender, Branding, and the Modern Music Industry: The Social Construction of Female Popular Music Stars*. New York: Routledge, 2013.

Luka, Mary Elizabeth. "Mapping CBC *ArtSpots*," in *Diverse Spaces: Examining Identity, Heritage and Community within Canadian Public Culture*, ed. Susan Ashley. Newcastle upon Tyne: Cambridge Scholars Publishing, 2013, 124–47.

Marx, Karl. "Letter to Annenkov" (1846). *Marx Engels Collected Works*. Trans. Peter and Betty Ross v. 38. International Publishers, 1975.

Mayer, Vicki. *Below the Line: Producers and Production Studies in the New Television Economy.* Durham, NC and London: Duke University Press, 2011.

Mayer, Vicki, Miranda Banks, and John T. Caldwell. "Production Studies: Roots and Routes," in *Production Studies: Cultural Studies of Media Industries*, eds. Vicki Mayer, Miranda Banks and John T. Caldwell Eds. New York: Routledge, 2009, 1–12.

McRobbie, Angela. *Feminism and Youth Culture: From "Jackie" to "Just Seventeen."* London: Macmillan, 1991.

Miller, Toby, Nitin Govil, Richard Maxwell, John McMurria and Ting Wang, eds. *Global Hollywood 2.* London: British Film Institute, 2005.

Moeller, Susan. *Compassion Fatigue: How the Media Sell Disease, Famine, War and Death.* London and New York: Routledge, 1999.

Morley, David. "Changing Paradigms in Audience Studies," in *Remote Control: Television, Audiences and Cultural Power.* Ellen Seiter, Hans Borchers, Gabriele Kreutzner and Eva-Marie Warth Eds. New York: Routledge, 1989, 16–43.

Mulvey, Laura. "Visual Pleasure and Narrative Cinema." *Screen* 16(3), 1975: 6–18.

Nixon, Sean. *Advertising Cultures: Gender, Commerce, Creativity.* London: Sage, 2003.

Ochs, Robyn and Sarah E. Rowley, eds. *Getting Bi: Voices of Bisexuals around the World* (2nd edition). Boston, MA: Bisexual Resource Center, 2009.

Ong, Jonathan C. "'Witnessing' or 'Mediating' Distant Suffering? Ethical Questions across Moments of Text, Production, and Reception." *Television & New Media* 15(3), 2014: 179–96.

O'Regan, Tom, Ben Goldsmith, and Susan Ward. *Local Hollywood: Global Film Production and the Gold Coast.* St. Lucia: University of Queensland Press, 2011.

Orgad, Shani. "Visualizers of Solidarity: Organizational Politics in Humanitarian and International Development NGOs." *Visual Communication* 12(3), 2013: 295–314.

Peters, J. D. "Witnessing." *Media, Culture and Society* 23, 2001: 707–23.

Pine, B. Joseph, II and James H. Gilmore. *The Experience Economy, Updated Edition.* Cambridge, MA: Harvard Business Review Press, 2011.

Powell, Helen ed., *Promotional Culture and Convergence: Markets, Methods, Media.* London and New York: Routledge, 2013.

Punathambekar, Aswin. *From Bombay to Bollywood: The Making of a Global Media Industry.* New York: New York University Press, 2013.

Redvall, Eva N. "Teaching Screenwriting in a Time of Storytelling Blindness: The Meeting of the Auteur and the Screenwriting Tradition in Danish Film-Making." *Journal of Screenwriting* 1, 2010: 57–79.

Rimban, L. "The Empire Strikes Back," in *From Loren to Marimar: Philippine Media in the 1990s*, ed. S. Coronel. Quezon City: Philippine Center for Investigative Journalism, 1999.

Rodrigo, R. *Kapitan: Geny Lopez and the Making of ABS-CBN.* Quezon City: ABS-CBN Publishing, 2006.

Ross, Andrew. *No-Collar: The Humane Workplace and Its Hidden Costs.* Philadelphia, PA: Temple University Press, 2004.

Scott, Martin. "The Mediation of Distant Suffering: An Empirical Contribution beyond Television News Texts." *Media, Culture & Society* 36(1), 2014: 3–19.

Seiter, Ellen. *Television and New Media Audiences.* Oxford: Oxford University Press, 1999.

Silverstone, Roger. *Media and Morality: On the Rise of the Mediapolis.* Cambridge: Polity, 2007.

Skeggs, Bev. *Class, Self, Culture.* London: Routledge, 2004.

Skeggs, Bev and Helen Wood. *Reacting to Reality Television: Performance, Audience and Value.* Abingdon: Routledge, 2012.

Spigel, Lynn. *TV by Design: Modern Art and the Rise of Network Television*. Chicago, IL and London: University of Chicago Press, 2008.

Stacey, Jackie. "Hollywood Memories." *Screen* 35(4), 1994: 317–35.

Steemers, Jeanette. *Creating Preschool Television: A Story of Commerce, Creativity and Curriculum*. Basingstoke: Palgrave Macmillan, 2010.

Strandvad, Sara Malou. *Inspiration for a New Sociology of Art: A Socio-material Study of Development Processes in the Danish Film Industry*, Copenhagen: CBS, 2009.

Sutton, Damian. "Cinema by Design: Hollywood as a Network Neighbourhood," in *Design and Creativity: Policy, Management and Practice*, eds. Guy Julier and Liz Moor. Oxford and New York: Berg, 2009: 174–90.

Szczepanik, Petr. "Globalization through the Eyes of Runners: Student Interns as Ethnographers on Runaway Productions in Prague." *Media Industries Journal* 1(1), 2013: 56–61.

Szczepanik Petr and Patrick Vonderau, eds. *Behind the Screen: Inside European Production Cultures*. New York: Palgrave MacMillan, 2013.

Tunstall, Jeremy. *Television Producers*. London: Routledge, 1993.

Uricchio, William. "Beyond the Great Divide: Collaborative Networks and the Challenge to the Dominant Conceptions of Creative Industries." *International Journal of Cultural Studies* 7(1), 2004: 79–90.

Van Dijck, José, and David Nieborg. "Wikinomics and Its Discontents: A Critical Analysis of Web 2.0 Business Manifestos." *New Media & Society* 11(5), 2009: 855–74.

Van Zoonen, Liesbet. "Feminist Internet Studies." *Feminist Media Studies* 1(1), 2001: 67–72.

Visser, Robin. *Cities Surround the Countryside: Urban Aesthetics in Postsocialist China*. Durham, NC and London: Duke University Press, 2010.

Wells, K. "The Melodrama of Being a Child: NGO Representations of Poverty." *Visual Communication* 12(3), 2013: 277–93.

West, Emily and Matthew P. McAllister, eds. *The Routledge Companion to Advertising and Promotional Culture*. London and New York: Routledge, 2013.

Williams, Raymond. *Television: Technology and Cultural Form*. London: Routledge, 1979.

Winship, Janice. *Inside Women's Magazines*. New York: Pandora Press, 1987.

Wood, Helen and Bev Skeggs. "Spectacular Morality," in *The Media and Social Theory*, eds. D. Hesmondhalgh and J. Toynbee. London and New York: Routledge, 2009: 177–93.

Zhang, Huijun, ed. *Xingshi zhuisu yu shijue chuangzuo: Zhang Yimou dianying chuangzuo yanjiu* [*The Pursuit of Form and Visual Production: Research on Zhang Yimou's Film Productions*]. Beijing: China Film Press, 2008.

LIST OF CONTRIBUTORS

Miranda Banks is Associate Professor of Visual and Media Arts at Emerson College and a research fellow in the Emerson Engagement Lab. She is author of *The Writers: A History of American Screenwriters and Their Guild* (Rutgers, 2015) and coeditor of *Production Studies: Cultural Studies of Media Industries* (Routledge, 2009). Her work appears in edited collections, as well as in the journals *Popular Communication, Television and New Media, Montage AV*, and *Cinema Journal*.

James Bennett is Head of Department, Media Arts and Reader in Television and Digital Culture. His work focuses on the production cultures and shape of television and celebrity in digital culture. He is the author of *Television Personalities: Stardom and the Small Screen* (Routledge, 2010) and editor (with Niki Strange) of *Television as Digital Media* (Duke, 2011). His latest edited collection is *Media Independence: Working with Freedom or Working for Free* (Routledge, 2014).

Tiziano Bonini, PhD in Media, Communication and Public Sphere at the University of Siena, 2008, is a Lecturer in Media Studies at IULM University of Milan. He has published extensively on radio and new media. His current research interests are the intersection between radio, the Internet, and social media; digital cultures and methodologies; public service media; production studies; and freelance work in creative industries.

Nicholas Boston is an Associate Professor in the Department of Journalism and Communication at the City University of New York—Lehman College. He is interested in the uses and effects of computer-mediated communication across a spectrum of contexts, including industry, intimacy, and migration. He holds an

MS in journalism from Columbia University and a PhD in sociology from Cambridge University. He is the author of *The Amorous Migrant: Race, Relationships and Resettlement* (Temple, 2015).

Bridget Conor is Lecturer in the Centre for Culture, Media and Creative Industries at King's College London and has previously taught at Goldsmiths College, Middlesex University and AUT University in Auckland. She is the author of *Screenwriting: Creative Labour and Professional Practice* (Routledge, 2014) and the coeditor, with Rosalind Gill and Stephanie Taylor, of *Gender and Creative Labour* (SRM, 2015).

Michael Curtin is the Duncan and Suzanne Mellichamp Professor in the Department of Film and Media Studies and Director of the Media Industries Project at UC Santa Barbara. His books include *The American Television Industry* and *Distribution Revolution: Conversations about the Digital Future of Film and Television*. He is working on *Media Capital: The Cultural Geography of Globalization*. Curtin is coeditor of *Media Industries*, the *Chinese Journal of Communication*, and the British Film Institute's *International Screen Industries*.

Mary Desjardins is an Associate Professor of Film and Media Studies at Dartmouth College. She is author of *Recycled Stars: Female Film Stardom in the Age of Television and Video* (Duke University Press, 2015) and coeditor of *Dietrich Icon* (Duke University Press, 2007). She has published widely in journals and essay collections on stardom, television and film history, and feminist filmmaking.

Brooke Erin Duffy, PhD, is an Assistant Professor at Temple University whose research interests include creative labor, feminist media studies, and digital culture. She is the author of *Remake, Remodel: Women's Magazines in the Digital Age* (University of Illinois Press, 2013) and has published articles in such journals as *Critical Studies in Media Communication, Communication, Culture & Critique*, and *The Communication Review*. Duffy holds a PhD from the University of Pennsylvania's Annenberg School for Communication.

Alessandro Gandini works as a Lecturer in PR and Media at Middlesex University, London, and is a Research Fellow on the EU-FP7 project "P2Pvalue" for the University of Milan. He holds a PhD in sociology and his research interests mainly concern the transformations of work in the digital age, reputation and social capital, digital cultures and methodologies.

Paul Grainge is an Associate Professor of Film and Television Studies at the University of Nottingham, where he is a member of the Institute for Screen Industries

Research. His books include *Promotional Screen Industries* (coauthored with Catherine Johnson, 2015), *Ephemeral Media: Transitory Screen Culture from Television to YouTube* (2011), *Brand Hollywood* (2008), *Film Histories: An Introduction and Reader* (2007), *Memory and Popular Film* (2003), and *Monochrome Memories* (2002).

Nina B. Huntemann is an Associate Professor of Media at Suffolk University and co-director of Women in Games Boston. She has coedited *Gaming Globally: Production, Play and Place* (Palgrave, 2013) and *Joystick Soldiers: The Politics of Play in Military Video Games* (Routledge, 2010). She is associate producer of *Joystick Warriors: Video Game Violence and the Culture of Militarism* (Media Education Foundation, 2013).

Deborah L. Jaramillo is an Assistant Professor of Film and Television Studies at Boston University. She is the author of *Ugly War Pretty Package: How CNN and FOX News Made the Invasion of Iraq High Concept* (Indiana University Press, 2009). Her current book project, *The Code*, examines the interactions between the NAB, the FCC, Congress, and the television audience in the years immediately preceding the adoption of the Television Code.

Alessandro Jedlowski is a Marie Curie/Cofund Postdoctoral Fellow in Anthropology at the University of Liège (Belgium). His research analyzes the political and economic dimensions of film production in the Nigerian video-film industry (Nollywood) compared to other emergent African video-film industries. He is author of "Small Screen Cinema: Informality and Remediation in Nollywood," in *Television and New Media*, and "From Nollywood to Nollyworld: Processes of Transnationalization in the Nigerian Video Film Industry," in *Global Nollywood* (2013).

Catherine Johnson is an Associate Professor of Film and Television Studies at the University of Nottingham, where she is a member of the Institute for Screen Industries Research. Her books include *Promotional Screen Industries* (coauthored with Paul Grainge, 2015), *Branding Television* (2012), *Transnational Television History* (2012), *Telefantasy* (2005), and *ITV Cultures: Independent Television Over Fifty Years* (2005).

Kristin J. Lieb is an Associate Professor of Marketing Communication at Emerson College. Before arriving at Emerson, Lieb held numerous marketing and business development positions in the music industry, including posts with Atomic Pop and Newbury Comics Interactive. She also worked as a researcher for Harvard Business School and as a freelance writer for *Billboard* and *Rolling Stone*. Lieb recently published her first book, *Gender, Branding, and the Modern Music Industry* (Routledge, 2013).

Dennis Lo is a doctoral candidate and Dissertation Year Fellow in Cinema Studies at the University of California, Los Angeles. He is currently completing a dissertation on the cultural politics of location shooting practices and representations of place in contemporary Chinese and Taiwanese cinemas, and has been published in six peer-reviewed journals, including *Film-Philosophy* and *Asian Cinema*. His highly interdisciplinary interests draw from a dual B.A.S. in film/media studies and physics at Stanford University.

Mary Elizabeth Luka, PhD, is a Postdoctoral Fellow in the Ted Rogers School of Management at Ryerson University. She is a published business and academic specialist in creative industries and strategic policy, planning and practice, with two decades of experience in broadcast, digital media production, and culture sector development, and an award-winning digital media producer-director.

Vicki Mayer is Professor of Communication at Tulane University. She has published widely on media production and producers, and is the author of *Below the Line: Producers and Production Studies in the New Television Economy* (Duke, 2011) and *Producing Dreams, Consuming Youth: Mexican Americans and Mass Media* (Rutgers, 2003). She is editor of the journal *Television & New Media*, and she directs the digital humanities projects MediaNOLA and New Orleans Historical.

Jonathan Corpus Ong is a Lecturer in Media and Communication at the University of Leicester. He is currently co-investigator to the ESRC-funded collaborative research "Humanitarian Technologies Project: Communications in the Wake of Typhoon Haiyan." He is also lead researcher of the DFID-funded project "Consulting Communities: Accountability after Haiyan and Hagupit." His first book, *The Poverty of Television: Suffering, Ethics and Media in the Philippines*, is forthcoming in 2015 from Anthem Press.

Alisa Perren is an Associate Professor in the Department of Radio-TV-Film at the University of Texas at Austin. She is coeditor of *Media Industries: History, Theory, and Method* and author of *Indie, Inc.: Miramax and the Transformation of Hollywood in the 1990s*. She is also a cofounder and co-managing editor for the peer-reviewed, open-access *Media Industries* journal.

Chris Peterson works, teaches, and researches at MIT. He earned his SM from MIT in comparative media studies in 2013, and his BA in critical legal studies from the University of Massachusetts at Amherst in 2009, where he also served on the Bargaining Committee of UAW 2322. He began making Twitter bots to procrastinate during the writing of his master's thesis; that a side project be more academically viable than a thesis seems less ironic than inevitable.

Eva Pjajčíková is a PhD student of film at Masaryk University, Brno, where she is preparing her thesis on Czech television screenwriting. During her nine-month internship on the television series called *The First Republic*, she worked as an assistant to the screenwriting team. Currently, she continues to work as a cowriter on the second season of the show.

Eva Novrup Redvall is an Associate Professor in Film and Media Studies at the University of Copenhagen, where she is head of the Research Priority Area on Creative Media Industries. Her research focuses on film and television production. Her latest books are *Writing and Producing Television Drama in Denmark: From the Kingdom to the Killing* (2013) and *Danish Directors 3: Dialogues on the New Danish Documentary Cinema* (coauthored with Mette Hjort and Ib Bondebjerg, 2014).

Naomi Sakr is a Professor of Media Policy at the Communication and Media Research Institute (CAMRI), University of Westminster, UK, and director of the CAMRI Arab Media Centre. She is the author of *Transformations in Egyptian Journalism* (2013), *Arab Television Today* (2007), and *Satellite Realms* (2001), and is editor or coeditor of *Women and Media in the Middle East* (2004), *Arab Media and Political Renewal* (2007), and *Arab Media Moguls* (2015).

Jeanette Steemers is a Professor of Media and Communications and Co-director of the Communications and Media Research Institute (CAMRI) at the University of Westminster, UK. Her books include *Changing Channels* (1998), *Selling Television* (2004), *European Television Industries* (2005, with P. Iosifides and M. Wheeler), and *Creating Preschool Television* (Palgrave, 2010). Her work on UK television exports and children's media industries has been funded by the British Academy, Leverhulme Trust, and Arts and Humanities Research Council.

Petr Szczepanik is an Associate Professor at Masaryk University, Brno. His current research focuses on the Czech (post)socialist production system, some of the results of which were published in *Behind the Screen: Inside European Production Culture* (Palgrave, 2013, coedited with Patrick Vonderau). He was also the main coordinator of an EU-funded project, "FIND" (www.projectfind.cz), which used student internships in production companies to combine job shadowing with ethnographic research of production cultures.

John Vanderhoef is a PhD candidate in the Department of Film and Media Studies at the University of California, Santa Barbara. He has published work in *Television and New Media, Spectator, Ada: A Journal of Gender, New Media, and Technology*, and *The Routledge Companion to Video Game Studies*. He has contributed to the Carsey-Wolf Center's Media Industries Project, and is on the editorial collective for *Media Fields Journal*.

Patrick Vonderau is a Professor in Cinema Studies at the Department for Media Studies at Stockholm University. His book publications include *Films that Sell: Moving Pictures and Advertising* (Palgrave/British Film Institute, forthcoming 2015), *Behind the Screen: Inside European Production Cultures* (Palgrave Macmillan, 2011), and *Films that Work: Industrial Film and the Productivity of Media* (Amsterdam University Press, 2009).

Anna Zoellner is a Lecturer in Media Industries at the University of Leeds with a professional background in television production. Her research interests are at the intersection of media industries, media production studies, cultural labor research, and television studies with a methodological interest in ethnography and internationally comparative research. Her work has been published in edited volumes and journals including *Mass Communication and Society, Journal for the Study of British Cultures* and *Journal of Media Practice*.

INDEX

Page numbers in *italic* followed by *b* indicate boxes; by *t* indicate tables.

#0080 - 061016 - C0 - 229/152/17 [19] - CB - 9781138831681